Guide to Fossil Man

Fourth Edition

Completely Revised and Enlarged

MICHAEL H. DAY

The University of Chicago Press

United Medical Schools of Guy's and St. Thomas's Hospitals,
of the Leakey Trust and is a past president of the Royal
of Great Britain.

The University of Chicago Press, Chicago 60637

Cassell Ltd., 1 St. Anne's Road, Eastbourne, East Sussex, BN21 3UN

Copyright © 1965, 1967, 1977, 1986 by Michael H. Day
All rights reserved. Published 1986

Reprinted 1988

Printed in Great Britain

95 94 93 92 91 90 89 88   5 4 3 2

Library of Congress Cataloging-in-Publication Data

Day, Michael H.
   Guide to fossil man.
   Includes bibliographical references and index.
   1. Fossil man.   I. Title.
GN282.D39   1986   569'.9   86-5548

ISBN 0-226-13889-5

Contents

List of Illustrations

Introduction to the First Edition

The study of human evolution presents many problems of peculiar difficulty, perhaps the greatest being the large and increasing number of specimens forming the evidence upon which the subject is based. In this book an attempt has been made to select, from the wide range of known material, the hominid fossils that best illustrate a significant stage or aspect of human palaeontology, the study of fossil man.

Anatomical examination of fossil bones and teeth can be revealing, tantalizing, exasperating. Always the temptation is to speculate beyond the facts, to argue from the particular to the general, to forget that one specimen represents a population and is therefore subject to the laws of biological variation. However, if these pitfalls are avoided, there remains an ever increasing body of knowledge of the anatomy of fossil man. Even so, anatomical knowledge is not enough upon which to base an assessment of the life of early man; other factors must be considered, the climate, the time relationships of different groups and the culture of the populations represented by the scant remains at our disposal.

It is the purpose of this book to bring together information from many disciplines and relate it for each of the 40 or so key sites which have yielded the bulk of significant hominid fossils.

November, 1965

Introduction to the Fourth Edition

It is almost 21 years since the first edition of this book was published; a period that has seen the most tremendous strides in the study of human evolution or, as it is now widely termed, palaeoanthropology. During this period not only the book but also the subject seems to have come of age. The approach of those who work in the subject has become sharper and more critical, new disciplines have arisen to make their contributions and scientists from all over the world have interested themselves in the search for the origins of man and his ancestors. This has in turn attracted increasing amounts of support from research foundations, universities and governments of both developed and developing countries. The result of this has been an enormous expansion in the literature of the subject in the form of new journals, books and conference volumes which threaten to engulf students and teachers, as well as researchers in the field.

In this edition, as in those before, the intention is to select those sites that are seminal to the study of the evolution of man; to draw attention to the best preserved and most significant fossils that they have produced; to set them in their environmental contexts and to assess their relationships in evolutionary terms. Almost 50 sites have been included, a number of which are long known and form the foundations of our knowledge; 15 are new to the book, many of them new to the science, others are included because they are now better documented or have assumed added significance in the light of developing theories.

New sites from Europe and the Middle East include Bilzingsleben, Salé, St Césaire and Shanidar, sites that contribute to the Neandertal and *Homo erectus* problems; from Africa, Middle Awash, Lake Baringo, West Turkana and Border Cave all contribute to our knowledge of the origins of the australopithecines, of *Homo erectus* and of *Homo sapiens*. New sites from the Far East and China include Sambungmachan and Hexian whilst the two most important sites in Australia have also been chosen. Longer known sites have been brought up to date and new information incorporated into the previous entries.

Since the last edition there have been many new technical developments such as trace element analysis of volcanic tuffs that allows geochemical stratigraphic correlation. The development and application of oxygen isotope analysis for dating the hominid fossil record, a new, enhanced radiocarbon dating method and the use of computer assisted tomography on fossils as well as the photogrammetric analysis of footprints, the counting of dental perikymata for ageing immature teeth and the use of energy dispersive X-ray microanalysis for relative dating have all proved themselves practical aids to increasing our knowledge of the subject. There have also been new theoretical approaches such as the widespread application of the cladistic method of taxonomy and the use of the principles of allometry in metrical analysis. The punctuated equilibrium theory of evolutionary tempo has been applied to the hominid fossil record. As always new approaches have their enthusiastic supporters but there are also those who are sceptical of the wilder claims made for some of the new theories.

The study of human evolution requires a basic knowledge of human anatomy, in particular osteology. No attempt is made here to cover the elements of these subjects— they are dealt with in all the standard works on human anatomy. It has been considered important, however, to retain and expand the introductory section. Such topics as normal variation, sexual variation, tooth form and dental terminology are still covered and for the first time, footprint analysis and nomenclature and taxonomy are included.

Looking back over the previous three editions I am struck by the rate of expansion of the subject of palaeoanthropology and the tremendous increase in the weight of evidence for the evolution of man and his hominid forebears that has resulted from research both in the field and the laboratory. Naturally this evidence also prompts new questions, but it is the privilege of mankind to be aware of itself and to seek its origins in the rocks of the past.

Acknowledgments

It is once again a great pleasure to record my most grateful thanks to all those who have helped me during the preparation of what is now the fourth edition of this book. I am most particularly grateful to my former Research Assistant, Wendy Bosler, who worked untiringly to assemble the literature and dealt with the extensive correspondence. I am also grateful to Joy Pollard and John Fenton who have worked hard on the illustrations, also to Audrey Besterman whose skill is reflected in the maps, charts and text figures. Finally, I am most grateful to Sheila Bishop, my secretary, who has wrestled with textual changes, fiendish tables, my handwriting and a new word processor without complaint and with great success.

For permission to examine original material in their care from almost all of the sites, for the provision of reprints and photographs, for valuable discussions and for reading and checking sections that relate to their areas of special knowledge I am grateful to the following colleagues: Professor Dr K.D. Adam, Dr P.B. Beaumont, Dr C.K. Brain, Dr G. Bräuer, Professor F.H. Brown, Dr G.R. Chapman, Dr R.J. Clarke, Professor Y. Coppens, Mr A. Currant, Mr X. Dong, Dr H.S. Green, Professor J.-L. Heim, Professor F. Clark Howell, Dr J.-J. Hublin, Professor T.K. Jacob, Professor J.J. Jaeger, Dr H.-E. Joachim, Dr D.C. Johanson, Dr R. Kraatz, Dr M.D. Leakey, Dr M.G. Leakey, Mr R.E. Leakey, Dr M.-A. de Lumley, Professor H. de Lumley, Miss T.I. Molleson, Dr F. Van Noten, Dr T. Partridge, Professor A. Poulianos, Dr B. Senut, Dr F.H. Smith, Dr C.B. Stringer, Dr H. Suzuki, Dr A. Thoma, Dr A. Thorne, Dr A.-M. Tillier, Professor P.V. Tobias, Dr E. Trinkaus, Professor R. Tuttle, Professor B. Vandermeersch, Dr E. Vlček, Dr E. Vrba, Dr T.D. White, Dr M.H. Wolpoff, Professor B.A. Wood, Professor Wu Rukang, Dr Wu Xinzhi.

If, despite all their help, there are still errors—and I am sure that there are—then they are my responsibility alone.

PART I
The Anatomy of Fossil Man

The Anatomy of Fossil Man

The principal evidence upon which direct knowledge of the evolution of man rests is provided by the anatomical examination of fossil hominid bones and teeth. Although skeletal and dental structure alone may appear to be limited sources of information, behavioural characteristics such as locomotor capability and dietary habit may be deducible from their study. The study of preserved hominid footprints can also contribute information on foot size and shape, stature, stance and gait.

In the past emphasis was placed upon the evolutionary significance of single features whose selective value was often obscure, for example, the variations in the arrangements of the skull sutures. Today, however, wider knowledge of the range of variation of single features in all primates has allowed these characteristics to be regarded in proper perspective.

The study of individual bones and teeth is of greater value, and an analysis of joint geometry and muscular mechanics can often strongly infer joint function. When there is available a group of bones that form a functional complex such as a hand, a foot, a pelvis, a cranium or jaws and teeth, then its examination will give the beginnings of an insight into the life of the hominid of which it once formed a part. With sufficient material knowledge of several functional complexes may be built up to provide almost the entire picture, morphological and functional. Such a process should stop short of modelling soft tissue features and hair distribution for which no direct evidence exists.

Bones

It is apparent that the study of fossil man requires a working knowledge of the skeleton of modern man; the terminology of human palaeontology closely parallels that of human osteology, but it is not within the scope of this book to describe the human skeleton, a topic dealt with in all standard anatomical texts. However, certain aspects of osteology perhaps acquire importance when set against a comparative background, and thus deserve emphasis.

Bone is living tissue, if it is cut, it bleeds; if broken, it heals. As with other living tissue it responds to stimuli; in particular it responds to mechanical stress, a principle embodied in Wolff's Law:

'The external form and internal architecture of a bone are related to the forces which act upon it.'

It follows that the shape of a bone, although primarily genetically determined, is capable of modification during life; at death the external form and the internal architecture will reflect the forces that it was called upon to resist during the latter part of its life. It is upon this premise that much of the interpretation of skeletal morphology depends.

Normal Skeletal Variation

It is a commonplace that no two people are exactly alike; neither are their skeletons nor the individual bones and teeth of which they are composed. Every morphological feature and every measurement forms but a part of the range of normal biological variation to be found within a population. Sampling techniques can be employed to define the approximate limits of this range of variation and the distribution of characters within it. Statistical methods can assist in the evaluation of observations and in the comparison of data, but hominid fossil bones and teeth are frequently too few in number to allow proper statistical comparisons. Often the most that can be achieved is to determine whether or not a given character (which may itself be at any point within its own range of normal variation) lies within the range of that character in allied forms.

In order to facilitate comparison, indices can be devised that allow two variables to be expressed as a single figure; length in terms of breadth (tooth crowns, crania), shaft thickness in terms of length (long bones). Comparison of indices allows specimens of differing absolute sizes to be compared in respect of a relative feature. This simple procedure, however, has its drawbacks and in recent years palaeoanthropologists have taken into account the methods of allometry in attempting to deal with the problems of size and shape.

Univariate statistical methods are frequently used to determine the significance of the differences between population means for single features, and also to determine the level of correlation between variables measured on a bone or a tooth. The more complex techniques of multivariate statistical analysis are also used in attempts to assess the significance of within-group and between-group variability for series of measurements taken from samples of several populations. In essence most of the methods involve an attempt to bring about a data reduction and often they permit a visualization of the data sets in two or more dimensions. One of the difficulties of using these methods stems from the multi-dimensional nature of the mathematical model so that a true visualization is not really possible or is even misleading. The statistics achieved (e.g. Hotelling's T^2, Mahalanobis' D^2 and others) may be regarded as measures of morphological distance and assigned levels of significance. Unfortunately their biological significance often remains obscure and may become the subject of controversy. This is sometimes the case when such measures are used as evidence in the taxonomic evaluation of scanty fossil remains, often themselves the subject of extensive reconstruction prior to measurement. Data drawn from limb bones may be expected to produce evidence that will relate to locomotor function, but the use of such evidence in a taxonomic evaluation may in turn depend upon the validity of locomotor evidence in taxonomy.

At best statistical evidence can only complement anatomical evidence and this applies only *when the measurements used have been taken directly from the original fossils* and due allowance has been made for speculative reconstructions and distortion. In the evaluation of fossil hominid remains nothing can replace an intimate familiarity with the anatomy of the specimens gained by study of the originals whenever possible. Casts and photographs have a place but they should never be used as primary sources of data in serious work. This does not mean that every worker has the right to take measurements on any specimen when agreed sets of dimensions are available; some of the most valuable and important specimens already show signs of 'caliper wear' and their dimensions are changing. Published work should always specify whether or not the observations quoted have been taken on the originals or on casts so that the reader can judge for himself the weight to put on the results. In this book most of the photographs have scales attached; they are there simply as scales and are not intended to be used as a means of taking measurements from the illustrations.

Sexual Variation

Sexual dimorphism is a common feature of primates including the hominids and modern man. Ranges of sexual dimorphism are known to vary quite widely both between primate species and within those species according to the feature that is being measured; therefore generalizations on the range of sexual dimorphism within a fossil hominid species, always known from limited material, can be hazardous. The placing of a boundary between two groups of fossils of similar morphology but of differing sizes, and the verification of this as an intraspecific (sexually dimorphic) division as opposed to an interspecies boundary, can be a difficult task.

Hominid sexual characters upon which some reliance can be placed are the morphological features of the bony pelvis. The necessity for a female pelvis whose inlet, cavity and outlet are sufficiently roomy to accommodate and transmit the head of a comparatively large-brained hominid foetus at childbirth has modified the shape of the pelvis. The male pelvis, with no reproductive function to parallel that of the female, evolves for efficiency in bipedal locomotion. In modern man this goes some way to explain the differences in peak achievements between men and women in running and jumping athletic activities. The female bony pelvis is a compromise between the needs of childbirth and those of locomotion with heavy selection pressure on the need for successful reproduction.

Age Variation

Growing Phase. Age changes in bones are well recognized during the period of skeletal development. Long bones ossify from centres which appear early in intra-uterine development near the mid-point of the cartilage pre-cursor of the shaft. The ossification process spreads from this diaphysial centre towards the ends of the bone; later new epiphysial centres appear at the ends. The cartilage plate separating the diaphysis from the epiphysis constitutes the growing zone. Additional bone is laid down beneath the periosteum which surrounds the shaft. Remodelling, by resorption and addition, modifies the structure until development is nearly complete, then the epiphysis fuses on to the shaft and the bone is adult.

The state of skeletal maturity allows some estimate to be made of age, although variability is common between individuals and between species. It is probably unwise to make estimates of the chronological age at death of an immature fossil bone on the basis of correlation with similar bones of modern man, other than in broad categories such as foetal, infant, juvenile and adolescent.

Mature Phase. During adult life age changes are comparatively few. Tooth attrition is continuous, but its rate is influenced by diet and the state of dental health. Typically, adult fossil hominid incisors are worn down so that in occlusion the bite is 'edge to edge'.

Skeletal changes during adult life include the gradual obliteration of the cranial sutures by fusion (synostosis) of adjacent bones. The sequence of closure has long been regarded as giving a guide to chronological age; however, it is in fact so unreliable in modern man that it is unwise to attempt to determine the age of an unknown fossil hominid by means of correlation, even if there were grounds for suggesting that such a correlation exists.

Senile Phase. The changes of senility are degenerative; they include osteoarthritis, osteoporosis and changes in the vertebral column which produce bent posture and loss of stature. Loss of teeth is sometimes associated with senility; complete tooth loss, with resorption of alveolar bone, considerably changes the stresses acting upon the mandible, and in turn leads to bone remodelling at the gonion and the temporo-mandibular joint.

However, since all of these 'senile' changes are pathological and may occur in individuals who are not old in a chronological sense, 'senile' skeletal or dental changes must be regarded cautiously as evidence of ageing in hominid fossil material.

Table 1   *Modern Human Postcranial Skeletal Maturation (Long bones)*

| | Appearance of Centres | | Fusion of Diaphysis |
Bone	Diaphysis	Epiphysis	and Epiphysis*
Clavicle	5–6/52 intrauterine life (i.u.)	c. 17–21	c. 20+
Humerus	8/52 i.u.	Upper 6/12–5	18–20
		Lower 18/12–12	14–16 (Med. epicond. c. 20)
Radius	8/52 i.u.	Upper 4–5*	14–17
		Lower 1	17–19
Ulna	8/52 i.u.	Upper 9–11*	14–16
		Lower 5–6*	17–18
Femur	7/52 i.u.	Upper 6/12–14	14–17
		Lower c. birth	16–18
Tibia	7/52 i.u.	Upper c. birth	16–18
		Lower 14/12	15–17
Fibula	8/52 i.u.	Upper 3–4	17–19
		Lower 1	15–17
Pelvis			
Ilium	8/52 i.u.	secondary centres c. puberty	Ischium-Pubis 7–8 Complete 15–25
Ischium	4/12 i.u.	secondary centres c. puberty	
Pubis	4–5/12 i.u.	secondary centres c. puberty	

*The lower figure applies to females   After Williams and Warwick (1980)

Teeth

Tooth morphology has played an important part in vertebrate palaeontology, if only because teeth preserve well and dental characters are easily identified. The human dentition is described fully in textbooks of dental anatomy, but it may be of value to draw attention to some features of anthropological interest.

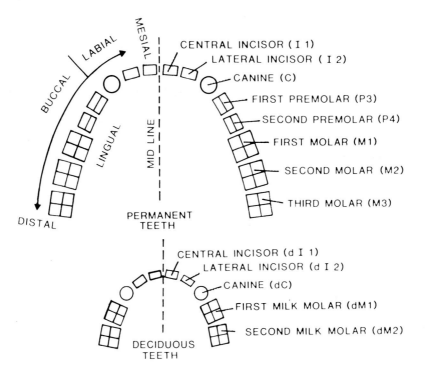

Fig. 1. The nomenclature of hominid upper and lower teeth.

Terminology

The hominid dental formula is the same as that of catarrhine monkeys and great apes.

Deciduous Teeth	Incisors (dI) $\frac{2}{2}$ Canines (dC) $\frac{1}{1}$ Molars (dM) $\frac{2}{2}$
Permanent Teeth	Incisors (I) $\frac{2}{2}$ Canines (C) $\frac{1}{1}$ Premolars (PM) $\frac{2}{2}$ Molars(M) $\frac{3}{3}$

That part of a tooth which projects above the gum is known as the crown; its surfaces are named mesial, distal, buccal, lingual labial and occlusal (Fig. 1).

In the case of premolars and molars, the biting or occlusal surface is modified by projections or cusps which are separated by fissures.

Premolar teeth are often referred to as 'third' or 'fourth' premolars, an indication that the Old World higher primate dental formula was derived from the generalized mammalian formula by loss of teeth and in particular by the loss of the first two premolars. Many publications refer to individual teeth by a shorthand method which indicates whether teeth are from the upper or lower dentition (e.g. PM_3 or $PM_{\overline{3}}$ meaning lower third premolar or M^1 or $M^{\underline{1}}$ meaning upper first molar).

The general nomenclature of mammalian molar crown morphology was developed by Cope and Osborn in the late nineteenth century, and enables any cusp or ridge to be identified. The primary distinction between upper and lower molar teeth is made by adding the suffix 'id' to the name of any part of a lower molar. This allows the same terms to apply to both upper and lower molar features yet remain clearly distinguishable. The basic structure is a three-cusped triangle or *Trigon* (*Trigonid*), whose apex is lingual in upper molars and buccal in lower molars. The apical cusp is the *Protocone* (*Protoconid*), the mesial cusp the *Paracone* (*Paraconid*) and the distal cusp the *Metacone* (*Metaconid*).

Distally the trigon (trigonid) is often extended by a basin-like *Talon* (*Talonid*) which carries a major cusp, the *Hypocone* (*Hypoconid*). The talonid frequently has a lingual *Entoconid* in addition to a hypoconid. Minor cusps which occur on ridges linking major cusps are distinguished by the suffix 'conule' (conulid), and are attributed to the nearest major cusp, for example *Protoconule* or *Hypoconulid*. A basal collar of enamel which may develop around a tooth is termed a cingulum (pl. cingula); minor cusps which arise from cingula are given the suffix 'style' (stylid) and are attributed to the related major cusp, for example *Parastyle* or *Parastylid*.

Although this terminology may appear complex it has the virtue of permitting direct reference to the features of tooth crown morphology in a wide range of mammals.

Hominid Dental Characters

The principal features of hominid dentition which distinguish it from that of the great apes are the regularly curved shape of the dental arcade, reduction in the size of incisors and canines, a non-sectorial first premolar, and premolar and molar teeth with a flat occlusal wear pattern. However, the hominoid lower molar cusp pattern is basically the same as that of a Miocene ape known as *Dryopithecus*; this arrangement consists of five cusps separated by grooves in the form of a Y (Y5), and is typical of modern apes. This persisting cusp and fissure pattern is commonly found in the lower molar teeth of fossil man, but in modern man there is frequently reduction or absence of the fifth cusp (hypoconulid) and the formation of a + fissure pattern (+ 5 or +4), particularly in the second and third molars.

Tooth Eruption

The times of eruption of modern human teeth have long been known to give an indication of age. Unfortunately the ranges of normal variation are apt to be very wide so that estimations of age based on correlation within this species tend to be unreliable. It is even more hazardous to attempt to correlate the ages of tooth eruption of fossil hominids with those of modern man, other than in broad general terms.

Table 2 (on page 11) gives the approximate ages of tooth eruption for modern man.

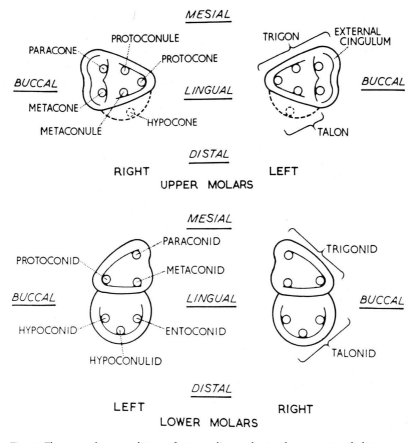

Fig. 2. The general nomenclature of mammalian molar tooth crown morphology (after Simpson, 1937).

The age at death of immature fossil hominids has been estimated by a new method that relies on the presence of two types of incremental growth lines within tooth enamel: enamel prism cross striations and the striae of Retzius. Cross striations result from circadian variation in the rate of matrix secretion by ameloblasts, or enamel forming cells. Striae of Retzius are coarser lines that pass obliquely from the enamel/dentine junction to the surface of the enamel where they become visible as perikymata. There are 7–8 cross striations between adjacent striae of Retzius that it is believed suggests a 7–8 day periodicity. On this basis it is possible to assess the age of the hominid by counting perikymata on immature teeth. Comparisons with dental eruption data taken from modern man has suggested that Plio-Pleistocene hominids have abbreviated growth periods relative to modern man and that previous estimates of the ages of some immature hominids were overestimates (Bromage and Dean, 1985).

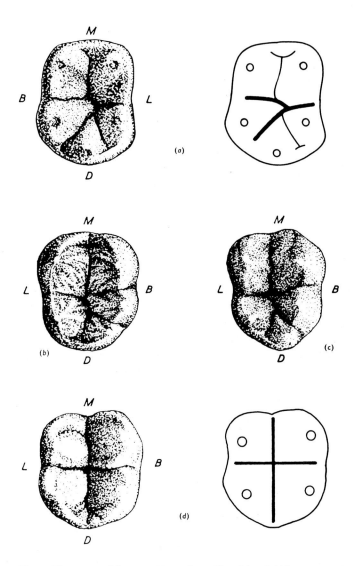

Fig. 3. The cusp and fissure pattern of pongid and hominid lower second permanent teeth. (a) *Dryopithecus* (Left, Y_5) (b) Modern chimpanzee (Right, Y_5) (c) Modern man (Right, Y_5) (d) Modern man (Right, $+4$).

Table 2   *Approximate Ages of Tooth Eruption in Modern Man*

Upper Deciduous Teeth								Months								
	4	6	8	10	12	14	16	18	20	22	24	26	28	30	32	34	36
dI¹		6—8															
dI²			8—10														
dC							16——20										
dM¹					12——16												
dM²									20————————30								

Upper Permanent Teeth							Years													
	4	5	6	7	8	9	10	11	12	13	14	15	16	17	18	19	20	21	22	23
I¹			6——8																	
I²				7——9																
C						9————12														
PM¹					10——12															
PM²					10——12															
M¹			6—7																	
M²						11——13														
M³														17————————21						

Footprints

Preserved prehistoric human footprints have been known from a number of cave sites in Europe for many years. (France: Tuc d'Audoubert, 1913, Ganties-Montespan, 1926, Bedeilhac, 1927; Cabreret, 1927; Aldène, 1948; Niaux, 1906 and 1949. Italy: Tana della Basura, 1950). All the sites are Upper Pleistocene and all the prints are attributable to *Homo sapiens*. The site studied in most detail is that of Niaux (Pâles, 1976).

Soft substrate footprints can give information on the shape and conformation of the foot, its length and breadth, the toe lengths, the toe projection formula and soft tissue details. Measurements of foot length can give estimates of standing height (stature) since in modern human bipeds foot length is 15–16 per cent of stature. Other formulae involving stride length (=approx. pace length × 2), foot length and relative stride length can suggest walking speed (Charteris, Wall and Nottrodt, 1981).

The mechanism of weight and force transmission to the ground during walking can also be investigated by means of photogrammetric contouring of both preserved and experimental footprints. Comparison of the preserved footprints with experimental modern human footprints can disclose similarities and differences in bipedal walking patterns (Day and Wickens, 1980).

The Plio-Pleistocene series of preserved hominid footprints from Laetoli (*q.v.*) are associated with the tracks of animals some of which are extinct, thus their contemporaneity is assured. Preserved footprints can provide, therefore, information concerning relative dating, soft tissue foot form, stature and gait. Preserved footprints provide the only means available of studying directly a contemporary record of hominid locomotor behaviour.

Nomenclature and Taxonomy

The need to create some order in the seeming chaos of the natural world by naming and classifying animals has a history at least as long as the writings of Aristotle. It was not until 1758 that Carl von Linné (Linnaeus) introduced the binary system of nomenclature in the 10th edition of his *Systema Naturae* to describe, name and classify living animals and plants. (It is worthy of note that at that time species were believed to be fixed and immutable and that Darwinian evolutionary theory was almost 100 years in the future.)

Today nomenclature and classification are distinct but related subjects. The naming of a new taxon must follow the rules of nomenclature as set out in the International Code of Zoological Nomenclature (Code Zoologique), a code adopted by successive International Congresses of Zoology and since 1973 by the Division of Zoology of the International Union of Biological Sciences.

The internationally accepted object of the code is to promote stability and universality in the scientific names of animals, and to ensure that the name of each taxon is unique and distinct. Duplications must be avoided and the international understanding and acceptance of names is a prime objective of the Code. Priority is the basic principle of zoological nomenclature. It follows that nomenclature, the naming of a taxon, is not simply a matter of choice and taste; if the rules of the Code are not followed the world of zoology will not accept the new name for the good reason that it will inevitably cause confusion and controversy. The history of palaeoanthropology is littered with nomenclatural solecisms not all of which are in the distant past.

Precision and consistency in the use of terms is also very important. *Taxonomy* is the theory and practice of classifying organisms; part of *systematics*, the study of the kinds and diversity of organisms. Classification is the application of taxonomic principles to the ranking of categories and the grouping of animals within those categories or taxa. This procedure is a matter of individual choice, usually based on common morphological features that indicate phylogenetic relationship or kinship. Almost 50 taxonomic units have been employed; 15 categories are enough for most purposes and six form the major units: Phylum, Class, Order, Family, Genus and Species. This expands to 15 within the Animal Kingdom by the addition of the prefixes Super-, Sub- and Infra- as shown opposite.

The original Linnean binomial system was designed for modern forms whose distinctiveness could be determined by their inability to breed with other species and produce like and fertile offspring. In palaeontology this possibility is denied to us yet the affinity of a modern hippopotamus to a fossil hippopotamus that was living some thousands of years ago cannot be denied. The Linnean system of classification based on similarity encourages natural classification, yet small evolutionary changes make precise delineation between successive fossil species difficult to determine. The concept of the palaeospecies, or chronospecies, evolving through time, is an attempt to deal with the problem of the application of the Linnean system to palaeontology.

An alternative approach is that of Hennig (1966). In this system taxonomic significance is attached to the appearance of new morphological features in an evolving lineage that may indicate a branch point on an evolutionary radiation of taxa. Features

Kingdom	Animalia
Phylum	Vertebrata
Subphylum	
Superclass	
Class	Mammalia
Subclass	
Superorder	
Order	Primates
Suborder	
Superfamily	Hominoidea
Family	Hominidae
Subfamily	Homininae
Genus	Homo
Subgenus	
Species	sapiens
Subspecies	sapiens

Homo sapiens sapiens—anatomically modern man

shared with previous evolutionary stages in a lineage are discounted as features of common inheritance. The sharing of new features is regarded as significant evidence of close kinship. The codification of these schemes allows diagrams, termed cladograms, to indicate relationships that are in no sense 'family trees' since a cladogram has no time axis. Cladistic or phylogenetic analysis can throw interesting and significant new light on the subject of primate taxonomy, particularly at the higher levels of taxonomic resolution; it is less effective when dealing with genera, species and subspecies. It can also produce inconsistent and confusing results when misused.

Linnean taxonomy, based on similarity, and Hennigian taxonomy, based on difference, are complementary approaches to the problems of understanding the natural world; they each have a contribution to make, they each have their difficulties. Neither one system nor the other is wholly right or wholly wrong, only the dogmatic application of either will lead to false conclusions; indeed, the literature has examples already.

References and Further Reading

Simpson, C. G. (1937) The beginning of the age of mammals. *Biol. Rev. 12*, 1–47.

Breathnach, A. S., Ed. (1958) Frazer's *Anatomy of the Human Skeleton*. 5th Ed. London: Churchill.

Martin, R. and Saller, K. (1959) *Lehrbuch der Anthropologie*. Stuttgart: Gustav Fischer Verlag.

Campbell, B. G. (1965) Nomenclature of the Hominidae. *R. anthrop. Inst. Occ. Pap. 22.*

Hennig, W. (1966) *Phylogenetic Systematics*. Urbana: University of Illinois.

Pâles, L. (1976) Les empreintes de pieds humains dans les cavernes. *Arch. Inst. Paléont. Hum. Mem.* 36. Paris: Masson.

Krogman, W. M. (1978) *The Human Skeleton in Forensic Medicine*. Springfield, Illinois: Charles C. Thomas.

Day, M. H. and Wickens, E. H. (1980) Laetoli Pliocene hominid footprints and bipedalism. *Nature 286*, 385–387.

Warwick, R. and Williams, P. L. (1980) *Gray's Anatomy*. 36th Ed. London: Longmans.

Charteris, J., Wall, J. C. and Nottrodt, J. W. (1981) Functional reconstruction of gait from the Pliocene hominid footprints at Laetoli, northern Tanzania. *Nature 290*, 496–498.

Osborn, J. W., Ed. (1981) *Dental Anatomy and Embryology*, Vol. 1, Book 2. Oxford:Blackwell.

Bromage, T. C. and Dean, M. C. (1985) Re-evaluation of the age at death of immature fossil hominids. *Nature 317*, 525–527.

International Commission on Zoological Nomenclature (1985) *International Code of Zoological Nomenclature*. 3rd Ed. Internat. Trust Zool. Nomen. Berkeley and Los Angeles: University of California Press.

PART II
The Fossil Hominids

The Name of the Finds

COUNTRY OF ORIGIN　　REGION

Synonyms and other names　The zoological names given to the specimens by other authors are quoted with the appropriate reference; in addition colloquial names in common use will be mentioned. Names given under this heading are not necessarily strict taxonomic synonyms.

Site　The location of the find. Distances are given in miles or kilometres according to the original publications.

Found by　The name of the field worker responsible for the find and the date.

Geology　A summary of the geology and stratigraphy of the site.

Associated finds　The artefacts and fossil fauna found with the remains.

Dating　An assessment of the dating of the specimens.

Morphology　A description of the specimens.

Dimensions　Selected dimensions are given, from measurement of the original bones, from published works and, on occasion, from measurement of casts. All measurements are in millimetres unless otherwise indicated.

Affinities　A summary of opinions on the nomenclature, classification and relationships of the finds.

Original　The address of the institution where the remains are usually kept.

Casts　Where possible the addresses are given of concerns or institutions where at one time or another casts might be obtained. No assurance can be given that casts are currently available from any of the sources mentioned.

References　The principal references to the literature concerning the find.

Europe

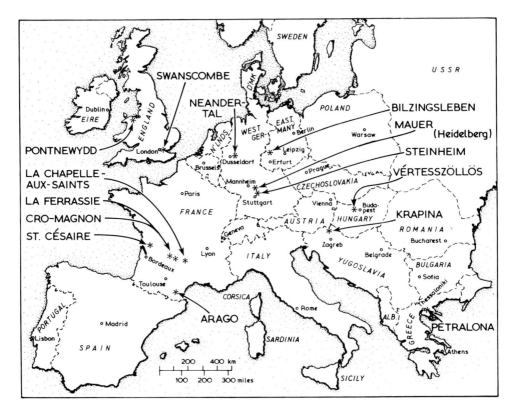

Fig. 4. Hominid fossil sites in Europe.

The Swanscombe Skull Fragments

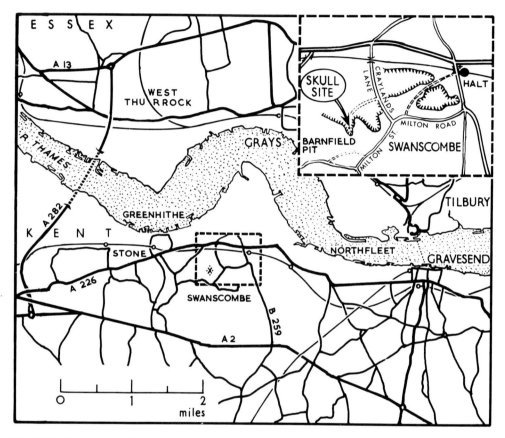

Fig. 5. The Swanscombe site.

Synonyms and other names *Homo cf. sapiens* (Le Gros Clark et al., 1938); Praesapiens man (Vallois, 1954); *Homo sapiens protosapiens* (Montandon, 1943); *Homo marstoni* (Paterson, 1940); *Homo swanscombensis* (Kennard, 1942); *Homo sapiens steinheimensis* (Campbell, 1964); Swanscombe man (Oakley, Campbell and Molleson, 1971).

Site Barnfield pit, half a mile south-west of All Saints Church, Swanscombe, Kent.

Found by A. T. Marston, 29th June, 1935; and 15th March, 1936; Mr and Mrs B. O. Wymer, A. Gibson and J. Wymer, 30th July, 1955.

Geology   The bones were found in river gravel 2 feet below the surface of the 100-foot terrace of the Thames in an oblique bed at the base of the Upper Middle Gravel.

Associated finds   The implements found with the remains include numerous hand-axes and flake tools, an industry equivalent to the Middle Acheulean culture (Breuil, Acheulean III).

The fossil mammalian fauna recovered from the Swanscombe interglacial deposits includes 26 species (Sutcliffe, 1964). Amongst those recognized from the Upper Middle Gravel are wolf (*Canis cf. lupus*), lion (*Panthera leo*), straight tusked elephant (*Palaeoloxodon antiquus*), Merck's rhinoceros (*Dicerorhinus kirchbergensis* = *mercki*), horse (*Equus cf. caballus*), fallow deer (*Dama dama*), giant deer (*Megaceros giganteus*), red deer (*Cervus elaphus*), giant ox (*Bos primigenius*) and hare (*Lepus sp.*). During 1968, 1969 and 1970 new excavations were conducted at Swanscombe (Waechter *et al.* 1969–1972) into the Lower Loam and Lower Gravels. Worked flint and mammalian bones were recovered.

The most significant finds were retrieved at the junction between the Lower Loam and Lower Gravels on what has been termed a 'floor'. On this floor was a skull of cave bear (*Ursus spelaeus*) and several bovid and cervid fragments.

Dating   On geological and faunal grounds, it seems probable that the deposit dates from the close of the Second Interglacial (Mindel–Riss or Penultimate Interglacial), a date which is confirmed by the type of tool culture associated with the remains (Wymer, 1974). The fluorine content of the skull fragments and the associated mammalian bones is similar, confirming the contemporaneity of the specimens (Oakley, 1949). More recently the Second Interglacial date of the Swanscombe fragments has been reaffirmed by Kurtén (1962), Oakley (1964), and Szabo and Collins (1975). An absolute age of about 225,000 years is suggested by thermoluminescence dating (Bridgland, *et al.*, 1985).

Morphology   The bones comprise an occipital (1935), a left parietal (1936) and a right parietal (1955). All three are almost complete and undistorted, the sutures are open and the bones clearly fit together; it is believed that they belong to a young adult. In general the bones are of modern form, but the parietals are exceptionally thick. The occipital shows no sign of a chignon and the transverse ridge—scarcely a torus—is more prominent at its ends than in its central portion. The occipital condyles and the orientation of the foramen magnum do not differ significantly from those features in *Homo sapiens*. The sphenoidal sinus must have been large as it extends into the basi-occiput. The parietals are quadrangular and marked

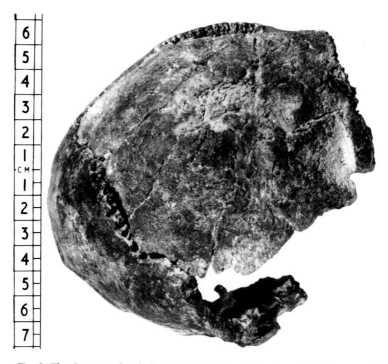

Fig. 6. The Swanscombe skull (right lateral view). *Courtesy of the Trustees of the British Museum (Nat. Hist.)*

Fig. 7. The Swanscombe skull (occipital view). *Courtesy of the Trustees of the British Museum (Nat. Hist.)*

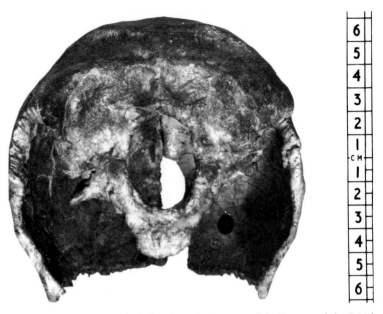

Fig. 8. The Swanscombe skull (basal view). *Courtesy of the Trustees of the British Museum (Nat. Hist.)*

by the temporal lines which are well separated from each other and pass below the parietal eminence. The parietal foramina are absent and the biasterionic breadth is large. Neither parietal has a Sylvian crest on its internal surface, but the meningeal vascular pattern is complex and of unusual form by comparison with modern human bones. The grooves for the dural venous sinuses are asymmetrical.

Dimensions

Swanscombe Committee (1938). Morant
Max. Length (181·5)   Max. Breadth (142)
Biasterionic Breadth 123·5?   Cranial Index 78?
Cranial Capacity (1,325 cc)   (Mesocephalic?)

Weiner and Campbell (1964)
Biasterionic Breadth 123·0   Max. Breadth (145)
? Close approximation
( ) Estimated

Affinities

The first two bones were studied by the Swanscombe Committee (Le Gros Clark *et al.*, 1938). In their report Morant showed that the metrical characters of the occipital and left parietal bones could not be distinguished from those of *Homo sapiens* with the exception of the biasterionic breadth; because of this difference and the thickness of the vault Morant suggested that the frontal bone might be like that of Steinheim man. This view has been re-expressed by Breitinger (1952 and 1955). Vallois (1954) saw no reason to suggest that

Swanscombe man had brow ridges and regards Swanscombe and Fontéchevade as 'Praesapiens' forms evolving in parallel with the Steinheim–Neandertal line. Le Gros Clark (1955) again drew attention to the similarities between the Swanscombe and Steinheim forms, referring to both as representatives of 'Pre-Mousterian and Early Mousterian *Homo sapiens*'. Other authors are less convinced of the sapient features of Swanscombe man and emphasize the Neandertal and primitive features of these remains (Breitinger, 1952 and 1955; Stewart, 1960). Howell (1960) affirmed that the known fragments from Swanscombe and Steinheim indicate that both forms represent the same hominid variety and that they 'deviate from the anatomically modern morphological pattern and, instead, are allied with early Neanderthal peoples'.

The Swanscombe site and fossil material were thoroughly reinvestigated in 1964 (Ovey *et al.*, 1964). Following a morphological, metrical and statistical reappraisal of the skull bones, Weiner and Campbell (1964) emphasized the degree of interrelatedness between the forms of *Homo*, i.e. Solo, Rhodesian, Neandertal and modern man. They suggest that it is not possible to maintain, in a taxonomic sense, strictly specific status for each of these forms, regarding them as a 'spectrum' of varieties within one species.

In an appraisal of the Vértesszöllös occipital (*q.v.*) Wolpoff (1971) has suggested that the Swanscombe skull probably represents a later female example of the same lineage. A lineage that he attributes to *Homo erectus*. More recently Wolpoff (1980) has emphasized again that the features of both Steinheim and Swanscombe lean towards those of *Homo erectus* where they differ from the Neandertals. However, Wolpoff does now admit to a preference for a *Homo sapiens* allocation for both specimens whilst considerig them to be female examples of an evolving lineage that includes Petralona (*q.v.*), Bilzingsleben (*q.v.*) and Vértesszöllös (*q.v.*). From recent work and from the literature several points stand out. The similarity between the Swanscombe and Steinheim skulls is reaffirmed by several authors (Santa Luca, 1978; Wolpoff, 1980; Stringer, Hublin & Vandermeersch, 1984). The Neandertal features of Swanscombe have been emphasized again (Santa Luca, 1978) and the feeling grows that Neandertal is a term that should be used only for European and Near Eastern fossils. The limited extent of the Swanscombe remains, the earliest of which have been known now for half a century, makes appraisal difficult. My view is that the skull can best be regarded as a female example of a *Homo erectus/Homo sapiens* transitional form that is at the root of the European Neandertal side branch.

Originals   British Museum (Natural History), Cromwell Road, South Kensington, London, S.W.7.

Casts   The University Museum, University of Pennsylvania, Philadelphia 4, Pennsylvania, U.S.A.

References   Smith, R. A. and Dewey, H. (1913) Stratification at Swanscombe. *Archaeologia 64*, 177–204.

Marston, A. T. (1936) Preliminary note on a new fossil human skull from Swanscombe, Kent. *Nature 138*, 200–201.

Marston, A. T. (1937) The Swanscombe skull. *J. R. anthrop. Inst. 67*, 339–406.

Clark, W. E. Le Gros, Oakley, K. P., Morant, G. M., King, W. B. R., Hawkes, C. F. C., *et al.* (1938) Report of the Swanscombe Committee. *J. R. anthrop. Inst. 68*, 17–98.

Paterson, T. T. (1940) Geology and early man. *Nature 146*, 12–15, 49–52.

Kennard, A. S. (1942) Faunas of the High Terrace at Swanscombe. *Proc. geol. Ass. Lond. 53*, 105.

Montandon, G. (1943) *L'Homme Préhistorique et les préhumains.* Paris: Payot.

Oakley, K. P., and Montagu, M. F. A. (1949) A reconsideration of the Galley Hill skeleton. *Bull. Br. Mus. Nat. Hist. 1*, 27–46.

Breitinger, E. (1952) Zur Morphologie und systematischer Stellung des Schädelfragmentes von Swanscombe. *Homo 3*, 131–133.

Oakley, K. P. (1952) Swanscombe man. *Proc. geol. Ass. Lond. 63*, 271–300.

Vallois, H. V. (1954) Neandertals and praesapiens. *J. R. anthrop. Inst. 84*, 111–130.

Breitinger, E. (1955) Das Schädelfragmentes von Swanscombe und das 'Praesapiens-problem'. *Mitt. anthrop. Ges. Wien 84/85*, 1–45.

Clark, W. E. Le Gros (1955) *The fossil evidence for human evolution.* Chicago: Chicago University Press.

Wymer, J. (1955) A further fragment of the Swanscombe skull. *Nature 176*, 426–427.

Oakley, K. P. (1957) Stratigraphical age of the Swanscombe skull. *Am. J. phys. Anthrop. 15*, 253–260.

Stewart, T. D. (1960) Indirect evidence of the primitiveness of the Swanscombe skull. *Am. J. phys. Anthrop. 18*, 363.

Howell, F. C. (1960) European and northwest African Middle Pleistocene hominids. *Curr. Anthrop. 1*, 195–232.

Kurtén, B. (1962) The relative ages of the australopithecines of Transvaal and the pithecanthropines of Java. In *Evolution und Hominisation*, 74–80. Ed. G. Kurth. Stuttgart: Gustav Fischer Verlag.

Ovey, C. D. Ed., (1964) *The Swanscombe Skull.* R. Anthrop. Inst., *Occ. Pap. No. 20.* London: Royal Anthropological Institute.

Conway, B. W. (1969) Preliminary geological investigation of Boyn Hill terrace deposits at Barnfield pit, Swanscombe, Kent, during 1968. *Proc. R. anthrop. Inst. of Gt Br. and Ir. 1968*, 59–61.

Waechter, J. D'A. (1969) Swanscombe 1968. *Proc. R. anthrop. Inst. Gt Br. and Ir. 1968*, 53–61.

Conway, B. W. (1970) Geological investigation of Boyn Hill terrace deposits at Barnfield pit, Swanscombe, Kent, during 1969. *Proc. R. anthrop. Inst. Gt Br. and Ir. 1969*, 90–92.

Newcomer, M. H. (1970) The method of excavation at Barnfield pit, Swanscombe (1969). *Proc. R. anthrop. Inst. Gt Br. and Ir. 1969*, 87–89.

Waechter, J. D'A. (1970) Swanscombe 1969. *Proc. R. anthrop. Inst. Gt Br. and Ir. 1969*, 83–85.

Conway, B. W. (1971) Geological investigation of Boyn Hill terrace deposits at Barnfield pit, Swanscombe, Kent, during 1970. *Proc. R. anthrop. Inst. Gt Br. and Ir. 1970*, 60–63.

Newcomer, M. H. (1971) Conjoined flakes from the Lower Loam, Barnfield pit, Swanscombe (1970). *Proc. R. anthrop. Inst. Gt Br. and Ir. 1970*, 51–59.

Oakley, K. P., Campbell, B. G. and Molleson, T. I. (1971) *Catalogue of Fossil Hominids Part II: Europe*. London: Trustees of the British Museum (Natural History).

Waechter, J. D'A. (1971) Swanscombe 1970. *Proc. R. anthrop. Inst. Gt Br. and Ir. 1970*, 43–49.

Wolpoff, M. H. (1971) Is Vértesszöllös an occipital of *Homo erectus? Nature 232*, 867–868.

Conway, B. W. (1972) Geological investigation of the Boyn Hill terrace deposits at Barnfield pit, Swanscombe, Kent, during 1971. *Proc. R. anthrop. Inst. Gt Br. and Ir. 1971*, 80–85.

Waechter, J. D'A. (1972) Swanscombe 1971. *Proc. R. anthrop. Inst. Gt Br. and Ir. 1971*, 73–78.

Szabo, B. J. and Collins, D. (1975) Ages of fossil bones from British Interglacial sites. *Nature 254*, 680–682.

Wymer, J. J. (1974) Clactonian and Acheulian industries in Britain—their chronology and significance. *Proc. geol. Ass. 85*, 391–421.

Santa Luca, A. P. (1978) A re-examination of presumed Neandertal-like fossils. *J. hum. Evol. 7*, 619–636.

Wolpoff, M. H. (1980) Cranial remains of Middle Pleistocene European hominids. *J. hum. Evol. 9*, 339–358.

Stringer, C. B., Hublin, J.-J. and Vandermeersch, B. (1984) The origin of anatomically modern humans in Western Europe. In *The Origins of Modern Humans*. Eds. F. H. Smith and F. Spencer. New York: Alan R. Liss.

Bridgland, D. R., Gibbard, P. L., Harding, P., Kemp, R. A. and Southgate, G. (1985) New information and results from recent excavations at Barnfield Pit, Swanscombe. *Q. Newsl. 46*, 25–39.

The Pontnewydd Remains

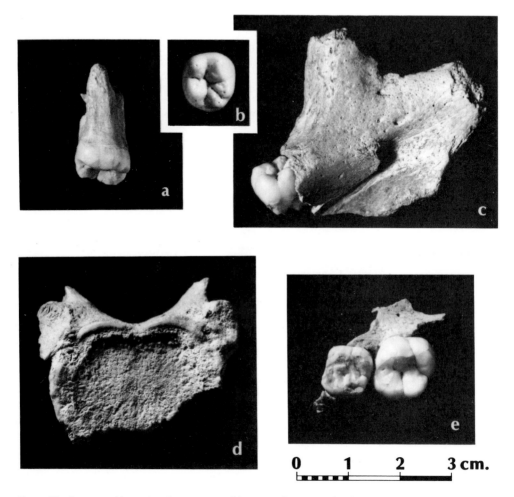

Fig. 9. The Pontnewydd remains. *By permission of the National Museum of Wales.*

Synonyms and other names *Homo* sp. indet. (Green *et al.*, 1981); Pontnewydd 1–6; PN1–PN6; Pontnewydd man.

Site Pontnewydd Cave is to be found in the lower Elwy valley of North Wales, near to the western edge of the vale of Clwyd about 5 miles from the town of Denbigh.

Found   H. S. Green and others.

1980—PN1
1981—PN2, PN3
1982—PN4
1983—PN5, PN6
1984—PN2, molar
1985—PN7

Geology   The cave is cut into the Carboniferous limestone scarp that forms one side of the valley of the river Elwy; its opening is about 50 m above the present level of the river. The valley contains drift deposits whose terraces approach the height of the cave entrance in places. The cave deposits are stratified and comprise Lower and Upper Sands and Gravels on the bedrock followed by an Intermediate Complex, Lower Breccia, *in situ* Stalagmite, Silt, Upper Breccia, Upper Clays and Sands capped by a Post Glacial stalagmitic floor. The molar tooth (PN1) was found in the Intermediate Complex; PN4–7 are from the Lower Breccia; and PN2 and 3 come from disturbed contexts.

Associated finds   The first occurrence of artefacts in deposits from Pontnewydd Cave were reported by Hughes and Thomas (1874). The artefacts were found in debris thrown out of the cave and they were made of a 'felstone' foreign to the site with evidence of intentional shaping. They are described as discoids, flakes and even scrapers that resemble 'common Le Mouster flints'. The new excavations have produced some 300 artefacts, mostly made of volcanic rock, including discoidal cores, Levallois cores, handaxes, cleavers, chopping tools, Mousterian points and scrapers (Green *et al.*, 1981; Green, 1981; Green, 1984).

The fossil mammalian remains originally reported from the site included a human tooth (now lost) and listed by Hughes and Thomas (1874). The recent excavations have recovered the following mammalian fossils from the Intermediate Complex, the lowest stratum to contain human remains: wolf (*Canis lupus*), bear (*Ursus sp.*), a felid (*Panthera* aff. *pardus*), a horse (*Equus sp.*), rhinoceros (*Dicerorhinus hemitoechus*), roe deer (*Capreolus capreolus*), beaver (*Castor fiber*), water vole (*Arvicola cantiana*), vole (*Microtus gregalis*) and wood mouse (*Apodemus cf. sylvaticus*) (Green *et al.*, 1981; Green, 1984). The overlying Lower Breccia did not produce roe deer, beaver or wood mouse but produced, in addition, Merck's rhinoceros (*Didermocerus cf. kirchbergensis*), red deer (*Cervus elaphus*), a bovine (*Bos* or *Bison sp.*), Norway lemming (*Lemmus lemmus*), northern vole (*Microtus oeconomus*) and pika (*Ochotona sp*).

Dating   The fauna recovered from the hominid levels inside the cave indicates a later Middle Pleistocene date with successive interglacial (Intermediate Complex) and cooler (Lower Breccia) conditions.

Uranium series dates and thermoluminescence analyses have combined with other evidence to suggest that the site was occupied before 225,000 years B.P. and perhaps during the interglacial period beginning about 250,000 years B.P. (Green *et al.*, 1981; Cook *et al.*, 1982; Green, 1984).

Morphology   The 'human molar' reported by Busk in Hughes and Thomas (1874) was said to be of 'very large size'. Despite a recent appeal it remains lost (Molleson, 1976). The hominid remains recovered in the recent excavations are dental, mandibular and vertebral.

Pontnewydd 1 (PN1)

Probably a left upper second molar from an adult. It has a large, low rectangular crown, a complete lingual root but broken buccal roots. The tooth has four cusps, the buccal being higher than the lingual. Occlusal attrition has exposed the dentine on the protocone. There is no Carabelli's cusp or pit on the lingual surface neither is there a cingulum. Radiographs show marked taurodontism of hour-glass shape (Stringer, in Green *et al.*, 1981).

Pontnewydd 2 (PN2)

This is an immature mandibular fragment and consists of part of the right ramus containing a rootless molar crown that is partly erupted. The head and neck of the right side of the mandible are broken off the condyloid process but the coronoid process is virtually intact. The external surface of the fragment is unremarkable but the internal surface is pierced by an inferior alveolar canal that is overhung by a lingular process. The groove for the mylohyoid vessels and nerve can be clearly seen on this surface, yet there is no sign of a crista entocoronoidea a crista entocondyloidea or a crista pharyngea. The age of the individual from this fragment has been given as about 11 years on modern human development patterns and the partly erupted molar has been identified as a third molar (Stringer, in Green 1984). An additional lower molar attributable to this individual was recovered from the same disturbed context in 1984.

Pontnewydd 3 (PN3)

Part of the body of a thoracic vertebra.

Pontnewydd 4 (PN4)

A right maxillary fragment containing a deciduous and a permanent molar tooth from an individual aged 8–9 years on the basis of modern human dental ages. The permanent molar shows taurodontism. The deciduous molar is very worn but its roots are not yet resorbed.

Pontnewydd 5, 6, 7 (PN5–7)

Three isolated teeth, all lower premolars, are large crowned. Two may be from a child of 8–12 years and the other from a somewhat older individual.

Dimensions   Stringer, in Green *et al.*, (1981); Green (1984)

PN1   *Left Upper second molar*

Mesiodistal length	10·9
Bucco-lingual breadth	12·9

PN2   *Mandibular fragment*

Minimum breadth of ramus	31·5

PN3   *Vertebral fragment*

Transverse breadth	35·2

PN4   *Deciduous molar (dM²)*

Mesiodistal length	9·2
Bucco-lingual breadth	10·25

Permanent molar (M¹)

Mesiodistal length	12·25
Bucco-lingual breadth	12·35

Affinities   Comparison of the Pontnewydd remains with other European fossil hominids confirms the presence of some Neandertal-like features in the upper molars; but the mandibular and vertebral fragment cannot be clearly identified as differing from the modern human condition. The scanty remains from the site preclude firm conclusions but the presence of marked taurodontism at this early stage, some 150,000 years before the appearance of 'classic' Neandertalers of the Fourth Glacial period (Würm or Last Glaciation) is of considerable interest. There are no features that would suggest strong affinity with *Homo erectus*. The unstratified fragments are too scanty to be positively excluded from representing anatomically modern *Homo sapiens* and thus cannot be assigned to any other taxon (Stringer *et al.*, 1984).

Originals   The National Museum of Wales, Cardiff.

Casts   The National Museum of Wales, Cardiff and the British Museum (Natural History).

References   Hughes, T. McK. and Thomas, D. R. (1874) On the occurrence of felstone implements of the Le Moustier type in Pontnewydd Cave, near Cefn, St Asaph. *J. anthrop. Inst.* 3, 387–390.

Molleson, T. (1976) Remains of Pleistocene man in Paviland and Pontnewydd Caves, Wales. *Trans. Br. Cave Res. Assoc.* 3, 112–116.

Green, H. S. (1981) The first Welshman: excavations at Pontnewydd. *Antiquity* 55, 184–195.

Green, H. S., Stringer, C. B., Collcutt, S. N., Currant, A. P., Huxtable, J., Schwarcz, H. P., Debenham, N., Embleton, C., Bull, P., Molleson, T. I. and Bevins, R. E. (1981) Pontnewydd Cave in Wales—a new Middle Pleistocene hominid site. *Nature* 294, 707–713.

Cook, J., Stringer, C. B., Currant, A. P., Schwarcz, H. P. and Wintle, A. G. (1982) A review of the chronology of the European Middle Pleistocene hominid record. *Yearb. phys. Anthrop.* 25, 19–65.

Green, H. S. (1984) *Pontnewydd Cave: A Lower Palaeolithic hominid site in Wales. The first report.* Cardiff: National Museum of Wales.

Stringer, C. B., Hublin, J.-J., and Vandermeersch, B. (1984) The origin of anatomically modern humans in Western Europe. In *The Origins of Modern Humans*, 51–135. Eds. F. H. Smith and F. Spencer. New York: Alan R. Liss.

The La Chapelle-aux-Saints Skeleton

FRANCE   LA CHAPELLE-AUX-SAINTS

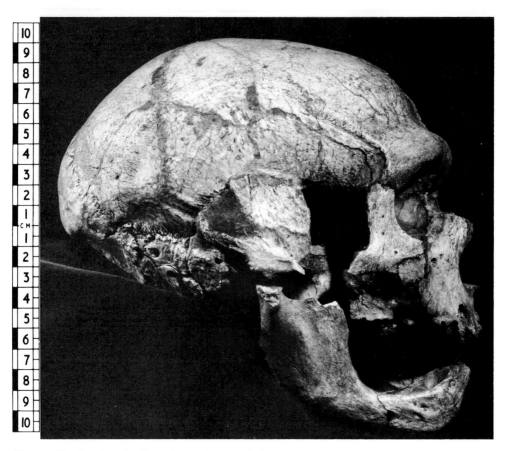

Fig. 10. The skull from La Chappelle-aux-Saints (right lateral view). *Courtesy of the Director of the Musée de l'Homme.*

Synonyms and other names	*Homo neanderthalensis* (Boule, 1911–1913); *Homo sapiens neanderthalensis* (Campbell, 1964); Neanderthal man; Neandertal man; La Chapelle-aux-Saints 1. (Oakley, Campbell and Molleson, 1971).
Site	Near the village of La Chapelle-aux-Saints, 25 miles south-east of Brive, Corrèze, France.
Found by	A. and J. Bouyssonie and L. Bardon, 3rd August, 1908.
Geology	The skeleton was found buried in the floor of a small cave hollowed

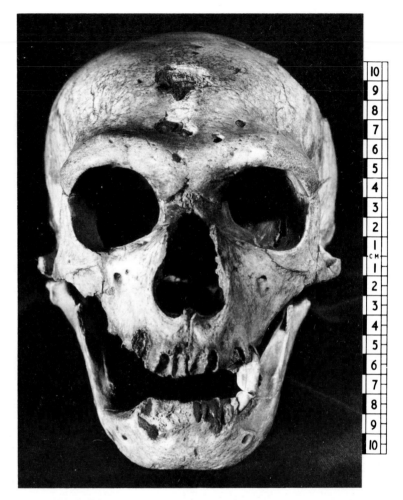

Fig. 11. The skull from La Chappelle-aux-Saints (frontal view). *Courtesy of the Director of the Musée de l'Homme.*

into the limestone of the Lower Lias, which rests upon Triassic sandstone. The skeleton was covered with calcareous clay containing stones which had fallen from the roof. The stratigraphy was carefully recorded whilst the remains were uncovered.

Associated finds With the bones were numerous flint tools of an evolved Mousterian culture including retouched blades, scrapers and keeled scrapers which are almost Aurignacian. In addition there were numerous fossil bones which belonged to mammals such as woolly rhinoceros (*Coelodonta antiquitatis*), reindeer (*Rangifer tarandus*), ibex (*Capra ibex*), hyena (*Crocuta crocuta*), marmot (*Arctomys marmotta*), wild horse (*Equus sp.*), bison (*Bison priscus*) and wolf (*Canis lupus*).

Dating   In view of the 'cold weather' fauna and the tool culture the skeleton has been attributed to the Upper Pleistocene, probably the Fourth Glacial period (Würm or Last Glaciation).

Morphology   The skeleton is almost complete and belonged to an adult male. It comprises the skull, twenty-one vertebrae, twenty ribs, one clavicle, two humeri, two radii, two ulnae, several hand bones including one scaphoid, one capitate, metacarpals I, II, III and V, as well as two proximal phalanges. The lower limbs are represented by two pelvic fragments, two femora, two patellae, parts of two tibiae, one fibula, one calcaneus, one talus, five metatarsals and several other fragmentary bones. The bones have been described by Boule (1911–1913) in detail.

The Skull

The skull is large and well preserved, having a low vault and a receding forehead. The supraorbital arches are large but the mastoid processes are small. The orbits are voluminous, the nose broad and the mandible stout but chinless. The central region of the face projects well forward. The occipital bone is prominent and protrudes into a typical bun shape and is surmounted by two suprainiac fossae.

The Teeth

The teeth are badly worn and some are missing. The extent of the damage is such that it has been believed that such a 'toothless' old man may have needed feeding on pap. A reappraisal of the dentition has suggested that he may have had intact upper and lower incisors, canine and premolar teeth on the left side and similar teeth in the maxilla of the right side. This would have been sufficient to allow mastication (Tappen, 1985).

The Postcranial Bones

In general the limb bones are short and thick, with strong markings and large joints. The humeri are straight but the femora are bowed; similarly the radii are curved, having a medial concavity. The tibiae are short and stout, and their upper ends appear to be bent backwards into a position of retroversion. The fibula is robust. The hand and foot bones are not unlike those of modern man; the scaphoid and capitate seem small, but the metacarpals are stout with large heads. The foot bones are rugged, the talus in particular being high and short-necked; the calcaneus is robust and has a prominent sustentacular shelf.

The vertebral column, as described by Boule (1911–1913), is said to have long, backwardly directed cervical spinous processes which are frequently bifid. The cervical and lumbar curvatures of the spine are obliterated and the remainder of the vertebrae are said to be short-bodied.

In view of the features of the post-cranial skeleton, Boule suggested that the stance of La Chapelle man (Neandertal man) was stooping with flexed hips and knees and jutting head carriage, and his undoubtedly bipedal gait imperfect and slouching. Examination of the skeleton (Arambourg, 1955; Cave and Straus, 1957; Patte, 1955, Dastugue and de Lumley 1976) has shown that there is evidence of gross deforming osteoarthritis present in the specimen and that Boule's reconstruction is faulty in a number of respects. The reasoning behind Boule's conclusion concerning the stance and gait of the La Chapelle Man, as well as his conclusion that the Neandertalers represent an extinct side branch, has been explained by Hammond (1982). He advances the view that these conclusions owe more to preconceived notions than to a dispassionate anatomical appraisal. Comparison with other Neandertal remains and a wider range of modern skeletal material has shown that many of the features recognized as being characteristically Neandertal fall within the range of modern human skeletal variation. Whilst Cave and Strauss (1957) do not deny the distinctive morphological characters of Neandertal man, they suggest that he stood and walked as does modern man.

A full re-evaluation of the La Chapelle skeleton has suggested that, whilst this individual did indeed suffer from degenerative joint disease, Boule's faulty postural reconstruction was not affected by the presence of this condition (Trinkaus, 1985).

Dimensions   Boule (1911–1913), Patte (1955)

Skull

Max. Length 208   Max. Breadth 156
Cranial Capacity 1,620 cc   Cranial Index 75·0
                                 (Dolichocephalic)
Symphysial Angle of Mandible 104°

Postcranial Bones

	Length	Circumference		Torsion
Right humerus	313		72	148°
Left humerus	—		65	—
Radius Length	235*	A/P diam.	12·0	Width 16·0
Ulna Length	255–260*	Upper Arm/Forearm		
		Carrying Angle	179°	
Capitate Length	24·0	Breadth	14·0	

* Restored.

	I	II	Metacarpals III	IV	V
Length	44·5	73·0*	71·0*	—	54·0
Min. diam.	11·0	7·5	8·0	—	6·5

Femur Length 430* (R)	A/P diam. 31·0 (L)	Trans. diam. 29·0 (L)
Tibiae —	Damaged —	
Talus Length/Breadth Index 107·5		Horiz. Angle of Neck 23°
Calcaneus Length 80*	Breadth 47	

*Restored.

Numerous measurements and indices relating to the La Chapelle skeleton are quoted by Patte (1955).

Affinities The similarities between the skeleton from Neandertal and that from La Chapelle-aux-Saints leave little doubt that they belong to the same species. Further finds have established that these men were widely distributed in Europe and the Near East during the Upper Pleistocene period. Their sudden disappearance and replacement by modern forms of man remains a topic for speculation and investigation. It is uncertain whether they became extinct because of the invasion of more advanced hominids, or became assimilated by the evolving population of modern man, or directly gave rise to modern man, an older view revived by Brace (1964). In a classification of the Hominidae, Campbell (1964) has identified Neandertal man as a subspecies of *Homo sapiens* (*Homo sapiens neanderthalensis*). The importance of the La Chapelle skeleton has rested in the depth of the original study by Boule (1911–1913) that made it the Neandertal 'reference specimen' for many years. There are now other specimens such as La Ferrassie (*q.v.*) and Shanidar (*q.v.*) that have given new insights into Neandertal morphology, a morphology well epitomized by Stringer, Hublin and Vandermeersch (1984). La Chapelle is now being viewed in a better perspective than before and its shortcomings as a Neandertal stereotype are being further exposed.

Original Musée de l'Homme, Palais de Chaillot, Paris–16ᵉ, France.

Casts 1 Musée de l'Homme, Paris   (Cranium and endocranium).
2 The University Museum, University of Pennsylvania, Philadelphia 4, Pennsylvania, U.S.A. (Restored skull only).

References Boule, M. (1908) L'Homme fossile de La Chapelle-aux-Saints (Corrèze). *C. r. Acad. Sci. Paris.* 147, 1349–1352.
Boule, M. (1908) L'Homme fossile de La Chapelle-aux-Saints. *Anthropologie* 19, 519–525.

Bouyssonie, A. and J. and Bardon, L. (1908) Découverte d'un squelette humain moustérien à La Chapelle-aux-Saints, Corrèze. *C. r. Acad. Sci. Paris* 147, 1414–1415.

Boule, M. (1911–1913) L'Homme fossile de La Chapelle-aux-Saints. *Annls Paléont. 6, 7, and 8.*

Hrdlička, A. (1930) The skeletal remains of early man. *Smithson. misc. Collns* 83, 1–379.

Arambourg, C. (1955) Sur l'attitude en station verticale, des Néanderthaliens. *C. r. Acad. Sci. Paris 240*, 804–806.

Patte, E. (1955) *Les Néanderthaliens: Anatomie, Physiologie, Comparaisons.* Paris: Masson et Cie.

Cave, A. J. E., and Straus, W. L. Jnr. (1957) Pathology and posture of Neanderthal man. *Q. Rev. Biol. 32*, 348–363.

Brace, C. L. (1964) A consideration of hominid catastrophism. *Curr. Anthrop. 5*, 3–43.

Campbell, B. (1964) Quantitative taxonomy and human evolution. In *Classification and Human Evolution*, 50–74. Ed. S. L. Washburn. London: Methuen and Co. Ltd.

Oakley, K. P., Campbell, B. G. and Molleson, T. I. (1971) *Catalogue of Fossil Hominids Part II: Europe.* London: Trustees of the British Museum (Natural History).

Dastugue, J. and De Lumley, M. A. (1976) Les Maladies des hommes préhistorique du Paléolithique et du Mesolithique. In *La Préhistoire Francaise*, 612–622. Ed. H. de Lumley. Paris: CNRS.

Hammond, M. (1982) The expulsion of the Neanderthals from human ancestry: Marcellin Boule and the social context of scientific research. *Soc. Stud. Sci. 12*, 1–36.

Trinkaus, E. (1983) Pathology and posture of the La Chapelle-aux-Saints Neandertal. *Am. J. phys. Anthrop. 60*, 262.

Stringer, C. B., Hublin, J.-J. and Vandermeersch, B. (1984) The origin of anatomically modern humans in Western Europe. In *The Origins of Modern Humans*, 51–135. Eds F. H. Smith and F. Spencer. New York: Alan R. Liss.

Tappen, N. C. (1985) The dentition of the 'Old Man' of La Chapelle-aux-Saints and inferences concerning Neandertal behaviour. *Am. J. phys. Anthrop. 67*, 43–50.

Trinkaus, E. (1985) Pathology and the posture of the La Chapelle-aux-Saints Neandertal. *Ibid*, 19–41.

The La Ferrassie Skeletons

FRANCE   LA FERRASSIE

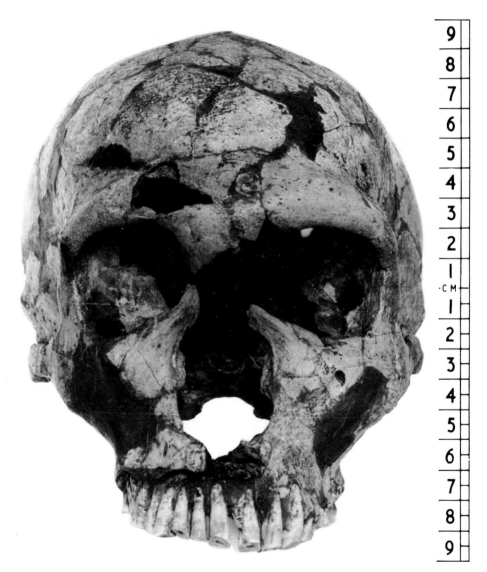

Fig. 12. The La Ferrassie I skull (frontal view). *Courtesy of the Director of the Musée de l'Homme.*

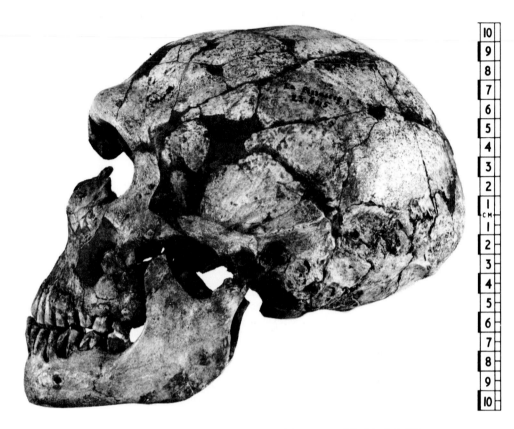

Fig. 13. The La Ferrassie I skull (left lateral view). *Courtesy of the Director of the Musée de l'Homme.*

Synonyms and other names	*Homo neanderthalensis* (Boule, 1911–1913); *Homo sapiens neanderthalensis* (Campbell, 1964) Neanderthal man; Neandertal man; Ferrassie 1 to 8.
Site	La Ferrassie, 3.5 km north of Bugue, Dordogne, France.
Found by	R. Capitan and D. Peyrony, 17 September 1909 (No. 1), September, 1910 (No. 2), 8 August 1912 (No. 3), 10 August 1912 (Nos. 4a and 4b), 26 April 1920 (No. 5), 1 July 1921 (No. 6). H. Delporte and co-workers September 1973 (No. 8) [No. 7 is now regarded as part of No. 3.]
Geology	The remains were in a rock shelter. The stratigraphy, determined by a group of eminent French prehistorians, was said to be the same as that found at La Chapelle-aux-Saints. The skeletons were found below three Perigordian layers, four Aurignacian levels and one Chatelperonian layer at the bottom of a layer containing Mousterian tools; this in turn rested upon another layer containing

Acheulean implements. The bones of the first skeleton were lying in anatomical relation with each other and the layers were undisturbed.

Associated finds   The tools found with the skeletons are of the Charentian Mousterian culture (Bourgon, 1957). The first mammalian bones recovered from the same deposit include those of mammoth (*Mammuthus primigenius*), hyena (*Crocuta crocuta*), pig (*Sus sp.*), ox (*Bos sp.*), red deer (*Cervus elaphus*) and horse (*Equus sp.*).

Dating   The tools and fauna suggest an Upper Pleistocene date for the remains, probably during the Fourth Glacial period (Würm II) (Vandermeersch, 1965), possibly > 38,000 years B.P. (Delporte *et al.* 1984).

Morphology   Originally only partly described (Boule, 1911–1913) the skeletons have now been reported more extensively (Heim, 1968, 1970, 1974, 1976, 1982a, b and e, 1984). La Ferrassie 1 is said to be the skeleton of an adult male and La Ferrassie 2 that of an adult female. La Ferrassie 3 is reported as the remains of a child of about 10 years of age, while number 4a is the remains of a foetus, 4b those of a neonate, La Ferrassie 5 the remains of a 6–7-month foetus and La Ferrassie 6 those of an infant of about three years. The adult skeletons are virtually complete while the immature skeletons are fragmentary. La Ferrassie 8 is the remains of an infant of 22–26 months.

The Skull

The male skull (No. 1) has stout supraorbital ridges, a flattened vault with recession of the forehead, a protuberant occiput and small mastoid processes. The hard palate is broad and limited by an almost parabolic dental arcade. The mandible is perhaps more modern than that of La Chapelle man. It has a feeble chin, a deep mandibular notch and large coronoid processes. The teeth are all in place in both jaws, with no diastema. All of the teeth are badly worn so that no details of crown morphology are discernible.

In occlusion there is slight anterior displacement of the mandible so that the lower incisors project slightly in front of the upper incisors (negative overjet or underbite).

It has been suggested that the wear of the adult dentition should indicate that this hominid made use of the teeth as a 'tool'; however, it is hard to distinguish this form of attrition from that caused by coarse particles in the diet (Wallace, 1975). This suggestion of non-masticatory tooth wear has been both contested (Wallace, 1975; Puech, 1981) and subsequently (Brace, Ryan and Smith, 1981) supported.

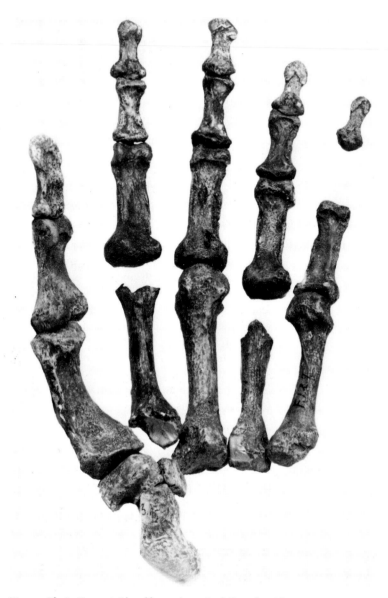

Fig. 14. The La Ferrassie I hand bones (an articulation of casts).

The Postcranial Bones

The limb bones resemble those of La Chapelle man in their principal features, tending to be robust with large joints. The tibiae have retroverted heads and the fibulae are stout.

The adult skeletons have well preserved feet and hands. Examination of the original foot bones (Nos. 1 and 2) shows that the great toe is not divergent, the longitudinal and transverse arches of the foot are well formed and that the general foot structure corresponds with that of modern man. These characteristics suggest that the stance and gait of La Ferrassie man differed little from that of *Homo sapiens*.

The hand bones are stout, the carpal arch is deep and the carpometacarpal joint of the thumb is saddle-shaped.

From a detailed metrical and morphological study of Neandertal hand bones, including those from La Ferrassie, Musgrave (1970 and 1971) concluded that the Neandertal hand shows unique features that may reflect environmental adaptations or the imperfect development of manual skill.

Dimensions Heim (1974)

Skull (La Ferrassie 1)

Max. Length 207·5   Max. Breadth 158
Cranial Capacity 1,681 cc.   Cranial Index 76·1
                                                 (Dolichocephalic)
Symphysial Angle of Mandible 85°

Postcranial Bones

	L.F. 1	L.F. 2
Right Humerus Max. Length	339	286
Left Humerus Max. Length	335	—
Right Tibia Max. Length)		302
Left Tibia Max. Length)	c. 370	300
Estimated Stature	1·7 m	1·48 m

Affinities The features of the skeletons indicate that they belong to the group of Neandertal men represented by the original Neandertal skeleton and the skeleton from La Chapelle-aux-Saints. This group is characterized by numerous skeletal similarities as well as by their general contemporaneity, and had led to their designation as 'classic' Neandertalers of the Würm glaciation. Campbell (1964) identified Neandertal man as a subspecies of *Homo sapiens* (*Homo sapiens neanderthalensis*).

Recent studies of sexual dimorphism in the skulls of Neandertal man (Smith, 1980; Heim, 1982c and d) and the postcranial bones (Smith, 1980; Trinkaus, 1980; Heim, 1983) have shown that it is very limited in amount. The preservation and completeness of the La Ferrassie I remains is such that Neandertal morphological features like the *sulcus axillaris teretis* of the axillary border of the scapula and the flattened superior pubic ramus, can be found in one specimen (Trinkaus, 1976, 1977). La Ferrassie is thus one of the most important Neandertal sites that has produced male and female adult skeletons and a unique collection of juvenile remains. The juvenile remains indicate a shortened growth period in these Neandertal children (Heim, 1981, 1984). It is also the first site at which intentional burial of Neandertals was established.

Originals   *Skeletons Nos. 1 to 4*—Musée de l'Homme, Palais de Chaillot, Paris–16ᵉ, France.

Skeletons Nos. 5 to 8—Musée des Eyzies, Les Eyzies, Dordogne, France.

Casts   Not available at present.

References   Capitan, L. and Peyrony, D. (1909) Deux squelettes humains au milieu de foyers de l'époque moustérienne. *Revue anthrop.* 19, 402–409.

Capitan, L. and Peyrony, D. (1911) Un nouveau squelette humain fossile. *Revue anthrop.* 21, 148–150.

Boule, M. (1911–1913) L'Homme fossile de La Chapelle-aux-Saints. *Annls Paléont.* 6, 7 and 8.

Capitan, L. and Peyrony, D. (1912) Station préhistorique de La Ferrassie. *Revue anthrop.* 22, 76–99.

Capitan, L. and Peyrony, D. (1912) Trois nouveaux squelettes humains fossiles. *Revue anthrop.* 22, 439–442.

Capitan, L. and Peyrony, D. (1921) Nouvelles fouilles à La Ferrassie, Dordogne. *C. r. Ass. fr. Avanc. Sci. 44ᵉ Session*, 540–542.

Capitan, L. and Peyrony, D. (1921) Découverte d'un sixième squelette moustérien à La Ferrassie, Dordogne. *Revue anthrop.* 31, 382–388.

Hrdlička, A. (1930) The skeletal remains of early man. *Smithson. misc. Collns.* 83, 1–379.

Patte, E. (1955) *Les Néanderthaliens: Anatomie, Physiologie, Comparaisons.* Paris: Masson et Cie.

Bourgon, M. (1957) Les industries moustériennes et prémoustériennes du Périgord. *Archs Inst. Paléont. hum.* 27, 141.

Campbell, B. (1964) Quantitative taxonomy and human evolution. In *Classification and Human Evolution*, 50–74. Ed. S.L. Washburn. London: Methuen and Co. Ltd.

Vandermeersch, B. (1965) Position stratigraphique et chronologie relative des restes humains du Paléolithique moyen dans le Sud-Ouest de la France. *Annls Paléont.* 51, 69–126.

Heim, J-L. (1968) Les restes neandertaliens de La Ferrassie. Nouvelles données sur la stratigraphie et inventaire des squelettes. *C. r. Acad. Sci., Paris.* 266, 576–578.

Anthony, J. and Heim, J-L. (1970) La morphologie encéphalique de l'Homme de La Ferrassie I. *C. r. Acad. Sci. Paris.* 271, 176–179.

Heim, J-L. (1970) L'encéphale Néandertalien de l'Homme de La Ferrassie. *Anthropologie* 74, 527–572.

Musgrave, J.H. (1970) An anatomical study of the hands of Pleistocene and Recent man. Ph.D. thesis, University of Cambridge.

Musgrave, J.H. (1971) How dextrous was Neanderthal man? *Nature* 233, 538–541.

Heim, J-L. (1974) Les hommes fossiles de La Ferrassie (Dordogne) et le problème de la définition des Néandertaliens classique. *Anthropologie*, 78, 81–112 and 321–378.

Wallace, J. A. (1975) Did La Ferrassie I use his teeth as a tool? *Curr. Anthrop.* *16*, 393–401.

Delporte, H. (1976) Les sépultures moustériennes de La Ferrassie. In *Les Sépultures Néandertaliennes*, 8–11. Ed. B. Vandermeersch. IXth Cong. UISPP Prétirage. Nice: CNRS.

Heim, J.-L. (1976) Les hommes fossiles de La Ferrassie. Tome 1. *Arch. Inst. Paléont. hum. Mem. 35*. Paris: Masson et Cie.

Trinkaus, E. (1976) The morphology of the European and Southwest Asian Neandertal pubic bones. *Am. J. phys. Anthrop. 44*, 95–104.

Trinkaus, E. (1977) A functional interpretation of the axillary border of the Neandertal scapula. *J. hum. Evol. 6*, 231–234.

Smith, F. H. (1980) Sexual differences in European Neanderthal crania with special reference to the Krapina remains. *J. hum. Evol. 9*, 359–375.

Trinkaus, E. (1980) Sexual differences in Neanderthal limb bones. *Ibid*, 377–397.

Brace, C. L., Ryan, A. S. and Smith, B. H. (1981) Tooth wear in La Ferrassie man: Comment. *Curr. Anthrop. 22*, 426–430.

Heim, J.-L. (1981) Les coroctères ontogeniques et biométrique de l'occipital néandertalien de La Ferrassie 8 (Dordogne). *C.r. Acad. Sci., Paris 293*. 195–198.

Puech, P.-F. (1981) *Ibid*, 424–426.

Heim, J.-L. (1982a) Les hommes fossiles de La Ferrassie II. Les squelettes d'adultes: Squelette des membres. *Arch. Inst. Paléont. hum. 38*, 1–272.

Heim, J.-L. (1982b) *Les Enfants Néandertaliens de La Ferrassie*. Paris: Masson et Cie.

Heim, J.-L. (1982c) Le dimorphisme sexuel du crâne des hommes de Néandertal. *L'Anthropologie 85*, 193–218.

Heim, J.-L. (1982d) *Ibid 85*, 451–469.

Heim, J.-L. (1982e) Les Hommes Fossiles de la Ferrassie, Tome II. *Arch. l'Inst. Paléont. hum. Mem. 38*. Paris: Masson et Cie.

Heim, J.-L. (1983) Les variations du squelette post-crânien des hommes de Néandertal suivant le sexe. *Ibid 87*, 5–26.

Delporte, H. *et al.* (1984) *Le grande abri de La Ferrassie*. Ed. H. Delporte. Études Quaternaires Mem. 7 Paris: Inst. Paléont.

Heim, J.-L. (1984) in *Le grand abri de la Ferrassie. Ibid.*.

Stringer, C. B., Hublin, J.-J. and Vandermeersch, B. (1984) The origin of anatomically modern humans in Western Europe. In *The Origins of Modern Humans*, 51–135. Eds F. H. Smith and F. Spencer. New York: Alan R. Liss.

The Cro-Magnon Remains

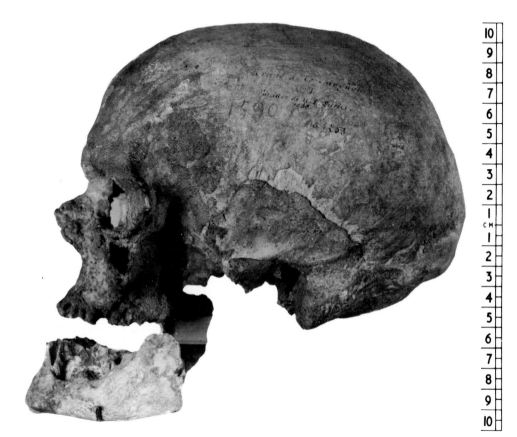

Fig. 15. The 'Old Man' from Cro-Magnon. *Courtesy of the Director of the Musée de l'Homme.*

Synonyms and other names	*Homo sapiens sapiens* Cro-magnon man; Le vieillard; The Old Man of Cro-Magnon; Cro-Magnon 1–5 (Oakley, Campbell and Molleson, 1971).
Site	Cro-Magnon, near Les Eyzies, Dordogne, France.
Found by	L. Lartet, 1868.
Geology	During the construction of a railway along the Vézère valley, excavation of a Cretaceous limestone cliff uncovered a rock shelter which had become filled by rock falls and debris. At the back of the shelter, under clearly recognizable occupation floors, were the

remains of four adult skeletons, one neonate and some fragmentary bones. It appeared that the bones had been deliberately buried.

Associated finds   With the skeletons were numerous flint tools of Aurignacian manufacture, and large numbers of sea shells, some of which were pierced. The fossil bones of mammals recovered from the site included reindeer (*Rangifer tarandus*), bison (*Bison priscus*), mammoth (*Mammuthus primigenius*) and horse (*Equus sp.*).

Dating   The bones, unearthed by L. Lartet, an experienced geologist, were stratigraphically contemporaneous with the deposit; the fauna and the tool culture suggested an Upper Pleistocene date for the burials, probably during the Fourth Glaciation (Würm or Last Glaciation).

Morphology   The best-preserved skull belonged to an adult male known colloquially as the 'Old Man' of Cro-Magnon, although he was possibly a little under 50 years of age at his death (Vallois, 1937). It was upon the description of this skeleton that the principal features of the 'Cro-Magnon race' were based.

Skull

The skull is virtually complete and undamaged except for missing mandibular condyles and a lack of teeth. The cranium is large and long with the vault somewhat flattened, and the outline of the skull from above is five-sided—the 'dolichopentagonal' form of some authors. In profile the forehead is steep and the superciliary ridges weak, the parieto-occipital region is curiously flattened in the midline and the parietal bosses are prominent. The face is broad and short with compressed rectangular orbits, whilst the tall narrow nasal opening and constricted nasal root make the nasal bones project. The subnasal maxilla slopes forward producing a moderate degree of alveolar prognathism. The bony palate is elevated centrally and grooved strongly for the palatal vessels and nerves. The dental arcade, as judged by the alveolar process of bone, is parabolic.

Postcranial Bones

The limb bones suggest that this individual was tall and muscular since the bones are long and the impressions for muscle and ligamentous attachments are strongly developed. The tibia is described as flattened and sabre-like (platycnemia), and the fibula deeply grooved.

Dimensions   *Skull*
Vallois and Billy (1965)
Max. Length 202   Max. Breadth 149·5

Cranial Capacity $\pm$ 1,600 cc   Cranial Index 74
(Dolichocephalic)

Postcranial Bones

Right Humerus Max. Length	no. 3 319
Left Humerus Max. Length	no. 3 320
Left Tibia Max. Length	no. 3 378

Affinities   There is no doubt that the general skeletal morphology of this Cro-Magnon man shows that he belongs to *Homo sapiens*, but several features of the bones when taken as a group serve to distinguish this skeleton from those representing modern man. This group of characteristics has been used to define the 'Cro-Magnon race' of the Upper Pleistocene. Skeletal remains having these general features have been collected from many parts of western Europe and North Africa, including France (Abri-Pataud, Dordogne; Bruniquel; Chancelade; Combe-Capelle; Gourdan; Les Hoteaux dans l'Ain; La Madeleine; and Solutré), Germany (Oberkassel; Stetten), Great Britain (Paviland, Glamorgan), Italy (Grimaldi), Czechoslovakia (Brno and Predmost; Moravia) and many other sites.

The remains from the Grottes des Enfants, Grimaldi, include two skeletons whose features have been regarded as negroid and thus may represent a distinct Upper Palaeolithic race; similarly the Chancelade remains have been likened to the skeletons of modern Eskimos and distinguished as the 'Chancelade race'. Whether or not these are valid distinctions it is apparent that European Upper Palaeolithic men exhibited a wide range of variation in skeletal form. Moreover, it is clear that they used stone and bone in a variety of ways, producing implements, ornamental objects and cave paintings. The tools made by these peoples have been classified in many ways but four main groups predominate: the Aurignacian, Gravettian (= Perigordian), Solutrean and Magdalenian cultures.

The origin of the Cro-Magnon people is still in some doubt because of the paucity of the fossil remains of their possible ancestors, similarly their relationship with the Neandertalers—at least some of whom were contemporaneous with Upper Pleistocene *Homo sapiens sapiens*—is an open question. It has been held variously that *Homo sapiens sapiens* displaced the Neandertalers who became extinct or that the spreading *Homo sapiens sapiens* population absorbed the Neandertalers or that *Homo sapiens sapiens* arose directly from a Neandertal stock. It seems likely that the first two of these possibilities may have taken place; the specialized nature of the Neandertal morphology would seem to preclude direct descent of *Homo sapiens sapiens* from Neandertal forebears. New assessments of the

Cro-Magnon remains have been given by Camps and Olivier (1970) and by Stringer, Hublin and Vandermeersch (1984).

A re-examination of the skeleton of the 'Old Man' (Cro-Magnon 1) by Dastugue (1967, 1982) has suggested that its bony abnormalities can all be ascribed to one pathological process and are the result of actinomycosis, a fungal infection by *Actinomyces israeli* that affects the mouth and can become generalized.

Originals Musée de l'Homme, Palais de Chaillot, Paris–16ᵉ, France.

Casts 1 Musée de l'Homme, Palais de Chaillot, Paris–16ᵉ, France. (Skull 1 and mandible, Skull 2 and Skull 3, one femur, two tibiae, one humerus, one ulna, one fibula).
2 The University Museum, University of Pennsylvania, Philadelphia 4, Pennsylvania, U.S.A.
(Skull 1 reconstruction).

References Broca, P. (1865–1875) On the human skulls and bones found in the cave of Cro-Magnon, near Les Eyzies. In *Reliquiae aquitanicae*, 97–122. E. Lartet and H. Christy. Ed. T. R. Jones. London: Williams and Norgate.

Broca, P. (1868) Sur les crânes et les ossements des Eyzies. *Bull. Soc. Anthrop. Paris 3*, 350–392.

Pruner, B. (1868) An account of the human bones found in the cave of Cro-Magnon in Dordogne. In *Reliquiae aquitanicoe*, 73–92. E. Lartet and H. Christy. Ed. T. R. Jones. London: Williams and Norgate.

Quatrefages, A. de and Hamy, E. (1874) La race de Cro-Magnon dans l'espace et dans le temps. *Bull. Soc. Anthrop. Paris 9*, 260–266.

Quatrefages, A. de and Hamy, E. (1882) Races humaines fossiles. In *Crania Ethnica*, 44–54 and 81–82. Paris: J. B. Baillière et Fils.

Morant, G. (1930–1931) Studies of Palaeolithic man, IV. *Ann. Eugen. Lond. 4*, 109–214.

Bonin, G. von (1935) European races of the Upper Palaeolithic. *Hum. Biol. 7*, 196–221.

Vallois, H. V. (1937) La durée de la vie chez l'homme fossile. *Anthropologie 47*, 499–532.

Vallois, H. V. and Billy, G. (1965) Nouvelles recherches sur les hommes fossiles de l'abri de Cro-Magnon. *Anthropologie 69*, 47–74.

Dastugue, J. (1967) Pathologie des hommes fossiles de l'abri de Cro-Magnon. *Anthropologie Paris 71*, 479–492.

Camps, G. and Olivier, G. (Eds) (1970) *L'Homme de Cro-Magnon; Anthropologie et Archéologie*. Paris: C.R.A.P.E.

Oakley, K. P., Campbell, B. G. and Molleson, T. I. (1971) *Catalogue of Fossil Hominids Part II: Europe*. London: Trustees of the British Museum (Natural History).

Wolpoff, M. H. (1980) *Paleoanthropology*. New York: Knopf.

Dastugue, J. (1982) Les maladies de nos ancêtres. *La Recherche, 13*, 980–988.

Stringer, C. B., Hublin, J.-J., and Vandermeersch, B. (1984) The origin of anatomically modern humans in Western Europe. In *The Origins of Modern Humans*, 51–135. Eds. F. H. Smith and F. Spencer. New York: Alan R. Liss.

The Arago Remains

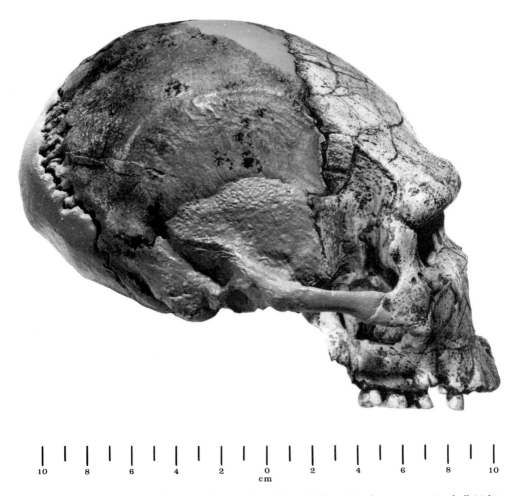

Fig. 16. The Arago XXI face and XLVII right parietal articulated with casts to form a composite skull (right lateral view). *Courtesy of the Director of the Musée de l'Homme.*

Synonyms and other names   Tautavel man; Arago man; Arago XXI and XLVII (skull), Arago II and XIII (mandibles), Arago XLIV (hip bone).

Site   Cave-site, Verdouble valley, at the southern tip of the Corbières mountain, near the village of Tautavel, 19 km northwest of Perpignan, Pyrénées-Orientales.

Found by   H. de Lumley, 1964– et seq.

Geology   The cave is in limestone and opens on to an escarpment about 50 m above the Verdouble river where it emerges on to the Tautavel plain. The cave is about 35 m deep and 10 m broad. There are 11 metres of deposits that contain over 20 occupation floors. The deposits have been divided into four units (I–IV) from below containing 12 beds (A–L). Unit I (L, K), Unit II (J, I, H), Unit III (G, F, E, D), Unit IV (C, B, A).

The Pleistocene deposits consist of sand and aeolian sandy loam overlaid by mineralized soil and a thick stalagmitic layer that sealed in the earlier deposits; a breccia, in turn, overlies the stalagmitic layer.

Associated finds   Mammalian faunal remains recovered from the site include wolf (*Canis lupus*), panther (*Felis pardus*), cave bear (*Ursus spelaeus*), wild boar (*Sus scrofa*), wild ox (*Bos primigenius*), red deer (*Cervus elaphus*), reindeer (*Rangifer tarandus*), ibex (*Capra ibex*), rhinoceros (*Rhinoceros mercki*), horse (*Equus caballus cf. mosbachensis*), elephant (*Elephas sp.*), beaver (*Castor fiber*), rabbit (*Oryctolagus cuniculus cuniculus*). Other remains include those of tortoise (*Testudo sp.*) and some birds (de Lumley, 1973). The rodent fauna has been studied by Chaline (1971, 1981) and is said to include *Pliomys lenki*, *Microtus ovalis*, *Microtus gregalis*, and *Pitmys marie-claudae*; an assemblage that indicates a cool environment. In addition to the faunal remains large assemblages of stone tools have been recovered from this site. Most of the tools have been attributed to the Tayacian with the exception of the upper levels which contained Middle Acheulean tools (de Lumley 1965 and 1971).

Dating   The dating of the hominid-bearing layers was originally given as the early part of the Third Glaciation (Riss Glaciation) on the basis of the fauna, particularly the rodents (de Lumley 1971 and 1973; Chaline, 1971). This assessment has been maintained by Chaline (1981) whilst others (de Lumley *et al.*, 1979; Guerin, 1981; Crégut, 1980 and 1981) have claimed an earlier date on faunal grounds, perhaps even as early as the Second Glaciation (Mindel Glaciation). The findings of Crégut with respect to the deer from Arago (1980, 1981) have not been substantiated. The dating of the Arago site remains uncertain on the basis of the faunal assemblage.

Morphology   *The Skull (Arago XXI and XLVII)*

The main specimen was found on a living floor amidst numerous fossil mammalian bones. It consists of a somewhat damaged and deformed face and partial vault. The frontal, sphenoid, zygomatic and maxillary bones are all present. Five teeth were in place, M^1–

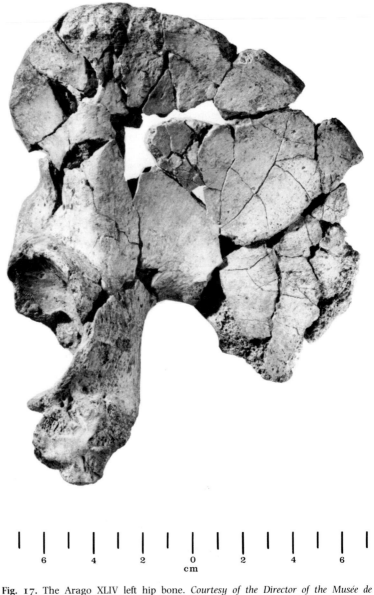

6   4   2   0   2   4   6
cm

Fig. 17. The Arago XLIV left hip bone. *Courtesy of the Director of the Musée de l'Homme.*

M³ on the right side and M¹ and M² on the left side. The third molar shows little sign of wear. The supraorbital torus is very prominent and is separated from the vault of the skull by a deep supratoral sulcus. The frontal recedes and the vault is somewhat flattened. Seen from above the postorbital constriction seems

Fig. 18. The Arago XIII mandible. *Courtesy of the Director of the Musée de l'Homme.*

marked but distortion of the frontal precludes a final judgement. The orbits are low and rectangular while the whole face seems to jut from the neurocranium, an appearance that is accentuated by the strong alveolar prognathism and flat anterior maxillary surface. The finds include a mandible with six teeth (Arago II), a half mandible with five teeth (Arago XIII) and numerous isolated teeth. The mandibles are large but may represent male and female dimorphs. The bodies of the mandibles are moderately robust and well marked by digastric fossae on the inferior borders; the muscular markings for the mylohyoid and genial muscles are well developed. The rami are high and broad with shallow mandibular notches and large condyles. The larger of the two specimens (Arago XIII) has a receding symphysial region and no chin whereas the smaller (Arago II) still recedes but appears to possess an *incurvatio mandibulae*. The larger specimen has a prominent *planum alveolare*.

The teeth differ in size in the two mandibles, the possible female (Arago II) having teeth of moderate size while those of the male (Arago XIII) are large. The male mandible possesses right PM_1–M_2 and the female mandible right M_1 and M_2.

The Arago XXI fronto-facial fragment, the Arago XLVII parietal and the Swanscombe occipital have been used to 'reconstruct' the skull of Arago man; from this Holloway (1982) has estimated a cranial capacity of between 1,100 and 1,200 cc whilst not accepting that the two Arago specimens need necessarily belong to one individual.

The postcranial bones recovered from the site include a left hip bone (Arago XLIV), three femoral fragments (Arago XLVIII, LI and LIII), a left fibular fragment (Arago XLIX), a left second metatarsal (Arago XLIII) and a hand terminal phalanx (Arago LII).

The hip bone and the femora bear resemblances to those of *Homo erectus* from Olduvai and Peking (Day 1982; Sigmon 1982).

Detailed descriptions and comparisons have been given for much of the Arago material in the two volumes of papers prepared for the CNRS Congress at Nice in 1982. Until full publication is achieved the 'Prétirage' to that meeting will remain the best source of information.

Dimensions   *Skull*

(Composite reconstruction
Arago XXI, XLVII and
Swanscombe occipital)

Max. length	198	Max. breadth	144
Cranial capacity	1,100–1,200 cc	Cranial Index	72.7
(Holloway, 1982)			

Mandibles

	Arago II		Arago XIII
Length	108	124.5	
Breadth	128	158	
Symphysial angle	103°	106°	

Affinities Initially the view was expressed that the Arago finds should be regarded as intermediate between *Homo erectus* and Neandertal man (de Lumley and de Lumley, 1973), a view with which Mann and Trinkaus (1973) agreed, suggesting that Arago II (mandible) has its closest resemblances with the Heidelberg mandible (*q.v.*) and the Montmaurin mandible. Howells (1971) drew attention to similarities between Arago and the *Homo erectus* remains from Ternifine (*q.v.*), Peking (*q.v.*) and Java (*q.v.*). The term 'Pre-neandertalers' figures in many writings about the Arago remains since it is a convenient, if non-committal, name. The Arago XLIV hip bone shows marked similarities to the *Homo erectus* hip bone from Olduvai Gorge (Olduvai Hominid 28 (*q.v.*)) and to the hip bone from Koobi Fora (KNM-ER 3228 (*q.v.*)) (Day, 1982; Sigmon, 1982). The femoral fragments from Arago show similarities to that of Olduvai Hominid 28 and to the Peking femora (*q.v.*) (Sigmon, 1982). This evidence would seem to suggest *Homo erectus* affinities. (Indeed the designation *Homo erectus tautavelensis* has already been suggested (Piveteau, 1982).) Others, however, favour the more modern features and emphasize the possible derived Neandertal characters of the mandible and the cranium that could link Arago Man to *Homo sapiens neanderthalensis* (Stringer, Hublin and Vandermeersch, 1984; Stringer, 1984).

My feeling is that these remains are best regarded as a European example of a *Homo erectus/Homo sapiens* transitional form that shows the mosaic evolutionary process to advantage. As a European fossil it will show, therefore, not only archaic *erectus* like features but also some derived characters that relate to cold adaptation in an early and primitive example of *Homo sapiens*.

Original Laboratoire de Géologie Historique, Faculté des Sciences, Place Victor Hugo, Marseille 3, France.

Casts Not available at present.

References de Lumley, H. and de Lumley, M–A. (1971) Découverte de restes humains anténéandertaliens datés du début de Riss à la Caune de l'Arago (Tautavel, Pyrénées-Orientales). *C.r. Acad. Sci. Paris 272*, 1729–1742.

Chaline, J. (1971) L'âge des Hominiens de la Caune de l'Arago à Tautavel (Pyrénées-Orientales), d'après l'étude des Rongeurs. *C.r. Acad. Sci. Paris 272*, 1743–1746.

Howells, W. W. (1971) Neanderthal man: facts and figures. *Proc. IX. Int. Cong. Anthrop. Ethnol. Sci. Chicago; U.S.A. Yearb. phys. Anthrop.* 7–18.

de Lumley, H. and de Lumley, M-A. (1973) Pre-Neanderthal human remains from Arago cave in South-eastern France. *Yearb. phys. Anthrop. 17*, 162–168.

Mann, A. and Trinkaus, E. (1973) Neanderthal and Neanderthal-like fossils from the Upper Pleistocene. *Yearb. phys. Anthrop. 17*, 169–193.

de Lumley, H. (1979) L'homme de Tautavel. *Les Dossiers de l'Archéologie 36*.

Crégut, E. (1980) La faune de mammifères du gisement pléistocène moyen antérissien de la Caune de l'Arago (Tautavel, Pyrénées-Orientales, France). *C.r. Acad. Sci. Paris 290*, 751–754.

Blackwell, B. (1981) Absolute dating and isotopic analyses in prehistory: methods and limits. *Geosci. Can. 8*, 174–175.

Crégut-Bonoure, E. (1981) Données de la faune de grands mammifères pour la biostratigraphie et l'environment du gisement Pléistocène moyen de la Caune de l'Arago à Tautavel. In *Datations absolutes et analyses isotopiques en Préhistoire*, 223–242. Eds. H. de Lumley and J. Labeyrie. Tautavel: CNRS.

de Lumley, H. and Labeyrie, J. Eds. (1981) *Datations absolues et analyses isotopiques en Préhistoire. Methodes et limites*. Tautavel, CNRS.

Chaline, J. (1981) Les rongeurs de la Caune de l'Arago à Tautavel et leur place dans la biostratigraphie Européenne. *Ibid* 193–203.

Guerin, C. (1981) Les rhinocéros (Mammalia, Perissodactylia) du gisement pléistocène moyen de la Caune de l'Arago à Tautavel. Signification stratigraphique by Claude Guerin. *Ibid*. 163–192.

Bouzat, J. (1982) *Le malaire de l'homme de Tautavel*. Prem. Congr. internat. Paleo. Hum. 1 Nice: Prétirage, 137–153.

Buyle-Bodin, Y. (1982) L'articulation temporo-mandibulaire chez les *Homo erectus* et les autres hominides fossiles. *Ibid*. 370–388.

Cook, J., Stringer, C. B., Currant, A. P., Schwarcz, H. P., Wintle, A. G. (1982) A review of the chronology of the European Middle Pleistocene hominid record. *Yearb. phys. Anthrop. 25*, 19–65.

Day, M. H. (1982) The *Homo erectus* pelvis: Punctuation or gradualism? *Congr. Internat. Paleo. Hum. 1* Nice: Prétirage, 411–421.

de Lumley, H., de Lumley, M.-A. and Fournier, A. (1982) La mandibule de l'homme de Tautavel. *Ibid*, 178–221.

de Lumley, M.-A. and Lamy, P. (1982) Le membre inferieur de l'homme de Tautavel. *Ibid*, 276–318.

de Lumley, M.-A. and Spitery, J. (1982) Le maxillaire de l'homme de Tautavel. *Ibid*, 154–177.

de Lumley, M.-A., Spitery, E. and Marart, B. (1982) Pathologie des *Homo erectus*. *Ibid*, 471–488.

Grimaud, D. (1982) Le parietal de l'homme de Tautavel. *Ibid*, 62–88.

Hemmer, H. (1982) Major factors in the evolution of hominid skull morphology—biological correlates and the position of the Anteneandertals. *Ibid*, 339–354.

Holloway, R. L. (1982) *Homo erectus* brain endocasts: volumetric and morphological observations with some comments on cerebral asymmetrics. *Ibid*, 355–369.

Lamy, P. (1982) Le Metatarsien Arago XLIII. *Ibid*, 319–336.

Lovejoy, C. O. (1982) Diaphyseal biomechanics of the locomotor skeleton of Tautavel man with comments on the evolution of skeletal changes in Late Pleistocene Man. *Ibid*, 447–470.

Puech, F. (1982) L'usure dentaire de l'homme de Tautavel. *Ibid*, 249–275.

Roth, H. (1982) Les arcades alveolaire et dentaire de l'homme de Tautavel. *Ibid*, 222–248.

Sigmon, B. (1982) Comparative morphology of the locomotor skeleton of *Homo erectus* and the other fossil hominids, with special reference to the Tautavel innominate and femora. *Ibid*, 422–446.

Spitery, J. (1982) Le frontal de l'homme de Tautavel. *Ibid*, 21–61.

Spitery, J. (1982) L'occipital de l'homme de Tautavel essai de reconstitution. *Ibid*, 89–109.

Spitery, J. (1982) La face de l'homme de Tautavel. *Ibid*, 110–136.

Wolpoff, M. H. (1982) The Arago dental sample in the context of hominid dental evolution. *Ibid*, 389–410.

Debenham, N. C. (1983) Reliability of thermoluminescence dating of stalagmitic calcite. *Nature 304*, 154–156.

Skinner, A. F. (1983) Overestimate of stalagmitic calcite ESR dates due to laboratory heating. *Nature 304*, 152–154.

Wintle, A. G. (1983) Dating Tautavel man. *Nature 304*, 118–119.

Stringer, C. B. (1984) The definition of *Homo erectus* and the existence of the species in Africa and Europe. *Cour. Forsch. Inst. Senck. 69*, 131–143.

Stringer, C. B., Hublin, J. J. and Vandermeersch, B. (1984) The origin of anatomically modern humans in Western Europe. In *The Origins of Modern Humans*, 51–135. (Eds) F. H. Smith and F. Spencer, New York: Alan R. Liss.

The St Césaire Skeleton

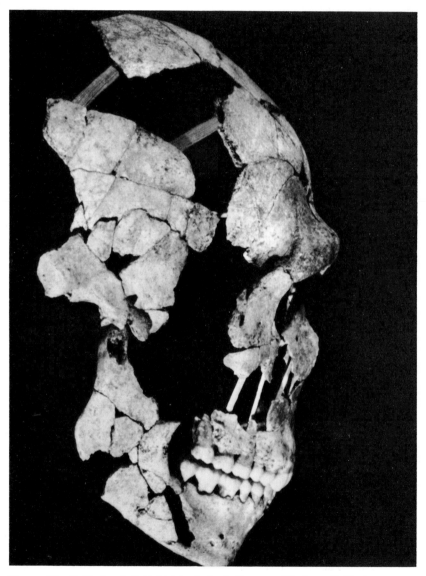

Fig. 19. The St Césaire skull (right lateral view). *Courtesy of Professor B. Vandermeersch.*

Synonyms and other names	The St Césaire Neandertal.
Site	Pierrot's Rock, a few hundred metres south of Saint-Césaire about 12 km from Saintes in Charente-Maritime.
Found by	F. Lévêque in July 1979 during a 'rescue dig' after the discovery of stone tools and fossil bones in the debris produced by a mechanical digger during a road widening project two years before.
Geology	The site is at the foot of a low cliff made of limestone along the course of a small stream, the Coran, which drains into the Charente. The archaeological layers are divided into two units A and B. The upper Unit A, 6 yellow layers that relate to the Upper Palaeolithic and the lower Unit B, 3 grey layers that relate to the Middle Palaeolithic. These two units rest on a red formation composed of a number of limestone gravels that appear sterile. The skeleton was recovered from Layer 5 of Unit A from a circular area about 70 cm in diameter.
Associated finds	Unit A, layer 1, is sterile in its upper two-thirds but its lower one-third contained a few stone tools of an evolved Aurignacian type. Similar tools were found in Layer 2. Layer 3 contained numerous fossil mammalian remains, particularly reindeer, as well as numerous stone tools. These implements included simple and re-touched burins, scraper blades, keeled scrapers, waisted blades and arrowheads with notched bases. These tools have been attributed to an older Aurignacian culture (Aurignacian I). Layer 4 contained keeled scrapers of an archaic Aurignacian or Protoaurignacian type while Layer 5, the layer that contained the human remains, disclosed points and backed blades attributed to the Châtelperronian culture. Layer 6 contained too few tools to characterize with certainty.
Unit B, Layer 1, contained darkly stained hearths and carbonized debris in its lower part, as well as an abundant fauna. The stone tools from Layers 1–3 are few but attributed to the Mousterian Culture. Layer 3 has produced at least one flat triangular biface (Lévêque and Vandermeersch 1980).
Dating	The dating of this site is of considerable importance since it may document the last appearance in the fossil record of Neandertals from Europe. So far the evidence put forward is biostratigraphical and archaeological. The skeleton was found in the upper of two Châtelperronian layers between the lower of these two layers and a later Aurignacian layer. There is no disagreement that this would suggest a date within the Fourth glaciation (Würm Glaciation) but where precisely within that glaciation is less certain. The relative

dating of the site is supported by pollen analyses (Leroi-Gourhan, 1984). Radiocarbon dates for the Châtelperronian lie between 34,000 and 31,000 years B.P. (ApSimon, 1980). If the St Césaire skeleton is confirmed as being of this age by other dating methods, such as radiocarbon, then the skeleton may well be the most recent Neandertal skeleton known.

Morphology   The remains consist of the right half of a cranium, the right half of a mandible including the symphysis and some postcranial bones including a radius, a scapula and some ribs, an ulna, some fragments of tibiae and the patellae. None of the vertebral column and none of the pelvis has been preserved. The skull possesses a receding frontal with a strongly marked supraorbital torus and a supratoral sulcus. The parietal bone is long and flat whilst the squamous temporal is low. The face has a voluminous orbit and a flattened maxilla without canine fossae. The mandible is long, chinless and with a very large retromolar space, indicating that the mid-facial region is pulled forward. The postcranial bones are robust and the radius shows marked curvature. These cranial, mandibular and skeletal characters are typical of the Neandertalers and suffice to ally the St Césaire skeleton with that population.

Dimensions   Not available at time of publication.

Affinities   The affinities of the St Césaire skeleton are not in doubt. It is clearly a Neandertal skeleton that bears many of the hallmarks of this group as set out by Stringer, Hublin and Vandermeersch (1984). What is of interest, however, is the light that it may throw upon the relationships between the Neandertalers and their successors *Homo sapiens sapiens* since the dating of the remains is late by Neandertal standards. The significance of the find was realized by Lévêque and Vandermeersch (1980 and 1981) and discussed by ApSimon (1981a and b), Wolpoff (1981) and Stringer, Kruszynski and Jacobi (1981). The Neandertal-modern *sapiens* transition could have taken several forms that can be paraphrased as evolutionary succession, displacement or absorption. A late survival of Neandertalers argues against the first of these hypotheses. (See the Neandertal Problem p. 407.)

Originals   At present under examination at the Laboratoire d'Anthropologie de l'Université de Bordeaux I.

Casts   Not available at time of publication.

References   Lévêque, F. and Vandermeersch, B. (1980) Les découvertes de restes humains dans un horizon castelperronien de Saint-Césaire (Charente-Maritime). *B. Bull. Soc. préhist. fr. 77*, 35.

Lévêque, F. and Vandermeersch, B. (1980) Découverte de restes humains dans un niveau castelperronien à Saint-Césaire (Charente-Maritime). *C.r. Acad. Sci. Paris* Série D *291*, 187–189.

ApSimon, A. M. (1980) The last Neanderthal in France? *Nature 287*, 271–272.

Lévêque, F. and Vandermeersch, B. (1981) Le néandertalien de Saint-Césaire. *La Recherche 12*, 242–244.

Wolpoff, M. H. (1981) Allez Neanderthal. *Nature 289*, 823. Also, Stringer, C. B., Kruszynski, R. G. and Jacobi, R. M. and reply by ApSimon, A. M.

Leroi-Gourhan, A. (1984) La place du Néandertalien de St Césaire dans la chronologie Würmienne. *Bull. Soc. préhist. fr. 81*, 7, 196–198.

Stringer, C. B., Hublin, J.-J. and Vandermeersch, B. (1984) The origin of anatomically modern humans in western Europe. In *The Origins of Modern Humans*, 51–135. Eds. F. H. Smith and F. Spencer, New York: Alan R. Liss.

The Bilzingsleben Remains

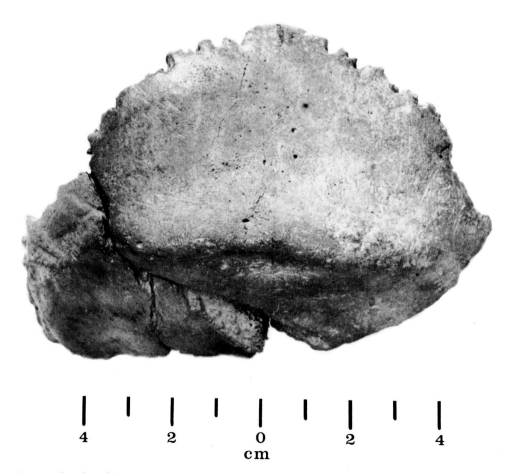

| 4 | 2 | 0 | 2 | 4 |

cm

Fig. 20. The Bilzingsleben occipital fragments (A1, A2). *Courtesy of E. Vlček.*

Synonyms and other names	*Homo erectus bilzingslebenensis* (Vlček, 1978); *Homo erectus* (Mania, Toepfer and Vlček, 1980); *Homo sapiens* (Stringer, Howell and Melentis, 1979); Bilzingsleben Man.
Site	A locality named Steinrinne, 1 km south of the village of Bilzingsleben in the district of Artern near Kindelbruck, Halle/Saale, on the north east border of the Thuringen Basin, 35 km north of Erfurt, German Democratic Republic.

Found by   A1—D. Mania 22 October 1972
              A2—D. Bauer 8 August 1974
              B1—H. Schroder 15 July 1975
              B2—Ch. Mania 15 August 1976
              B3—W. Hansch 26 July 1979
              C1—D. Mania and J. Suess 3 July 1976
              D1—W. Kukkenburg 5 July 1977
              D2—After 1983

                                  (Vlček, 1983)

Geology   The deposits from which the skull fragments were recovered occur in the Steinrinne travertine quarry and cover a plateau of Triassic (Lower Keuper) marls and dolomites at about 35 m above the river Wipper. The valley shows four Pleistocene river gravel terraces at the 30, 20, 10 and 2–5 metre levels; these terraces are usually attributed to the Second Glaciation (Elsterian), Third Glaciation (Saalian) and Fourth Glaciation (Warthian and Vistulian) in order from older to younger (Mania, 1977). The hominid skull fragments, stone tools, and animal bones were found under the quarry bottom in a sandy travertine at the base of a travertine complex on the 30 m terrace of the Wipper river.

Associated finds   The bones of fossil mammals recovered from the site indicate an interglacial fauna and include straight tusked elephant (*Palaeoloxodon antiquus*), rhinoceros (*Dicerorhinus kirchbergensis*), wild horse (*Equus sp.*), wild ox (*Bos*), red deer (*Cervus elaphas*), pig (*Sus scrofa*), monkey (*Macaca*), bear (*Ursus sp.*), wild cat (*Felis silvestris*), beaver (*Castor fiber*) and giant beaver (*Trogontherium cuvierii*). The flora is also interglacial in character and includes oak (*Quercus*), lime (*Tilia*), maple (*Acer*), hazel (*Corylus*), firethorn (*Pyracantha*), and box (*Buxus*). The stone and bone tools consist of a flint flake industry of Micro-Clactonian character, quartzite chopping tools, antler clubs and retouched bone implements (Vlček and Mania, 1977; Vlček, 1978).

Dating   The geological age of the deposits at Bilzingsleben has been the source of debate for many years, the only clear consensus being that the travertine sequence containing the archaeological remains must be younger than the Second Glaciation (Mindel Glaciation) in age. An earlier assessment gave the stratigraphic age as Third Interglacial (Riss/Würm Interglacial) (Toepfer, 1960). Later excavations have suggested that the stratigraphic sequence is entirely Second Interglacial (Mindel/Riss Interglacial) on the basis of geomorphological evidence (Mania *et al.*, 1980), botanical evidence (Mai, 1980) the evidence of molluscs (Mania, 1980) and small mammals (Heinrich, 1980 Cook *et al.*, 1982).

Harmon *et al.* (1980) have published Uranium Series dates on

Fig. 21. The Bilzingsleben glabellar fragment (B1). *Courtesy of E. Vlček.*

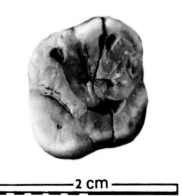

Fig. 22. The Bilzingsleben right upper molar (C1). *Courtesy of E. Vlček.*

samples from Bilzingsleben and give an absolute age of 228,000 years B.P. ($+17,000$ or $-12,000$) from ^{230}Thorium/^{234}Uranium analyses. This date and the evidence of an interglacial flora and fauna allows them to correlate the Bilzingsleben travertine deposits with 'Stage 7' of the marine oxygen isotope record of Second Interglacial (Mindel/Riss Interglacial) age. This precise correlation with 'Stage 7' is debatable (Stringer, 1981; Cook *et al.*, 1982) since further Uranium Series determinations by Schwarcz give ages of more than 350,000 years but it seems that the site is clearly Middle Pleistocene and most likely of Second Interglacial (Mindel/Riss Interglacial) age.

Morphology *The Skull*

The remains from Bilzingsleben consist of two occipital fragments (A1, A2), a glabellar fragment (B1), frontal fragments (B2 and B3), a right upper molar (C1), a right parietal fragment (D1) and a parietal fragment of indeterminate side. There are also teeth from at least two individuals (Vlček, 1979; Vlček and Mania, 1979; Vlček, 1983a; Vlček, 1983b). The skull fragments seem likely to represent one skull in that there are no duplications or morphological inconsistencies. The occipital fragments fit together to disclose an angulated robust occipital bone that bears a continuous occipital torus and a supratoral sulcus. The inion would seem to coincide with the opisthocranium. The nuchal plane displays muscle attachments for semispinalis capitis and superior oblique muscles while the superior nuchal line shows the attachment of splenius capitus and parallel to it the occipital attachment of sternocleidomastoid. The fragments are very thick.

The glabellar fragment is heavy and displays a continuous supraorbital torus (in vertical view) and a minimal glabellar depression in frontal view but there is no central supratoral sulcus in the midline. The nasal root is broad and shows an opening into the frontal sinuses which are developed within the supraorbital torus. The second frontal fragment is unremarkable.

The Tooth

The upper molar consists of two fragments of the crown without roots (C1). The crown has suffered much attrition with dentinal exposure. The pulp cavity is large (Vlček, 1978; Mania, Toepfer and Vlček, 1980).

Dimensions Vlček (1978)

Skull

A1 and A2

Lambda—Asterion chord	86
Lambda—Asterion arc	100

Inion—Asterion chord	76
Inion—Asterion arc	81
Lambda—Inion chord	51
Lambda—Inion arc	53

Occipital Thickness

| At Lambda | 11 |
| At Inion | 17 |

B1 and B2

Thickness of supraorbital torus	32
Height of supraorbital torus	21
Interorbital width	34

Tooth

Upper Tooth (Crown Dimensions)

Bilzingsleben (C_1)	M^1 or M^2
l	12
b	13

Affinities   The early publications concerning the Bilzingsleben find by the finders and their collaborators are in no doubt as to the taxonomic attribution of the remains to *Homo erectus* (Mania, 1975; Mania

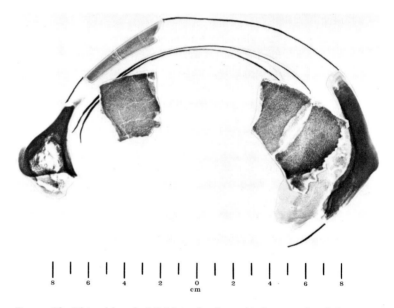

Fig. 23. The Bilzingsleben skull (left lateral radiograph). *Courtesy of E. Vlček.*

and Vlček, 1977; Vlček and Mania, 1977; Vlček, 1978). Later monographic study of the site and the remains confirms this attribution and its geographic subspecific name *Homo erectus bilzingslebenensis*. The basis for this specific attribution is given as comparison with finds from Java, China, East and South Africa. Comparisons from Europe have included Swanscombe (*q.v.*), Steinheim (*q.v.*), Vértesszöllös (*q.v.*), Arago (*q.v.*) and Ehringsdorf. Basic similarities are seen with Olduvai Hominid 9 (*q.v.*) and with Sangiran 17 (*q.v.*). The principal features that are emphasized are the occipital and supraorbital tori and their likeness to the *Homo erectus* sample examined as well as their differences from the European early sapients such as Swanscombe and Steinheim. It is concluded that Bilzingsleben man belongs to *Homo erectus* yet shows sufficient distinction from the Javan and Chinese examples of this taxon to allow the establishment of a new subspecies *Homo erectus bilzingslebenensis*. It is also concluded that *Homo erectus* represented by Bilzingsleben man and Vértesszöllös man were contemporary with *Homo sapiens steinheimensis* represented by Swanscombe and Steinheim man (Vlček, 1978).

Wolpoff (1980) is in no doubt that the Bilzingsleben skull fragments are 'indistinguishable in any meaningful sense' from those of *Homo erectus*. These taxonomic opinions have been questioned and the 'gracility' of the Bilzingsleben occipital torus and other resemblances to the Petralona skull (*q.v.*), the Arago skull and the Vértesszöllös specimen are emphasized even to the extent of classifying these remains as a unit outside *Homo erectus* yet within an archaic form of *Homo sapiens*. The absence of Neandertal or modern characters in the available remains has been reaffirmed (Stringer, Hublin and Vandermeersch, 1984).

In summary, it seems that there is no doubt whatsoever that the Bilzingsleben remains available to us are overwhelmingly similar to those of *Homo erectus* and on this basis can easily be included in that taxon. What is less certain is whether the features that we have are new features distinctive to *Homo erectus* and thus diagnostic of that taxon alone. On the basis that taxonomic opinions must be based on morphological judgement of the available evidence, then it seems to me that we have clear evidence of affinity to *Homo erectus* and no evidence of either modern (i.e. sapient) or Neandertal features in the specimen to suggest affinities to either of these groups.

If this is accepted then the Linnean system of taxonomy by resemblance would place the remains in *Homo erectus*. Those who favour the Hennigian system of taxonomy, based on the first appearance of new features, would find these remains hard to classify other than to genus.

Originals   Landesmuseum für Vorgeschichte, Richard Wagner Strasse 10, Halle/Saale, GDR.

Casts   As above.

References   Toepfer, V. (1960) Das letztinterglaziale mikrolithische Paläolithikum von Bilzingsleben, Kr Artern. *Ausgr. Funde* 5, 7–11.

Mania, D. (1975) Bilzingsleben (Thuringen): Eine neue altpälaeolithische Fundstelle mit Knochenresten des *Homo erectus*. *Archäologisches Korrespondenzblatt* 5, 263–272.

Mania, D. (1977) Die Altpälaolithische Travertinfundstelle von Bilzingsleben, Kr. Artern. *Ethnogr.-archaol. Z.* 18, 5–24.

Mania, D. and Vlček, E. (1977) Altpälaolithische Funde mit *Homo erectus* von Bilzingsleben (DDR). *Archeol. Rozhl.* 29, 603–616.

Vlček, E. and Mania, D. (1977) Ein neuer fund von *Homo erectus* in Europa: Bilzingsleben (DDR). *Anthropologie* 15, 159–169.

Vlček, E. (1978) A new discovery of *Homo erectus* in central Europe. *J. hum. Evol.* 7, 239–251.

Stringer, C. B., Howell, F. C. and Melentis, J. K. (1979) The significance of the fossil hominid skull from Petralona, Greece. *J. archaeol. Sci.* 6, 235–253.

Vlček, E. (1979) '*Homo erectus bilzingslebenensis*' – Eine neue form des mittelpleistozänen Menschen in Europa. *Ethnogr.-Archäol. Z.* 20, 634–661.

Mania, D. and Vlček, E. (1979) Hominidenreste aus dem mittelpleistozänen Travertinkomplex bei Bilzingsleben. 3. Mitteilung. *Z. Archäol.* 13, 113–122.

Harmon, R. S., Glazek, J. and Nowak, K. (1980) ^{230}Th/^{234}U dating of travertine from the Bilzingsleben archaeological site. *Nature 284*, 132–135.

Heinrich, W. D. (1980) Kleinsangerfunde aus dem Travertin komplex von Bilzingsleben. *Ethnogr.-Archäol. Z.* 21, 36–41.

Mai, D. H. (1980) Pflanzenreste des mittel pleistozänen Travertins von Bilzingsleben. *Ibid*, 21, 4–16.

Mania, D. (1980) Die Mollusken fauna aus dem Travertinkomplex von Bilzingsleben. *Ibid*, 20, 585–606.

Mania, D., Toepfer, V. and Vlček, E. (1980) *Bilzingsleben I*. Berlin: Veb Deutscher Verlag der Wissenschaften.

Wolpoff, M. H. (1980) Cranial remains of Middle Pleistocene European hominids. *J. hum. Evol.* 9, 339–358.

Stringer, C. B. (1981) The dating of European Middle Pleistocene hominids and the existence of *Homo erectus* in Europe. *Anthropologie (Brno)* 19, 3–14.

Cook, J., Stringer, C. B., Currant, A. P., Schwarcz, H. P. and Wintle, A. G. (1982) A review of the chronology of the European Middle Pleistocene hominid record. *Yearb. phys. Anthrop.* 25, 19–65.

Mai, D. H., Mania, D., Notzold, T., Toepfer, V., Vlček, E. and Heinrich, W.-D. (1983) *Bilzingsleben II*. Berlin: Veb Deutscher Verlag der Wissenschaften.

Vlček, E. (1983a) Uber einen weiteren Schädelrest des *Homo erectus* von Bilzingsleben 4. Mitteilung. *Ethnogr.-Archäol. Z.* 24, 321–325.

Vlček, E. (1983b) Die neufunde vom *Homo erectus* aus dem mittelpleistozänen travertinkomplex bei Bilzingsleben aus den Jahren 1977 bis 1979. In *Bilzingsleben II*. D. H. Mai, D. Mania, T. Notzold, V. Toepfer, E. Vlček and W.-D. Heinrich. Berlin: Veb Deutscher Verlag der Wissenschaften.

Stringer, C.B., Hublin, J.-J. and Vandermeersch, B. (1984) The origin of anatomically modern humans in Western Europe. In *The Origins of Modern Humans*, 51–135. Eds. F.H. Smith and F. Spencer. New York: Alan R. Liss.

The Neandertal Skeleton

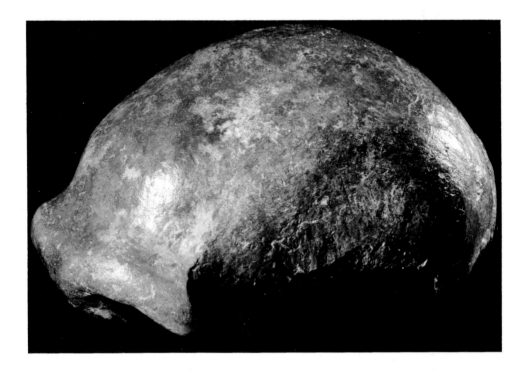

8		6		4		2		0		2		4		6		8

cm

Fig. 24. The Neandertal calotte. *Courtesy of Dr H.-E. Joachim, Director, Reinisches Landesmuseum.*

Synonyms and other names   *Homo neanderthalensis* (King, 1864a, b); *Homo sapiens neanderthalensis* (Campbell, 1964)
Neanderthal man; Neandertal man.
Numerous other names have been proposed for Neandertal forms, amongst them *Homo primigenius, Homo antiquus, Homo incipiens, Homo europaeus, Homo mousteriensis.* None of them precedes the name given by King and none is in common use.

Site   The Neandertal valley, near Hochdal, about seven miles east of Dusseldorf, towards Wuppertal.

Found by   Workmen; recognized by von Fuhlrott, August, 1856.

Geology   The skeleton was uncovered when a cave deposit was disturbed during quarrying operations. The cave (Feldhofer grotto) was in Devonian limestone which formed the walls of the valley. Most of the valley no longer exists, neither does the cave. It is likely that much of the skeleton was lost before its significance was appreciated.

Associated finds   Neither artefacts nor fossil mammalian bones were found with the remains.

Dating   This find was perhaps the earliest acceptable example of fossil man, but because of the circumstances of the find, the lack of stratigraphy or associated tools and the absence of a fossil fauna it was impossible to date the skeleton with any confidence. It is likely that the man from Neandertal died during the Fourth Glaciation (Würm or Last Glaciation).

Morphology   The parts of the skeleton which have been preserved include the skull cap, one clavicle, one scapula, five ribs, two humeri, one radius, two ulnae, two femora and part of the pelvis.

The Calotte

The vault of the skull is low, the supraorbital ridges large and the occipital bone prominent. The sagittal suture and most of the coronal suture are obliterated, but the lambdoid suture is apparently still open. This degree of sutural fusion has led to the suggestion that the age at death was about 50 years.

The Postcranial Bones

The limb bones are of rugged construction, having stout tuberosities and impressive muscular markings. The humeri are straight and cylindrical, but the radius is curved with an internal concavity. The radial tuberosity is very large, adumbrating a powerful biceps muscle. The left elbow was the site of an injury which severely limited movement at the joint. The femur is cylindrical and has the beginnings of a third trochanter.

Recent studies of 13 Neandertal skulls and postcranial skeletons have shown that sexual dimorphism in Neandertals is similar in range to that of modern human populations. In the skull the overall dimensions and the breadth of the supraorbital torus show sexual differences whilst in the postcranial skeleton the major differences between males and females are found in the length of the long bones, the size of the hands and feet, the form of the thorax and the breadth of the shoulders (Heim, 1981a and b, 1983).

Dimensions   Hrdlička (1930)

The Calotte

Length 201   Breadth 147
Cranial Index 73·1 (Dolichocephalic)
Cranial Capacity 1,033 cc (Schaafhausen, 1858)
               1,230 cc (Huxley, 1863)
               1,234 cc (Schwalbe)

Postcranial Bones

	Length	*Mid-shaft diameter*	
Humerus	312	26 ⎫	Schaafhausen, 1858
Femur	438	30 ⎭	
Radius	239	15·5	

Affinities   The principal importance of this find is, perhaps, its historical interest, for in the years following *The Origin of Species* it caused intense controversy. Fuhlrott was willing to accept the antiquity of the bones and their contemporaneity with the mammoth, Virchow (1872) believed that the skull was pathological, whilst Blake (1864) considered that it belonged to an imbecile. Schaafhausen (1858) said that the bones were those of an ancient savage and barbarous race, but Huxley (1863) recognized the primitive features of the skeleton and could not accept that it was an intermediate form between man and apes; thus he proposed that Neandertal man was an example of reversion towards a previous simian ancestor. King (1864) decided that the characters of the Neandertal remains were so different from those of contemporary man that he proposed the name *Homo neanderthalensis*. The controversy continued unabated for many years until further finds convinced the sceptics that fossil man existed; of particular importance in this respect was the discovery of the La Chapelle-aux-Saints skeleton (*q.v.*) which shares numerous features with the Neandertal remains. Boule was in no doubt that they were co-specific, since then many Neandertal skulls, skeletons and parts of skeletons have been found in Europe and the Near East as well as remains from Africa and Asia which have been regarded by some anthropologists as being Neandertaloid. The suggestion has been revived that the Neandertal morphology may be due to pathological change, one view impugning Vitamin D deficiency in youth (rickets) (Ivanhoe, 1970) and another syphilis (Wright, 1971). Neither suggestion was adequately supported, or justified, subsequently.

The phylogenetic position of the Neandertal skeleton has been reviewed recently (Schott, 1982) and an historical survey has been given of the Neandertalers as a whole (Spencer, 1984).

A general review of current theories relating to the origin of the Neandertal group will be given later (p. 413).

Original   Rheinisches Landesmuseum, Bonn, West Germany.

Casts   1. F. Krantz, Rheinisches Mineralienkontor, Bonn, West Germany. (Calotte and postcranial bones.)

2. The University Museum, University of Pennsylvania, Philadelphia 4, Pennsylvania, U.S.A. (Calotte and endocranial cast.)

References   Schaafhausen, H. (1858) Zur Kenntnis der ältesten Rassenschädel. *Archiv. Anat. Phys. wiss. Medicin*, 453–478.

Fuhlrott, C. von (1859) Menschliche Uebereste aus einer Felsengrotte des Düsselthals. *Verh. naturk. Ver. der preuss. Rheinl. 16*, 131–153.

Huxley, T. H. (1863) *Evidence as to Man's Place in Nature*. London: Williams and Norgate.

King, W. (1864a) On the Neanderthal skull, or reasons for believing it to belong to the Clydian Period, and to a species different from that represented by man. *Rep. Br. Ass. Advmt. Sci.* (Notices and abstracts).

King, W. (1864b) The reputed fossil man of the Neanderthal. *Q. J. Sci. 1*, 88–97.

Blake, C. C. (1864) On the alleged peculiar characters and assumed antiquity of the human cranium from the Neanderthal. *J. anthrop. Soc. Lond. 2*, 139–157.

Virchow, R. (1872) Untersuchung des Neanderthal-Schädels. *Z. Ethn. 4*, 157–165.

Hrdlička, A. (1930) The skeletal remains of early man. *Smithson. misc. Coll. 83*, 1–379.

Campbell, B. (1964) Quantitative taxonomy and human evolution. In *Classification and Human Evolution*, 50–74. Ed. S. L. Washburn. London: Methuen and Co. Ltd.

Ivanhoe, F. (1970) Was Virchow right about Neanderthal? *Nature 277*, 577–579.

Wright, D. J. M. (1971) Syphilis and Neanderthal man. *Nature 229*, 409.

Heim, J.-L. (1981a, b) Le dimorphisme sexuel du crâne des hommes de Neandertal. Part I. *L'Anthropologie (Paris) 85*, 193–218. Part II. *Ibid. 85*, 451–469.

Schott, L. (1982) Contemporary and modern attitudes on the morphology and phylogenetic position of the skeletal find of 1856 from the Neanderthal Valley. *Humanbiol. Budapest 9*, 61–67.

Heim, J.-L. (1983) Les variations du squelette post-crânien des hommes de Neandertal suivant le sexe. *L'Anthropologie (Paris) 87*, 5–26.

Spencer, F. (1984) The Neandertals and their evolutionary significance: a brief historical survey. In *The Origins of Modern Humans*, 1–49. Eds. F. H. Smith and F. Spencer. New York: Alan R. Liss.

The Mauer Mandible

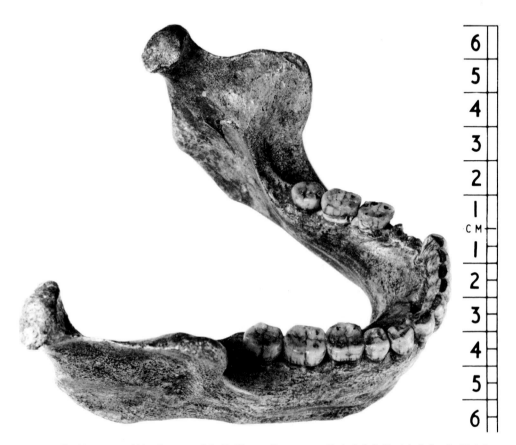

Fig. 25. The Mauer mandible. *Courtesy of Dr R. Kraatz, Conservator, Geologisch-Paläontologisches Institut der Universität, Heidelberg.*

Synonyms and other names	*Homo heidelbergensis* (Schoetensack, 1908); *Palaeanthropus heidelbergensis* (Bonarelli, 1909a); *Homo (Euranthropus) heidelbergensis* (Arambourg, 1957) Heidelberg man; Mauer man. Several other generic names have been proposed such as *Pseudhomo*, *Europanthropus*, *Rhenanthropus* and *Maueranthropus*. None has gained acceptance.
Site	The Rösch sandpit, half a mile north of the village of Mauer, three

miles south of Neckargemund and about six miles south-east of Heidelberg, West Germany.

Found by   The mandible was found by a workman on the 21st October, 1907. It was shown to O. Schoetensack. (It is uncertain whether the fossil was seen *in situ* by Schoetensack.)

Geology   The deposits exposed at the pit consist of a lower series of river sands, the Mauer sands, from the bed of the Neckar river. These sands are overlain by two layers of silt or loess which are approximately 50 feet thick and rest upon sandstone gravel. The mandible was found 80 feet from the surface, on a collapse about 3 feet from the base of the layer.

New excavations at the site have been reported (Müller-Beck, 1964, 1976 and 1977).

Associated finds   With the mandible was a well preserved fossil fauna of mammalian bones showing no evidence of water rolling. This fauna included Etruscan rhinoceros (*Dicerorhinus etruscus*), red deer (*Cervus elaphus*), straight-tusked elephant (*Palaeoloxodon antiquus*), bison (*Bison priscus*), moose (*Alces latifrons*), roe deer (*Capreolus capreolus*), horse (*Equus mosbachensis*), primitive bear (*Ursus sp.*) and beaver (*Castor fiber*). Less frequently there were carnivores including lion and primitive wolf.

No artefacts were found with the mandible.

Dating   The fauna is post-Villafranchian and pre-Second Interglacial (Mindel–Riss or Penultimate Interglacial), suggesting that the climate was probably warm/temperate. The stratigraphy and fauna indicates that the Mauer sands were laid most probably during the First Interglacial or possibly during an interstadial within the Second Glaciation. Oakley (1964) confidently attributed Heidelberg man to the First Interglacial period.

The Lower Sands have been said to document an important faunal event (von Koenigswald, 1973) that may correlate with palynological data from Norfolk, England (Stuart and West, 1976). This may indicate that the Mauer site should be attributed to the latter part of the First Interglacial. No absolute dates are available for the site (Cook *et al.*, 1982).

Morphology   *Mandible*

The mandible is large and stoutly built with broad ascending rami and rounded angles. The body is thick and particularly deep in the region of the premolars and molars; the mental symphysis is buttressed on its inner aspect but there is no simian shelf and no chin. The coronoid processes point forwards and laterally and the mandibular notches are shallow. The inner aspect of the bone shows well-marked genial tubercles, and on each side a mylohyoid ridge above a shallow submandibular fossa. On the rami the openings of the inferior dental canals are overhung by lingular processes. On the left the groove for the mylohyoid nerve and vessels is particularly prominent.

Muscular markings include roughenings for the medial pterygoids, pits for the lateral pterygoids and marked inferior depressions for the digastric muscles. The mental foramina are multiple (Howell, 1960). With the exception of those for the masseters, the muscular impresses are in keeping with the size of the bone.

Teeth

The dental arcade is parabolic and the tooth row has no diastema. The permanent dentition is complete although the premolars and first two molars of the left side are broken. The teeth appear small and lie within the crown dimension ranges of modern man; however, only the molars are said to lie within the range of size variation of the Peking *Homo erectus*. The molar cusp pattern is dryopithecine. The molar teeth decrease in size in the order $M2 > M3 > M1$, and all four are well worn. None of the molars has a cingulum or any sign of secondary enamel wrinkling. The premolars are bicuspid and the incisors somewhat swollen posteriorly, although not shovelled. The pulp cavities are moderately enlarged (taurodontism).

Molar Cusp Pattern (Howell, 1960)

	Lower Molars Left	Right
M_1	Sub Y5	Sub Y5
M_2	+5	+5
M_3	+5	+5

Dimensions

	Boule and Vallois (1957)	Wust (1951)	Howell (1960)
Symphysial Height	—	37·0	34·0
Body Height (Behind M1)	—	35·5 (M2)	34·3
Body Thickness	23·0 (M3)	19·5 (PM1)	22·0 (M1)
Ramus Height	66·0	69·0	71·0
Ramus Breadth	60·0	51·0	52·0
Mandibular Angle	—	—	105°
Total Length	—	126·0	120·0
Bicondylar Breadth	—	130·0	133·0

Teeth   Howell (1960)

		Lower Teeth (Crown Dimensions)				
		PM1	PM2	M1	M2	M3
Left	l	7·3	—	11·1	12·9	11·5
Side	b	—	—	—	—	11·3
Right	l	8·1	7·5	11·6	12·7	12·2
Side	b	9·0	9·2	11·2	12·0	10·9

These figures broadly correspond to those of Schoetensack (1908), differing principally in terminology and in Howell's reluctance to measure broken teeth.

Affinities   This is an important, but isolated, mandible whose morphology shows a number of points of similarity with the mandibles of pithecanthropines (*Homo erectus*) of approximately equivalent Middle Pleistocene age. The skull to which it belongs is unknown.

For many years the relationships of the jaw have been discussed because of its combination of relatively advanced teeth in a mandible which has such archaic features as a receding chin and broad rami. Howell (1960) reappraised the Mauer mandible and, concluding that its dental and mandibular morphology shows 'fundamental differences' from those of Java and Peking man, he tentatively suggested that Mauer man belongs to the lineage represented later by the Montmaurin mandible and the early Neandertalers. An alternative view places Mauer man within a larger group which could include the hominids from Java, Peking and Ternifine (Mayr, 1963). However, it has been suggested that the available material neither justifies the inclusion of Mauer man in any of the recently proposed subspecies of *Homo erectus*, nor warrants it being placed in a subspecific category of its own (Campbell, 1964).

Opinion is divided still on the placing of the Mauer jaw within *Homo erectus* (Wolpoff, 1980; Campbell, 1985 and Kraatz, 1985) or with the Arago remains (*q.v.*) and the Petralona remains (*q.v.*) (Stringer, 1981) in line with the view that *Homo erectus* has not yet been clearly demonstrated from a European site (Stringer, Howell and Melentis, 1979; Howell, 1981; Howell, 1982). The jaw may, therefore, represent an archaic 'sapient' or a 'preneandertaler'. The problem of *Homo erectus* as a taxon has been explored in several recent publications with implications for the Mauer jaw (Howells, 1980, Howells, 1981; Andrews, 1984; Day, 1984; Stringer, 1984 and Wood, 1984). In summary, this is an isolated mandible whose provenance, dating and taxonomic attribution are uncertain and about which opinion is divided. Until the skull and/or the postcranial bones are known the affinities of the Mauer jaw will remain in doubt.

Original   Geologisch-Paläontologisches Institut der Universität, Heidelberg, West Germany.

Casts   1. F. Krantz, Rheinisches Mineralien-Kontor, Bonn, West Germany.
2. The University Museum, University of Pennsylvania, Philadelphia 4, Pennsylvania, U.S.A.

References   Schoetensack, O. (1908) *Der Unterkiefer des* Homo heidelbergensis *aus den Sanden von Mauer bei Heidelberg*, 1–67. Leipzig: Wilhelm Englemann.

Bonarelli, G. (1909a) *Palaeanthropus (n.g.) heidelbergensis* (Schoet.) *Riv. ital. Paleont. 15*, 26–31.

Bonarelli, G. (1909b) Le razze umane e le loro probabili affinita. *Boll. Soc. geogr. ital. 10*, 827–851, 953–979.

Weinert, H. (1937) Dem Unterkiefer von Mauer zur 30 jahrigen Wiederkehr seiner Entdeckung. *Z. Morph. Anthrop. 37*, 102–113.

Wust, K. (1951) Über den Unterkiefer von Mauer (Heidelberg) im Vergleich zu anderen fossilen und mit besonderer Berucksichtigung der phyletischen Stellung des Heidelberger Fossils. *Z. Morph. Anthr. 42*, 1–112.

Boule, M. and Vallois, H. V. (1957) *Fossil Men*. London: Thames and Hudson.

Arambourg, C. (1957) 'Les Pithécanthropiens', 33–41. In *Mélanges Pittard*. Brive-la-Gaillarde. Nizet.

Howell, F. C. (1960) European and northwest African Middle Pleistocene hominids. *Curr. Anthrop. 1*, 195–232.

Mayr, E. (1963) *Animal Species and their Evolution*. London: Oxford University Press.

Campbell, B. (1964) Quantitative taxonomy and human evolution. In *Classification and Human Evolution* 50–74. Ed. S. L. Washburn. London: Methuen and Co. Ltd.

Oakley, K. P. (1964) *Frameworks for Dating Fossil Man*. London: Weidenfeld and Nicolson.

Müller-Beck, H.-J. (1964) Zur stratigraphischen Stellung des *Homo heidelbergensis. Jb. Rom-Germ. Zmus. (Mainz) 11*, 15–33.

Koenigswald, B. von (1973) Verönderungen in der Kleinsäuger-fauna von Mitteleuropa zwischen Cromer und Eem (Pleistozän). *Eisalter, Gegenw. 23/24*, 159–167.

Müller-Beck, H.-J. (1976) Zum Problem der frühen Artefakte Mitteleuropas. In *Les Prèmieres industries de l'Europe*, 24–34. Ed. K. Valoch. Nice: Colloque 8 UISPP Cong.

Stuart, A. J. and West, R. G. (1976) Late Cromerian fauna and flora at Ostend, Norfolk. *Geol. Mag. 1*, 469–473.

Müller-Beck, H.-J. (1977) Zum Problem der 'faustkeil-freien altpäläolithischen Industrien' in Mitteleuropa. *Ethnogr.-Archäol. Z. 18*, 39–56.

Stringer, C. B., Howell, F. C. and Melentis, J. K. (1979) The significance of the fossil hominid skull from Petralona, Greece. *J. archaeol. Sci. 6*, 235–253.

Howells, W. W. (1980) *Homo erectus* – Who, when and where: A survey. *Yearb. phys. Anthrop. 23*, 1–23.

Wolpoff, M. H. (1980) Cranial remains of Middle Pleistocene European Hominids. *J. hum. Evol. 9*, 339–358.

Howell, F. C. (1981) Some views of *Homo erectus* with special reference to its occurrence in Europe. In *Homo erectus*. Eds. B. A. Sigmon and J. S. Cybulski. Toronto: Univ. of Toronto Press.

Howells, W. W. (1981) *Homo erectus* in human descent: ideas and problems. In *homo erectus*. Eds. B. A. Sigmon and J. S. Cybulski. Toronto: Univ. of Toronto Press.

Stringer, C. B. (1981) The dating of European Middle Pleistocene hominids and the existence of *Homo erectus* in Europe. *Anthropologie (Brno)* 19, 3–14.

Cook, J., Stringer, C. B., Currant, A. P., Schwarcz, H. P. and Wintle, A. G. (1982) A review of the chronology of the European Middle Pleistocene hominid record. *Yearb. phys. Anthrop.* 25, 19–65.

Howell, F. C. (1982) Pers. Comm. to Nice UISPP Congress delegates.

Andrews, P. (1984) On the characters that define *Homo erectus*. *Cour. Forsch. Senck.* 69, 167–175.

Day, M. H. (1984) The postcranial remains of *Homo erectus* from Africa, Asia and possibly Europe, 113–121. *Ibid.*

Stringer, C. B. (1984) The definition of *Homo erectus* and the existence of the species in Africa and Europe, 131–143. *Ibid.*

Wood, B. A. (1984) The origins of *Homo erectus*. 99–111. *Ibid.*

Campbell, B. (1985) *Human Evolution*. New York: Aldine.

Kraatz, R. (1985) A review of recent research on Heidelberg Man, *Homo erectus heidelbergensis*. In *Ancestors*, 268–271. Ed. E. Delson, New York: Alan R. Liss.

The Steinheim Calvaria

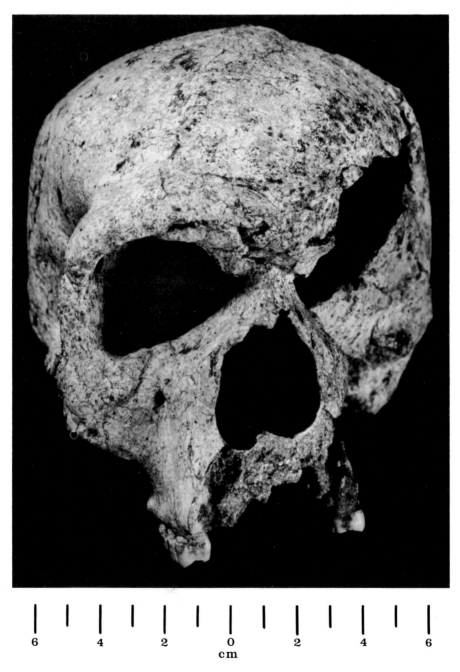

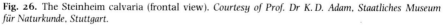

Fig. 26. The Steinheim calvaria (frontal view). *Courtesy of Prof. Dr K. D. Adam, Staatliches Museum für Naturkunde, Stuttgart.*

Synonyms   *Homo steinheimensis* (Berckhemer, 1936); *Homo (Protanthropus)*
steinheimensis (Berckhemer, 1937); *Homo cf. sapiens* (Le Gros Clark,
1955); *Homo sapiens steinheimensis* (Campbell, 1964)
Steinheim man.

Site   The Sigrist gravel pit, Steinheim on the river Murr, about 12 miles
north of Stuttgart, Wurttemberg, West Germany.

Found by   Karl Sigrist Jr, 24th July, 1933. Unearthed by F. Berckhemer.

Geology   The calvaria was found in Pleistocene gravels washed down by the
River Murr and deposited at Steinheim. The Sigrist pit shows several
distinct strata of sands and gravels overlain by a layer of loess;
these have been studied in detail by Berckhemer (1925) and others
who demonstrated that the gravels are of two types and contain
two separate faunal groups. This work has been continued and
amplified by Adam (1954a and b) who suggests that four layers
can be distinguished, each characterized by its contained fauna, in
particular by the elephant remains.

Associated finds   The layers have been named and characterized in the following
way:
1. *Younger Mammoth Gravels*
Containing steppe-mammoth (*Mammuthus primigenius*) and woolly
rhinoceros (*Coelodonta antiquitatis*).
2. *Main Mammoth Gravels*
Containing steppe-mammoth (*Mammuthus trogonherii-primigenius*),
bison (*Bison priscus*), horse (*Equus steinheimensis*) and woolly rhinoceros (*Coelodonta antiquitatis*).
3. *Straight-tusked Elephant Gravels*
Containing straight-tusked elephant (*Palaeoloxodon antiquus*), bear
(*Ursus arctos*), wild ox (*Bos primigenius*) and lion (*Felis sp.*). It was
in this layer that Steinheim man was found.
4. *Older Mammoth Gravels*
Containing steppe-mammoth (*Mammuthus trogontherii*), horse
(*Equus cf. mosbachensis*), rhinoceros (*Didermocerus kirchbergensis*),
bison (*Bison priscus*) and red deer (*Cervus elaphus*). According to
Adam (1954a) the fauna in Gravel 3 is clear evidence of an interglacial woodland environment at the time the deposit was laid
down, for the straight-tusked forest elephant is almost confined to
this layer whilst the steppe-mammoth occurs in each of the other
three layers.
Itermann (1961) has described a pebble tool culture from the interglacial gravels of the Lower Murr River and attributed it to Steinheim man. This claim has been dismissed on the grounds that the
'tools' have been incorrectly identified (Adam, 1973).

Dating   In the past opinion has varied regarding the dating of this find, the gravels having been assigned by some to the Second (Mindel–Riss) and by others to the Third (Riss–Würm) Interglacials. In view of the evidence given above and other evidence, Howell (1960) states that there can be no question that the gravels in which the Steinheim calvaria was found are other than of Second Interglacial age (Great, Mindel–Riss or Penultimate Interglacial); this has been reaffirmed by Kurtén (1962), Oakley (1964) and Adam (1985).

Morphology   *Calvaria*

A detailed description of the specimen has not yet been published, but several reports have appeared (Berckhemer, 1933, *et seq.*). A longer account was published by Weinert (1936). The specimen, which is distorted and damaged, consists of the cranial and facial skeleton of a young adult. The left orbit, temporal and infratemporal regions and part of the left maxilla are missing, as is the premaxillary region of both sides. The base of the skull is broken away around the foramen magnum, but it is well preserved in its anterior portion. The upper right second premolar tooth and all of the molar teeth are in place.

The vault of the skull is long, narrow and moderately flattened; the supraorbital torus is pronounced, the nasal opening wide and the root of the nose depressed. In lateral view the degree of facial prognathism is small, the mastoid processes small but well defined and the occipital region well rounded. There is no occipital chignon but a low torus extends to the asterion. The greatest width of the cranium is its biparietal diameter.

Teeth

The premolar crown is symmetrical but has a large buccal cusp and a smaller lingual cusp. The molars decrease in size in the order M1 > M2 > M3. The third molar is markedly smaller than the other two and all are moderately taurodont.

Dimensions

Cranium	Weinert (1936)	Howell (1960)	Wolpoff (1980)
Length	184	185	179
Breadth	132–133	116	130
Cranial Index	72·0	62·5	72·6
Cranial Capacity	1,070 cc	1,150–1,175 cc	—

Affinities   The precise relationships of this form are uncertain. The skull has a few resemblances to known *Homo erectus* skulls of the Middle Pleistocene, such as a small cranial capacity, yet it has some features that it shares with the Neandertals such as the heavy supraorbital torus and the broad nasal opening. Its principal resem-

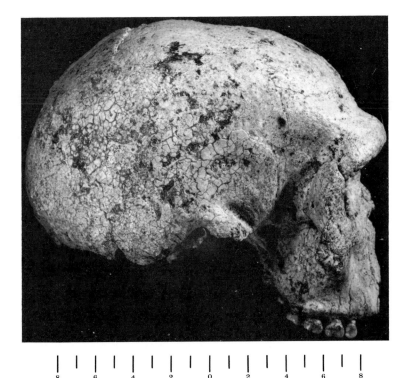

Fig. 27. The Steinheim Calvaria (right lateral view). *Courtesy of Prof. Dr K. D. Adam, Staatliches Museum für Naturkunde, Stuttgart.*

blance is to the Swanscombe skull (*q.v.*) which has been attributed to *Homo sapiens* (Howell, 1960; Stringer, 1978; Wolpoff, 1980), an affinity based on such features as the high position of the maximum breadth, the occipital contour and the form of thickness of the skull vault bones. The teeth are small and sapient in form although moderately taurodont. Wolpoff (1980) advances the view that Steinheim, Swanscombe and Arago (*q.v.*) represent female examples of European Middle Pleistocene hominids whilst skulls from Petralona (*q.v.*) Bilzingsleben (*q.v.*) and Vértesszöllös (*q.v.*) represent male counterparts of populations that exhibit wide sexual dimorphism. The difficulties of incorporating these remains into a taxonomic scheme led to the suggestion that hominids dated to before the end of the Second Glaciation (Mindel Glaciation) should be attributed to *Homo erectus* and those that are post Second Glaciation (Mindel Glaciation) should be attributed to *Homo sapiens*. The weaknesses and problems associated with this approach have been exposed by Stringer (1981), who does not accept that the evidence for the presence of *Homo erectus* in Europe is conclusive. The opposite view is taken by Vlček (1978) on the basis of the Bilzingsleben skull (*q.v.*) which is attributed to *Homo erectus*.

In a recent review (Stringer, Hublin and Vandermeersch, 1984) the question is left unresolved and the identification of Neandertal features such as nasal form, occipital torus morphology and supra-iniac fossa is left open, indeed their recognition as new features (apomorphic) or features of common inheritance (plesiomorphic) is also left open.

My view is that the Steinheim skull can best be regarded as a female example of a *Homo erectus/Homo sapiens* transitional form that is at the root of the European Neandertal side branch.

Original   Institut für Anthropologie und Humangenetik der Universität, Tübingen 74, West Germany.

Casts   1. Staatliches Museum für Naturkunde, Stuttgart, West Germany. (Calvaria and reconstruction.)
2. The University Museum, University of Pennsylvania, Philadelphia 4, Pennsylvania, U.S.A. (Calvaria.)

References   Berckhemer, F. (1925) Eine Riesenhirschstange aus den diluvialen Schottern von Steinheim a.d. Murr. *Jh. Ver. vater I. Naturk. Württ. 81*, 99–108.
Berckhemer, F. (1933) Ein Menschen-Schädel aus den diluvialen Schottern von Steinheim a.d. Murr. *Anthrop. Anz. 10*, 318–321.
Berckhemer, F. (1936) Der Urmenschenschädel aus den zwischeneiszeitlichen Fluss—Schottern von Steinheim a.d. Murr. *Forschn. Fortschr. 12*, 349–350.
Weinert, H. (1936) Der Urmenschenschädel von Steinheim. *Z. Morph. Anthrop. 35*, 463–518.
Berckhemer, F. (1937) Bermerkungen zu H. Weinerts' Abhandlung 'Der Urmenschenschädel von Steinheim'. *Verh. Ges. phys. Anthrop. 2*, 49–58.
Adam, K.D. (1954a) Die mittelpleistozänen Faunen von Steinheim an der Murr (Württemberg). *Quaternaria 1*, 131–144.
Adam, K.D. (1954b) Die zeitliche Stellung der Urmenschen-Fundschicht von Steinheim an der Murr innerhalb des Pleistozäns. *Eiszeitalter Gegenw. 4/5*, 18–21.
Clark, W.E. le Gros (1955) *The Fossil Evidence for Human Evolution*. Chicago: Chicago University Press.
Weiner, J.S. (1958) The pattern of evolutionary development of the genus *Homo. S. Afr. J. med. Sci. 23*, 111–120.
Howell, F.C. (1960) European and northwest African Middle Pleistocene hominids. *Curr. Anthrop. 1*, 195–232.
Napier, J.R., and Weiner, J.S. (1962) Olduvai Gorge and human origins. *Antiquity 36*, 41–47.
Kurtén, B. (1962) The relative ages of the australopithecines of Transvaal and the pithecanthropines of Java. In *Evolution und Hominisation*, 74–80. Ed. G. Kurth. Stuttgart: Gustav Fischer Verlag.
Campbell, B. (1964) Quantitative taxonomy and human evolution. In *Classification and Human Evolution*, 50–74. Ed. S.L. Washburn. London: Methuen and Co. Ltd.

Oakley, K. P. (1964) *Frameworks for Dating Fossil Man*. London: Weidenfeld and Nicolson.

Itermann, J. (1961) Uber 'Alteste Steinwerkzeuge'. 8 Abb. – *Heimarkalender 1961 des Selfkantkreises Geilenkirchen-Heinsberg*, Geilenkirchen & Heinsberg *11*, 11–13.

Itermann, J. (1962) Ein Faustkeil des '*Homo steinheimensis*'. 3 Abb – *Eiszeitalter und Gegenwart. Jbr Deutschen Qverei. Ohringen/Wurtt. 13*, 19–23.

Adam, K. D. (1973) Die 'Artefakte des Homo steinheimensis' als Belege urgeschichtlichen Irrens. *Stuttg. Beitr. Naturk.*, B, *6*, 1–99.

Stringer, C. B. (1978) Some problems in Middle and Upper Pleistocene hominid relationships. In *Recent Advances in Primatology, Vol. 3 Evolution*, 395–418. Eds. D. J. Chivers and K. Joysey. London: Academic Press.

Vlček, E. (1978) A new discovery of *Homo erectus* in central Europe. *J. hum. Evol. 7*, 239–251.

Wolpoff, M. H. (1980) Cranial remains of Middle Pleistocene European hominids. *J. hum. Evol. 9*, 339–358.

Stringer, C. B. (1981) The dating of European Middle Pleistocene hominids and the existence of *Homo erectus* in Europe. *Anthropologie (Brno) 19*, 3–14.

Stringer, C. B., Hublin, J.-J. and Vandermeersch, B. (1984) The origin of anatomically modern humans in Western Europe. in *The Origins of Modern Humans*, 51–135. Eds. F. H. Smith and F. Spencer, New York: Alan R. Liss.

Adam, K. D. (1985) The chronological and systematic position of the Steinheim skull. In *Ancestors*, 271–276. Ed. E. Delson. New York: Alan R. Liss.

The Krapina Remains

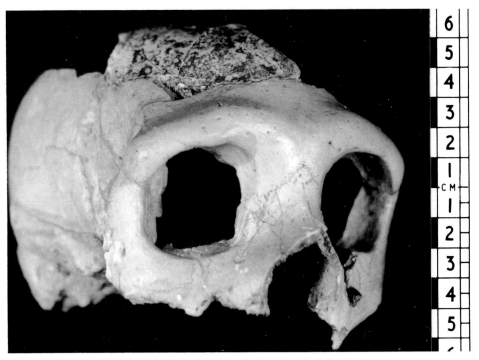

Fig. 28. The Krapina craniofacial fragment (cranium C). *Courtesy of Dr F. Smith.*

Synonyms and other names	*Homo primigenius var. krapinensis* (Gorjanovič-Kramberger, 1906) *Homo neandertalensis var. krapinensis* (Skerlj, 1953).
Site	Near the river Krapinica, a tributary of the Drave, which runs through the small town of Krapina, 25 miles northwest of Zagreb, Yugoslavia.
Found by	K. Gorjanovič-Kramberger, September, 1899–July, 1905.
Geology	The remains were discovered during the excavation of a rock shelter that had become filled by fallen debris. The deposits have been divided into 13 stratigraphic units the upper nine of which contain artefacts. The stratigraphic levels for all the hominid remains are not known, but levels 3 and 4 seem to have produced most of the specimens (Gorjanovič-Kramberger, 1906; Malez, 1970a, 1978).

Associated finds It is believed that large numbers of stone implements were recovered from the site but relatively few have been described; they appear to be of Mousterian type and include points and scrapers. In addition Acheulean and 'pre-Aurignacian' tools have been mentioned (Skerlj, 1953). A few tools of Upper Palaeolithic type are known from the upper levels but no clear Upper Palaeolithic culture is present at the site (Malez, 1970c; Smith, 1982).

Fossil mammalian bones found at the site included those of Merck's rhinoceros (*Dicerorhinus mercki*), cave bear (*Ursus spelaeus*), wild ox (*Bos primigenius*), beaver (*Castor fiber*), marmot (*Marmotta marmotta*) and red deer (*Cervus elaphus*).

The faunal complex from the hominid levels indicates a warm or moderate climate (Malez, 1970b, 1978).

Dating Originally the site was attributed to an early Interglacial date, First or Second Interglacial (Günz–Mindel or Mindel–Riss); a conclusion attributed to Gorjanovič–Kramberger by Skerlj (1953). However, other authors have regarded the site as being somewhat later, e.g. Third Interglacial (Riss–Würm) (Skerlj, 1953; Le Gros Clark, 1964); end of Third Interglacial and early stages of Würm I (Zeuner, 1940; Coon, 1962; Oakley, 1964); Göttweiger Interstadial of Würm Glaciation (Guenther, 1959).

The upper 9 stratigraphic units have been correlated with the Third Interglacial (Riss–Würm Interglacial) and the Fourth Glaciation (Lower Würm–Würm Interstadial). The hominid levels have been correlated with the end of the Third Interglacial (Riss–Würm Interglacial) (Malez, 1970a; 1978). No reliable absolute dates have been given for the site.

Morphology The bones from Krapina are numerous but badly fragmented. They comprise the remains of at least 13 men, women and children; some of the bones show evidence of having been burned. Almost all the bones of the skeleton are represented, some several times, and there are many teeth.

Skulls

Five skulls (A, B, C, D and E) are complete enough for study but only one (Skull C) gives any idea of the form of the cranium and face. This specimen consists of the upper part of the face together with part of the frontal bone, and the right temporal and parietal bones. It is probably the skull of an adolescent. The supraorbital ridges are separated by grooves from the somewhat retreating forehead. The bones of the vault are of modern form but the mastoid process is small.

Other features of the skull include lambdoid flattening and occipital bunning in the juvenile B skull. The faces are large with large frontal sinuses restricted to the torus, forward projection of the face with no nasal root depression or canine fossae.

The lower part of the Krapina face is represented by six maxillae (A–F) and nine mandibles (A–J, less I). These bones indicate that the palate was broad.

Cranial sexual dimorphism has been demonstrated in 13 of the Krapina specimens (Smith, 1976a, 1980, 1984).

Mandibles

The most complete adult mandible (J) has a parabolic dental arcade bearing the permanent dentition, lacking only the first premolars and the left third molar. The body is relatively stout but there is no mandibular torus or simian shelf. The condyles are flattened, although this is probably due to osteoarthritis of the temporomandibular joint. In some specimens the mental foramina are large and single, in others small and multiple.

There are no chins or even true submental trigons and the symphyses angle forward from the base to the alveolar margins. Clearly the face is pulled forward (Alexeev, 1979) and a retromolar space is present in those specimens where the region is preserved.

The Teeth

The Upper Incisors are moderately shovelled and several have basal 'finger-like' tubercles.

The Canines resemble those of modern man but some have ridged margins.

The Premolars are bicusped, symmetrical and taurodont.

The Molars have four or five cusps, well-marked anterior foveae and, in unworn teeth, secondary wrinkling of the enamel. An upper left first molar has a distinct Carabelli cusp and pit, whilst both upper and lower third molars show some reduction in size. Taurodontism is extreme in these molar teeth (Kallay, 1963).

Dental wear (Smith, 1976b), dental eruption, ageing and demographic characters (Wolpoff, 1979) as well as dental size (Brace, 1979) have all been the subject of study from this population of 279 teeth.

Postcranial Bones

Amongst the large collection are vertebrae, ribs, clavicles, scapulae, humeri, radii, ulnae, hand bones; also innominate bones, femora, patellae, tibiae, a fibula, a calcaneus, tali and other foot bones. Many of the bones are broken and incomplete.

Inventories of the upper limb bones (Smith, 1976c), the hand bones (Musgrave, 1977) and the lower limb bones (Trinkaus, 1975) have been given. In general terms the Krapina people show a complex of features similar to other Neandertals including barrel-shaped chests, great muscularity and robustness of the skeleton, and large joints. Where these bones do not display the coarse modelling and large joints typical of Western Neandertalers it seems likely that it is due to the predominance of sub-adult material in the sample (Smith, 1984).

In general there is little to distinguish these bones from their counterparts in modern man.

Dimensions   Selected from Gorjanovič-Kramberger (1906)

Skull C (Reconstructed)

Max. Length 178
Max. Breadth 149
Cranial Index 83·7 (Brachycephalic)

Mandible J

Symphysial Height 42·3
Symphysial Thickness 15·0
Coronoid Height 73·0
Ramus Breadth (Middle) 37·0

Teeth

Lower Permanent Molars (Crown Dimensions)

Mandible J		M1	M2	M3
Left	l	11·0	12·5	—
Side	b	11·1	11·5	—
Right	l	11·4	11·5	11·6
Side	b	11·3	12·2	c10·3

Numerous other dental dimensions have been published (Wolpoff, 1979; Smith, 1984).

Postcranial Bones

Clavicle (complete)	Length	149·5 (adult)
Clavicle (complete)	Length	59·4 (child)
Capitate	Length	27·5
	Breadth	17·6
Innominate bone (left)	Acetabular dia.	53·5
Innominate bone (right)	Acetbular dia.	57·0
Femora	Mean dia. of head I	52·7
	Mean dia. of head II	44·3
Talus	Length	53·3
	Breadth	42·5
	L/B Index	79·7

Cuboid   Length   37·5
                                          Breadth 27·4

Numerous other measurements were given but many of them are of little value for comparative purposes since they are not standard dimensions.

Affinities   It has become clear in recent years that early opinions of the advanced morphology of the Krapina people were not soundly based, neither was the view that the remains antedate the 'classic Neandertalers'. Whilst a few features such as occipital bunning and mid-facial projection may not be as marked or as well expressed as in Western Neandertals, it is said that the Krapina population does not differ significantly in total morphological pattern from Western Neandertals. There is no basis for regarding Krapina as an example of a 'progressive' or early modern group of *Homo sapiens sapiens*. They are regarded as belonging to *Homo sapiens neanderthalensis* (Smith, 1984).

The question of cannibalism and the dismemberment of the corpses of the Krapina people has been suggested on the grounds of fragmentation, cut marks and bone splitting (Ullrich, 1978a and b). This has been discounted by Trinkaus (1985) on the basis that there is no evidence of damage that cannot be explained in other ways than cannibalism.

Originals   National Museum of Geology and Palaeontology, Zagreb, Yugoslavia.

Casts   National Museum of Geology and Palaeontology, Zagreb, Yugoslavia (Cranio-facial fragment, two mandibles, one femur).

References   Gorjanovič-Kramberger, K. (1899) Vorläufige Mitteilung über den Krapina-fund. *Mitt. anthrop. Ges. Wien 29*, 1, 65–68.

Gorjanovič-Kramberger, K. (1900) Der diluviale Mensch aus Krapina in Kroatien. *Mitt. anthrop. Ges. Wien 30*, 1, 203.

Gorjanovič-Kramberger, K. (1901–1905) Der paläolithische Mensch und seine Zeitgenossen aus dem Diluvium von Krapina in Kroatien. *Mitt. anthrop. Ges. Wien 31*, 164–197. 32, 189–216, 34, 187–199. 35, 197–229.

Gorjanovič-Kramberger, K. (1906) *Der diluviale Mensch von Krapina in Kroatia. Ein Beitrag zur Paläoanthropologie.* Wiesbaden: C. W. Kreidels Verlag.

Zeuner, F. C. (1940) *The age of Neanderthal man with notes on the Cotte de St. Brelade, Jersey, C.I.* London: Occ. Paper No 3 Univ. of London, Inst. of Archaeol.

Skerlj, B. (1953) In *Catalogue des hommes fossiles.* Eds.H. V. Vallois and H. L. Movius, Jnr. *C.r. Int. geol. Cong. Algiers 1952.* Section 5, 250–251.

Coon, C. S. (1962) *The Origin of Races.* London: Jonathan Cape.

Guenther, E. W. (1959) Zur Alters datierung der diluvialen Fundstelle von Krapina in Kroatien. In *Bericht über die 6 Tagung der Deutschen Gesellschaft für Anthropologie, Göttingen, 202–209* (cited by Brace, 1964).

Clark, W. E. le Gros (1964) *The Fossil Evidence for Human Evolution.* 2nd Ed. p. 76. Chicago: Chicago University Press.

Kallay, J. (1963) Radiographic study of the Neanderthal teeth from Krapina, Croatia. In *Dental Anthropology,* 75–86. Ed. D. Brothwell, Oxford: Pergamon Press.

Brace, C. L. (1964) The fate of the 'Classic' Neanderthals: A consideration of hominid catastrophism. *Curr. Anthrop. 5, no. 1,* 3–43.

Campbell, B. (1964) Quantitative taxonomy and human evolution. In *Classification and Human Evolution, 50–74.* Ed. S. L. Washburn. London: Methuen and Co. Ltd.

Oakley, K. P. (1964) *Frameworks for Dating Fossil Man,* 303. London: Weidenfeld and Nicolson.

Malez, M. (1970a) Novi pogledi na stratigrafiju krapinakog nalazista (German summary). In *Krapina 1899–1969,* 13–44. Ed. M. Malez. Zagreb: Jugoslavenska Akademija Znanosti i Umjetnosti.

Malez, M. (1970b) Rezultati revizije pleistocenske faune iz Krapine. *Ibid,* 45–56.

Malez, M. (1970c) Paleolitska kulture Krapine u svjetlu noviijh istrazivanja. *Ibid.,* 57–129.

Trinkaus, E. (1975) The Neandertals from Krapina, northern Yugoslavia: An inventory of the lower limb remains. *Z. Morph. Anthrop. 67,* 44–59.

Smith, F. H. (1976a) The Neandertal remains from Krapina: A descriptive and comparative study. *Univ. Tenn. Dep. Anthrop. Rep. Invest. 15,* 1–359.

Smith, F. H. (1976b) On anterior tooth wear at Krapina and Ochoz. *Curr. Anthropol. 17,* 167–168.

Smith, F. H. (1976c) The Neandertal remains from Krapina, northern Yugoslavia; An inventory of the upper limb remains. *Z. Morph. Anthrop. 67,* 275–90.

Musgrave, J. (1977) The Neandertals from Krapina, northern Yugoslavia: An inventory of the handbones. *Z. Morph. Anthrop. 68,* 150–171.

Malez, M. (1978) Stratigrafski paleofaunski, i paleolitski odnosi krapinokog nalizista. In *Krapinski Pracovjek i Evolucija Hominida,* 61–102 (German summary). Ed. M. Malez. Zagreb: Jugoslavenska Akademija Znanosti i Umjetnosi.

Smith, F. H. (1978) Some conclusions regarding the morphology and significance of the Krapina Neandertal remains. In *Krapinski Pracovjek i Evolucija Hominida,* 61–102 (German summary). Ed. M. Malez. Zagreb: Jugoslavenska Akademija Znanosti i Umjetnosi.

Ullrich, H. (1978a) Zur frage des kannibalismus beim Neandertaler von Krapina. *Zentralinstitut fur alte geschichte und archäologie, Der Akademie der Wissenschaften der DDR, Berlin,* 7–15.

Ullrich, H. (1978b) Kannibalismus und Leichenzerstuckelung beim neandertaler von Krapina. *Krapinski Pracovjek I Evolucija Hominida 5,* 293–318.

Alexeev, V. P. (1979) Horizontal profile of the Neandertal crania from Krapina comparatively considered. *Coll. Anthropol. 3,* 7–13.

Brace, C. L. (1979) Krapina 'classic' Neanderthals and the evolution of the European face. *J. hum. Evol. 8,* 527–550.

Wolpoff, M. H. (1979) The Krapina dental remains. *Am. J. phys. Anthrop. 50,* 67–114.

Smith, F. H. (1980) Sexual differences in European Neandertal crania with special reference to the Krapina remains. *J. hum. Evol.* 9, 359–375.

Smith, F. H. (1982) Upper Pleistocene hominid evolution in south-central Europe: A review of the evidence and analysis of trends. *Curr. Anthrop.* 23, 667–703.

Smith, F. H. (1984) Fossil hominids from the Upper Pleistocene of central Europe and the origin of modern Europeans. In *The Origins of Modern Humans*, 137–209. Eds. F. H. Smith and F. Spencer. New York: Alan R. Liss.

Trinkaus, E. (1985) Cannibalism and burial at Krapina. *J. hum. Evol.* 14, 203–216.

The Petralona Cranium

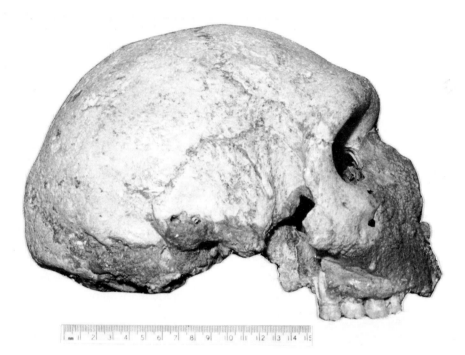

Fig. 29. The Petralona cranium (right lateral view). *Courtesy of Dr C. B. Stringer.*

Synonyms and other names Petralona 1; *Homo erectus petraloniensis* (Murrill, 1983).

Site Near Petralona, 37 km south-east of Thessalonika, Khalkidhiki, eastern Greece.

Found by J. Malkotsis, J. Stathis, B. Avaramis, Chr. and Const. Sarijanides and St Hantzaridés; 16th September, 1960.

Geology Katsika Hill lies about 37 km to the south-east of Thessalonika and consists of Mesozoic calcareous deposits. A stalagmitic cave was found accidentally in the hillside in May 1959, and later when the opening in the cave was enlarged and the cave explored fossil mammalian bones and teeth were found. Further exploration of the cave led to the discovery of the skull (Kokkoros and Kanellis, 1960). Further details of the geology and stratigraphy of the site are given in Poulianos, A. (1971, 1978, 1983; Kurtén and Poulianos, A.,

1977). Five principal groups of strata are recognized (A–E from above downwards) containing 27 sub-strata made up of breccias, red earths, clays, and earths variously containing stalagmitic material, blackened fire-stones and ashes. Layers 1–10 (from above downwards) are said to show signs of human habitation.

Layer 11 is said to correlate with the 'Mausoleum' or cavity within the cave system that contained the skull (Poulianos, A., 1983; Poulianos, N., 1983). This correlation has been seriously questioned (Wintle and Jacobs, 1982; Cook *et al.*, 1982; Stringer, 1983).

Associated finds Some stone tools and bone artefacts were recovered from the cave (Marinos, Yannoulis and Sotiradis, 1965; Poulianos, 1971). The tools have been ascribed to an early Mousterian culture and include quartz 'balls', scrapers and chopping tools made from imported materials. In addition some bone awls and bone scrapers were found. The more elaborate tools seem to come from higher in the sequence than those that are more simple in form. Tools made from limestone, bauxite and quartz have been claimed from the site and two levels of technology, the 'Petralonian' and the 'Crenian', have been described (Poulianos, N., 1978; Poulianos, A., 1983). Examination of these tools shows that, whilst many are unlikely to be artefacts, some undoubtedly are human work. The claim that they are between 600,000 and 1,000,000 years old (Poulianos, N., 1983) must be evaluated in conjunction with other dating evidence (see below).

The mammalian remains found in the Petralona cave deposits include those of cave bear (*Ursus spelaeus*), red deer (*Cervus elaphus*), and cave lion (*Panthera leo spelaea*) (Kokkoros and Kanellis, 1960). Later when the cave was investigated in greater detail further fossil mammals were identified including horse (*Equus*), fallow deer (*Dama dama*), giant deer (*Megaceros*), wild ox (*Bos primigenius*) and wild goat (*Capra caucasica*) (Sickenberg, 1964). Further finds that have been reported include wolf (*Canis lupus*), three species of hyena (*Hyena brevirostris, H. perrieri* and *Crocuta crocuta*) and rhinoceros (*cf. Dicerorhinus hemitoechus*) (Fortelius and Poulianos, N., 1979). Small vertebrates have also been reported from the site as being of Middle Pleistocene character (Poulianos, A., 1967; Kretzoi, 1977; Kretzoi and Poulianos, N., 1981). Following detailed study of the carnivores (Schutt, 1971; Kurtén and Poulianos, A., 1977, 1981; Kurtén, 1983) three superimposed faunas are recognized. It is claimed that the entire sequence antedates the later Middle Pleistocene and that the Petralona skull is associated with the earliest of these faunas.

Dating The precise dating of the cave site is a matter of dispute. The fauna was at first said to indicate a date of either the end of the Third

Fig. 30. The Petralona cranium (occipital view). *Courtesy of Dr C. B. Stringer.*

Interglacial (Riss–Würm) period or the beginning of the Last Glacial (Würm) period (Poulianos, 1967). It was suggested later that a maximum date for the skull should be taken as 70,000 years B.P. (Poulianos, 1971). However, Sickenberg (1971) concluded that the Petralona fauna could well be pre-Second Glaciation (Mindel) in age. The carnivore study confirmed a possible Middle Pleistocene date for the cave deposits as did a uranium/thorium analysis of stalagmite from the floor claimed to be above the skull layer (Kurtén and Poulianos, 1977). It was then claimed that on the basis of new data from stalagmite dated by the Electron Spin Resonance method (Ikeya, 1977) an age of 700,000 ± 50,000 years B.P. should be given for Petralona man (Poulianos, A., 1978). This assertion is also based upon a reported palaeomagnetic reversal below Layer 11 and correlation of the fauna with those from other early sites that predate a palaeomagnetic reversal (Kurtén and Poulianos, A., 1977). This claim has been disputed by several authors (Stringer, 1981; Wintle and Jacobs, 1982; Cook *et al.*, 1982; Stringer, 1983). Cook *et al.* (1982) are most trenchant in their criticism and maintain that a date of 700,000 years or more B.P. for the Petralona cranium depends firstly, upon a clear association between the cranium and a given layer, secondly, that a correlation can be shown between that layer and the sequence elsewhere in the cave that contains the studied fauna; thirdly, that the fauna can be shown to predate 'Cromerian' faunas such as West Runton, Süssenborn and Stránská skála and fourthly that the palaeomagnetic reversal at Stránska skála dates the fauna there and represents the Bruhnes–Matuyama boundary c. 700,000 years B.P. If any point in this chain is broken, the Kurtén and Poulianos (1977) claim must fail. Cook *et al.* (1982) claim that there is no published evidence that establishes a Lower Pleistocene age for the fauna from Petralona or for the hominid cranium. Attempts to establish the absolute date of the site have proved equally controversial (Ikeya, 1980; Hennig *et al.*, 1981; Poulianos, A., 1982; Liritzis, 1982; Ikeya, 1982; Hennig *et al.*, 1982) and absolute dates given range from 160,000 years B.P. to 620,000 years B.P. In 1982 the 3rd European Anthropological Congress was held at Petralona and many papers given dealt with the dating of the site, its fauna and stratigraphy as well as the cranium itself (Proceedings of the 3rd European Anthropological Congress – *Anthropos 10*, 1983). The debate at this meeting has been summarized elsewhere (Day, 1982) but a consensus view of the date for the Petralona cranium would be about 350–400,000 years B.P. This is clearly not accepted by Poulianos, A. (1984) who, in an astonishing paper impervious to previous criticisms, reasserts his claim for Petralona man as a European Lower Pleistocene hominid who was the world's oldest known fire-maker.

Morphology   The skull was found 'suspended in the air (twenty-four centimetres above the floor) attached to a stalactitic column ...' (Poulianos, 1971). In the same paper it is stated that the whole skeleton was found nearby lying on its right side in a contracted position. Unfortunately the postcranial skeleton either never existed or was not preserved.

The cranium was covered with a calcareous incrustation that had served to preserve even the more fragile portions of the face. The only parts of the cranium that are missing are part of the right zygomatic bone and parts of both mastoid processes. The mandible has not been recovered. When the incrustation was removed from the cranial vault the shape of the skull emerged. It has large supraorbital ridges and a low vault with a retreating forehead. The occipital region is protuberant and leads down to a flattened nuchal plane. The face is large in most of its dimensions, but particularly so in the breadth of the upper face; the size of the mandible is estimated to have exceeded all known Neandertal jaws in terms of its bicondylar breadth. Even the Heidelberg jaw (*q.v.*) is said to be too small to match the Petralona maxillae (Stringer, 1974). A detailed description has been given by Stringer, Howell and Melentis

(1979) and this has been expanded following the exposure of the face by further cleaning (Stringer, 1983). The cranium was also described by Murrill (1981). Radiographs of the skull have disclosed remarkable pneumatization of the mastoid and temporal bones as well as huge frontal air sinuses.

Affinities The first opinions (Kokkoros and Kanellis, 1960) suggested that the Petralona cranium is of Neandertal type, a view that was confirmed later by Bostanci (1964). Later authors have differed widely in their views, some supporting the Neandertal affinities (Jelinek, 1969; Brose and Wolpoff, 1971; de Bonis and Melentis, 1982) whilst others have drawn attention to features that the Petralona cranium shares with the Kabwe cranium (*q.v.*) (Breitinger, 1964; Bostanci, 1964; Yrson, 1964; Stringer, 1974; Stringer *et al.*, 1979; Murrill, 1975, 1981, 1983; de Bonis and Melentis, 1982; Stringer, 1983; Van Vark, 1983). At the same time, almost all have conceded some *Homo erectus* features and Hemmer (1972) even suggested that it should be regarded as an advanced example of *Homo erectus*, a view that was moderated later (Hemmer, 1982).

This lack of consensus has been addressed by Stringer *et al.* (1979) and Stringer (1983) after detailed examination and analysis. The mosaic of features shown by this cranium has been considered in the light of the modern debate concerning *Homo erectus* and its occurrence in Europe (Howell, 1982; Stringer, 1984; Wood, 1984; Andrews, 1984). (See also 'The *Homo erectus* problem'—this volume.)

The outcome is that the Petralona cranium, at first regarded as best assigned to '*Homo sapiens but of the most primitive grade*' (italics mine) (Stringer *et al.*, 1979), is later conceded by them to be more Neandertal-like in the face and, with the Kabwe cranium and Arago 21 (*q.v.*), to be a member of an 'undifferentiated archaic hominid group which can be distinguished from typical *Homo erectus* fossils . . . [and] from both Neandertals and modern *Homo sapiens*.'

The problems encountered in trying to assess the affinities of the Petralona cranium epitomizes one of the central problems of palaeoanthropology today, how to deal in phylogenetic and taxonomic terms with fossils that show a mosaic of features. It seems clear, however, that the Petralona cranium represents a population that is not simply another 'classic' Neandertaler but may represent a population of early forms comparable to the Kabwe (Rhodesian) population from Africa and related to possible European equivalents such as Vértesszöllös, Arago 21, Mauer and Bilzingsleben (*q.v.*).

Dimensions

Skull	Poulianos (1971)	Stringer *et al.* (1979)
Max. Length	209	209
Max. Breadth	149	150 (bi-parietal)

Cranial Index   71·6   71·7
                       (Dolichocephalic)
Cranial Capacity   1,220 cc   1,190–1,210 cc

Original   Geological and Palaeontological Institute of the University of Thessalonika.

Casts   Not available at present.

References Anon (1959) Newsletter *Makedonia:* Thessalonika (in Greek).

Kokkoros, P. and Kanellis, A. (1960) Découverte d'un crane d'homme paléolithique dans la peninsule Chalcidique. *Anthropologie 64*, 132–147.

Bostanci, E. (1964) An examination of the Neanderthal type fossil skull found in the Chalcidique peninsula. *Belleten Turk Tarih Kurumu Bosimeni 28*, 373–381.

Breitinger, E. (1964) Report to the Moscow Anthropological Congress (quoted by Poulianos, 1967).

Sickenberg, O. (1964) Die Saugetierfauna der Hohle Petralona bei Thessaloniki. *Geol. Geophys. Res. 9*, 1–16.

Yryson, M.J. (1964) Report to the Moscow Anthropological Congress (quoted by Poulianos, 1967).

Marinos, G., Yannoulis, P. and Sotiradis, L. (1965) Palaeoanthropologische untersuchungen in der Hohle von Petralona-Chalkidi. (In Greek with a German summary.) *Wiss. Phys. Math. Fak. Univ. Thassaloniki*, 149–204.

Poulianos, A.N. (1967) The place of Petralonian man among Palaeoanthropoi. *Anthropos (Brno) 19*, 216–221.

Jelinek, J. (1969) Neanderthal man and *Homo sapiens* in Central and Eastern Europe. *Curr. Anthrop. 10*, 475–503.

Brose, D.S. and Wolpoff, M.H. (1971) Early Upper Palaeolithic man and late Middle Palaeolithic tools. *Am. Anthrop. 73*, 1156–1194.

Poulianos, A.N. (1971) Petralona: a Middle Pleistocene cave in Greece. *Archaeology 24*, 6–11.

Schutt, G. (1971) Die Hyänen der Mosbacher Sonde (Altpleistozän, Wiesbaden/Hessen) mit einem Beitrag zur Stammesgeschichte der Gattung Crocuta. *Mainz. Naturw. Arch. 10:* 29–76.

Hemmer, H. (1972) Notes sur la position phylétique de l'homme de Petralona. *Anthropologie 76*, 155–162.

Stringer, C.B. (1974) A multivariate study of the Petralona skull. *J. hum. Evol. 3*, 397–404.

Murrill, R.L. (1975) A comparison of the Rhodesian and Petralona upper jaws in relation to other Pleistocene hominids. *Z. Morph. Anthr. 66* (2), 176–187.

Ikeya, M. (1977) Electron Spin Resonance dating of Petralona. *Anthropos 4*, 152–168.

Kretzoi, M. (1977) The fauna of small vertebrates of the Middle Pleistocene at Petralona. *Anthropos 4*, 131–143.

Kurtén, B. and Poulianos, A.N. (1977) New stratigraphic and faunal material from Petrolona cave with reference to the carnivora. *Anthropos 4*, 47–130.

Poulianos, A.N. (1978) Stratigraphy and age of the Petralonian Archanthropus. *Anthropos 5*, 37–46.

Poulianos, N. (1978) The oldest artifacts in Petralona Cave. *Anthropos 5*, 74–80.

Fortelius, M. and Poulianos, N. A. (1979) *Dicerorhinus* cf. *hemitoechus* (Mammalia, Perrissodactyla) from the Middle Pleistocene cave at Petralona-Chalkidiki—N. Greece. *Anthropos 6*, 15–43.

Stringer, C. B., Howell, F. C. and Melentis, J. K. (1979) The significance of the fossil hominid skull from Petralona, Greece. *J. arch. Sci. 6*, 235–253.

Ikeya, M. (1980) ESR dating of carbonates at Petralona Cave. *Anthropos 7*, 143–151.

Hennig, G. J., Herr, W., Weber, E. and Xirotiris, N. I. (1981) ESR-dating of the fossil hominid cranium from Petralona Cave, Greece. *Nature 292*, 533–536.

Kretzoi, M. and Poulianos, N. A. (1981) Remarks on the Middle and Lower Pleistocene vertebrate fauna in the Petralona Cave. *Anthropos 8*, 57–72.

Kurtén, B. and Poulianos, A. N. (1981) Fossil Carnivora of Petralona Cave (status 1980). *Anthropos 8*, 9–56.

Murrill, R. I. (1981) *Petralona Man*, Springfield: Charles C. Thomas.

Holloway, R. L. (1981) The Indonesian *Homo erectus* brain endocasts revisited. *Am. J. phys. Anthrop. 55*, 505–521.

Stringer, C. B. (1981) The dating of European Middle Pleistocene hominids and the existence of *Homo erectus* in Europe. *Anthropologie (Brno) 19*, 2–14.

Day, M. H. (1982) Greek Fireworks. *Nature 300*, 484.

De Bonis, L. and Melentis, J. (1982) L'homme de Petralona: comparisons avec l'homme de Tautavel. *Congr. Int. Palaeont. hum. Nice.* Prétirage, 847–874.

Cook, J., Stringer, C. B. Currant, A. P., Schwarcz, H. P. and Wintle, A. G. (1982) A review of the chronology of the European Middle Pleistocene hominid record. *Yearbk. phys. Anthrop. 25*, 19–65.

Hemmer, H. (1982) Major factors in the evolution of hominid skull morphology, biological correlates and the position of the Anteneandertals. *Congr. Int. Palaedont. hum. Nice.* Prétirage, 339–354.

Hennig, G. J., Herr, W., Weber, E. and Xirotiris, N. I. (1982) Petralona Cave dating controversy. *Nature 299*, 281–282.

Howell, F. C. (1982) Pers. Comm. to delegates. *Cong. Int. Paléont. hum.* 1, Nice.

Ikeya, M. (1982) Petralona Cave dating controversy. *Nature 299*, 281.

Liritzis, Y. (1982) Petralona Cave dating controversy. *Ibid*, 280–281.

Poulianos, A. (1982) Petralona Cave dating controversy. *Ibid*, 280.

Wintle, A. G. and Jacobs, J. A. (1982) A critical review of the dating evidence for Petralona Cave. *J. arch. Sci. 9*, 39–47.

Kurtén, B. (1983) Faunal sequence in Petralona Cave. *Anthropos 10*, 53–59.

Kurtén, B. (1983) The age of Petralona Cave. *Anthropos 10*, 16–17.

Poulianos, A. N. (1983) On the stratigraphy and dating of the Petralonian Man. *Anthropos 10*, 49–52.

Poulianos, N. A. (1983) Biostratigraphy and tool distribution of Petralona Cave (Section b). *Anthropos 10*, 74–83.

Murrill, R. I. (1983) On the dating of the fossil hominid Petralona Skull. *Anthropos 10*, 12–15.

Stringer, C. B. (1983) Some further notes on the morphology and dating of the Petralona hominid. *J. hum. Evol. 12*, 731–742.

Van Vark, G. N. (1983) On the phylogenetic position of the Petralona Skull. *Anthropos 10*, 88–92.

Andrews, P. (1984) On the characters that define *Homo erectus. Cour. Forsch. Senck.* 69, 167–175.

Poulianos, A. N. (1984) Once more on the age and stratigraphy of the Petralonian man. *J. hum. Evol.* 13, 465–467.

Stringer, C. B. (1984) The definition of *Homo erectus* and the existence of the species in Africa and Europe. *Cour. Forsch. Senck.* 69, 131–143.

Wood, B. A. (1984) The origins of *Homo erectus. Ibid*, 99–111.

The Vértesszöllös Remains

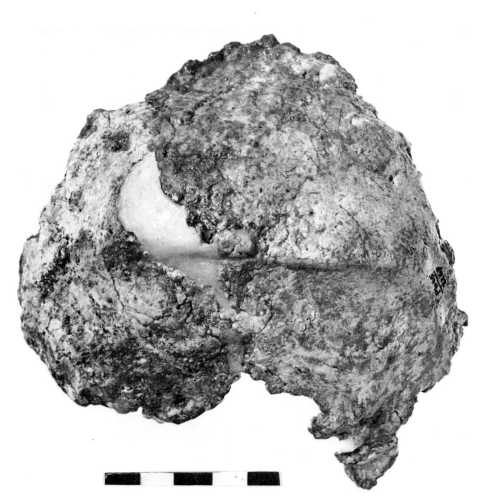

Fig. 31. The Vértesszöllös Occipital (external aspect). *Courtesy of Dr Andor Thoma.*

Synonyms and other names	*Homo (erectus seu sapiens) palaeohungaricus* (Thoma, 1966); *Homo erectus* (Wolpoff, 1971a); Vértesszöllös man.
Site	Near the village of Vértesszöllös about 50 km to the west of Budapest, Hungary.
Found by	Dr Laslo Vertes and his team from the Hungarian National Museum. Vértesszöllös I (excavated in 1964, recognized in 1965) and in 1965 on the 21st August, Vértesszöllös II.

Geology   The site lies at the foot of the Gerecse mountains in a quarry cut into the travertine deposits of the fourth terrace of the Danube system.

Associated finds   Four occupation layers were recognized in the deposits, each of dried mud that may have come from thermal springs. The lowest level (Level I) was 5 cm thick and contained the human remains. Numerous artefacts were found, 'pebble-tools' and 'chopper-tools' as well as numerous flakes many of which were of small size (Buda Industry). Perhaps a 'microlithic variant of the industrial traditions of Afro-asia' (Kretzoi and Vertes, 1965).

The faunal remains of both large and small vertebrates were re-covered from the site and are of early Middle Pleistocene character. The large vertebrates include wolf (*Canis lupus mosbachensis*), lion (*Panthera leo*), bears (*Ursus stehlini* and *Ursus deningeri*), wild horse (*Equus mosbachensis*), roe deer (*Capreolus capreolus*), hyena (*Hyaena brevirostris*) and giant beaver (*Trogontherium schmerlingi*) (Kretzoi and Vertes, 1965; Kahlke, 1975). The micro-mammalian fauna was also rich.

Dating   The deposits underlie the Mindel loess and are within the fourth, or Mindelian terrace of the river Danube. The lower two occupation layers are said to correspond to a mild climate whereas the upper two layers correspond to a period of colder conditions. The presence of imprints of beech leaves from the lower layers suggests that the remains should be dated to a warm phase within the Second Glaciation (Mindel or Elster Glaciation). On the basis of a thorium/uranium estimation, Cherdyntsev, Kazachevsky and Kuzmina (1965) have given the date of the remains as approximately 350,000 years B.P.

A recent reappraisal of the dating of the Vértesszöllös travertines, by uranium-series analysis, has suggested that the deposits are much younger than formerly believed at 185,00 years ± 25,000 years B.P. (Schwarcz and Latham, 1984). Palaeomagnetic studies on the Vértesszöllös travertines confirm that they are normally magnetized and within the Bruhnes normal period at less than 730,000 years B.P. (Latham and Schwarcz, 1983).

Morphology   *Vértesszöllös I*

The first finds of human remains were several fragments of deci-duous teeth from the lower dentition of a child. They include a left lower deciduous canine crown, a damaged deciduous second molar crown and two other tooth fragments (Thoma, 1967).

Vértesszöllös II

The second find was an adult occipital bone broken into two frag-ments, an upper right portion and a lower left portion. The two

Fig. 32. The Vértesszöllös Occipital (right lateral view). *Courtesy of Dr Andor Thoma.*

parts fitted together leaving a small gap in the central region; the fragments were located by the internal vascular markings. The region of the lambda was slightly deformed by the downward and forward displacement of the sublambdatic apex. In profile the bone can be divided into two parts, an upper curved occipital portion and a lower flattened nuchal portion, along the line of a well marked and undivided occipital torus. The nuchal plane is incomplete and does not include the foramen magnum whose borders are broken away, nevertheless it was possible to reconstruct the position of the opisthion with a reasonable degree of certainty.

The corners of the lambdoid sutures are well preserved and correspond to the asterion of each side, however, there are Wormian bones at lambda which render its exact location dubious. The attachments of the suboccipital muscles are well impressed on the nuchal plane, but the thickness of the bone bordering the foramen magnum does not constitute a postcondyloid tuberosity. There is a well marked occipitomastoid crest.

Internally the cerebellar fossae are small by comparison with the fossae for the occipital poles of the cerebral hemispheres, while the internal occipital protuberance lies well below the inion. The venous sinus impressions are distinct, the superior sagittal sinus passing directly into the right transverse sinus. Both transverse sinuses run directly on to the temporal bone at a point below each asterion without marking the parietal bones. It has been suggested that the occipital bone bears cut-marks in the region of the attachment of the cervical muscles, cut marks that result from the transection of these muscles. Subsequent speculation gives this as evidence that Vértesszöllős man was the victim of cannibalism (Ullrich, 1979).

Dimensions   Thoma (1966)

Occipital Bone

Biasterionic breadth 126·5; Lambda-opisthion chord 102; Lambda-inion chord 73; Inion-opisthion chord 56.
Cranial capacity estimated as in excess of 1,400 cc.

Teeth

	Lower Teeth (Crown Dimensions)		
Vértesszöllös	I	dc_1	dm_2
	l	6·7	10·3
	b	5·4	6·4*

*damaged.

Wolpoff (1977)

Occipital bone
Biasterionic breadth 128·3; Lambda-inion chord 73·0;
Inion-opisthion chord 53·0 or 56·0.
Cranial capacity 1,115–1,437 cc

Affinities   The remains have been studied by Thoma (1966, 1967, 1969 and 1972). Thoma also commented on Wolpoff (1977) denying that it belongs to *Homo erectus* (Thoma, 1978). In his view the occipital bone belonged to a male of under 30 years of age. In his description Thoma draws attention to the thickness and breadth of the bone, as well as the undivided occipital torus, as being primitive characters whereas the height and curvature of the upper segment of the bone are modern features. Similarly in his view the configuration of the brain is primitive while the capacity is large. However, the morphological comparisons and the metrical analyses taken together are said to indicate that whilst this man took his origin from

Homo erectus he had differentiated from this group and thus occupies a phyletic position at the beginning of the progressive line represented by Swanscombe, Fontéchevade and Quinzano (Thoma, 1966). Subsequently Stęślicka (1968) has stated that the occipital bone indicates Neandertal affinities on the basis of its dimensions and proportions; on the other hand Wolpoff (1971a and b, 1977) takes the view that the teeth and occipital bone together should be allocated to *Homo erectus*.

In a survey of *Homo erectus* sites and fossils (Howells, 1980) it is suggested that *Vértesszöllös* shares the *erectus*—like characteristics of similar parts from Petralona (*q.v.*) and Arago, although the features of these skulls are mixed. Stringer, Howell and Melentis (1979) suggest that the Vértesszöllös occipital shares 'grade characteristics' with Petralona; thus it is best regarded as a primitive form of *Homo sapiens*, a position not far from that of Thoma (1966).

Originals The Hungarian National Museum, Budapest, Hungary.

Casts Not generally available at present.

References Cherdyntsev, I., Kazachevsky, V., and Kuzmina, E. A. (1965) Age of Pleistocene Carbonate Formation according to Thorium and Uranium Isotopes. *Geokhimiya* 9, 1085–1092.

Kretzoi, M., and Vertes, L. (1965) Upper Biharian (Intermindel) Pebble-industry occupation site in western Hungary. *Curr. Anthrop.* 6, 74–87.

Thoma, A. (1966) L'occipital de l'homme Mindelien de Vértesszöllös. *Anthropologie 70*, 495–533.

Thoma, A. (1967) Human teeth from the Lower Palaeolithic of Hungary. *Z. Morph. Anthrop. 58*, 152–180.

Stęślicka, W. (1968) W. sprawie Stanowiska Systematycznego Dolnoplejstocénskiej Kości Potylicznej Z Vértesszöllös *Przeg. Antrop. 2*, 267–274.

Thoma, A. (1969) Biometrische Studie über das Occipitale von Vértesszöllös. *Z. Morph. Anthr. 60*, 229–241.

Thoma, A. (1969) Le caractère aromorphotique de l'évolution humaine à la lumière des nouveaux fossiles. *Symp. Biol. Hung. 9*, 39–46.

Wolpoff, M. H. (1971a) Is Vértesszöllös an occipital of European *Homo erectus? Nature 232*, 567–568.

Wolpoff, M. H. (1971b) Vértesszöllös and the presapiens theory. *Am. J. phys. Anthrop. 35*, 209–215.

Stringer, C. B., Howell, F. C. and Melentis, J. K. 1970 The significance of the fossil hominid skull from Petralona, Greece. *J. archaeol. Sci. 6*, 235–253.

Thoma, A. (1972) On Vértesszöllös man. *Nature, 236*, 464–465.

Kahlke, H. D. (1975) The macrofaunas of continental Europe during the Middle Pleistocene: Stratigraphic sequence and problems of intercorrelation. In *After the Australopithecines*, 309–374. Eds. K. Butzer and G. L. Isaac. The Hague: Mouton.

Wolpoff, M. H. (1977) Some Notes on the Vértesszöllös occipital. *Am. J. phys. Anthrop. 47*, 357–364.

Thoma, A. (1978) Some notes on the Vértesszöllös occipital. *J. hum. Evol. 7*, 323–325.

Ullrich, H. von (1979) Artifizielle Veronderungen am occipitale von Vértesszöllös . *Anthrop. Kozl.*, *23*, 3–10.

Howells, W. W. (1980) *Homo erectus*—Who, when and where: a survey. *Yearb. phys. Anthrop. 23*, 1–23.

Latham, A. G. and Schwarcz, H. P. Magnetic polarity of travertine samples from Vértesszöllös . In *The Vértesszöllös Prehistoric Site*. Eds. M. Kretzoi and C. Dobosi (In prep.).

Schwarcz, H. P. and Latham, A. G. (1984) Uranium-series age determination of travertines from the site of Vértesszöllös, Hungary. *J. archaeol. Sci. 11*, 327–336.

Near East

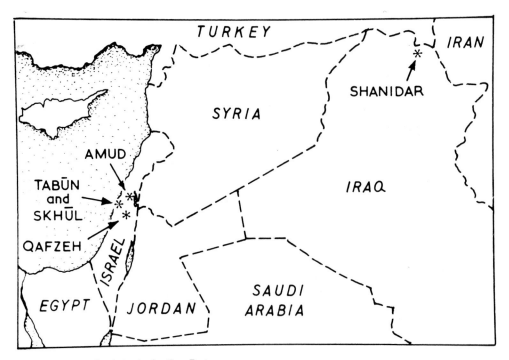

Fig. 33. Hominid fossil sites in the Near East.

The Tabūn Remains

ISRAEL   MOUNT CARMEL

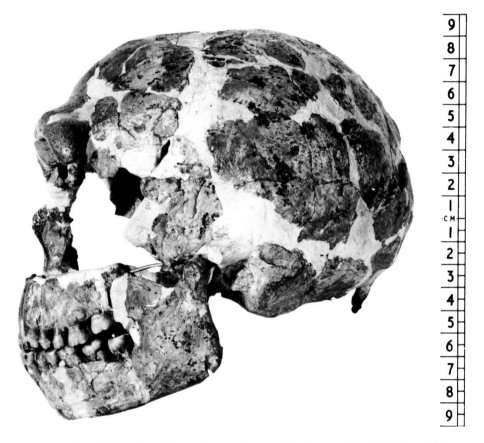

Fig. 34. The Tabūn (C1) cranium (left lateral view). *Courtesy of the Trustees of the British Museum (Nat. Hist.)*

Synonyms and other names	*Palaeoanthropus palestinensis* (McCown and Keith, 1939); Tabūn I (C1) and II (C2); Mount Carmel man.
Site	Mugharet et-Tabūn, Wadi el-Mughara, Mount Carmel, south-east of Haifa, Israel.
Found by	Joint Expedition of the British School of Archaeology in Jerusalem and the American School of Prehistoric Research, directed by D. A. E. Garrod (1929–1934).

Geology   The Tabūn Cave is situated in a former wave—cut cliff overlooking the Wadi el-Mughara. This cave, like others, is hollowed into a steep limestone escarpment at the foot of Mount Carmel. Excavations of the floor of the Tabūn Cave have disclosed a number of archaeological layers characterized by the tools and fossil mammalian bones which they contained (Garrod and Bate, 1937). During the excavation a female skeleton and a male mandible were uncovered and other fragmentary hominid bones.

New excavations (Jelinek *et al.*, 1973; Jelinek, 1982) have added to knowledge of the site in terms of its detailed geology, stratigraphy and sedimentology, as well as in other ways.

Associated finds   The occupation levels originally recognized were lettered A–G working from above downwards in a 25 metre section. These contained several types of stone tools.

Uppermost layer—A	Iron age and recent artefacts
Upper layers—B, C and D	Levalloiso-Mousterian flake tools
Lower layers—E and F	Upper Acheulean hand-axes, retouched flakes (Yabrudian)
Lowermost layer—G	Tayacian tools, poor quantity and quality. (Garrod and Bate, 1937).

More recent excavations have recognized 85 geological beds in a 10 metre section at the centre of the old profile with 300 contextural associations of artefacts recorded. No new hominine remains were recovered (Jelinek, 1982).

The mammalian fossil fauna, principally from Garrod and Bate's layers C and D—the layers which contained the bulk of the hominid remains—was extensive and included hippopotamus (*Hippopotamus amphibius*), wild boar (*Sus gadarensis*), red deer (*Cervus elaphus*), fallow deer (*Dama dama mesopotamica*), wild ox (*Bos sp.*), gazelle (*Gazella sp.*), wild ass (*Equus hemionus*), hyaena (*Crocuta crocuta*), rhinoceros (*Dicerorhinus cf. hemitoechus*) and roe deer (*Capreolus capreolus*). The so-called faunal break between layers C and B described by Bate may be the result of a change in the use of the cave (Jelinek *et al.*, 1973).

Dating   Originally Garrod and Bate (1937) suggested that layers C and D belonged to the latter part of the Third Interglacial (Riss–Würm or Last Interglacial) and that the faunal break was evidence of the onset of the Würm Glaciation; however, carbon 14 dating of layer C at 45,000(± 2,000) years B.P. has altered this view. Later Garrod (1962), has suggested that Tabūn C should be attributed to the second part of the Würm Glaciation and that the faunal break above this level was evidence of the onset of an interstadial period. However, Vogel and Waterbolk (1963) gave a radiocarbon date of 40,900 years B.P. ± 1,000 years for level C, the hominid layer for Tabūn I (C1) and Tabūn II (C2).

Even the oldest radiocarbon date given from Bed C (*c.* 51,000 B.P.) has been considered as a minimum date (Farrand, 1979). In the same paper, sedimentological studies indicate that the changes in the Tabūn deposits between C and D may not be climatic but due to changes in cave configuration. The lower part of layer B is given by Farrand (1979) as 'not younger' than 39,700 years B.P. and thus by implication the age of the hominid-bearing layers is greater. Amino acid racemization dates given for the site (Bada and Helfmann, 1976; Masters, 1982) of 51,000 years B.P. are generally confirmative. Jelinek (1982) however, places the Tabūn material from layer C between 50,000–60,000 years B.P. whilst that from layer D may be as old as 70,000–80,000 B.P..

Morphology Tabūn I (C1) is an almost complete adult female skeleton aged about 30 years. Tabūn II (C2) is an isolated mandible believed to be male. In addition there are five other specimens of postcranial bones, at least some of which may belong to a further individual. The remains have been described in a lengthy monograph by Keith and McCown (1939).

Tabūn I

The skull was in fragments when found and needed extensive restoration. The cranium as restored is small and low-vaulted with a pronounced frontal torus, and the outline of the skull from above is shaped so that its maximum breadth is towards the back. There is no marked 'bun-formation', but an occipital torus denotes powerful nuchal muscles. The mastoid process is small. The face is orthognathous and appears to be bent backwards to lie beneath the skull base.

The mandible has a stout body, broad rami and widely separated condyles. The symphysis is oblique and there is no chin. The mental foramina are double.

Tabūn II

The second individual is represented by a robust mandible which has a broad ramus and a better-developed chin.

Teeth

Tabūn I has a complete dentition, except for lack of the upper right third molar. The incisors are worn but lingual tubercles are present on both incisors and canines. The premolars are not remarkable

other than they have some buccal swelling of the crown. The first
two molars have four-cusped square crowns with well marked oblique ridges, but the third molars are triangular, lacking hypocones.
A Carabelli pit is present on the first and second upper molars but
it is absent on the third upper molars. The Tabūn II mandible has
very worn teeth but the lingual tubercles are less developed than
those of Tabūn I. All the teeth are present in the Tabūn II mandible
except for the left lateral incisor, and in general the crown morphology of the lower teeth of Tabūn I and II is similar. The isolated
teeth have corresponding characteristics, the molars having a dryopithecine cusp pattern.

The Postcranial Bones

The long bones of the Tabūn I skeleton tend to be short, robust and
somewhat bowed. In particular the radius and ulna are stout and
curved. The vertebral column is modern in form but the bones of
the shoulder are stout with strong muscular markings reminiscent
of the bones of the 'classic Neandertalers'. The pelvic girdle is low
and narrow with flattened pubic rami. The tibia has a somewhat
retroverted head, otherwise it is of modern form.

Dimensions McCown and Keith (1939)

Tabūn I Skull

Max. Length 183   Max. Breadth 141
Cranial Index 77·0 (Mesocephalic)
Cranial Capacity 1,271 cc (Pearson's formula)

Tabūn I and II Mandibles	*Tabūn I*	*Tabūn II*
Symphysial Angle	61°	72°
Bicondylar Breadth	(133)	(130)
Length	(95)	(119)

Teeth

				Upper Teeth (Crown Dimensions)				
Tabūn I	I^1	I^2	C	PM^1	PM^2	M^1	M^2	M^3
l	9·0	7·3	7·9	7·5	6·5	10·8	10·5	8·3
b	8·2	7·7	8·8	9·8	9·6	11·5	11·7	10·2
Side	R	L	R	R	R	L	R	L

				Lower Teeth (Crown Dimensions)				
Tabūn I	I_1	I_2	C	PM_1	PM_2	M_1	M_2	M_3
l	5·7	6·7	8·0	7·0	5·9	10·0	11·2	10·9
b	7·0	7·6	8·3	8·5	8·7	10·5	10·6	9·8
Side	R	R	R	R	R	R	R	L

Tabūn II		I1	I2	C	PM₁	PM₂	M₁	M₂	M₃
				Lower Teeth (Crown Dimensions)					
Right	l	5·9	6·1	8·0	7·8	7·9	11·0	10·8	11·5
Side	b	8·0	8·2	9·0	9·0	9·5	11·0	11·0	10·8

Tabūn I Postcranial Bones

Length of Humerus	287	Left
Length of Radius	222	Left
Length of Ulna	243	Left
Length of Femur	(416)	Right
Length of Tibia	310	Left

( ) Approximate measurement

Affinities The Tabūn and Skhūl remains were found in separate caves literally within yards of each other. Both groups of bones were described by McCown and Keith (1939) in the same monograph. It is convenient to discuss their relationships together, despite the suggestion that chronologically they may be separated by 10,000 years (Higgs, 1961).

Originals *Tabūn I* and some isolated specimens from Layer C: British Museum (Natural History), Cromwell Road, South Kensington, London, S.W.7.

Tabūn II and some other fragments: Museum of the Department of Antiquities, Jerusalem.

The remaining specimens: Peabody Museum, Harvard University, Cambridge, Mass., U.S.A.

Casts Tabūn II, mandible: The University Museum, University of Pennsylvania, Philadelphia 4, Pennsylvania, U.S.A.

References
Garrod, D. A. E. and Bate, D. M. A. (1937) *The Stone Age of Mount Carmel.* Vol. I Excavations at the Wady el-Mughara. Oxford: The Clarendon Press.

McCown, T. D. and Keith, A. (1939) *The Stone Age of Mount Carmel.* Vol. 2 The fossil human remains from the Levalloiso-Mousterain. Oxford: The Clarendon Press.

Higgs, E. S. (1961) Some Pleistocene faunas of the Mediterranean coastal areas. *Proc. prehist. Soc. 27,* 144–154.

Brothwell, D. R. (1961) The people of Mount Carmel. *Proc. prehist. Soc. 27,* 155–159

Higgs, E. S., and Brothwell, D. R. (1961) North Africa and Mount Carmel: Recent developments. *Man 61,* 138–139.

Garrod, D. A. E. (1962) The Middle Palaeolithic of the Near East and the problem of Mount Carmel man. *J.R. anthrop. Inst. 92,* 232–259.

Vogel, J. C. and Waterbolk, H. T. (1963) Gröningen radiocarbon dates. *Radiocarbon 5,* 172.

Jelinek, A. J., Farrand, W. R., Haas, G., Horowitz, A. and Goldberg, P. (1973) New Excavations at the Tabūn Cave, Mount Carmel, Israel 1967–1972: A preliminary report. *Paleorient. 1,* 151–183.

Bada, J. L. and Helfman, P. M. (1976) Application of amino acid racemization in paleoanthropology and archaeology. *Union Internationale des Sciences Préhistoriques et Protohistoriques*, IXᵉ Congrès, Nice, Colloque I, 39–62.

Farrand, W. R. (1979) Chronology and palaeoenvironment of Levantine prehistoric sites as seen from sediment studies. *J. arch. Sci.* 6, 369–392.

Jelinek, J. (1982) The Tabūn Cave and Paleolithic man in the Levant. *Science* 216, 1369–1375.

Masters, P. (1982) An amino acid racemization chronology for Tabūn. In *The Transition from the Lower to Middle Palaeolithic and the Origin of Modern Man* 151, 43–54. Ed. A. Ronen. Oxford: *Br. arch.* Reports. Int. Ser.

The Skhūl Remains

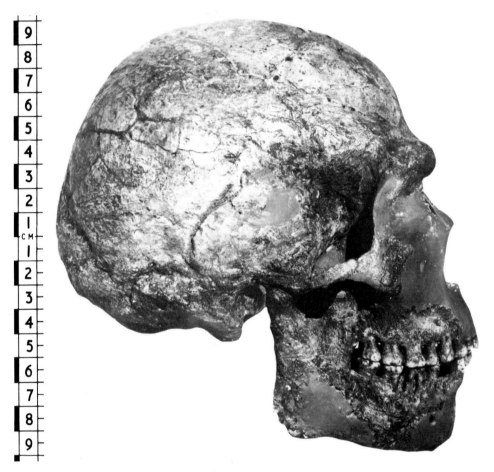

Fig. 35. The Skhūl V skull reconstructed by C. E. Snow (right lateral view). *Courtesy of the Trustees of the British Museum (Nat. Hist.)*

Synonyms and other names	*Palaeoanthropus palestinensis* (McCown and Keith, 1939) Mount Carmel man.
Site	Mugharet es-Skhūl, Wadi el-Mughara, Mount Carmel, south-east of Haifa, Israel.
Found by	Joint expedition of the British School of Archaeology in Jerusalem and the American School of Prehistoric Research, directed by D. A. E. Garrod (1929–1934).

Geology   The western slope of Mount Carmel overlooking the Wadi el-Mug-hara is penetrated by a number of caves which are hollowed into a steep limestone escarpment. The smallest cave, really a rock shelter, is the Mugharet es-Skhūl. Excavation of the limestone breccia which formed the cave floor uncovered several archaeological layers containing flint tools and fossil mammalian bones. Amongst these remains there were a number of hominid bones belonging to at least ten individuals who appeared to have been intentionally buried. Most of the bones were in proper relation with each other showing little sign of disturbance, but no grave furniture or grave outline was found. The only object directly related to the skeletons was a wild boar mandible in the arms of Skhūl V. Stratigraphically the burials were all contemporaneous with the deposit.

Associated finds   The flint implements recovered from the cave all belong to the Levalloiso-Mousterian culture. No Acheulean tools precede them as in the Tabūn cave. The principal finds were made in layers B1 and B2 and consist of Mousterian points, racloirs (scrapers), Levallois flakes, cores and burins.

The fossil mammalian fauna included wild ox (*Bos sp.*), hyaena (*Crocuta sp.*), hippopotamus (*Hippopotamus amphibius*), rhinoceros (*Didermocerus cf. hemitoechus*), wild ass (*Equus hemionus*), gazelle (*Gazella sp.*), fallow deer (*Dama dama mesopotamica*), roe deer (*Capreolus capreolus*), red deer (*Cervus elaphus*), boar (*Sus gadarensis*) and small carnivores (*Felis sp.*). The wild ox was the commonest species in the assemblage.

Dating   The fauna of the Skhūl cave deposit has been correlated with the fauna of Tabūn layer C. Likewise, the tools found at the Tabūn and the Skhūl skeleton levels are almost indistinguishable in their workmanship. In view of these findings Garrod and Bate (1937) believed that the two sites were contemporaneous and could be attributed to the end of the Third Interglacial (Riss–Würm or Last Interglacial). By correlating the faunal changes found at several Mediterranean coastal sites, Higgs (1961) produced evidence which led him to suggest that the Skhūl site may be as much as 10,000 years more recent than the Tabūn site, and thus within the Gottweiger Interstadial (Higgs and Brothwell, 1961). This view was rejected by Garrod (1962) who maintained that the Tabūn and Skhūl remains were broadly contemporaneous.

There would seem to be little further chance for correlative analysis since all the deposits at Skhūl have been removed by previous excavations (Farrand, 1979). Amino acid racemization dates given for material from Skhūl range from 33,000 years B.P. to 55,000 years B.P. (Masters, 1982).

Morphology The remains uncovered in the Skhūl cave have been identified by McCown and Keith (1939) as follows:

Designation	Status	Sex	Age in years	Bones
Skhūl I	Infant	?♂	4–4½	Skeleton
Skhūl II	Adult	♀	30–40	Skeleton
Skhūl III	Adult	♂	—	Left leg bones
Skhūl IV	Adult	♂	40–50	Skeleton
Skhūl V	Adult	♂	30–40	Skeleton
Skhūl VI	Adult	♂	30–35	Skeleton
Skhūl VII	Adult	♀	35–40	Skeleton
Skhūl VIII	Child	?♂	8–10	Lower limb bones
Skhūl IX	Adult	♂	Approx. 50	Incomplete skeleton
Skhūl X	Infant	?♂	5–5½	Mandible and humeral fragment only

In addition there were sixteen isolated specimens.

Skull

The best-preserved skull is that which belongs to Skhūl V. The cranial vault of this specimen is high, the supraorbital torus marked and the occipital region full and rounded. The facial skeleton is somewhat prognathic and meets the vault at the depressed nasal root. The bony palate is broad but the temporomandibular joint and the mastoid process are of modern form. The external auditory meatus is tall but the greater wing of the sphenoid and the orbital process of the zygomatic bone have some archaic features. The angle of the cranial base (basispheniod/basioccipital angle) is modern, as is the plane of the foramen magnum.

Mandible

In general the Skhūl mandibles have chins although this feature is poorly marked in Skhūl V. The mental foramina are single and the mandibular condyles do not differ appreciably from those of modern man, but some of the specimens have traits which recall the Tabūn mandibles.

Teeth

The teeth of the Skhūl specimens are worn but do not differ very much from the teeth of the Tabūn skull and mandible. Individual variation is discernible in that Skhūl VII has teeth with a few archaic features whereas Skhūl IV and V have more modern teeth. Skhūl V has bony evidence of dental sepsis in the form of several apical abscess cavities and the bony changes of pyorrhoea, but no dental caries.

Postcranial Bones

The postcranial bones have mixed characteristics, the majority being very like those of modern man but others resembling those of the Tabūn skeleton. The Skhūl long bones are long and slender contrasting with the stout, curved and big-jointed bones of the so-called 'classic Neandertaler'. The hands are large and broad with well developed thumbs. Similarly the feet are large, stoutly constructed and well arched, without doubt feet well adapted to a propulsive bipedal gait. The axial skeleton has few distinctive features but the fourth segment of the sternum of Skhūl IV is long and resembles that of the Tabūn skeleton. The ribs are variable in form, Skhūl V ribs having a thicker and more rounded cross-section than those of Skhūl IV which are flattened and modern.

Dimensions   McCown and Keith (1939)

Skulls (Unrestored)	*Skhūl IV*	*Skhūl V*
Max. Length	(206)	192
Max. Breadth	(148)	143
Cranial Index	71·8	74·5
Cranial Capacity (Pearson's formula)	1,554 cc	1,518 cc

Mandibles		
Bicondylar Width	(132)	(133)
Length	(118)	109
Symphysial Angle	75°	69°

Postcranial Bones		
Length of Humerus	—	Left 379
Length of Ulna	—	Right 270
Length of Radius	—	Right 236
Length of Femur	—	Right and Left (518)
Length of Tibia	—	Left (412)

( ) Approximate measurement

Teeth

Skhūl V		*Upper Teeth (Crown Dimensions)*							
		I^1	I^2	C	PM^1	PM^2	M^1	M^2	M^3
Right	l	8·5	7·0	8·7	8·2	7·0	11·0	10·8	9·1
Side	b	7·5	7·2	9·5	10·8	10·8	12·5	12·2	11·8

Skhūl V		*Lower Teeth (Crown Dimensions)*							
		I_1	I_2	C	PM_1	PM_2	M_1	M_2	M_3
	l	5·0	6·4	8·0	8·2	7·7	11·3	11·6	11·4
	b	6·4	7·0	9·0	9·2	9·1	11·5	11·4	10·5
Side		L	R	R	L	R	R	R	R

Skhūl V (Restored by C. E. Snow, 1953)

Skull	Before restoration	After restoration
Length	192	192
Breadth	143	144
Cranial Index	74·5	75·0
Cranial Capacity (Water displacement of cavity cast)	1,450 cc	—
(Pearson's formula)	1,518 cc	1,518 cc

Mandible

Length	109	107
Bicondylar Width	(132)	131

Postcranial Bones

Humerus	(Left)	379	378
Ulna	(Right)	270	(280)
Radius	(Right)	236	(254)
Femur	(Right)	518	(505)
Tibia	(Left)	412	(438)

(   ) Approximate measurement

Affinities   At first, McCown and Keith (1939) considered that the Tabūn and Skhūl remains belonged to two distinct peoples, but later they concluded that the burials represented one population of a single species or race. None the less, anatomically the Skhūl skeletons were considered to be of a later type, representing one extreme of a highly variable series. McCown and Keith rejected hybridization as an explanation for supposed Neandertal and Cro-Magnon features. The dating of the Skhūl site to the Third Interglacial (Riss–Würm Interglacial) was doubted by Howell (1958) and rejected by Higgs (1961) in favour of a later date within the Fourth Glaciation (Würm Glaciation). The essentially modern form of the Skhūl remains now seems to be established (Howell, 1958; Brothwell, 1961; Howells, 1970; Santa Luca, 1978; Stringer, 1978; Trinkaus, 1984).

Once the difference in date between the sites had been accepted and the differences in the morphology of the Tabūn and Skhūl remains recognized as broadly Neandertal and modern sapient respectively, the field of speculation was open with regard to their evolutionary relationships. Several schemes have been proposed. One suggests local morphological and cultural continuity from Neandertal to modern sapient (Wolpoff, 1980; Jelinek, 1982). A similar view recognizes *in situ* change but sees no evidence of transitional morphology in the material from both sites (Trinkaus, 1984). Another view favours replacement of the earlier Neandertal Tabūn population by more modern forms; or even the opposite, with a later Neandertal arrival after modern man (as evidenced by Jebel Kafzeh) was in the Levant (Vandermeersch, 1979). Most recently it has been accepted that no transitional fossils can be recognized from the area. Neither can unequivocal directional trends from Neandertal to modern man be recognized in the area as a whole including Shanidar (*q.v.*) (Stringer, Hublin and Vandermeersch, 1984).

Recent work has clarified the position of the Mount Carmel remains, at least to this extent. The two hominid sites are of differing ages, Skhūl being the younger, both within the Fourth Glaciation (Würm Glaciation) between 30,000–60,000 years B.P. Anatomically the Skhūl remains, if not totally modern, are very advanced in this direction and similar to the remains from Jebel Qafzeh (*q.v.*). The Near Eastern Neandertals such as Galilee, Tabūn and Shanidar (*q.v.*) are less florid in their features than their European relations. The precise relationship between the remains from Tabūn and Skhūl remains obscure.

Originals   *Skhūl I and IV:* Museum of the Department of Antiquities, Jerusalem. *Skhūl IX:* British Museum (Natural History), Cromwell Road, South Kensington, London, S.W.7.
Skhūl II, III, V, VI, VII, VIII and isolated teeth: Peabody Museum, Harvard University, Cambridge, Mass., U.S.A.

Casts   *Skhūl I, IV and V, also Skhūl V* (C. E. Snow reconstruction): The University Museum, University of Pennsylvania, Philadelphia 4, Pennsylvania, U.S.A.

References   Garrod, D. A. E. and Bate, D. M. A. (1937) *The Stone Age of Mount Carmel.* Vol. I Excavations at the Wady el-Mughara. Oxford: The Clarendon Press.

McCown, T. D. and Keith, A. (1939) *The Stone Age of Mount Carmel.* Vol. II The fossil human remains from the Levalloiso-Mousterian. Oxford: The Clarendon Press.

Snow, C. E. (1953) The Ancient Palestinian Skhūl V reconstruction. *Am. Sch. prehist. Res. Bull. 17*, 5–12.

Higgs, E. S. (1961) Some Pleistocene faunas of the Mediterranean coastal areas. *Proc. prehist. Soc. 27*, 144–154.

Brothwell, D. R. (1961) The people of Mount Carmel. *Proc. prehist. Soc. 27*, 155–159.

Higgs, E. S. and Brothwell, D. R. (1961) North Africa and Mount Carmel: Recent developments. *Man 61*, 138–139.

Garrod, D. A. E. (1962) The Middle Palaeolithic of the Near East and the problem of Mount Carmel man. *J. R. anthrop. Inst. 92*, 232–259.

Howell, F. C. (1958) Upper Pleistocene men of the southwest Asian Mousterian. In *Hundert Jahre Neanderthaler.* Ed. G. H. R. von Koenigswald. Utrecht: Kemink en Zoon.

Howells, W. W. (1970) Mount Carmel man: morphological relationships. *Proc. Int. Congr. anthrop. ethnol. Sci., 8 Tokyo and Kyoto, 1968.* Vol. 1 Anthropology.

Santa Luca, A. P. (1978) A re-examination of presumed Neandertal fossils. *J. hum. Evol. 7*, 619–636.

Stringer, C. B. (1978) Some problems in Middle and Upper Pleistocene hominid relationships. In *Recent Advances in Primatology*. Eds. D. J. Chivers and K. A. Joysey. London: Academic Press.

Farrand, W. R. (1979) Chronology and palaeoenvironment of Levantine prehistoric sites as seen from sediment studies. *J. arch. Sci. 6*, 369–392.

Wolpoff, M. H. (1980) *Paleoanthropology*. New York: Knopf.

Jelinek, A. J. (1982) The Tabūn cave and paleolithic man in the Levant. *Science 216*, 1369–1375.

Masters, P. (1982) An amino acid racemization chronology for Tabūn In *The Transition from the Lower to Middle Palaeolithic and the Origin of Modern Man 151*, 43–54. Ed. A. Ronen. Oxford: Br. Arch. rep. Int. Series.

Trinkaus, E. (1984) Western Asia. In *The Origins of Modern Humans*. Eds. F. H. Smith and F. Spencer. New York: Alan R. Liss.

The Jebel Qafzeh Remains

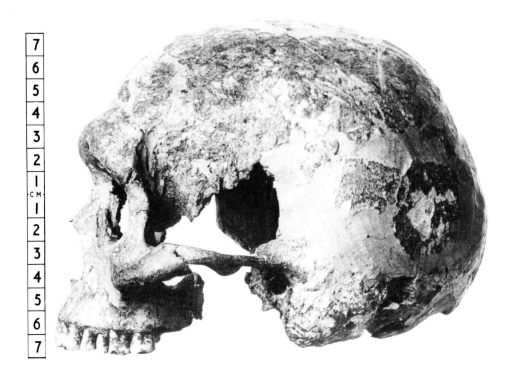

Fig. 36. The Jebel Qafzeh VI skull (left lateral view). *Courtesy of Professor B. Vandermeersch.*

Synonyms and other names *Homo sapiens sapiens* (Vandermeersch, 1971); Jebel Qafza man; Djebel Qafzeh man.

Site A cave site 2·5 km from Nazareth, towards the south, on the south-west flank of Mount Qafzeh, Israel.

Found by Qafzeh 1 and 2, R. Neuville, 1933; Qafzeh 3–7, R. Neuville and M. Stekelis, 1934 (Qafzeh 3–6) and 1935 (Qafzeh 7); Qafzeh 8–11, B. Vandermeersch, 1966 (Qafzeh 8), 1969 (Qafzeh 9 and 10), 1970 (Qafzeh 11). Further specimens have been recovered since 1970.

Geology The Jebel Qafzeh cave is extremely large, about 20 m broad and 12 m deep. It communicates with the exterior through a big 'vestibule' which gives place to a slope. In all, 24 layers have been described including breccias, stalagmitic layers and limestone layers of differing colours, that have been numbered I–XXIV from above downwards. Layers I–III correspond to breccias against the rock wall and layers IV–VII are relatively recent. Below these layers are a series of occupation levels, IX–XVIII, containing stone tools and hearths. Bed XVII, the layer containing Qafzeh 8–10, is split into two by a layer of yellow gravel. Layer XVII of Vandermeersch (1966) corresponds with Layer L of Neuville in its upper portion and the yellow gravel corresponds with Layer M of Neuville. Qafzeh 3, 6 and 7 are believed to come from the same layer (XVII) from the examination of the site records kept by Neuville (Vandermeersch, 1971). Qafzeh 4 and 5 are less certain in their provenance since they were recovered from a trial excavation in front of the vestibule. With this reservation it seems likely that they also derive from Layer XVII. Qafzeh 8, 9 and 10 were burials in the deposits of the vestibule area, Qafzeh 8 a contracted burial on its right side, Qafzeh 9 semi-flexed like number 8 and Qafzeh 10 an infant in a strongly flexed position. Finally the remains of a child, Qafzeh 11, were recovered from Layer XXII from a grave containing some offerings.

Associated finds   The stone tools recovered from the Jebel Qafzeh site were of Levalloiso-Mousterian type; a rich industry containing denticulate tools, scrapers, Levallois points, backed knives and burins of Upper Palaeolithic character (Ronen and Vandermeersch, 1972).

The faunal remains found at this site include the remains of horse (*Equus*), rhinoceros (*Rhinoceros*), fallow deer (*Dama*), wild ox (*Bos*) and gazelle (*Gazella*), as well as some bird remains (Vandermeersch, 1966 and 1970). A more extensive faunal list resulted from the early excavation (Picard, 1937) and from a later study (Bouchud, 1971).

Dating   On the basis of the stratigraphy and the fauna the date of the Jebel Qafzeh has been given as the Last Pluvial of the Würm Glaciation (Vandermeersch, 1966) and as the end of the Last Interpluvial of the Würm Glaciation (Howell, 1959). Sedimentary studies revealed differences between deposits inside the cave and those from the 'terrace' and it remains to be demonstrated that the Mousterian industries of the inner chamber and of the 'terrace' were contemporaneous (Farrand, 1979). Amino-acid dating (Bada and Helfman, 1976) gave ages of 32–39,000 years B.P. for animal bones from Bed 9, but human remains from Bed XVII (Terrace) gave 27–33,000 years B.P. which seems far too young for the Mousterian industry in that layer. Revised dates were given following refinements to the amino-acid racemization technique used, and the ages for the same material were raised to 39–78,000 years B.P.; these dates are also regarded as unsatisfactory (Masters, 1982). An archaeological appraisal of the age of the site has been given and two hypotheses emerged (Bar Yosef and Vandermeersch 1981). One gives an age of *c.* 100,000 years B.P. for Tabūn D and Qafzeh XXIV–XV, whilst the other gives 70–80,000 years B.P. for the same sites and layers. On the balance of evidence the authors favour the older date. There are no radiocarbon dates for the site.

Morphology   The remains recovered from Jebel Qafzeh have been identified as follows:

Designation	Status	Bones	First reference
Qafzeh 1	Adult	Frontal	Neuville, 1934
Qafzeh 2	Adult	Calotte, mandible, teeth	Neuville, 1934
Qafzeh 3	Adult	Incomplete skeleton	Köppel, 1935
Qafzeh 4	Infant	Palate, mandible, teeth	Köppel, 1935
Qafzeh 4a	Infant	Left iliac bone, right temporal, right incus	Arensburg and Tillier 1983
Qafzeh 5	Adult	Calotte, palate, teeth	Köppel, 1935
Qafzeh 6	Adult	Cranium, teeth	Köppel, 1935
Qafzeh 7	Adult	Cranial fragments, palate, teeth, mandible, clavicle, phalanges	Köppel, 1935
Qafzeh 8	Adult	Incomplete skeleton	Vandermeersch, 1966
Qafzeh 9	Adult	Incomplete skeleton	Vandermeersch, 1969
Qafzeh 10	Infant	Skeleton	Vandermeersch, 1969
Qafzeh 11	Child (10)	Skeleton	Vandermeersch, 1970

A reappraisal of Qafzeh 4 has disclosed that the remains are mixed and a new child aged three years (Qafzeh 4a) has been described (Arensburg and Tillier, 1983). Detailed description and comparison of the Qafzeh remains have been given by Vandermeersch (1981) and the Qafzeh 11 child has been compared with other Neandertal children of approximately the same age (Tillier, 1984).

Skull

Qafzeh 6 has been carefully restored and described (Vallois and Vandermeersch, 1972). It appears to be that of a young adult male on the basis of its skull form and the state of its teeth and sutures. The skull is a little distorted and some surface details are missing as well as much of the skull base, but sufficient remains of both vault and face to permit a satisfactory reconstruction.

The skull is generally robust and large with a high well-rounded vault, a modest supraorbital torus and no supratoral groove. The occipital bone is full and rounded with a low position of the inion and no evidence of an occipital chignon. In general form the neurocranium is long and broad with little or no postorbital waisting, well defined parietal bosses high on the bones and well marked mastoid processes that are broad based. The face is large and low

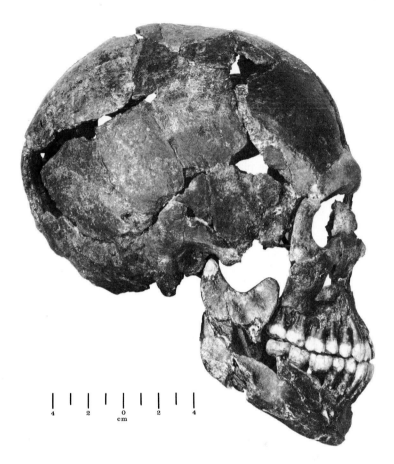

Fig. 37. The Jebel Qafzeh IX skull (right lateral view). *Courtesy of Professor B. Vandermeersch.*

with quadrangular orbits that slope downwards and laterally; the nasal cavity appears large both below and above giving rise to marked interorbital separation. The maxillae are large with canine fossae and well defined maxillozygomatic angulation. In lateral view the face is virtually orthognathic with little or no projection of the central region of the face. In basal view the skull shows a wide shallow digastric groove, an elongated narrow and deep temporomandibular glenoid and a prolonged postglenoid process. The palate is wide and shallow. Three middle ear ossicles from the site have also been described (Arensburg and Nathan, 1972; Arensburg and Tillier, 1983).

Mandible

The mandibular remains (Qafzeh 8 and 9) suggest that the jaws

were tall and robust without trace of a *planum alveolare* but with
well marked chins. The digastric fossae are placed on the internal
aspect of the symphysial region and face both downwards and
backwards.

Teeth

The Qafzeh 6 palate lacks both right premolars, the right lateral
incisor and both third molars. In general all the teeth are large and
heavily worn with dentinal exposure in all but the second molars.
The plane of incisal wear is oblique and the incisors are not shovelled. The premolars are bicuspid, the first molars have four cusps
including a hypocone but the second molars lack a hypocone and
are consequently tritubercular. The right third molar possessed
three roots. No details of the lower teeth are available.

Postcranial Bones

In a detailed appraisal of the postcranial remains Vandermeersch
(1981) concludes that their features are principally those of modern
man; very few can be said to be Neandertal in character.

Dimensions   Vallois and Vandermeersch (1972)
Qafzeh 6
Max. Length 196   Max. Breadth 145·5
Cranial Index 73·7   Cranial Capacity 1568 cc

Teeth

Qafzeh 6		I^1	I^2	Upper Teeth (Crown Dimensions) C	PM^1	PM^2	M^1	M^2	M^3
Right	l	10·0	—	8·5	—	—	11·0	10·5	—
side	b	—	—	10·0	—	—	12·5	13·0	—
Left	l	10·5	8·5	8·5	7·0	6·5	11·0	10·5	—
side	b	—	8·0	10·0	10·0	10·0	13·0	13·0	—

Affinities   The full description of the Qafzeh remains (Vallois and Vandermeersch, 1972; Vandermeersch and Tillier, 1977; Tillier, 1979;
Vandermeersch, 1981; Arensburg and Tillier, 1983; Tillier, 1984)
confirm the opinions given in earlier publications, that although
the material shows some archaic features, its affinities lie nearer to
modern *Homo sapiens* than to the classic Neandertal variety of this
species. Indeed, Vandermeersch (1981) is in no doubt that they
belong to *Homo sapiens sapiens* similar in type to specimens from
Cro-Magnon and Skhūl (*q.v.*) and contrasts them with the remains
from Tabūn, Amud and Shanidar (*q.v.*) which he sees as having clear
affinities with the Neandertalers. Other authors who concur with

this general view include Howells (1974), and Stringer (1974) but Thoma (1965) regards the Qafzeh remains as Proto-Cro-Magnon in the same way that he regards the Skhūl population. Thoma sees in the latter remains signs of hybridization that occur again in the Jebel Qafzeh remains but this time the Cro-Magnon character of the skulls is, to him, even more pronounced. Only Brose and Wolpoff (1971) would include Jebel Qafzeh in a 'non-classic' Neandertal group that comprises a wide range of African, Asian and Near Eastern fossil men. This viewpoint has been severely criticized (Howells, 1974).

Recently, Trinkaus (1984) has discussed the mosaic of anatomical change that has characterized the Levantine archaic and anatomically modern *Homo sapiens* groups and has concluded that *in situ* local continuity of local populations best fits the available facts. He regards Qafzeh and Skhūl as the earliest of these anatomically modern groups.

The significance of the Jebel Qafzeh site rests also on the combination of the supposed date (Last Glaciation), the tool culture (Levalloiso-Mousterian) and the taxonomy of the remains (*Homo sapiens sapiens*), contradicting an older view that only Neandertal man was responsible for Mousterian tools.

Originals	Laboratoire de Paléontologie des Vertébrés et de Paléontologie Humaine. 4 Place Jussien, 75230, Paris.
Casts	Not available at present.

References Neuville, R. (1934) Le préhistorique de Palestine. *Rev. Bibliq. 43*, 249.

Köppel, R. (1935) Das Alter der neuentdeckten Schädel von Nazareth. *Biblica* 16, 58–73.

Neuville, R. (1936) Excavations in Palestine 1934–5. *Q. Dep. Antiq. Palest.* 5, 199.

Picard, L. (1937) Inferences on the problem of the Pleistocene climate of Palestine and Syria drawn from flora, fauna and stratigraphy. *Proc. prehist. Soc. 3*, 58–70.

Neuville, R. (1951) Le Paléolithique et le Mésolithique du désert de Judée. *Archs. Inst. Paléont. hum. 24*, 179–184.

Howell, F. C. (1959) Upper Pleistocene stratigraphy and early man in the Levant. *Proc. Am. phil. Soc. 103*, 12–13.

Thoma, A. (1965) La définition des Néanderthaliens et la position des hommes fossiles de Palestine. *Anthropologie, 69*, 519–534.

Vandermeersch, B. (1966) Nouvelles découvertes de restes humains dans les couches Levalloiso-Moustériennes du gisement de Qafzeh (Israël). *C.r. Acad. Sci. Paris. 262*, 1434–1436.

Vandermeersch B. (1969) Les nouveaux squelettes moustériens découverts à Qafzeh (Israël) et leur signification. *C.r. Acad. Sci. Paris., 268*, 2562–2565.

Vandermeersch B. (1970) Une sépulture moustérienne avec offrandes découverte dans la grotte de Qafzeh. *C.r. Acad. Sci. Paris. 270*, 298–301.

Vandermeersch B. (1971) Récentes découvertes de squelettes humains à Qafzeh (Israël): essai d'interprétation. In *Origine de l'homme moderne (Écologie et conservation 3)*, 49–54: UNESCO.

Bouchud, J. (1971) Étude préliminaire de la faune du Djebel Qafzeh prés de Nazareth (Israël). In *Proc. VIIIᵉ Cong. INQUA*. Paris: Assoc. Franç. pour l'Étude du Quaternaire.

Brose, D. S. and Wolpof, M. H. (1971) Early Upper Paleolithic man and Late Middle Pleistocene tools. *Am. Anthrop.* 73, 1156–1194.

Arensburg, B. and Nathan, H. (1972) A propos de deux osselets de l'oreille moyenne d'un néanderthaloide trouvés à Qafzeh. *Anthropologie 70*, 301–307.

Ronen, A. and Vandermeersch, B. (1972) The Upper Paleolithic in the cave of Qafzeh (Israel). *Quaternaria* 16, 189–202.

Vallois, H. V. and Vandermeersch, B. (1972) Le crâne mousterien de Qafzeh (Homo VI), *Anthropologie 76*, 71–96.

Howells, W. W. (1974) Neanderthals: names, hypotheses and scientific method. *Am. Anthrop. 76*, 24–38.

Stringer, C. B. (1974) Population relationships of Later Pleistocene hominids: a multivariate study of available crania. *J. archaeol. Sci. 1*, 317–342.

Bada, J. L. and Helfman, P. M. (1976) Application of amino acid racemization in paleoanthropology and archaeology. *Union Internationale des Sciences Préhistoriques et Protohistoriques*. Congres, 9, Nice, Colloque I, 39–62.

Vandermeersch, B. and Tillier, A. M. (1977) Étude preliminaire d'une mandibule d'adolescent provenant des niveaux de Qafzeh (Israel). *Eretz Israël, Archaeol. Hist. Geog. Studies 13*, 177–183.

Farrand, W. R. (1979) Chronology and palaeoenvironment of Levantine prehistoric sites as seen from sediment studies. *J. arch. Sci. 6*, 369–392.

Tillier, A. M. (1979) Restes craniens de l'enfant mousterien *Homo 4* de Qafzeh (Israël): la mandibule et les maxillaires. *Paleorient. V*, 67–85.

Bar Yosef, O. and Vandermeersch, B. (1981) Notes concerning the possible age of the Mousterian layers in Qafzeh Cave. In *Préhistoire du Levant*, 281–285. Eds. P. Sanlaville and Cauvin. Paris: CNRS.

Vandermeersch, B. (1981) *Les Hommes fossilles de Qafzeh (Israel)*. Thèse Doctorate d'Etat 1977. Cahiers de Paléontologie (Paléoanthropologie) p. 310. Ed. du CNRS.

Masters, P. (1982) An amino acid racemization chronology for Tabūn. In *The Transition from the Lower to Middle Palaeolithic and the Origin of Modern Man 151*, 43–54. Ed. A. Ronen. Oxford: Br. arch. Rep. Int. Series.

Arensburg, B. and Tillier, A.M. (1983) A New Mousterian Child from Qafzeh (Israël): Qafzeh 4a. *Bull. Mém. Soc. Anthrop. Paris 10* (série XIII), 61–69.

Tillier, A. M. (1984) L'enfant *Homo 11* de Qafzeh (Israel) et son apport à la compréhension des modalités de la croissances des squelettes Moustériens. *Palorient. 10*, 7–47.

Trinkaus, E. (1984) Western Asia. In *The Origins of Modern Humans*. Eds. F. H. Smith and F. Spencer. New York: Alan R. Liss.

The Amud Remains

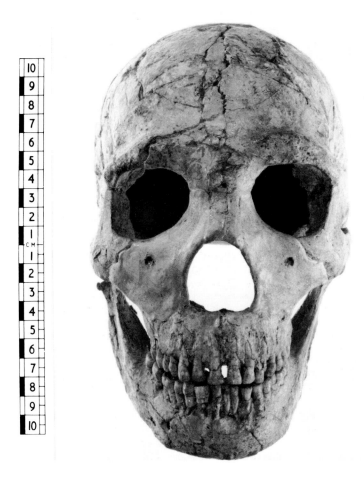

Fig. 38. The Amud I skull (frontal view). *Courtesy of Prof. Hisashi Suzuki.*

Synonyms and other names	Amud I–IV; Amud man.
Site	A cave site on the lower course of the Wadi Amud, 10 km. north of the town of Tiberias, 50 km east-north-east of Haifa. The cave is situated 3 km from the mouth of the wadi which opens into Lake Tiberias.

Found by   Tokyo University Scientific Expedition to Western Asia (28th June–17th July, 1961). Director: H. Suzuki.

Geology   The deposits in the Amud area consist of Upper Cretaceous and Eocene limestones the upper part of which is exposed in the lower part of the Amud gorge. Around the cave the limestone is overlain by veneers of gravels, basaltic lava flows, lacustrine silts, sands and other non-marine sediments. These are probably of Quaternary or Neogene age. The slopes nearby are covered with a calcareous layer termed the Nari crust. The stratigraphy has been disturbed in places by the tectonic activity of the Rift valley. The limestone series is divided into four from above downwards; 'Massive' limestone, 'Bedded' limestone, 'Weakly Bedded' limestone and 'Irregularly Bedded' limestone. Below these layers there is chalk with layers of flint. The Amud cave opens between the 'Massive' and 'Bedded' layers and comprises a semicircular depression about 12 m by 10 m the outer half of which is covered by cave deposits while the inner half is exposed limestone. The cave deposits consist of two layers separated by an erosional unconformity. Layer A is recent and contains potsherds but layer B is made up of loose calcareous silts with limestone rubble. Layer B comprises strata (1–4) from above downwards and Amud I was found as a contracted burial just below the top of layer B1.

Associated finds   Layer B is said to be a palaeolithic horizon representing a single industrial cycle throughout which there is a mixture of Levalloiso-Mousterian and Upper Palaeolithic stone tools. The former group includes retouched points and racloirs while the latter includes end-scrapers and burins. The form and proportions of these tools may indicate a transitional or intermediate industry between the Middle and Upper Palaeolithic industries of the region, or a mixed assemblage. The mammalian faunal remains are scanty and fragmented but fossils representing gazelle (*Gazella cf. subgutturosa*), fallow deer (*Dama mesopotamica*), wild ox (*Bos sp.*), wild pig (*Sus sp.*), wild goat (*Capra sp.*) and horse (*Equus sp.*) have been found as well as some birds and reptiles (Suzuki and Takai, 1970).

Dating   Consideration of the fauna and the tools recovered from the Amud site indicate a date within the Interstadial between the Early and Main Fourth Glaciation (Würm).

Physical methods that support this date include uranium/ionium growth which gives a date of $27,000 \pm 500$ years B.P. and uranium fission track which gives a date of $28,000 \pm 9,800$ years B.P. Radiocarbon dates range from $5,710 \pm 80$ years B.P. for Upper B1 to $18,300 \pm 400$ years B.P. for Basal B4. These dates are believed to

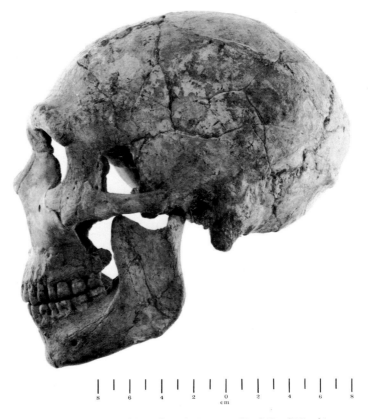

Fig. 39. The Amud I skull (left lateral view). *Courtesy of Prof. Hisashi Suzuki.*

be too 'young' as the result of contamination by younger carbon (Suzuki and Takai, 1970).

Morphology   Amud I is the skeleton of an adult male of approximately 25 years of age. The skull was badly crushed laterally and the postcranial bones were highly fragmented. Amud II consists of an adult right maxillary fragmented and Amud III and IV are skull fragments of infants.

Amud I Skull

This skull has been reconstructed using the Shanidar material to assist with missing areas. The vault is almost complete but much of the base is missing; the dentition is complete but a good deal of the palate and the central part of the face are missing. The mandible is intact.

The vault of the skull is rounded with a receding forehead, a divided supraorbital torus, prominent mastoid processes and a rounded occipital bone. The cranial capacity, by water displacement of the cavity endocast, is very large (1,740 cc), indeed it is the largest known capacity of all the fossil hominids.

The face is long and narrow, the vault is long and wide and the mandible is long as well as having a very large bicondylar breadth. The dental arcade is U-shaped and rather short and the mandibular symphysial region does not recede but neither is there a well marked chin.

Teeth

Both the upper and lower dentitions are complete (thirty two teeth in all) but there has been a good deal of post-mortem distortion of the tooth alignment. In lateral view the occlusal plane appears to be almost flat.

The incisors and canines are broad labio-lingually with well developed lingual tubercles. The premolars are bicuspid and the second premolars (PM2) are larger than the first premolars (PM1) in both upper and lower jaws. The first and second upper molars have large hypocones and the mesiodistal lengths of the lingual sides are longer than those of the buccal sides. Both upper molars are reduced in size.

The lower first molars have a Y5 cusp pattern while the lower second molar on the left has a +4 pattern and the second molar on the right an X4 pattern. Both lower third molars have five cusps and a median lingual accessory cuspule.

An isolated molar was also recovered from the site.

Postcranial Bones

Loss of the ends of most of the limb bones renders length assessments and therefore height estimates hazardous. However, a standing height of 172·3–177·8 cm has been given. In general the long bones are relatively long and slender, the hand is large with large joints and the pelvis (although badly broken) appears narrow, but with a typical superior pubic ramus (Trinkaus, 1976). An error in the attribution to side (left) of the first metacarpal has been corrected (right) (Kimura, 1976).

Dimensions   Suzuki and Takai (1970)

Amud I Skull

Max. Length 215   Max. Breadth 154
Cranial Index 71·6   Cranial Capacity 1,740 cc
    (Dolichocephalic)

Amud I Mandible

Length 119   Bicondylar Breadth 145

Amud I Teeth

		Upper Teeth (Crown Dimensions)							
		I^1	I^2	C	PM^1	PM^2	M^1	M^2	M^3
Right	l	9·3	7·7	8·5	7·3	6·6	10·7	10·4	6·8
Side	b	8·2	8·4	9·5	10·4	10·1	12·4	12·3	7·7
Left	l	—	7·7	8·5	7·4	6·6	10·7	10·4	8·5
Side	b	—	8·4	9·5	10·6	10·0	12·5	12·2	11·0

		Lower Teeth (Crown Dimensions)							
		I_1	I_2	C	PM_1	PM_2	M_1	M_2	M_3
Right	l	—	6·3	—	(7·5)	6·9	(11·0)	11·3	11·6
Side	b	—	7·5	—	9·1	8·5	10·8	10·3	10·5
Left	l	(5·0)	(6·1)	7·6	(7·4)	(6·5)	(10·9)	(10·5)	11·8
Side	b	(7·2)	7·5	9·1	8·9	8·5	10·8	10·8	10·8

( ) Approximate measurement

Amud I Postcranial Bones

Femur Maximum Estimated Length 489
Tibia Maximum Estimated Length 386

Affinities The overall characteristics of the Amud remains seem to suggest that they are part of the Near Eastern Neandertal group. Amud man is said to be closest to the Shanidar and Tabūn remains (*q.v.*) but a little more advanced, showing affinities to the Skhūl and Qafzeh remains (*q.v.*) (Suzuki and Takai, 1970). Howells (1974) and Stringer (1974) include Amud as a Near Eastern Neandertaler with Tabūn and Shanidar, an opinion echoed by Trinkaus (1984). It seems that Amud man was part of the evolving Near Eastern populations displaying a mixture of morphological characters most of which are best compared with those of 'classic' Neandertalers whilst some are reflected in later human material.

The Amud remains have closest affinities to the Tabūn and Shanidar specimens (*q.v.*) and to European 'classic' Neandertalers such as La Chapelle-aux-Saints, La Ferrassie and Neandertal (*q.v.*).

Originals Amud I is held at the Rockefeller Museum, Jerusalem.

Casts Not generally available at present.

References Vallois, H. V. (1962) Un nouveau Néanderthaloide en Palestine. *Anthropologie* 66, 405–406.

Suzuki, H. and Takai, F. (Eds.) (1970) *The Amud Man and his Cave Site.* Tokyo: Keigaku Publishing Co.

Howells, W. W. (1974) Neanderthals: names, hypotheses and scientific method. *Am. Anthrop. 76,* 24–38.

Stringer, C. B. (1974) Population relationships of Later Pleistocene hominids: a multivariate study of available crania. *J. archaeol. Sci. 1,* 317–342.

Kimura, T. (1976) Correction to the Metacarpale I of the Amud Man. *J. anthrop. Soc. Nippon 84,* 48–54.

Trinkaus, E. (1976) The Morphology of European and Southwest Asian Neandertal pubic bones. *Am. J. phys. Anthrop. 44,* 95–104.

Trinkaus, E. (1984) Western Asia. In *The Origins of Modern Humans.* Eds. F. H. Smith and F. Spencer. New York: Alan R. Liss.

The Shanidar Remains

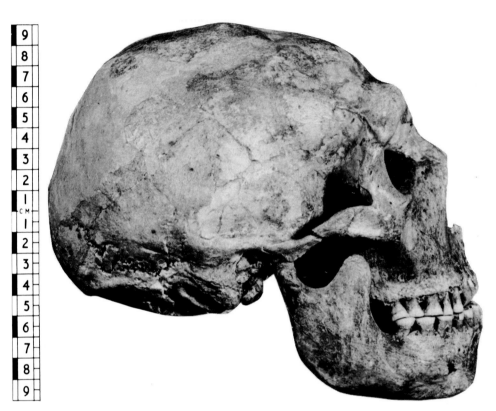

Fig. 40. The Shanidar I skull (right lateral view). *Courtesy of E. Trinkaus.*

Synonyms and other names
Homo sapiens shanidarensis (Senyürek, 1957); *Homo sapiens neanderthalensis* (Stringer and Trinkaus, 1981); The Shanidar Neandertals; Shanidar 1–9.

Site
The Shanidar valley in the Zagros mountains about 13·5 km northwest of the confluence of the Greater Zab and Rowanduz rivers about 400 km north of Baghdad, Republic of Iraq.

Found by
R. Solecki and his co-workers 1951–1960. Shanidar 1, 27th April, 1957; Shanidar 2, 23rd May, 1957; Shanidar 3, 16th April, 1957; Shanidar 4, 3rd August, 1960; Shanidar 5, 7th August, 1960; Shanidar 6, 9th August, 1960; Shanidar 7, 22nd June, 1953; Shanidar 8, 4–15th August, 1960; Shanidar 9, August 1960.

Geology   The remains were found in the deposits within a large cave at the foot of Baradost Mountain. The cave opening faces south and is about 25 m wide. Inside the cave is 40 m deep, 53 m wide and 8 m high. In winter time today it is still used by Barzani Kurdish shepherds, their families and flocks for shelter. About 36 square m of the central area has been excavated 14 m down to bedrock. The cave deposits consist of loamy soils containing boulders and rocks that have fallen from the roof. Five archaeological layers have been described and termed Layers A, B1, B2, C and D. These layers contained faunal remains, 28 modern human burials and 9 sets of remains known as the Shanidar Neandertals (Solecki, 1957, 1960, 1963).

Associated finds   The upper 3 Layers (A, B1, and B2) contained relatively recent artefacts and numerous hearths and have been described as Neolithic, Proto-Neolithic and Mesolithic (Solecki, 1963). Layer C contained Upper Palaeolithic tools of an industry termed the Baradostian, an industry that recalls the Levantine Aurignacian in that it comprises numerous burins, end scrapers and used blade cores (Solecki, 1963). Layer D, the largest layer, is Middle Palaeolithic and contained a Mousterian culture with many points and scrapers; it seemed generally similar in character throughout the layer (Solecki, 1963; Akazawa, 1975). There are many hearths in Layer C as well as in those above. Layer D, the lowest, also contained Mousterian tools homogeneous throughout the layer (Solecki, 1963).

The faunal remains identified from the site include red sheep (*Ovis orientalis*), wild goat (*Capra hirca*), wild boar (*Sus scrofa*), red deer (*Cervus elaphus*), fallow deer (*Dama mesopotamica*), roe deer (*Capreolus capreolus*), wolf (*Canis lupus*), golden jackal (*Canis aureus*), tawny fox (*Vulpes vulpes*), brown bear (*Ursus arctus*), marten (*Martes foina*), beaver (*Castor fiber*), gerbil (*Meriones sp.*), tortoise (*Testudo graeca*), snails (*Helix salomonica*) and river clams (*Unio tigridis*) as well as numerous rodent bones, some avian bones and remains of fish (Reed and Braidwood, 1960; Perkins, 1964 and Evins, 1981). All of the fauna is currently extant but not local to the site. Pollen analyses of samples from the Shanidar 4 burial site suggest that flowers were placed in the grave (Leroi-Gourhan, 1975; Solecki, 1975).

Dating   Radiocarbon dates from Layers C and D range from 26,500 years B.P. ± 1,500–50,600 years B.P. ± 3,000 (Rubin and Suess, 1955; Broecker and Kulp, 1957; Rubin and Alexander, 1960; Vogel and Waterbolk, 1963). Climatic correlations (Solecki, 1963) on the basis of pollen analysis and radiocarbon dates and an assumption of constant depositional rates in the cave, has suggested a date of 60–70,000 B.P. for the middle of Layer D and 100,000 years B.P. for the bottom of Layer D. This suggested date should be regarded with caution, whilst generally acceptable within the framework of the Levantine Neandertal sites such as Amud and Tabūn (*q.v.*) (Trinkaus, 1983).

Morphology Nine partial skeletons have been recovered from Layer D. Their numbering, extent, age and sex determinations are as follows:

Table 3 Layer D Recoveries

Original Designation	Number Trinkaus (1983)	Sex	Age in years	Bones
Shanidar I or 1	1	♂	30–45	Skull; skeleton
Shanidar II or 2	2	♂	20–30	Skull, vertebrae, some limb bones
Shanidar III or 3	3	♂	40–50	Teeth, postcranial bones
Shanidar IV	4	♂	30–45	Skull; skeleton
Shanidar V	5	♂	35–50	Cranium, some limb bones
Shanidar VI	6	♀	20–35	Skull; skeleton
'child'	7	?	6–9 (months)	Skull; some limb bones
Shanidar VII	8	♀	Young adult	Cranium; some limb bones
Shanidar VIII	9	?	6–12 (months)	Cervical and thoracic vertebrae

(Based on Trinkaus, 1983)

The material has been described anatomically by Stewart (1958–1977) and Trinkaus (1978–1983).

Cranium

The best preserved cranium is that which belongs to Shanidar 1. It is a large skull with features that are widely recognized as those of the Neandertalers. These features include a long low cranial vault, a large supraorbital torus, a prognathic mid-facial region with a retromolar space, a transverse occipital torus and developed occipitomastoid crests and a rounded vault profile in occipital view.

Mandible

The Shanidar 1 mandible is virtually complete. It is large, elongate and chinless with definite but moderate muscular and other anatomical features on the external surface. Internally the features are more marked such as the mylohyoid line and the attachments of medial pterygoid muscle. The form of this mandible is typically Neandertal in that it is robust, with well marked muscle attachments and an alveolar process that bears a dental arcade well in front of the mandibular ramus.

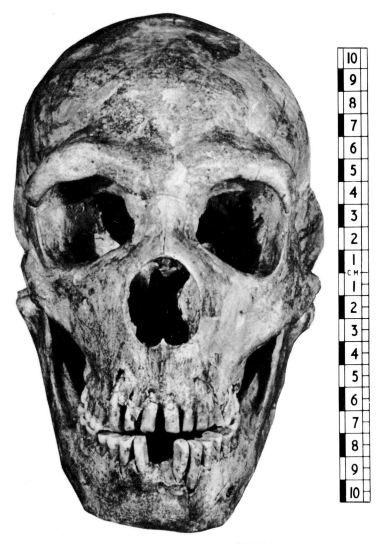

Fig. 41. The Shanidar I skull (frontal view). *Courtesy of E. Trinkaus.*

Teeth

Ninety-six permanent teeth are known from six of the seven adults. Shanidar 1 and 2 have virtually complete dentitions. All of the Shanidar Neandertals show considerable dental attrition so that much of the crown cusp and fissure morphology is lost. The anterior teeth are large as are their posterior molars by comparison with modern man. There is a moderate degree of taurodontism and some evidence of non-dietary use of the anterior teeth as indicated by the form of the attrition (Trinkaus, 1978, 1983).

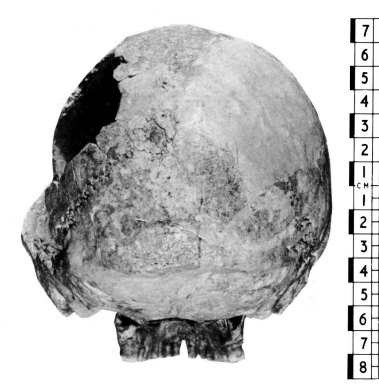

Fig. 42. The Shanidar I skull (occipital view). *Courtesy of E. Trinkaus.*

Postcranial Bones

The vertebral columns of the Shanidar Neandertals are similar to those of modern man but with a marked tendency to robustness. The ribs are thick. The upper limb bones disclose a pattern of morphology close to that of other Neandertals of the Near East and of Europe. This pattern includes powerful shoulders, arms and hands built for grasping, pulling and lifting. The lower limb remains conform to the pattern of Neandertal man in that they are robust, powerfully muscled and in keeping with upright posture and bipedal gait. In addition it seems that the distribution of muscularity is such that powerful acceleration would have been possible in running, jumping or climbing.

Dimensions Trinkaus (1983)
Shanidar 1

Skull

Max. Length 207·2   Max. Breadth (154)

Cranial Index 74·3

Cranial Capacity 1,600 cc
(Stewart, 1977). Water
displacement of restored endocast.

Mandible

Bicondylar breadth 142·8   Length 90·0
Symphysial angle 65°

Postcranial Bones

Max. length of Humerus   243·2
Max. length of Ulna   270·2
Max. length of Radius   224·4
Max. length of Femur   437·5
Max. length of Tibia   333·0
Max. length of Fibula   275·0

Teeth (Trinkaus, 1978)
Shanidar 1

| | | Upper Teeth (Crown Dimensions) | | | | | | | |
		I^1	I^2	C	PM^1	PM^2	M^1	M^2	M^3
Right	l	—	—	—	7·0	6·8	10·3	0·1	9·7
side	b	(7·7)	(8·9)	(9·5)	10·4	9·7	12·3	11·8	11·6
Left	l	—	—	—	—	(6·2)	10·7	10·1	9·4
side	b	(7·5)	(8·7)	(10·0)	(9·6)	10·0	11·7	11·9	11·6

| | | Lower Teeth (Crown Dimensions) | | | | | | | |
		I_1	I_2	C	PM_1	PM_2	M_1	M_2	M_3
Right	l	—	—	—	7·7	7·5	10·5	11·0	11·6
side	b	—	(8·5)	9·0	8·4	8·1	10·4	11·0	10·9
Left	l	—	—	—	6·5	6·8	10·5	10·9	11·5
side	b	—	(8·4)	(9·8)	8·5	8·8	10·0	10·8	10·8

( ) Approximate measurements

Affinities   The affinities of the Shanidar remains seem to have been so plain
to all since their discovery that there has been little or no discussion
in the literature. Initially, the 'child' (Shanidar 7) was attributed to
a geographic subspecies of *Homo sapiens*, *Homo sapiens shanidarensis*
(Senyurek, 1959). Later authors have scarcely bothered to refer to
the taxonomic position. They have confined their attentions to phylogenetic speculations and to the view that *in situ* local change
may have been responsible for evolution towards anatomically
modern man in the Near East whilst local variability is recognized
(Stringer and Trinkaus, 1981; Trinkaus, 1984). Clearly the Shanidar
Neandertals have most in common with other early Levantine
Neandertal populations such as those represented by remains from
Tabūn and Amud (*q.v.*) .

The assemblage from Shanidar is of value for two other reasons; one, the level of skeletal pathology in this group due to trauma and arthritis and two, the possibility that the crania of two of them were artificially deformed for cultural or aesthetic reasons (Trinkaus and Zimmerman, 1982; Trinkaus, 1982a, 1983). Skulls 1 and 5 show prebregmatic grooving that may have resulted from head binding in infancy or maternal pressure—but another explanation may be the carriage of loads by means of a head strap, 'Kikuyu style'.

Originals The Iraq Museum, Baghdad, Republic of Iraq. University of New Mexico, Albuquerque, USA (No. 3).

Casts Not generally available.

References
Rubin, M. and Suess, H. E. (1955) U.S. geological survey radiocarbon dates II. *Science 121* 481–488.

Broecker, W. S. and Kulp, J. L. (1957) Lamont natural radiocarbon measurements IV. *Science 126*, 1324–1334.

Senyürek, M. S. (1957) The skeleton of the fossil infant found in Shanidar cave, northern Iraq. *Anatolia 2*, 49–55.

Senyürek, M. S. (1959) A study of the deciduous teeth of the fossil Shanidar infant. A comparative study of the milk teeth of fossil men. *Pubs Fac. Lang. Hist. Geog. Univ Ankara, Palaeoanthrop. Div.* 2 1–174.

Solecki, R. S. (1957) Shanidar cave. *Scient. Am. 197*, 58–64.

Stewart, T. D. (1958) First view of the restored Shanidar I skull. *Sumer 14*, 90–96 (Reprinted in *A. Rep. Smithson. Inst. 1958*, 473–480).

Stewart, T. D. (1959) Restoration and study of the Shanidar I Neanderthal skeleton in Baghdad, Iraq. *Yearb. Am. phil. Soc. 1958*, 274–278.

Reed, C. A. and Braidwood, R. J. (1960) Toward the reconstruction of the environmental sequence in northeastern Iraq. In *Prehistoric Investigations in Iraqi Kurdistan.* Eds. R. J. Braidwood and B. Howe. Studies in ancient Oriental Civilization *31*, 163–173.

Rubin, M. and Alexander, C. (1960) U.S. geological survey radiocarbon dates II. *Science 2* 129–185.

Solecki, R. S. (1960) Three adult Neanderthal skeletons from Shanidar cave, northern Iraq. *A. Rep. Smithson. Inst. 1959*, 603–635.

Stewart, T. D. (1961) The skull of Shanidar II. *Sumer 17*, 97–106. (Reprinted in *A. Rep. Smithson. Inst. 1961*, 521–533.

Stewart, T. D. (1962a) Neanderthal cervical vertebrae with special attention to the Shanidar Neanderthals from Iraq. *Biblica primatol. 1*, 130–154.

Stewart, T. D. (1962b) Neanderthal scapulae with special attention to the Shanidar Neanderthals from Iraq. *Anthropos, 57*, 779–800.

Solecki, R. S. (1963) Prehistory in Shanidar valley, northern Iraq. *Science 139* 179–193.

Stewart, T. D. (1963) Shanidar skeleton IV and VI. *Sumer 19*, 8–26.

Vogel, J. C. and Waterbolk, H. T. (1963) Groningen radiocarbon dates IV. *Radiocarbon 5* 163–202.

Perkins, D. Jr. (1964) Prehistoric fauna from Shanidar. *Science 144*, 1565–1566.

Akazawa, T. (1975) Preliminary notes on the Middle Pleistocene assemblage from the Shanidar Cave. *Sumer* 31 3–10.

Leroi-Gourhan, A. (1975) The flowers found with Shanidar IV, a Neanderthal burial in Iraq. *Science* 190, 562–564.

Solecki, R. S. (1975) Shanidar IV, a Neanderthal flower burial in northern Iraq. *Science* 190, 880–881.

Stewart, T. D. (1977) The Neanderthal skeletal remains from Shanidar cave, Iraq: a summary of the findings to date. *Proc. Am. phil. Soc.* 121, 121–165.

Trinkaus, E. (1978a) A preliminary description of the Shanidar 5 Neandertal partial skeleton. In *Recent Advances in Primatology* Vol. 3., 431–433. Eds. D. J. Chivers and K. A. Joysey. London: Academic Press.

Trinkaus, E. (1978b) Dental remains from the Shanidar adult Neanderthals. *J. hum. Evol.* 7, 369–382.

Evins, M. A. (1981) A study of the fauna from the Mousterian deposits of Shanidar Cave, Northeastern Iraq. MA thesis, Univ. Chicago.

Stringer, C. B. and Trinkaus, E. (1981) The Shanidar Neanderthal crania. In *Aspects of Human Evolution*, 129–165. Ed. C. B. Stringer. London: Taylor and Francis.

Trinkaus, E. (1982a) Artificial cranial deformation of the Shanidar 1 and 5 Neandertals. *Curr. Anthrop.* 23, 198–199.

Trinkaus, E. (1982) The Shanidar 3 Neandertal. *Am. J. phys. Anthrop.* 57, 37–60.

Trinkaus, E. and Zimmerman, M. R. (1982) Trauma among the Shanidar Neandertals. *Am. J. phys. Anthrop.* 57, 61–76.

Trinkaus, E. (1983) *The Shanidar Neandertals.* New York: Academic Pres.

Northwest Africa

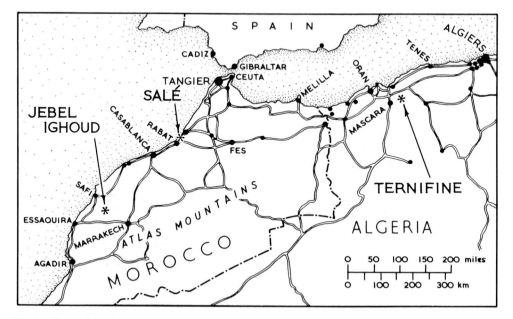

Fig. 43. Hominid fossil sites in North Africa.

The Ternifine Remains

Fig. 44. The Ternifine I mandible (right lateral view). *Courtesy of the late Prof. C. Arambourg.*

Synonyms and other names *Atlanthropus mauritanicus* (Arambourg, 1954); *Homo erectus* (Campbell, 1972, Tillier, 1980); Ternifine man.

Site Ternifine, near the village of Palikao, 11 miles east of Mascara, Oran, Algeria.

Found by C. Arambourg and R. Hoffstetter, July, 1954: C. Arambourg, 1955.

Geology Commercial excavation of a large hill of sand exposed the bed of a Pleistocene artesian lake containing fossil bones and stone tools. The level of the water table made it necessary for pumps to be used in the recent exposure of the lower layers.

Associated finds   Several hundred implements were recovered from the site, made principally of quartzite and sandstone but occasionally of poor-quality flint. The tools included primitive biface hand-axes, scrapers and a type of small axe with a curved blade; an industry described as Acheuléen II (Balout and Tixier, 1957). The associated fossil fauna was rich and varied containing many extinct forms suggestive of a tropical savannah environment. The predominant mammals were hippopotamus (*Hippopotamus amphibius*), elephant (*Loxodonta atlantica*), early zebra (*Equus mauritanicus*), rhinoceros (*Ceratotherium simum mauritanicum*), camel (*Camelus thomasi*), several antelopes and numerous carnivores. In addition, several species of particular importance were identified, a sabre-toothed cat (*Homotherium latidens*), giant wart-hog (*Afrochoerus sp.*) and a giant baboon (*cf. Simopithecus*).

Dating   The character of the fauna, especially the presence of the last three species, in conjunction with the type of industry, allowed Arambourg (1955a) to establish an early Middle Pleistocene date for these deposits.

Morphology   Arambourg (1963)
The hominid bones which were discovered comprise three mandibles, a parietal bone and some isolated teeth.

Mandibles

The mandibles are all adult and remarkable for their size and robustness. Nos. I and III are probably male, whereas No. II despite its great size is probably female. In all three specimens the borders of the bodies of the mandibles are parallel, the symphyses slope backwards, so that there are no chins, but a sub-mental trigone is present in Nos. II and III. The dental arcades are parabolic and there are several mental foramina in Nos. I and III. The body of No. I is strengthened by a prominent marginal torus. The rami are broken, but enough remains to suggest some variability; none the less they are all broad with marked impresses for masseter and medial pterygoid muscles.

Teeth

The incisors and canines are known only from the two worn specimens present in No. III. Little more can be said than that they appear hominid. The premolars are large, the first having an asymmetrical crown with a prominent buccal cusp and a smaller lingual cusp more distally placed. The second premolars have large buccal and lingual cusps placed opposite to each other, and large posterior foveae. The premolar teeth have large labial cingula whilst the

Fig. 45. The Ternifine II mandible (occlusal view). *Courtesy of the late Prof. C. Arambourg.*

second premolar, which is little worn, shows marked secondary enamel wrinkling.

The molar teeth are large and decrease in size in the order M2 > M1 > M3. The cusp pattern is dryopithecine (Y5 or +5), sixth cusps being present in No. II (M2, M3) and No. III (?M3) (Howell, 1960). It is probable that secondary enamel wrinkling was present on the occlusal surfaces of the molars as shown by those which are least worn; signs of a buccal cingulum are present on some of the molar teeth. Four of the isolated teeth are deciduous upper molars whose degree of development suggests that they may have belonged to one individual of from 8–10 years of age. These two dental features are typical of all the North African sample until modern people (see Tillier, p. 419). The status of *H. erectus* may be due to the jaw and parietal morphology.

The Parietal (Arambourg, 1955c)

The parietal is young, for all its sutures were open at the time of death. Its thickness is within the range of variation found in modern man. The parietal curve indicates that the vault was probably low and that the widest diameter of the cranium was bitemporal rather than biparietal. The temporal lines are well inscribed and testify to the power of the temporalis muscle. Internally the bone is heaped to form a prominent Sylvian crest whilst the middle meningeal pattern is primitive in its design, the principal division of the vessel having occurred before it reached the parietal bone. Thereafter, the anterior and bregmatic branches are weak but the temporal branch is stronger.

Dimensions   Arambourg (1955b) and Howell (1960)

Mandibles	No. I	No. II	No. III
Symphysial height	39	35	39
Body height (Behind M1)	35	34	38
Body thickness (Behind M1)	19	16	20
Ramus height	—	72	93
Ramus breadth	—	45	48
Mandibular angle	—	98°	111°
Total length	110	110	129
Bicondylar breadth	—	—	158

Mandibles	Lower Teeth No. I	(Crown Dimensions) No. II	No. III
PM1 l	8·5	9·0	8·0
b	9·0	11·2	10·0
PM2 l	8·0	9·5	8·2
b	10·0	10·5	10·0
M1 l	12·8	14·0	12·0
b	12·0	13·0	11·8
M2 l	13·0	14·2	12·0
b	13·7	13·7	12·1
M3 l	12·0	13·2	8·0
b	12·5	12·5	11·5

Affinities   The similarities between the Ternifine mandibles and those of Zhoukoudian Locality I (*Homo erectus*) are particularly striking. Features such as the mandibular torus, the shape of the dental arcade and the mental trigone, the form of the first premolar, the molar size order, the enamel wrinkling and the presence of cingular ridges, all argue for their morphological relationship. These likenesses were recognized by Arambourg (1954), but the Ternifine remains have been provisionally named *Atlanthropus mauritanicus*. They are now widely regarded as belonging to *Homo erectus*. Howell (1960) also accepted the resemblances between the Ternifine and Zhoukoudian mandibles and asserted that 'there are no differences between the Ternifine and Zhoukoudian Locality I people which might not be expected within a single polytypic species, populations of which were widely separated geographically'.

Originals   Institut de Paléontologie, 8, Rue de Buffon, Paris–5ᵉ, France.

Casts   Not generally available at present.

References   Arambourg, C. and Hoffstetter, R. (1954) Découverte, en Afrique du Nord, de restes humains du Paléolithic inférieur. *C.r. Acad. Sci. Paris* 239, 72–74.
Arambourg, C. (1954) L'hominien fossile de Ternifine (Algérie). *C.r. Acad. Sci. Paris* 239, 893–895.
Arambourg, C.(1955a) A recent discovery in human paleontology: *Atlanthropus* of Ternifine (Algeria). *Am. J. phys. Anthrop. 13*, 191–202.

Arambourg, C.(1955b) Une nouvelle mandibule 'd'Atlanthropus' au gisement de Ternifine. *C.r. Acad. Sci. Paris 241*, 895–897.

Arambourg, C. (1955c) Le pariétal de *l'Atlanthropus mauritanicus. C.r. Acad. Sci. Paris 241*, 980–982.

Arambourg, C.(1956) Une IIIème mandibule d' 'Atlanthropus' découverte à Ternifine. *Quaternaria 3*, 1–4.

Balout, L. and Tixier, J. (1957) L'Acheuléen de Ternifine. *C.r. Cong. préhist. Fr. 15, 1956*, 214–218.

Howell, F.C. (1960) European and northwest African Middle Pleistocene hominids. *Curr. Anthrop. 1*, 195–232.

Arambourg, C.(1963) Le gisement de Ternifine. Part I C. Arambourg and R. Hoffstetter, Part II C. Arambourg. *Archs Inst. Paléont. hum. 32*, 1–190.

Tillier, A.-M. (1980) Les dents d'enfant de Ternifine (Pleistocene moyen d'Algérie). *Anthropologie* (Paris) *84*, 413–421.

The Jebel Ighoud Remains

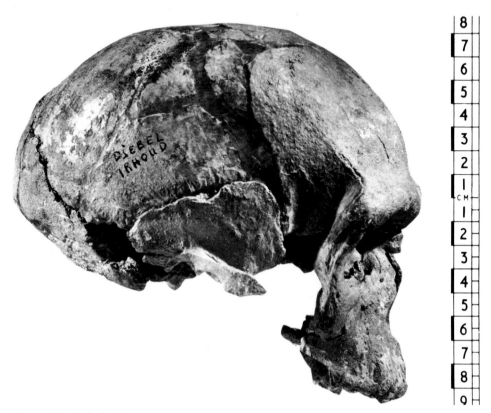

Fig. 46. The Jebel Ighoud I cranium (right lateral view). *Courtesy of the Director of the Musée de l'Homme.*

Synonyms and other names	Ighoud 1–3; Ighoud man; Neandertal man (Ennouchi, 1962b); *Homo sapiens sapiens* (Hublin and Tiller 1981).
Site	At a barytes mine, Jebel Ighoud, 60 km south-east of Safi, Morocco.
Found by	Ighoud 1. Workmen 1961, investigated by E. Ennouchi 1962. Ighoud 2. Workmen and E. Ennouchi, 1968. Ighoud 3. E. Ennouchi 1968.
Geology	The deposits containing the Jebel Ighoud remains were fissure fillings within the Pre-Cambrian limestone of the barytes mine; the filling material was made up of red clay, rock fragments and fossil bones. The fissure (8 m in height by 5 m in breadth) that contained

the remains must have been originally a cave or a cavity open above by means of a narrow neck. The working gallery of the mine exposed the fissure and its filling in cross-section and the remains were found near the floor.

Associated finds Following the recovery of the second skull (Ighoud 2) an abundant flint industry was recovered whose character has been given as Levalloiso-Mousterian. Some rare quartzite implements have also been recovered as well as a number of eggshell fragments from the egg of a large bird. It has been suggested that the egg could have served as a receptacle.

The fauna that was recovered includes gazelles (*Gazella atlantica, G. cuvieri, G. dorcas*), rhinoceros (*Rhinoceros sp.*), horse (*Equus mauritanicus*), wild dog (*Canis anthus*), bovids (*Alcelaphus bubalis, Connochaetes taurinus, Bos ibericus, Bos primigenius*) and wild ass (*Asinus africanus*) (Ennouchi, 1962b).

Dating The only dating evidence that is available is that based on the faunal list and the stone tool descriptions given above. The conclusion drawn from this was that the site is 'indisputably' Middle Pleistocene (Ennouchi, 1963). However, Oakley (1964) has suggested a considerably younger age on the basis of sea level changes. No chemical, radiometric or other evidence has been put forward so far as to the date of the site other than an attempt to use the radiocarbon method. This resulted in the conclusion that the date of the site was beyond the capacity of this method (Ennouchi, 1968).

Morphology The remains identified from the Jebel Ighoud site comprise two skulls (Ighoud 1 and 2) and an immature mandible (Ighoud 3).

Skull

The first skull lacks a mandible and all the upper teeth are broken off at the tooth necks. Much of the base is missing including the area of the foramen magnum. The skull is said to have belonged to an adult male of about 35 years of age and shows a continuous supraorbital torus surmounted by a supratoral sulcus. The frontal profile retreats and leads on to a generally flattened vault and a flattened lambdoid region. The face shows subnasal prognathism with a large palate and large temporomandibular glenoid cavities. The orbits are large, square and widely separated by a large nasal cavity.

The second skull is a calvaria with all of the face below the brow ridge missing, as is much of the base. The left side retains much of the occipital bone and the left half of the foramen magnum is complete. In many respects the second specimen resembles the first

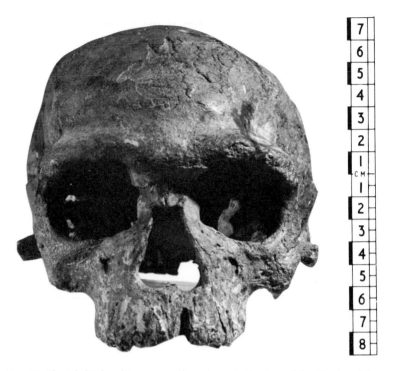

Fig. 47. The Jebel Ighoud I cranium (frontal view). *Courtesy of the Director of the Musée de l'Homme.*

but may have belonged to a younger individual (perhaps 20–25 years of age) and has a slight indentation of the supraorbital torus centrally and an 'open' metopic suture. The walls of both skulls are thick but the former specimen is more robust than the latter.

Teeth

There are no complete teeth present in either skull but from the retained roots and the spaces left for the crowns it appears that they may have been large. Both premolars of Ighoud 1 are double rooted (Ennouchi, 1962 a and b, 1968).

Mandible

Ighoud 3 is a broken juvenile mandible containing both deciduous and permanent teeth. The body of the mandible is intact on the left but broken through at its junction with the ramus on the right. On both sides the first permanent molars are in place and on the left the second deciduous molar is also retained. The remaining deciduous teeth that had erupted are broken off and many of their roots are present in their alveoli. Skiagrams of the mandible disclose the germ of the left second permanent molar in its crypt and on the right the germs of the first and second permanent premolars (En-nouchi, 1969).

Following a detailed comparative study it has been concluded that, like the teeth, the mandible is robust but that its features are distinct from Neandertal morphology. The probable age of the child is given as 8–9 years at death (Hublin and Tillier, 1981).

Dimensions   Ennouchi (1962 a, b and c, 1969)

Skulls

	Jebel Ighoud 1	Jebel Ighoud 2
Max. Length	198	197
Max. Breadth	145	148
Cranial Index	73·2	75·1
Cranial Capacity (Ighoud 1)	1,480 cc	(Displacement method)
	1,305 cc	(Holloway, 1981)

Mandible (Ighoud 3)

Hublin and Tillier (1981)

Ramus height	47·9
Ramus breadth	33·2
Symphysial height	26·7

Teeth (Ighoud 3)

		I_1	I_2	C	PM_1	PM_2	M_1	M_2	M_3
			Lower Teeth (Crown Dimensions)						
Left	l	—	—	9·4	—	—	14·5	—	—
side	b	—	—	8·8	—	—	12·2	—	—
Right	l	—	—	—	—	—	14·4	—	—
side	b	—	7·2	—	—	—	12·3	—	—

Left Second Deciduous Molar	Length	11·3
	Breadth	10·4

Affinities   The first opinion given by the finder of these remains was that they were Neandertal in the classic sense and thus akin to La Chappelle and La Ferrassie (*q.v.*) (Ennouchi, 1962b), and in his subsequent publications there seems to be no basic change in that view. Piveteau (1967), however, does not fully accept that interpretation, neither does Howells (1973, 1974), both authors emphasizing 'modern' features in the skulls. Howells particularly notes the divergence in facial and occipital morphology between the Jebel Ighoud skulls and such Near Eastern Neandertals as Tabūn, Shanidar and Amud (*q.v.*). Stringer (1974, 1978), after extensive metrical analyses, concluded that the general relationships of the Ighoud material were closest to those of Saccopastore, Amud and Skhūl 5 and that it represented a generalized Upper Pleistocene hominid, not a Neandertal.

The recent study of the mandible leaves no doubt that neither it nor the skulls show any specialized Neandertal features, and it is claimed that such archaic features as are shown do not exclude the material from *Homo sapiens sapiens* (Hublin and Tillier, 1981).

In summary the few opinions that have been given would seem to be against those of the finder in terms of relationship to the classic Neandertals and favour slightly more 'modern' affinities.

Originals   Laboratory of Geology, University Mohammed V, Avenue Moulay-Cherriff, Rabat, Morocco.

Casts   Not generally available.

References   Ennouchi, E. (1962a) Un crâne d'Homme ancien au Jebel Irhoud (Maroc). *C.r. Acad. Sci. Paris 254*, 4330–4332.

Ennouchi, E. (1962b) Un Néanderthalien; L'Homme du Jebel Irhoud (Maroc). *Anthropologie 66*, 279–299.

Ennouchi, E. (1963) Les Néanderthaliens du Jebel Irhoud (Maroc). *C.r. Acad. Sci. Paris. 256*, 2459–2460.

Oakley, K. P. (1964) *Frameworks for Dating Fossil Man.* London: Weidenfeld & Nicolson.

Piveteau, J. (1967) Un parietal humain de la grotte du Lazaret (Alpes-Maritimes). *Annls Paléont. 53*, 165–169.

Ennouchi, E. (1968) Le deuxième crâne de L'Homme d'Irhoud. *Annls Paléont. (Vertébrés) 54*, 117–128.

Ennouchi, E. (1969) Présence d'un enfant Néanderthalien au Jebel Irhoud (Maroc). *Annls Paléont. (Vertébrés) 54*, 251–265.

Howells, W. W. (1973) *Evolution of the Genus* Homo. Reading, Mass.: Addison Wesley.

Howells, W. W. (1974) Neanderthals: names, hypotheses and scientific method. *Am. Anthrop. 76*, 24–38.

Stringer, C. B. (1974) Population relationships of Later Pleistocene hominids: a multivariate study of available crania. *J. archaeol. Sci. 1*, 317–342.

Stringer, C. B. (1978) Some problems in Middle and Upper Pleistocene relationships. In *Recent Advances in Primatology*, 395–418. Eds. D. J. Chivers and K. A. Joysey. London: Academic Press.

Holloway, R. L. (1981) Volumetric asymmetry determinations on recent hominid endocasts: Spy I and II, Djebel Irhoud I, and the Sale *Home erectus* specimens, with some notes on Neandertal brain size. *Am. J. phys. Anthrop. 55*, 385–393.

Hublin, J.-J. and Tillier, A. M. (1981) The Mousterian Juvenile Mandible from Irhoud (Morocco): A Phylogenetic Interpretation. In *Aspects of Human Evolution*, 167–185. Ed. C. B. Stringer. London: Taylor and Francis.

The Salé Calvaria

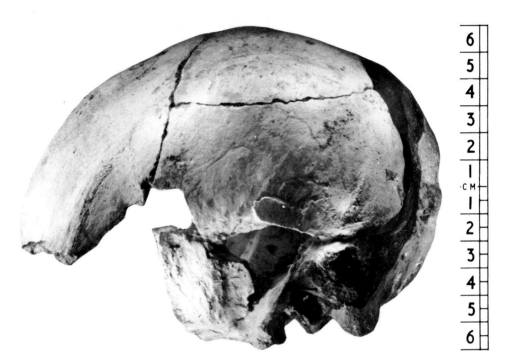

Fig. 48. The Salé calvaria (left lateral view). *Courtesy of Dr J. J. Hublin.*

Synonyms and other names	*Homo erectus* (Jaeger, J.-J., 1975); Salé man.
Site	In an open quarry near Douar Caïd bel Aroussi (El Hamra) several kilometres to the north of Salé, near Rabat, Morocco.
Found by	J.-J. Jaeger and M. Abdeslem Dakka, 1971.
Geology	The deposits containing the remains consist of an ancient cemented dune sandstone situated about 1·5 km from the modern seashore cliffs at a height of 30–40 m above sea-level.
Associated finds	There were no stone tools directly associated with the remains. The large mammals found in the deposits include rhinoceros (*Ceratotherium simum*), wild horse (*Equus cf. mauritanicus*) and a bovid (*Connochaetes taurinus*). The small mammals include *Paraethomys* and *Ellobius*.

Dating   The stratigraphy of the Moroccan littoral is defined by a series of marine transgressions and retreats figured in Jaeger (1981). The Salé site was said at first to represent the Tensiftien transgression of the Upper Middle Pleistocene (Jaeger, 1975; 1981). Later correlations have indicated that the Anfatien transgression could be as old as 400,000 years B.P. In this event the Salé site could be of that age (Hublin, 1985).

Morphology   Jaeger (1975, 1981).

Skull

On the basis of dental attrition and vault sutural closure the Salé calvarium belonged to an adult. It is a low and flattened skull with a retreating frontal and a cranial capacity of 930–960 cc, estimated by water displacement of a natural endocast. Holloway (1981) gives a cranial capacity of 860 cc. The walls of the vault are thick and there is marked postorbital constriction; the greatest breadth of the cranium is at the base. There is a weak occipital torus but the position of the inion is a matter of some debate, since the nuchal region shows some abnormality or pathological feature that confuses the anatomy (Hublin, 1985). The meningeal vascular pattern is relatively simple (Saban, 1982, 1984) and the temporal squama are low.

There are other morphological features that are more modern, such as the degree of parietal bossing, and the proportions of the basioccipital and basisphenoid. It is unsafe to use the occipital features (Hublin, 1985).

Teeth

The left maxilla contains the upper second incisor, the canine, the two premolars and two molars. There is also a fragment of the right upper third molar. The teeth are heavily worn with dentinal exposure; they are robust teeth similar in size to those known from *Homo erectus.*

The degree of attrition is such that the incisor and canine are worn down to their necks and appear round in section, cusp and fissure details are obscure.

Dimensions   Jaeger (1975)

Skull

Max. length	(>168)
Max. breadth	134
Cranial Capacity	930–960 cc
Cranial Capacity (Holloway, 1981)	860 cc
( ) Approximate measurement	

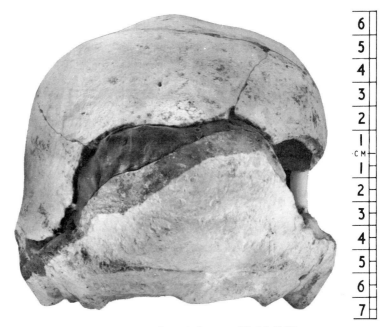

Fig. 49. The Salé calvaria (occipital view). *Courtesy of Dr J. J. Hublin.*

Teeth

Salé		I¹	I²	C	PM¹	PM²	M¹	M²	M³
			Upper Teeth (Crown Dimensions)						
Left	l	—	6·5	8·5	8·7	8·0	11·8	11·5	—
side	b	—	7·8	10·7	12·1	12·2	13·8	13·8	—
Right	l	—	—	—	—	—	—	—	11·2
side	b	—	—	—	—	—	—	—	15·1

Affinities In the initial description (Jaeger, 1975) the principal characters of the Salé specimen were clearly outlined and they are overwhelmingly those of *Homo erectus*. In particular, the small size of the skull, its small cranial capacity, the thickness of its walls and the low position of its maximum breadth are a few of the most telling *Homo erectus* features. On the other hand it has a rounded occiput and some evidence of what is termed parietal 'bossing' as well as a well developed and vertically orientated mastoid process. This assessment led the finder to attribute the skull to *Homo erectus* of an evolved type. This position is maintained later and the Salé skull allied with the remains from Rabat and Sidi Abderrahman (Casablanca) within *Homo erectus*.

Recently Hublin (1985) has drawn attention to the problems associated with the occipital bone in this specimen and states that '. . . in taxonomic discussions about the Salé specimen it is necessary to ignore all the characters of this area as well as measurements involving inion, or at least be very cautious in using them'. In this case most of the modern features of the skull disappear. Hublin also states that 'taking into account only the shared derived features, Salé should be considered as a primitive *Homo sapiens* although most of its features are "erectus" features'. (Hublin 1985). Examination of the skull reveals the numerous features of *Homo erectus* that are present, also the abnormal occipital. It is unsafe to conclude anything very much from this bone and certainly unsafe to state that it is of modern form. The parietal 'bosses' have been termed modern features; but the occipital view of the vault reveals the 'tent-shaped' outline of the skull which is quite distinct from that of *Homo sapiens* in whom the parietal bosses are high on the vault and reflect the increased cranial capacity of the species. The 'bosses' on the Salé cranium do not seem to be equivalent to those of modern man and the cranial capacity is very small. My view, therefore, is that the Salé calvarium is another example of *Homo erectus* from the north African littoral on the basis of numerous similarities with other specimens of the species recognized from Africa and Asia. Those who prefer to base their taxonomic judgements alone on the first appearance of 'new' features may regard this skull as a primitive form of *Homo sapiens*, but the 'new' features that are cited should not include the occipital morphology.

Originals   Laboratoire de Paléontologie des Vertébrés et de Paléontologie Humaine, Université de Paris VI.

Casts   Not generally available.

References   Jaeger, J.-J. (1975) Decouverte d'un Crâne d'Hominide dans le Pleistocene Moyen du Maroc. In *Problémes actuels de Paléontologie—Evolution des Vertébrés.* 897–902. Colloque internationaux CNRS No. 218.

Jaeger, J.-J. (1981) Les hommes fossiles du Pleistocene moyen du Maghreb dans leur cadre géologique, chronologique, et paléoecologique. In *Homo erectus*. Eds. B. A. Sigmon and J. S. Cybulski. Toronto: Univ. Toronto Press.

Holloway, R. H. (1981) Volumetric and asymmetry determinations on recent hominid endocasts: Spy I and II, Djebel Ighoud I and the Salé *Homo erectus* specimens with some notes on Neandertal brain size. *Am. J. phys. Anthrop*, 55, 385–393.

Saban, R. (1982) Les empreintes endocrâniennes, des veines méningées moyennes et les étapes de l'évolution humaine. *Ann. Paléontol. 68*, 171–220.

Saban, R. (1984) *Anatomie et évolution des veines méningées moyennes chez le hommes fossils*. Paris: CTHS, La Documentation France.

Hublin, J.-J. (1985) Human fossils from the north African Middle Pleistocene and the Origin of *Homo sapiens*. In *Ancestors* 238–288. Ed. E. Delson. New York: Alan R. Liss.

East Africa

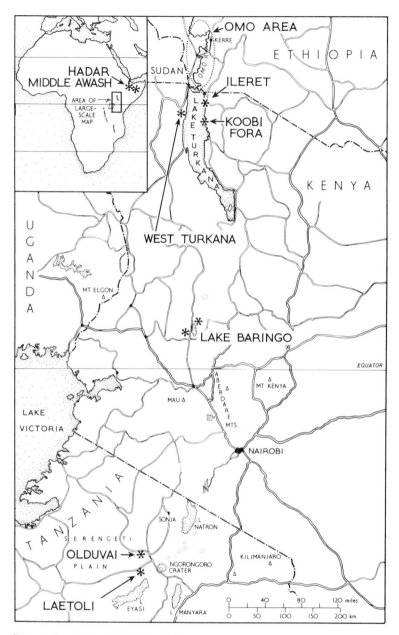

Fig. 50. Hominid fossil sites in East Africa.

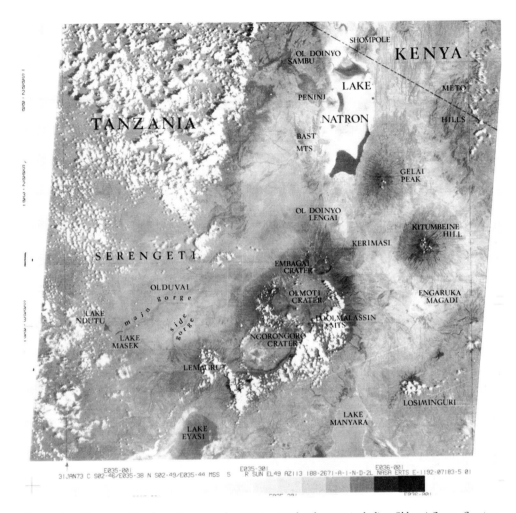

Fig. 51. Satellite view of Northern Tanzania showing geographic features including Olduvai Gorge. *Courtesy of the National Aeronautical Space Administration, USA (Original image). Reproduction by Courtesy of the USA Geological Survey, Earth Resources Observation Systems Data Center.*

The Olduvai Remains

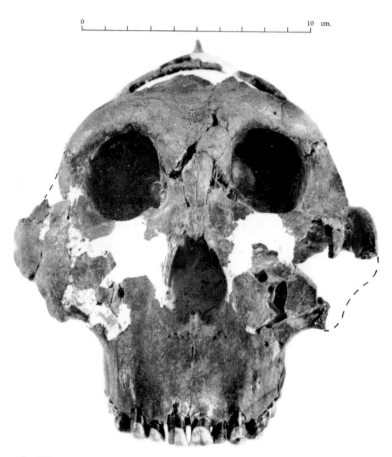

Fig. 52. The Olduvai Hominid 5 cranium (frontal view). *Courtesy of Prof. P. V. Tobias, photographed by R. Klomfass.*

Synonyms and other names

1. *Zinjanthropus boisei* (Leakey, 1959); *Paranthropus boisei* (Robinson, 1960); *Australopithecus (Zinjanthropus) boisei* (Leakey, Tobias and Napier, 1964); *Australopithecus boisei* (Tobias, 1967).

2. *Homo habilis* (Leakey, Tobias and Napier, 1964); *Homo africanus* (Robinson, 1972).

3. *Homo leakeyi* (Heberer, 1963); *Homo erectus* (Leakey, M.D., 1971a).

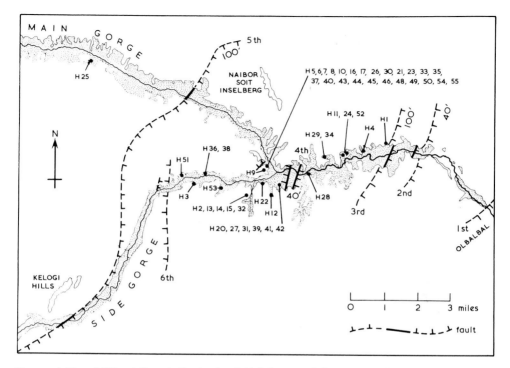

Fig. 53. A Map of Olduvai Gorge indicating hominid find sites and the positions of geological faults in the area.

Site   Olduvai Gorge, Tanzania, East Africa, 110 miles southwest of Nairobi.

Geology   Olduvai Gorge* is a canyon, in places as much as 300 ft. deep, about 30 miles long cut into the Serengeti Plain north of Lake Eyasi and west of Ngorongoro Crater. Extending westwards from the Ol Balbal depression it forms a forked gorge cut solely by erosion. The fossiliferous strata, which rest on a lava base in the eastern part of the gorge, are bedded and consist of a series of lacustrine. fluviatile and wind-blown deposits some of which are volcanic tuffs. The strata have been numbered from below upwards I–IV followed by the Masek, Ndutu and Naisiusiu Beds. Thus Olduvai contains a stratigraphic record of about the past two million years in a rather small basin that has been the site of periodic deformation and faulting. A perennial saline lake was present during Bed I and Lower Bed II times, but it was reduced by earth movements after the deposition of Lower Bed II. Subsequently the lake was inconstant and moved progressively eastward.

* Ol Duvai means 'The place of the wild sisal'; it still grows in the gorge.

Bed I is distinguished from Bed II by a flagstone layer chosen by Reck and Leakey in 1931 as a matter of convenience. For many years it appeared that this arbitrary line coincided with a major faunal change; it is now clear that geologically, faunally and culturally, Lower Bed II belongs with Bed I.

Since 1935 the site has been excavated by the late Dr L. S. B. Leakey and his wife, Dr M. D. Leakey; it has produced a prodigious quantity of mammalian fossils and stone tools. The most interesting bones, from an anthropological point of view, are those of fossil hominids. These hominids have been numbered and a complete list of them is included as a table with some details of the relevant stratum, locality, taxonomic attribution and associated industry. The map shows the position of some of the find-sites as well as the major faults. The geology of the Olduvai area has been described in detail (Hay, 1963 and 1976) and the fossil hominids, up to Hominid 46, have been published in stratigraphic context (Leakey, 1978).

Found by

Apart from Olduvai Hominid 1, which was found by H. Reck in 1913, all of the Olduvai Hominids have been found by the late Dr L. S. B. Leakey or by Dr M. D. Leakey and their co-workers during and since 1935.

Associated finds

Stone Tools

Bed I (Leakey 1966, 1971a)
The stone tools recovered from this layer belong to an industry termed the Oldowan. It is best known for its choppers, primitive tools made by flaking one edge of a water worn cobble to form a jagged cutting edge. There are some other small tools such as scrapers and chisels that were used for lighter work.

Bed II (Leakey 1971a)
Two differing industries occur in Bed II, the Developed Oldowan and the Acheulean. The Developed Oldowan is directly evolved from the Oldowan of Bed I and has the same tool-types with the addition of a few small and crudely made hand-axes.

In the Acheulean the characteristic tools are hand-axes and cleavers. They are made from large flakes and resemble some of the hand-axes found in Bed IV.

Bed III
The artefacts recovered from Bed III at site JK2 include hand-axes, heavy duty picks, choppers, small scrapers and borers as well as cores and flakes (Kleindienst, 1973).

Bed IV
Two contemporary industries have been recovered from Bed IV. One appears to be a derivative of the Developed Oldowan from Bed II and consists of relatively few small and rather poorly made

hand-axes. The Acheulean variant consists of tools that are boldly flaked (WK) and have refined secondary flaking (HEB). These tools are very similar to the Lower Acheulean cleavers and hand-axes from Bed II (Leakey, 1971b).

Masek Beds

One site at Olduvai represents a later phase of the Acheulean in this area. The characteristic tools are very large hand-axes usually made of quartzite very finely trimmed. In addition there are many small scrapers but no cleavers. The latest phases of the Acheulean are post-Masek, i.e. HK and TK Fish gully—both in hillwash.

Ndutu Beds (Upper)

The tools from this bed are Middle Stone Age tools made by a prepared core or Levallois technique recognized from many parts of Africa, Europe and elsewhere. No tools are known from the Lower Ndutu Beds.

Naisiusiu Beds

The tools from these beds are relatively recent and consist of small crescents and other geometric forms made from chert, obsidian and quartzite.

Faunal Remains
Bed I and Lower Bed II

The fossil mammalian fauna recovered from Bed I and Lower Bed II is extensive. It includes two proboscidians (*Deinotherium bozasi* and *Elephas recki*), several archaic pigs (including *Mesochoerus sp.*, *Notochoerus sp.*, *Potamochoerus sp.* and *Metridiochoerus sp.*), several bovids and giraffids, and many other forms such as rodents, carnivores, primates and equids. There were also numerous remains of small amphibia, reptiles and fish (Leakey, 1965; Gentry and Gentry 1978; Andrews, 1983).

Pollen studies on material from Bed I and Lower Bed II suggest that climatic conditions at that time would have been favourable for the development of more montane forest near Olduvai than at present (Bonnefille, 1984).

Upper Bed II

The mammalian fauna of Upper Bed II contains many giant herbivores including hippopotamus (*Hippopotamus gorgops*), pigs (*Stylochoerus nicoli, Mesochoerus olduvaiensis, Potamochoerus majus*), a giant bovid (*Pelorovis oldowayensis*), equids (*Equus oldowayensis, Stylohipparion albertense*); also large carnivores, rhinoceroses and primates (Leakey, 1965).

Bed III

The fauna known from Bed III includes hippopotami, bovids and equids. In addition there were Lagomorpha, Rodentia, Carnivora, Perissodactyla and Proboscidea (Kleindienst, 1973).

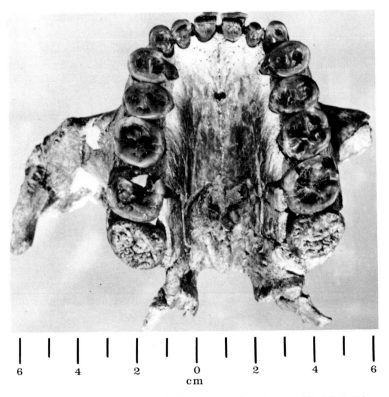

6   4   2   0   2   4   6
cm

Fig. 54. The palate and dentition of Olduvai Hominid 5. *Courtesy of Prof. P. V. Tobias, photographed by R. Klomfass.*

Bed IV
Most of the animals found in Bed III and upper Bed II persist into Bed IV, but crocodiles and catfish are more common.

Masek
Fauna of this period is only known from one site. It includes some of the same animals that are found in Bed IV, notably the suids *Mesochoerus* and *Stylochoerus*, as well as *Phacochoerus* and a gerbil.

Ndutu
Living species of animals are found in the upper Ndutu Beds. The fauna from the Lower Ndutu Beds is virtually unknown except for a giant form of *Theropithecus*.

Naisiusiu
Fauna from one excavated site consists of extant species, including Burchell's zebra, living on the Serengeti Plain today. Studies on animal bones from Beds I and II suggest that hominids of that time were using stone tools to break bones and to cut flesh from bones, presumably for use as food (Burn, 1981; Potts and Shipman, 1981).

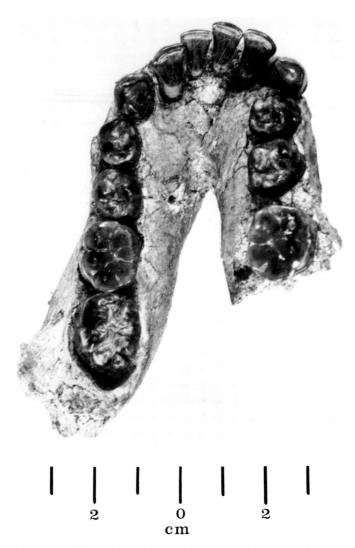

2   0   2

cm

Fig. 55. The Olduvai Hominid 7 mandible. *Courtesy of Prof. P. V. Tobias, photographed by A. R. Hughes.*

Dating An early potassium-argon date from a layer near the base of Bed I was given as 1·7 million years B.P. (Leakey, Evernden and Curtis, 1961); this age was disputed (von Koenigswald, Gentner and Lippolt, 1961) but subsequent work has produced a series of dates for the Olduvai stratigraphic units based on potassium-argon, geomagnetic polarity, fission track, C^{14}, aminoacid racemization as well as sedimentation rates. Bed I (approx. 2·1–1·7 m.y. B.P.), Bed II (1·7–1·15 m.y. B.P.), Bed III (1·15–0·8 m.y. B.P.), Bed IV (0·8–0·6 m.y.

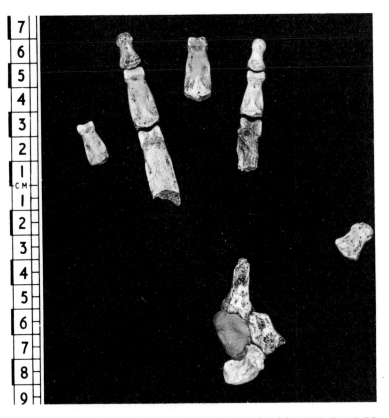

Fig. 56. A reconstruction of the Olduvai Hominid 7 hand by M.H. Day & J.L. Scheuer.

B.P.), the Masek Beds (0·6–0·4 m.y. B.P.), the Ndutu Beds (approx. 400,000–32,000 years B.P.) and the Naisiusiu Beds (22,000–15,000 years B.P.) (Hay, 1976; Hay, 1978).

Morphology   1. *Olduvai Hominid 5*

This skull was recovered in 1959 from site FLK Bed I. The skull is almost complete with an intact upper dentition, only the mandible is lacking. It is probably male and belonged to a young adult whose third molars had erupted, but had not come into wear; the sutures of the skull are still open. The skull has been fully described (Tobias, 1967). The cranial vault is low and the brow ridges are strongly marked; the facial skeleton and palate are large and the teeth robust. Anteroposterior dental disproportion is marked in that the incisors and canines are relatively small while the molars and premolars are large. The premolars show marked 'molarization' and the third molars are heavily wrinkled. A particularly striking fea-

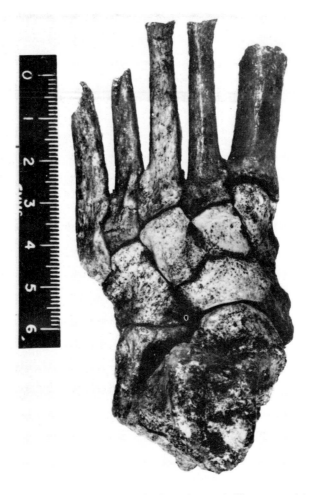

Fig. 57. The Olduvai Hominid 8 foot. *Photographed by courtesy of the late Prof. L. S. B. Leakey.*

ture of the skull is the great development around the cranium of muscular ridges such as the sagittal, occipital and supramastoid crests which were probably associated with a heavy mandible and powerful muscles of mastication. The mastoid processes are large and laterally prominent.

Olduvai Hominid 20

This femoral fragment was recovered from site HWK as a surface find that is believed to have come from Upper Bed I or Lower Bed II.

The fragment consists of the upper end of the shaft, greater trochanter, lesser trochanter and neck of a robust left femur. The head of the bone is missing as well as small portions of both greater and lesser trochanters. The neck of the bone is flattened, the lesser trochanter posteriorly directed and the greater trochanter lacks lateral flare. The relative length of the neck of the bone is high by comparison with those of modern man and the great apes (Day, 1969).

2. Olduvai Hominid 7

The remains described under this number come from site FLKNN Bed I, and comprise parts of a juvenile individual. They include a damaged mandible with a partial dentition (third molar not yet erupted), a pair of parietals, an occipital fragment, fragments of both right and left petrous portions of the temporal bones, several other skull fragments and a group of hand bones (Leakey, 1960, 1961a and b). (Of the original twenty-one 'hand' bones six are non-hominid and one appears to be a vertebral fragment.) Of the fifteen left for consideration seven are clearly juvenile, six are of uncertain age and two are adult. It may be that the adult bones should be excluded from further consideration (Day, 1976; Susman and Creel, 1979). Of the thirteen that are left one is clearly left sided, four are right sided and all are juvenile or possibly juvenile. Most economically at least two hands are involved.

The *mandible* was broken prior to fossilization and the right side of the body has been displaced medially. The body is very stout but its depth cannot be determined since the lower border and part of the symphysial region are missing. Both rami and their coronoid and condyloid processes are also absent. All of the permanent teeth are present in the mandible with the exception of the right second molar and both third molars. Sufficient bone is present distal to the left second molar to establish that the third molar is unerupted. The incisors are hominid in their general structure, but at least one of the premolars is elongated in that the mesiodistal length of its crown is greater than its buccolingual width. The second molar crown is larger than the first on the left side and the molar cusp pattern is basically dryopithecine.

The *parietals* are thin and immature and have no sign of a sagittal crest or marked temporal lines. Restoration was facilitated by the fortunate preservation of the entire coronal and temporal borders of the left bone and the entire occipital border of the right bone. Moreover the anterior part of the sagittal border of the left parietal bone and the posterior part of this border of the right parietal bone were preserved. Thus although the bones have no point of contact, reconstruction of the vault could proceed. The volume of the biparietal endocast has been estimated by water displacement and by other methods with varying results (see page 173) (Leakey, 1961a; Tobias, 1964b; Wolpoff, 1981; Vaisnys, Lieberman and Pilbeam, 1984).

The *hand* was powerfully built, capable of strong finger flexion and possessed an opposable thumb; deductions based upon the morphology of the finger bones, the presence of a well defined saddle surface on the trapezium and a thumb terminal phalanx that is stout and broad (Napier, 1962; Day, 1976). Following a comparative study it has been suggested that the Olduvai Hominid 7 juvenile hand has features indicative of 'suspensory behaviors' that are not primitive retentions of 'pongid-like features' (Susman and Stern, 1979).

Olduvai Hominid 8

This specimen was recovered from site FLKNN, Bed I (Leakey, 1960); all of the bones were found within the area of one square foot. It comprises the bones of a foot, including all the left tarsal and metatarsal bones, of an adult individual; all the phalanges, the metatarsal heads and the posterior portion of the calcaneum are missing. It is clear from examination of this foot when articulated that it has most of the specializations associated with the plantigrade propulsive feet of man (Day and Napier, 1964). The presence of an articular facet between the bases of the first and second metatarsals demonstrated unequivocally the absence of hallucial divergence which characterizes non-human primate feet. The distal row of tarsal bones forms a well marked transverse arch; the ligamentous and muscular impressions upon the bones provide evidence for the static and dynamic support of the arches of the foot. In short the foot is non-prehensile and adapted for upright stance and bipedal gait. This conclusion has been confirmed by further studies (Susman and Stern, 1982). These authors consider, however, that the foot is sub-adult and may even be part of one individual represented by the OH 7 hand and the OH 35 tibia and fibula—an interesting speculation that seems insufficiently supported by the evidence to be fully convincing.

Olduvai Hominid 10

This specimen was recovered from site FLK (North) at the top of Bed I. It is the terminal phalanx of a right great toe. The bone is short, broad and flattened; its head bears a prominent tubercle for the support of the nail while its base has stout tubercles for the collateral ligaments. The long axis of the bone shows a valgus deviation and the shaft shows lateral torsion. It is believed that this terminal phalanx provides further evidence for an advanced form of bipedal gait in the early hominid forms which were evolving in

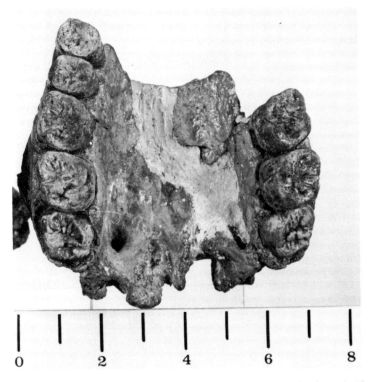

Fig. 58. The palate and dentition of Olduvai Hominid 13 (occlusal view). *Photographed by courtesy of Dr M. D. Leakey.*

East Africa during the Lower Pleistocene (Day and Napier, 1966; Day, 1967).

Olduvai Hominid 13

This skull was found at site MNK in Lower Bed II. It consists of the greater part of the mandible including the complete dentition, the greater part of the maxillae, most of the occipital, the right parietal and temporal bones, parts of the left parietal and temporal bones as well as frontal fragments and many other bone fragments. It has been possible to reconstruct the dental arcades and to place them into occlusion and to attempt a reconstruction of the skull vault. The teeth are elongated mesiodistally and narrowed labiolingually (Leakey and Leakey, 1964).

Olduvai Hominid 24

This skull was recovered from Lower Bed I at site DK East. The specimen includes the greater part of the vault, much of the occipital bone, nearly all of the sphenoid, nearly all of the right temporal bone and a considerable part of the face and palate.

Fig. 59. The Olduvai Hominid 10 toe bone. *Photographed by courtesy of Dr M. D. Leakey.*

Unfortunately the skull was badly crushed while in the deposit and despite a remarkable reconstruction it retains a good deal of distortion. In particular the reconstructed vault remains flattened from above downwards and this has resulted in the occiput protruding further posteriorly than it should. The face is concave when viewed in profile with no nasal protrusion and the supraorbital ridge is prominent and continuous across a marked glabellar protrusion. From above, the vault outline shows considerable postorbital waisting, but this may appear exaggerated since the vault is much reconstructed and asymmetrical. As the earliest of the hominids recovered from Olduvai it has been described in some detail in the preliminary communication (Leakey, Clarke and Leakey, 1971).

Olduvai Hominid 35

Early in 1960 a tibia and fibula were found on the same living floor as the Olduvai Hominid 5 skull at site FLK (Leakey, 1960). The upper ends of both bones are missing but the lower articular surfaces are intact allowing them to be fitted together. In a preliminary assessment the bones were described as being well adapted to bipedal gait at the ankle, but less well adapted at the knee. It was concluded that while this form was an habitual bipedal walker, the gait may have differed considerably from that of man (Davis, 1964).

Subsequent examination of the upper end of the tibia has suggested an alternative explanation of part of the anatomy which may detract from the view that the leg was less well adapted for bipedalism at the knee (Day, 1976). In a new study the bipedal adaptations of the tibia and fibula have been confirmed (Susman and Stern, 1982).

Olduvai Hominid 48

A clavicle was recovered from site FLKNN in Bed I (Leakey, 1960). As originally described it is said to have overall similarities to that of man (Leakey, Tobias and Napier 1964). Subsequent examination has done little to alter that view (Day, 1976).

3. Olduvai Hominid 9

This find consists of the greater part of a thick calvaria that was recovered from site LLK, Upper Bed II. It lacks a face, base and part of the vault. The frontal region is flattened, the nuchal crest is prominent, the inion coincides with the opisthocranion and the nuchal plane is flattened. The small mastoid processes are surmounted by supramastoid crests that are continuous with the nuchal crest and the brow ridges are large and flaring (Leakey, 1961a).

Olduvai Hominid 28

This femoral shaft and hip bone were recovered together *in situ* from Bed IV at site WK. The femur lacks a head, greater trochanter and the lower end. It is flattened throughout with acute medial and lateral borders, it has a convexity of the medial border and the narrowest point of the shaft is distally placed. The hip bone is represented by the major parts of its iliac and ischial portions, the pubic portion is missing. The bone is stoutly constructed with prominent muscular markings and a large acetabulum indicating a large femoral head. The iliac pillar is massive and the ischium medially rotated (Day, 1971).

Olduvai Hominid 36

An almost complete ulna was recovered from site SC, Upper Bed II. The most striking features of the bone are its general robustness, the strength of its muscular markings and the degree of its curvature in the anteroposterior plane throughout its length. When viewed posteriorly the bone shows a typical ulnar sigmoid. The trochlear notch is unusual in several respects; in particular it has a smooth vertical ridge or keel dividing the articular surface into a small medial portion and a large lateral portion while the gape of the trochlear notch is small in relation to the overall size of the bone.

Fig. 60. The Olduvai Hominid 9 calvaria reconstructed by Professor P. V. Tobias and A. R. Hughes. *Courtesy of the late Dr L. S. B. Leakey and Professor P. V. Tobias, photographed by A. R. Hughes.*

Dimensions

1. *Olduvai Hominid 5*

Tobias (1963, 1967)

Maximum Length (Glabella-Opisthocranion)	173·0
Maximum Breadth (Supramastoid)	139·5
Maximum Height (Basion to a point vertically above it in the	
coronal plane) Left of sagittal crest	92·0
Right of sagittal crest	90·5
Cranial Capacity	530 cc

2. *Olduvai Hominid 7*

Skull

Estimated Cranial Capacity 673·5–680·8 cc (Central values) Range of estimates 642·7–723·6 cc (Tobias, 1964b, 1965c, 1966b; Holloway, 1965, 1966); 657 cc (Tobias, 1968) 687 cc (Tobias, 1971); 580–600 cc (Wolpoff, 1981); 690 cc, range 538–868 cc (Vaišnys, Lieberman and Pilbeam, 1984).

Mandible

Dimensions not available.

Teeth

Tobias and von Koenigswald (1964)

				Lower Teeth (Crown Dimensions)				
	I_1	I_2	C	PM_1	PM_2	M_1	M_2	M_3
Left l	*	*	*	9·6	10·3	14·3	15·6	—
side b	*	*	*	10·3	10·7	12·2	13·5	—
Right l	*	*	*	9·9	11·1	14·3	—	—
side b	*	*	*	10·1	10·7	12·4	—	—

*Unpublished

Postcranial Bones

Hand

Specimen	Digit	Inter-artic length	Width (med./lat.)	Depth (ant./post.)
D	II	18·5	9·8	4·3
F	III	25·1	11·8	5·0
E	IV	24·9	11·4	4·9
G	V	17·8	9·0	3·9

Olduvai Hominid 10

Max. Length 17·5   Max. Breadth 18·3
Length/Breadth Index 104·5   Valgus Deviation 2°
Lateral Torsion 13°

Olduvai Hominid 13

Teeth

Tobias and von Koenigswald (1964)

		Upper and Lower Teeth (Crown Dimensions)				
		PM1	PM2	M1	M2	M3
Upper teeth	l	8·3	8·7	12·5	12·8	12·0
	b	11·4	11·5	12·6	13·8	13·1
Lower teeth	l	—	8·9	12·7	13·8	14·6
	b	—	9·8	11·6	12·2	12·5

Cranial Capacity (reconstructed skull) 650 cc (Holloway, 1973)

Olduvai Hominid 24

Skull

Leakey, Clarke and Leakey (1971)
Maximum Length (Glabella to inion chord)   147*
Maximum Breadth (Bimastoid)   122*
Cranial Capacity   590 cc*
      (Holloway, 1973)

3. *Olduvai Hominid 9*

Skull

Length 209   Breadth 150   Cranial Index c. 72

*Skull reconstructed with considerable residual distortion.

Olduvai Hominid 28

Day (1971)

Femur

Length (reconstructed)	456
Mid-shaft Diam. (sagittal)	24·7
(transverse)	32·7
Platymeric Index	62·3
Pilastric Index	75·5

Affinities 1. In the original description of the Olduvai Hominid 5 skull it was stated that, while the new skull belonged patently to the sub-family Australopithecinae, it differed from both *Australopithecus* and *Paranthropus* 'much more than these two genera differ from each other' (Leakey, 1959). On these grounds the new genus *Zinjanthropus* was created; the specific name *boisei* was given after a benefactor. Robinson (1960) believed that the cranial and dental characters of this skull are typically those of *Paranthropus* and proposed that *Zinjanthropus* be included in this genus (*Paranthropus boisei*). Following the discovery of further hominid remains in Bed I (*Homo habilis*), Leakey, Tobias and Napier (1964) recognized the genus *Australopithecus* as having three sub-genera within the family Hominidae, i.e. *Australopithecus*, *Paranthropus* and *Zinjanthropus*. Thus 'Zinjanthropus' was accepted as an East African australopithecine, sub-generically distinct from the South African forms. Later Tobias (1967) formally sank the sub-genus 'Zinjanthropus' and retained Hominid 5 within the genus and species *Australopithecus boisei*.
Olduvai Hominid 20 has been attributed to *Australopithecus cf. boisei* until further material is available for comparison.

2. Following the discovery and preliminary evaluation of this material it was considered that this form was not an australopithecine and that sufficient evidence was available on which to create a new species of the genus *Homo* in the light of a revision of the diagnosis of the genus. This revision and a definition of the new species was given by Leakey, Tobias and Napier (1964) and Olduvai Hominid 7 was designated the type specimen (juvenile mandible, skull bones and hand bones). Hominids 4, 6, 8, 13 and 48 (formerly included in Hominid 8) were declared paratypes of the new species which was named *Homo habilis*.
A debate ensued regarding the taxonomic status of *Homo habilis* during which Leakey, Tobias and Napier vigorously defended the new species (Tobias, 1965a, 1965b, 1966a; Leakey, 1964a and b; Napier, 1965) against several others who did not believe the new species to be a valid taxon or who felt that the evidence presented

for this step was inadequate (Robinson, 1965a and b, 1966; Campbell, 1964; Oakley, 1964; Le Gros Clark, 1964). Subsequently the intensity of the debate declined but it would be premature even now to say that it is resolved (Stringer, 1985). Reassessment of the Olduvai postcranial material in the light of that from East Rudolf has led to the suggestion that the Olduvai material may well be a mixture of hominine and australopithecine bones (Day, 1976).

3. Of this group of material Hominid 9, a calvaria, was at first likened to the 'Pithecanthropines' although some resemblance to later forms was suggested (Leakey, 1961a). Later it was accepted as an example of *Homo erectus* and was so attributed (Leakey, 1971a). Detailed studies of Hominid 9 and another specimen, Hominid 12, from the later Lower Pleistocene confirm their attribution to *Homo erectus* (Rightmire, 1979). Computerized tomography of the Hominid 9 calvarium has produced serial sections of the skull that are facilitating comparisons (Maier and Nkini, 1984). Middle Pleistocene specimens (Hominids 11, 15, 22, 23, 25, 29, 51, 59) from the Upper bed at Olduvai have been studied recently. Whilst most of these specimens are fragmentary several show affinities to *Homo erectus* remains from Ternifine and Peking (*q.v.*) (Rightmire, 1980).

On the basis of the similarities between the Hominid 28 femur and those from Peking both the Hominid 28 femur and its associated pelvic fragment have been attributed to *Homo erectus* (Day, 1971). Doubts have been cast on this attribution on the grounds that the pelvic specimen is 'merely aberrant', and that the anatomical association of the femoral and the pelvic fragment has been assumed (Brain, Vrba and Robinson, 1974). Since the two specimens were recovered from the same level within one square metre of the deposit (Leakey, 1971b), a second specimen with almost identical features has been recovered from East Rudolf (Leakey, 1976) and a third from Arago (*q.v.*) (Day, 1982), the doubts may well be assuaged.

A valuable, but brief, history of the site, and the investigations performed there, has been given (Leakey, 1978).

Originals   Property of the Government of Tanzania, East Africa, housed in the National Museum, Dar-es-Salaam; at present some specimens are held at the National Museum of Kenya, Nairobi.

Casts   The Supervisor, Casting Department, National Museum of Kenya, P.O. Box 40658, Nairobi, Kenya.

Table 4   *The Olduvai Hominids*

No.	Attribution	Stratum; Locality	Remains	Date	Associated Industry
O.H. 1	H. sapiens	Intrusive burial, Bed II: RK	Complete skeleton	1913	Nil
O.H. 2	cf. H. erectus	Surface, Bed IV, MNK	Two vault fragments	1935	Inferred Acheulean
O.H. 3	cf. Australopithecus	In situ, Upper Bed II; BK	One deciduous canine One deciduous molar	1955	Developed Oldowan
O.H. 4	H. habilis	In situ, Lower Bed I and surface; MK	One molar, two broken teeth	1959	Inferred Oldowan
O.H. 5*	A. boisei	Surface, Bed I; FLK	Almost complete cranium	1959/60	Oldowan
O.H. 6	H. habilis	Surface, Middle Bed I	Two teeth, skull fragments	1959/60	Inferred Oldowan
O.H. 7*	H. habilis (type)	In situ, Middle Bed I; FLK NN	Mandible, parietals, hand bones	1960	Oldowan
O.H. 8*	H. habilis	In situ, Middle Bed I; FLK NN	Foot	1960	Oldowan
O.H. 9*	H. erectus	Surface, Upper Bed II; LLK	Calvaria	1960	Nil
O.H. 10*	?	Upper Bed I; FLK North	Terminal phalanx great toe	1961	Oldowan
O.H. 11	Homo sp.	Surface, possibly from Lower Ndutu Beds; DK	Palate and maxillary arch	1962	Nil
O.H. 12	H. erectus	Surface, Bed IV; VEK	Palate, maxillary arch and cranial fragments	1962	Inferred Acheulean
O.H. 13*	H. habilis	In situ, Lower Middle Bed II; MNK	Mandible, parietals, occipital, maxilla and many cranial fragments	1963	Oldowan
O.H. 14	?	Surface, inferred Lower Middle Bed II; MNK	?	1963	?Inferred Oldowan
O.H. 15	cf. H. erectus	In situ, Lower Middle Bed II; MNK	One worn canine, two molars	1963	Indet.
O.H. 16	?	In situ, Base Bed II; FLK Maiko Gully	Many skull fragments, upper and lower dentition	1963	Inferred Oldowan
O.H. 17	?	Surface; FLK Maiko Gully	Part of a deciduous molar	1963	Nil
O.H. 18					
O.H. 19					
O.H. 20*	A. cf. boisei	Surface, inferred Lower Bed II/Upper Bed I; HWK	Neck of femur	1959	Inferred Developed Oldowan A or Oldowan
O.H. 21	cf. H. habilis	Surface, Bed I; FLK North	Upper molar	1968	Nil
O.H. 22	cf. H. erectus	Surface, indeterminate gravel? Bed IV (VEK/MNK)	Right half of mandible	1968	Nil
O.H. 23	cf. H. erectus	In situ, Masek Beds; FLK	Left mandibular fragment	1968	Acheulean
O.H. 24*	H. habilis	Surface, Lower Bed I; DK East	Cranium with some teeth	1968	Inferred Oldowan
O.H. 25	Indet.	Surface, Bed IV; Geol. Loc. 54	Parietal fragment (juv.)	1968	Inferred Acheulean
O.H. 26	?A. boisei	Surface, Upper Bed I Lower II; FLK West	Large unworn third molar	1969	Nil
O.H. 27	cf. H. habilis	Upper Bed I; Surface HWK	Unworn third molar	1969	Inferred Developed Oldowan A
O.H. 28*	H. erectus	In situ, Bed IV; WK	Left innominate, left femoral shaft	1970	Acheulean
O.H. 29	cf. H. erectus	In situ, Bed III; JK West	Molar fragment, 2 incisors and phalanx	1969	Acheulean
O.H. 30	Indet.	Surface, Lower Bed II; Maiko Gully North	Teeth, permanent and deciduous, cranial fragments	1969	Inferred Oldowan
O.H. 31	Indet.	Surface, Upper Bed I; HWK East	Part of a molar tooth	1969	Nil
O.H. 32	Indet.	Surface, Middle Bed II; MNK	Part of a molar tooth	1969	Nil
O.H. 33	Indet.	Surface, Bed I; FLK NN	Thin skull fragments	1969	Nil
O.H. 34	Homo sp.	In situ, Bed III; JK West	Femur and part tibia shaft	1962	Acheulean
O.H. 35*	H. habilis	In situ, Middle Bed I; FLK	Tibia and fibula	1960	Oldowan
O.H. 36*	H. erectus	Bed II (Tuff IID); SC	Almost complete ulna	1970–71	?
O.H. 37	?	Surface, FLK; ex-Bed II	Left half mandible	1971	?
O.H. 38					
O.H. 39	?	Surface, ex Upper Bed I; (Matrix) HWK EE	Partial permanent and deciduous dentition	1972	Nil
O.H. 40	?	Surface, lower Bed II; FLK South	Broken molar (possibly dm²)	1972	Nil

Table 4   *The Olduvai Hominids (continued)*

No.	Attribution	Stratum; Locality	Remains	Date	Associated Industry
O.H. 41	H. habilis	In situ, lower Bed II; HWK EE	Left M¹ or M²	1972	Oldowan
O.H. 42	?	Surface, upper Bed I; HWK EE	Broken premolar	1972	Nil
O.H. 43	?	In situ, Bed I; FLK NN	2 left metatarsals	1960	Oldowan
O.H. 44	H. habilis	Surface, Bed I; FLK at site of O.H. 5	Right M¹	1970	Nil
O.H. 45	H. habilis	In situ, Bed I; FLK NN	Left germ M¹	1960	Nil
O.H. 46	cf. A. boisei	In situ, Bed I; FLK NN	Broken crown of molar or premolar	1960	Nil
O.H. 47					
O.H. 48*	?H. habilis	In situ, Middle Bed I; FLK NN	Clavicle	1960	Oldowan
O.H. 49	?H. habilis	In situ, Middle Bed I; FLK NN	Part radius shaft	1960	Oldowan
O.H. 50	?	In situ, Middle Bed I; FLK NN	Part rib shaft	1960	Oldowan
O.H. 51	cf. H. erectus	Surface, Bed III; GTC	Part left side of mandible with P₄, M₁	1974	Nil
O.H. 52	cf. H. habilis	Surface, lower Bed I; DK East	Incomplete left temporal	1969	Nil
O.H. 53	?	In situ, Middle Bed II; SHK	Shaft of right femur	1957	Developed Oldowan
O.H. 54	?	Surface, Bed I; Maiko Gully	Half lower M₁ or M₂	1969	Nil
O.H. 55	H. habilis	Surface, Bed I; FLK South	Crown of molar, weathered	1976	Nil
O.H. 56	cf. H. habilis	In situ at Site DK below Tuff IB	Three conjoining fragments of left parietal in region of bregma	1976	—
O.H. 57	?	Site HWKE. Surface, Lower Bed II, about 100 m. South of O.H. 31	Crown of lower P³ or P⁴	1977	—
O.H. 58	?	Surface of Bed I at base of JK Cliff	Lateral half of crown of unerupted premolar	1977	—
O.H. 59	?	In situ in JK Bed III	Crown of upper left central incisor	1962	—
O.H. 60	cf. A. boisei	FLK, bottom of gully	Large M3	1982	—
O.H. 61	Homo sapiens	In situ at Site MCK. Holocene	Skeleton (crouched burial)	1982	—

References   Leakey, L. S. B. (1959) A new fossil skull from Olduvai, *Nature 201*, 967–970.

Leakey, L. S. B. (1960) Recent discoveries at Olduvai Gorge. *Nature 188*, 1050–1052.

Robinson, J. T. (1960) The affinities of the new Olduvai australopithecine. *Nature 186*, 456–458.

Koenigswald, G. H. R. von, Gentner, W. and Lippolt, H. J. (1961) Age of the basalt flow at Olduvai, East Africa. *Nature 192*, 720–721.

Leakey, L. S. B. (1961a) New finds at Olduvai Gorge. *Nature 189*, 649–650.

Leakey, L. S. B. (1961b) The juvenile mandible from Olduvai. *Nature 191*, 417–418.

Leakey, L. S. B., Evernden, J. F., and Curtis, G. H. (1961) Age of Bed I, Olduvai Gorge, Tanganyika. *Nature 191*, 478–479.

Napier, J. R. (1962) Fossil hand bones from Olduvai Gorge. *Nature 196*, 409–411.

Hay, R. I. (1963) Stratigraphy of Bed I through IV, Olduvai Gorge, Tanganyika. *Science N.Y. 139*, 829–833.

Heberer, G. (1963) Uber einen neuen archanthropinen Typus aus der Oldoway Schlucht. *Z. Morph. Anthr. 53*, 171–177.

Tobias, P. V. (1963) Cranial capacity of Zinjanthropus and other australopithecines. *Nature 197*, 743–746.

Campbell, B. G. (1964) Just another man-ape? *Discovery* (June issue).

Clark, W. E. Le Gros (1964) Letter. *Discovery* (July issue).

Davis, P. R. (1964) Hominid fossil from Bed I, Olduvai Gorge, Tanganyika. A tibia and fibula. *Nature 201*, 967–970.

Day, M. H. and Napier, J. R. (1964) Hominid fossils from Bed I, Olduvai Gorge, Tanganyika. Fossil foot bones. *Nature 201*, 967–970.

Leakey, L. S. B. (1964a) Letter. *Discovery* (August issue).

Leakey, L. S. B. (1964b) Letter. *Discovery* (October issue).

Leakey, L. S. B. and Leakey, M. D. (1964) Recent discoveries of fossil hominids in Tanganyika; at Olduvai and near Lake Natron. *Nature 202*, 5–7.

Leakey, L. S. B., Tobias, P. V. and Napier, J. R. (1964) A new species of the genus *Homo* from Olduvai Gorge. *Nature 202*, 7–9.

Napier, J. R. (1964) Five steps to man. *Discovery* (June issue).

Oakley, K. P. (1964) Letter. *Discovery* (September issue).

Tobias, P. V. (1964a) Letter. *Discovery* (September issue).

Tobias, P. V. (1964b) The Olduvai Bed I hominine with special reference to its cranial capacity. *Nature 202*, 3–4.

Tobias, P. V. and Koenigswald, G. H. R. Von (1964) Comparison between the Olduvai hominines and those of Java and some implications for hominid phylogeny. *Nature 204*, 515–518.

Holloway, R. L. (1965) Cranial capacity of the hominine from Olduvai, Bed I. *Nature 208*, 205–206.

Leakey, L. S. B. (1965) *Olduvai Gorge 1951–1961, Vol. 1*. Cambridge University Press.

Napier, J. R. (1965) Curr. Anthrop. Comment. *Curr. Anthrop. 6*, 402–403.

Robinson, J. T. (1965a) *Homo 'habilis'* and the australopithecines. *Nature 205*, 121–124.

Robinson, J. T. (1965b) Curr. Anthrop. Comment. *Curr. Anthrop 6*, 403–406.

Tobias, P. V. (1965a) New discoveries in Tanganyika: their bearing on hominid evolution. *Curr. Anthrop 6*, 391–399.

Tobias, P. V. (1965b) New discoveries in Tanganyika: their bearing on hominid evolution. Curr. Anthrop. comment. *Curr. Anthrop. 6*, 406–411.

Tobias, P. V. (1965c) Cranial capacity of the hominine from Olduvai, Bed I. *Nature 208*, 206.

Day, M. H. and Napier, J. R. (1966) A hominid toe bone from Bed I, Olduvai Gorge, Tanzania. *Nature 211*, 929–930.

Leakey, M. D. (1966) A review of the Oldowan culture from Olduvai Gorge, Tanzania. *Nature 210*, 462–466.

Robinson, J. T. (1966) The distinctiveness of *Homo habilis*. *Nature 209*, 957–960.

Tobias, P. V. (1966a) The distinctiveness of *Homo habilis*. *Nature 209*, 953–957.

Tobias, P. V. (1966b) Cranial capacity of the Olduvai Bed I hominine. *Nature 210*, 1108–1109.

Day, M. H. (1967) Olduvai Hominid 10: a multivariate analysis. *Nature 215*, 323–324.

Tobias, P. V. (1967) *Olduvai Gorge, Vol. 2*. Cambridge: Cambridge University Press.

Tobias, P. V. (1968) Cranial capacity in anthropoid apes, *Australopithecus* and *Homo habilis*, with comments on skewed samples. *S. Afr. J. Sci. 64*, 81–91.

Day, M. H. (1969) Femoral fragment of a robust australopithecine from Olduvai Gorge, Tanzania. *Nature 221*, 230–233.

Day, M. H. (1971) Postcranial remains of *Homo erectus* from Bed IV, Olduvai Gorge, Tanzania. *Nature 232*, 383–387.

Leakey, M. D. (1971a) *Olduvai Gorge, Vol. 3*. Cambridge: Cambridge University Press.

Leakey, M. D. (1971b) Discovery of postcranial remains of *Homo erectus* and associated artefacts in Bed IV at Olduvai Gorge, Tanzania. *Nature 232,* 380–383.

Leakey, M. D., Clarke, R. J. and Leakey, L. S. B. (1971) New hominid skull from Bed I, Olduvai Gorge, Tanzania. *Nature 232,* 308–312.

Tobias, P. V. (1971) *The Brain in Hominid Evolution.* New York: Columbia University Press.

Robinson, J. T. (1972) *Early Hominid Posture and Locomotion.* Chicago: Chicago University Press.

Holloway, R. L. (1973) New endocranial values for the East African early hominids. *Nature 243,* 97–99.

Kleindienst, M. R. (1973) Excavations at Site J.K.2, Olduvai Gorge, Tanzania, 1961–1962: the geological setting. *Quaternia 17,* 145–208.

Brain, C. K., Vrba, E. S. and Robinson, J. T. (1974) A new hominid innominate bone from Swartkrans. *Ann. Transv. Mus. 29,* 55–63.

Day, M. H. (1976) Hominid postcranial material from Bed I, Olduvai Gorge. In *Perspectives on Human Evolution Vol. III: Human Origins,* 363–374. Eds. G. L. Isaac, and E. R. McCown, Menlo Park, Cal: W. A. Benjamin Inc.

Hay, R. L. (1976) *Geology of the Olduvai Gorge: a study of the Sedimentation in a Semiarid Basin.* Berkeley: University of California Press.

Leakey, R. E. F. and Findlater, I. (1976) New hominid fossils from the Koobi Fora Formation in Northern Kenya. *Nature 261,* 574–6.

Gentry, A. W. and Gentry, A. (1978) The Bovidae (Mammalia) of Olduvai Gorge, Tanzania. Parts 1 and 2. *Bull. Br. Mus. (Nat. Hist.) 29,* 289–446; *30,* 1–83.

Hay, R. L. (1978) Olduvai Gorge: stratigraphy, age and environments. In *Geological Background to Fossil Man.* Ed. W. W. Bishop.

Leakey, M. D. (1978) Olduvai fossil hominids: their stratigraphic positions and associations. In *Early Hominids of Africa,* 3–16. Ed. C. T. Jolly. Duckworth.

Leakey, M. D. (1978) Olduvai Gorge 1911–75: a history of the investigations. In *Geological Background to Fossil Man,* 151–155. Ed. W. W. Bishop. Edinburgh: Scottish Academic Press.

Rightmire, G. P. (1979) Cranial remains of *Homo erectus* from Beds II and IV, Olduvai Gorge, Tanzania. *Am. J. phys. Anthrop. 51,* 99–116.

Susman, R. L. and Creel, N. (1979) Functional and morphological affinities of the subadult hand (OH 7) from Olduvai Gorge. *Am. J. phys. Anthrop. 51,* 311–332.

Susman, R. L. and Stern, J. T. (1979) Telemetered electromyography of flexor digitorum profundus and flexor digitorum superficialis in *Pan troglodytes* and implications for interpretation of the OH 7 hand. *Am. J. phys. Anthrop. 50,* 565–574.

Rightmire, G. P. (1980) Middle Pleistocene hominids from Olduvai Gorge, Northern Tanzania. *Am. J. phys. Anthrop. 53,* 225–241.

Bunn, H. T. (1981) Archaeological evidence for meat-eating by Plio-Pleistocene hominids from Koobi Fora and Olduvai Gorge. *Nature 291,* 574–577.

Potts, R. and Shipman, P. (1981) Cutmarks made by stone tools on bones from Olduvai Gorge, Tanzania. *Nature 291,* 557–580.

Wolpoff, M. H. (1981) Cranial capacity estimates for Olduvai Hominid 7. *Am. J. phys. Anthrop. 56,* 297–304.

Susman, R. L. and Stern, J. T. (1982) Functional morphology of *Homo habilis. Science 217,* 931–934.

Andrews, P. (1983) Small mammal faunal diversity at Olduvai Gorge,

Tanzania. In *Animals and Archaeology: 1. Hunters and Their Prey*, 77–85. Ed. J. Clutton-Brock and C. Grigson. Oxford: BAR Internat. Series 163.

Bonnefille, R. (1984) Palynological research at Olduvai Gorge. *Res. Reps.* 17, Washington: National Geographic Society.

Maier, W. and Nkini, A. (1984) Olduvai Hominid 9: new results of investigation. *Cour. Forsch. Inst. Senck.* 69, 123–130.

Vaisnys, J. R., Lieberman, D. and Pilbeam, D. (1984) An alternative method of estimating the cranial capacity of Olduvai Hominid 7. *Am. J. phys. Anthrop.* 65, 71–81.

The Laetoli Remains

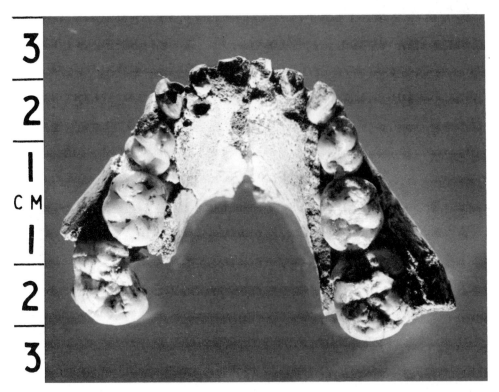

Fig. 61. The Laetoli Hominid 2 juvenile mandible and dentition (occlusal view). *Courtesy of Dr M. D. Leakey.*

Synonyms and other names
1. *Cf. Homo* sp. (Leakey, M.D., Hay, Curtis, Jackes and White, 1976); *Australopithecus afarensis* (Johanson, White and Coppens, 1978); *Homo antiquus* (Ferguson, 1984).
2. Hominidae. Genus and *sp.* indet. (Leakey and Hay, 1979).
3. *Homo sapiens* (Day, Leakey and Magori, 1980).

Site
Laetoli, southern Serengeti Plains, northern Tanzania, 20–30 miles from the camp-site at Olduvai Gorge.

Found by
Dr Mary Leakey and her co-workers, 1974–1975.

Geology
1. Recent work on the geology of the Laetoli area has shown that the Laetolil Beds (formerly referred to variously as the Garusi or Vogel River series) proved to be far thicker than previously recog-

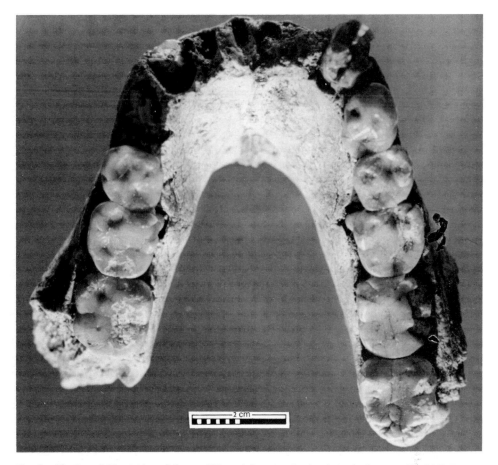

Fig. 62. The Laetoli Hominid 4 adult mandible and dentition (occlusal view). *Courtesy of Dr M. D. Leakey.*

nized. The lavas and agglomerates noted by Kent (1941) overlie an irregular surface deeply eroded into the Laetolil Beds. The 130 m section of the Laetolil Beds is divisible into an upper half, three quarters of which consists of aeolian tuff, and a lower half consisting of interbedded 'air-fall' and aeolian tuff with minor conglomerate and breccia. Nearly all of the hominid remains and most of the faunal remains come from the uppermost 44 to 59 m of the aeolian tuffs.

2. More than 50 widespread air fall tuffs have been recognized in the Laetolil Beds; one of these tuffs (Tuff 7; the Footprint Tuff) is divisible into two units of differing lithology. Tuff 7 is the site of numerous animal footprints preserved by the cementation of composite ash falls of carbonatite ash and melilite lava globules. Footprints were made on at least ten differing surfaces (Hay and Leakey, 1982).

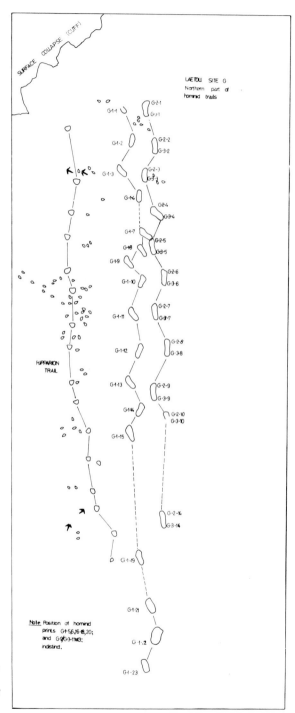

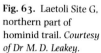

Fig. 63. Laetoli Site G, northern part of hominid trail. *Courtesy of Dr M. D. Leakey.*

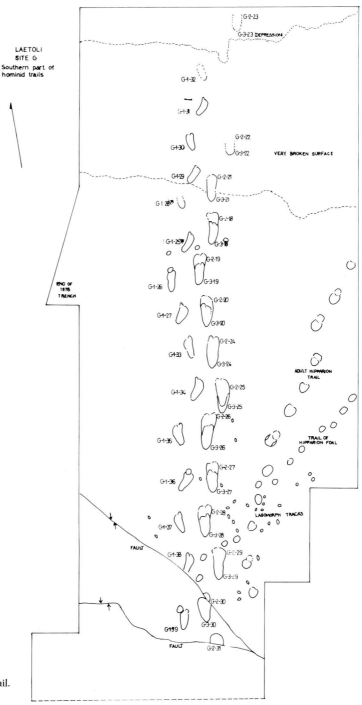

Fig. 64. Laetoli Site G,
southern part of hominid trail.
Courtesy of Dr M. D. Leakey.

3. The Ngaloba Beds overlie the vogesite lavas which separate them from the underlying Ndolanya and Laetolil Beds. The Ngaloba Beds are stream deposits of sandstone and claystone, only patches of which are preserved; they consist of redeposited detritus eroded from the underlying Ndolanya and Laetolil Beds (Day, Leakey and Magori, 1980).

Associated finds   1. No stone tools have been recovered from this site up to the present. Fossils have been recovered in the area on several occasions, including a hominid fragment, by Kohl-Larsen in 1938–1939. Later, discrepancies were noted in the fauna by Dietrich (1942) and Maglio (1969) who both suggested two faunal assemblages of differing ages. In the recent work fossils from the Laetolil Beds were noted as being distinctively coloured and of a chalky texture. Representatives of vertebrate groups, assigned to these Beds include bovids, lagomorphs, giraffids, rhinocerotids, equids, suids, proboscidians, rodents and carnivores. Some genera have now been excluded from former lists given by Dietrich (*op. cit.*) and Hopwood (in Leakey, 1951); these include *Theropithecus*, *Tragelaphus*, *Equus* and *Phacochoerus*.

2. No stone tools have been recovered from the Footprint Tuff. An extensive fauna has been identified from the preserved footprints including proboscidians, chalicotheres, birds, monkeys, carnivores, equids, rhinoceroses, suids, giraffids, bovids and hominids. The presence of these records of the fauna in solidified ash ensures the contemporaneity of the faunal assemblage.

3. The stone tools found in the Upper Ngaloba Beds include 392 artefacts both *in situ* and on the surface. The industry is attributed to the Middle Stone Age cultural complex similar to that recovered from the Lake Eyasi foreshore and from the Upper Ndutu Beds at Olduvai Gorge.

The faunal remains include reptilian, avian and mammalian fossils, none of which are from extinct forms.

Dating   1. Stratigraphically the Laetolil Beds underlie Bed I and Bed II, Olduvai Gorge. Potassium-argon dating of a series of suitable deposits from the site established the age of the upper fossiliferous part of the Laetolil Beds at 3·6–3·75 m.y. B.P.

2. The dating of the Footprint Tuff is given as the same as that of the Laetolil Beds of which it forms a part, 3·6–3·75 m.y. B.P.

3. The Upper Ngaloba Beds at Laetoli contain a vitric tuff which is trachytic and contains the pyroclastic minerals biotite and anorthoclase; it has been tentatively correlated with the marker tuff in the lower unit of the Ndutu Beds at Olduvai Gorge. This is the only trachytic tuff younger than Bed III Olduvai Gorge and its age is estimated at 120,000 ± 30,000 years B.P.

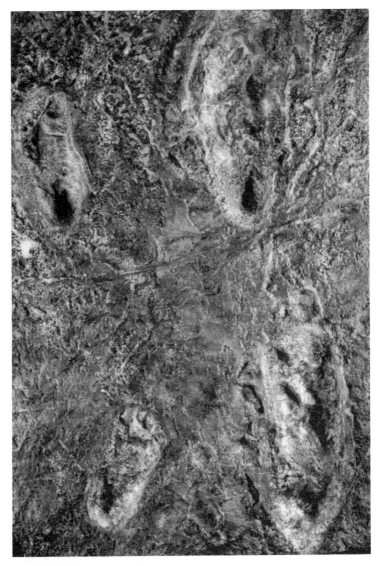

Fig. 65. Hominid footprints at Site G, Laetoli. Left side prints G-1-35 and G-1-36; right side prints at G-2-3-26 and G-2-3-27. *Photograph of a cast.*

Morphology   1. Thirty new hominid specimens were recovered from the Laetoli site between 1935 and 1979; the remains include mandibles, maxillae, isolated teeth and a juvenile partial skeleton.

L.H.2

This specimen consists of the body of the mandible of an infant and contains part of both the permanent and deciduous dentitions. The mandibular symphysis is incompletely fused in the specimen and both of the rami are missing. The symphysial region shows a concave *planum alveolare* and an incipient superior transverse torus.

The deciduous incisors are unknown but the right deciduous canine is present as a damaged but sharp conical tooth; the lower first deciduous molar has four or five main cusps and a lingually directed anterior fovea; the lower second deciduous molar has a sixth cusp. The lower first permanent molar is square with five cusps present.

L.H.4

This specimen consists of the body and part of the dentition of an adult mandible. The rami are missing. Much of the anterior dentition has been lost post-mortem except for the right lateral incisor which appears to have been lost during life. There seems to be evidence of periodontal disease in relation to this tooth and several others. The teeth appear to have been arranged in an evenly rounded dental arcade and there is development of both superior and inferior transverse tori. The basal contour of the body of the mandible is wide with marked lateral eversion posteriorly. The lower first premolars have large buccal cusps and weak lingual cusps placed obliquely giving the tooth an irregular shape; the lower second premolars are square with buccal and lingual cusps and moderate talonids. The lower molars increase in size progressively from the first to the third and show a square occlusal outline with five cusps and no trace of a sixth cusp. The fissure pattern is Y_5.

A suggestion that the younger Laetolil hominid had a unique anterior dental cutting complex (Wolpoff, 1979) has been denied (White, 1981a). A hominid canine from Laetoli found by L. S. B. Leakey and held by the British Museum (Natural History) has been recognized and assigned to *Australopithecus afarensis* (White, 1981b). A study of dental microwear including specimens from Laetoli indicates dental wear similar to that of baboons; dietary and behavioural parallels are suggested (Puech and Albertine, 1984). These specimens have been described in detail (White, 1977). Additional specimens have been recovered between 1976 and 1979 including a number of teeth, mandibular fragments and maxillary fragments as well as an immature partial skeleton. This unusual specimen includes the cranial, dental and postcranial remains of an infant or very young child. All the new specimens have been described in detail (White, 1980).

2. Two groups of hominid footprint trails from sites (A) and (G). Those from site (A) are not hominid and should be discounted, but those from site (G) are unequivocally bipedal hominid footprints. The site (G) trails include the tracks of three individuals: one small,

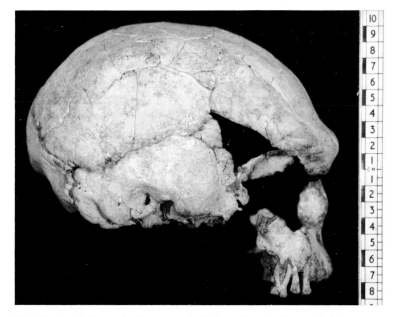

Fig. 66. Laetoli Hominid 18 cranium (right lateral view). *Photographed by courtesy of Dr M. D. Leakey.*

on the left, and one large on the right; the third individual's prints are to be found superimposed on those of the larger individual on the right. Details of the footprints, as analysed by photogrammetry, have been given and comparisons drawn with modern human experimental footprints (Day and Wickens, 1980; Day, 1985).

These studies conclude that the form of the foot, and the mechanism of force and weight transference through the foot during bipedal walking, are remarkably similar to those of the modern human habitually unshod.

3. The Laetoli Hominid 18 skull is almost complete and includes the bones of the vault, much of the base, both temporal bones, part of the sphenoid and much of the face including the palate and part of the upper dentition. There are some signs of post-mortem deformation of the vault. The skull shows marked recession of the forehead, a rounded occiput and a small mastoid process. The supraorbital torus is divided, the frontal bone is very slightly keeled and there are some mid-parietal swellings. On the right there is a prominent occipitomastoid crest (Day, Leakey and Magori; Magori and Day, 1983a; Magori and Day, 1983b).

Dimensions   1. To be found in White (1977, 1980).

2. Av. footprint length of smallest individual 185

Av. footprint length of one of larger individuals 215
Av. stride length of smallest individual 387.
Av. stride length of one of larger individuals 472
(Leakey and Hay, 1979).
Stature estimates

Smaller	1·15–1·34 m
Larger	1·34–1·54 m

(White, 1980)

LH 18

Magori and Day (1983)
3. *Skull*

Max. length 205	Max. breadth 140
Cranial Index 68·2	Cranial Capacity 1200 cc

Affinities   1. In the preliminary description it was suggested that the Laetoli specimens represent one group of hominids only and that the variation shown in the sample is either individual or sexual in origin. Some similarities to the South African gracile *Australopithecus africanus* material have been noted as well as some to specimens attributed to the genus *Homo* from Koobi Fora. Marked differences are suggested between the Laetoli material and robust australopithecine specimens from both East and South Africa. In addition some similarities are claimed for the Laetoli hominids to specimens of *Homo* from both East Africa and Asia (Leakey, M. D. *et al.*, 1976). Later all of the Laetoli hominids were included within a new species, *Australopithecus afarensis*, the type specimen of which has been designated from this collection; it is the mandible LH 4. Other specimens included within this new taxon have been found at Hadar in Ethiopia (*q.v.*) as well as two specimens referred to as *Meganthropus africanus* also from Laetoli (Johanson *et al.*, 1978). Owing to nomenclatural and taxonomic procedural irregularities resulting from the prior, but valid, publication of the new name by a journalist, LH 4 is a lectotype and the type series are paralectotypes, since a holotype can only be designated in the original publication of a new taxon (Day, Leakey, M. D. and Olson, 1980). These nomenclatural and taxonomic criticisms have been rejected, but without debate (White, Johanson and Kimbel, 1981).

The taxonomic position of the Laetoli hominids is unclear since it is now mixed with that of the Hadar hominids (*q.v.*) which are more numerous and provide better opportunities for anatomical appraisal and taxonomic judgement. On the other hand, the Laetoli hominids are a little older and the Laetolil Beds also contain the footprints (*vide infra*). The problem of australopithecine taxonomy and relationships will be discussed in more detail elsewhere (p. 405).

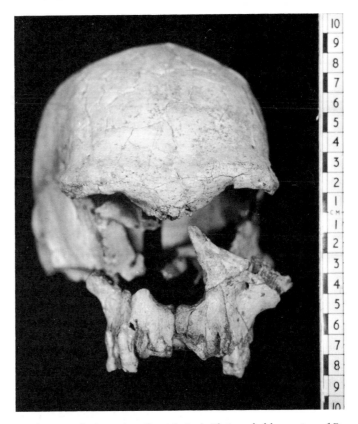

Fig. 67. Laetoli Hominid 18 cranium (frontal view). *Photographed by courtesy of Dr M. D. Leakey.*

2. It is very hard indeed to attribute affinities to the creatures who made the footprint trails; other than to say that they were clearly made by upright bipedal creatures capable of weight and force transference to the ground in an extraordinarily human-like manner (Day and Wickens, 1980; Day, 1985). Secondly, their stature may be calculated from footprint measurements and the application of formulae (White, 1980) and thirdly that gait analysis indicates short strides relative to stature and on this occasion a 'strolling' walking speed consistent with a modern human pattern of gait (Charteris, Wall and Nottrodt, 1981).

These characteristics of stance and gait are indeed those of hominids, but it must be remembered that definitions of hominid taxa themselves often contain these attributes as criteria. Footprints are acceptable as evidence of both behaviour and morphology, and this evidence points to members of the Family Hominidae as being responsible for the Laetoli trails. Whether they belong to the genus *Australopithecus* or to the genus *Homo* is uncertain at present.

Table 5   *Fossil Hominid Remains from Laetoli*

Specimen Numbers	Year Found	Parts Found	Localities	Stratigraphic Position	Discoverers
B.M.N.H.: M.42323	1935	Left lower canine	Unknown	Presumed surface of Laetoli Beds	Member of L. S. B. Leakey's expedition
Garusi I	1939	Right maxillary frag. P³– P⁴	Unknown	Presumed surface of Laetolil Beds	Member of Kohl-Larsen's expedition
Garusi II	1939	Left M³	Unknown	Presumed surface of Laetolil Beds	Member of Kohl-Larsen's expedition
L.H. 1	1974	Right P⁴	Loc. 1	Surface, Laetolil Beds, ca. 1·2 m. above Tuff 7	M. Mwoka
L.H. 2	1974	Juvenile mandible	Loc. 3	*In situ*, ca. 0·5 m. above Tuff 7	M. Muluila
L.H. 3 a–t	1974–75	Partial upper and lower dentitions	Loc. 7	*In situ*, between Tuffs 7 and 8	M. Mwoka
L.H. 4	1974	Adult mandible	Loc. 7	Surface, Laetolil Beds, 1·2 m. below Tuff 7	M. Muluila
L.H. 5	1974	Right maxillary frag. I²– M¹	Loc. 8	Surface, Laetolil Beds, ca. 1·8 m. below Tuff 7	M. Muluila
L.H. 6 a–e	1974–75	Partial upper and lower dentition	Loc. 7	*In situ*, ca. 0·5 m above Tuff 7	M. Mwoka
L.H. 7	1975	Right M¹ or M² fragment	Loc. 5	Surface, Laetolil Beds, ca. 0·6 m. above Tuff 5	M. Mwoka
L.H. 8	1975	Right M² and M³	Loc. 11	Surface, Laetolil Beds, ca. 0·9 m. above Tuff 7	E. Kandindi
L.H. 9	1975	Invalid, part of L.H. 3/6 dentition	—	—	—
L.H. 10	1975	Left mandibular fragment	Loc. 10W	Surface, Laetolil Beds, 5·5 m. below Tuff 3	E. Kandindi
L.H. 11	1975	Left M²	Loc. 10W	Surface, Laetolil Beds, 7·3 m. below Tuff 3	E. Kandindi
LH.12	1975	Left M³ fragment	Loc. 5	Surface, Laetolil Beds, 1·8 m. below Tuff	E. Kandindi
L.H. 13	1975	Right mandibular fragment	Loc. 8	Surface, Laetolil Beds, ca. 3 m. below Tuff 7	M. Jackes
L.H. 14 a–k	1975–76	Partial lower dentition	Loc. 19	Surface, Laetolil Beds, ca. 3 m. above Tuff 5	E. Kandindi
L.H. 15	1976	Left M₃	Loc. 1	Surface, Laetolil Beds, 9 m. above Tuff 8	Mrs Luce
L.H. 16	1976	Left M₁	Loc. 6	Surface, Laetolil Beds, just below Tuff 6	L. Kangiran
L.H. 17	1976	Left M¹ or M²	Loc. 9	Surface, between Tuffs 5 and 8	A. Mwongela
L.H. 18	1976	Cranium, *H. sapiens*	Loc. 2 South	*In situ*, Upper Ngaloba Beds (Pleistocene)	E. Kandindi
L.H. 19	1976	Left M₂	Loc. 8	Surface, Laetolil Beds, between Tuffs 5 and 6	M. Mwoka
L.H. 20	1976	Invalid (cercopithecoid incisor)	—	—	—
L.H. 21	1976	Partial immature skeleton	Loc. 12E	Surface, Laetolil Beds, between Tuffs 6 and 7	M. Mwoka
L.H. 22	1977	Right P⁴, M¹ (same individual as L.H. 8)	Loc. 11	Surface, Laetoli Beds, ca. 0·9 m. above Tuff 7	E. Kandindi
L.H. 23	1978	Left M₂	Loc. 8	Surface, Laetolil Beds, ca. 1·3 m. below Tuff 7	M. Mwoka
L.H. 24	1978	Left P₃	Loc. 10E	Surface, Laetolil Beds, ca. 2 m. below Tuff 7	E. Kandindi
L.H. 25	1978	Right P₃	Loc. 2	Surface, Laetolil Beds, just above Tuff 6	M. Mwoka
L.H. 26	1978	Right M²	Loc. 6	Surface, Laetolil Beds, ca. 3·7 m. below Tuff 7	J. Masovo
L.H. 27	1979	Right M³ (same individual as L.H. 5)	Loc. 8	Surface, Laetolil Beds, ca. 2 m. below Tuff 7	N. Mbuika
L.H. 28	1979	Right M² (same individual as L.H. 5)	Loc. 8	Surface, Laetolil Beds, ca. 2 m. below Tuff 7	P. Sila
L.H. 29	1979	Left mandibular fragment, M₁–M₃, *Homo* cf. *erectus*	Loc. 8	Surface, lower part of exposures, near Garusi river (Pleistocene)	M. Mwoka
L.H. 30	1975	Left dec. upper canine, synonymous with 3/6 (c)	Loc. 7	Surface, Laetolil Beds, probably between Tuffs 6 and 8	Member of M. D. Leakey's expedition

3. The affinities of the Laetoli Hominid 18 skull lie clearly with archaic *Homo sapiens*. Its morphology is largely modern yet it retains some archaic features. It is quite unlike *Homo erectus* or Neandertal crania having its greatest similarities to other archaic sapient crania from Africa such as the Eyasi, Kabwe (*q.v.*) and Omo I (*q.v.*) skulls. LH18 is a good example of the mosaic evolutionary process in hominid evolution.

Originals 1. At present being studied at the National Museum of Kenya, Nairobi, to be housed with 3 in the National Museum of Tanzania, Dar-es-Salaam.

Casts Available from the Casting Director National Museum of Kenya, Nairobi, Kenya.

References Kent, P. E. (1941) The recent history and Pleistocene deposits of the plateau north of Lake Eyasi, Tanganyika. *Geol. Mag. Lond. 78*, 173–184.

Dietrich, W. O. (1942) Altestquartäre Saügetiere aus der südleichen Serengeti Deutsche-Ostafrika. *Palaeontographica 94A*, 43–133.

Hopwood, A. T. (1951) The Olduvai Fauna. In L. S. B. Leakey, *Olduvai Gorge*, 20–24. Cambridge: Cambridge University Press.

Maglio, V. J. (1969) The status of the East African elephant '*Archidiskodon exoptatus*' Dietrich 1942. *Breviosa 336*, 1–25.

Leakey, M. D., Hay, R. I., Curtis, G. H., Drake, R. E., Jackes, M. K. and White, T. D. (1976) Fossil hominids from the Laetolil Beds. *Nature 262*, 460–66.

White, T. D. (1977) New fossil hominids from Laetoli, Tanzania. *Am. J. phys. Anthrop. 46*, 197–229.

Johanson, D. C., White, T. D. and Coppens, Y. (1978) A new species of the genus *Australopithecus* (Primates: Hominidae) from the Pliocene of Eastern Africa. *Kirtlandia, 28*, 1–14.

Johanson, D. C. and White, T. D. (1979) A systematic assessment of early African hominids. *Science 202*, 321–330.

Leakey, M. D. and Hay, R. L. (1979) Pliocene footprints in the Laetolil Beds at Laetoli, northern Tanzania. *Nature 278*, 317–323.

Wolpoff, M. H. (1979) Anterior dental cutting in the Laetolil hominids and the evolution of the bicuspid P3. *Am. J. phys. Anthrop. 51*, 233–234.

Day, M. H., Leakey, M. D. and Magori, C. (1980) A new hominid fossil skull (LH 18) from the Ngaloba Beds, Laetoli, northern Tanzania. *Nature 284*, 55–56.

Day, M. H. and Wickens, E. H. (1980) Laetoli Pliocene hominid footprints and bipedalism. *Nature 286*, 385–387.

White, T. D. (1980) Evolutionary implications of Pliocene hominid footprints. *Science 208*, 175–176.

Charteris, J., Wall, J. C. and Nottrodt, J. W. (1981) Functional reconstruction of gait from the Pliocene hominid footprints at Laetoli, northern Tanzania. *Nature 290*, 496–498.

White, T. D. (1981a) On the evidence for 'Anterior Dental Cutting' in Laetoli hominids. *Am. J. phys. Anthrop. 54*, 107–108.

White, T. D. (1981b) Primitive hominid canine from Tanzania. *Science 213*, 348–349.

White, T. D., Johanson, D. C. and Kimbel, W. H. (1981) *Australopithecus africanus*: its phyletic position reconsidered. *S. Afr. J. Sci. 77*, 445–470.

Hay, R. L. and Leakey, M. D. (1982) The fossil footprints of Laetoli. *Sci. Am.* 246, 50–57.

Magori, C. C. and Day, M. H. (1983a) Laetoli Hominid 18: an early *Homo sapiens* skull. *J. hum. Evol.* 12, 747–753.

Magori, C. C. and Day, M. H. (1983b) An early *Homo sapiens* skull from the Ngaloba Beds, Laetoli, northern Tanzania. *Anthropus*, 10, 143–183.

Ferguson, W. W. (1984) Revision of fossil hominid jaws from the Plio/ Pleistocene of Hadar, in Ethiopia including a new species of the genus *Homo* (Hominoidea: Homininae). *Primates* 25, 519–529.

Puech, P.-F. and Albertini, H. (1984) Dental microwear and mechanisms in early hominids from Laetoli and Hadar. *Am. J. phys. Anthrop.* 65, 87– 91.

Day, M. H. (1985) Hominid locomotion—from Taung to the Laetoli footprints. In *Hominid Evolution: Past, Present and Future*. Ed. P. V. Tobias. New York: Alan R. Liss.

The Koobi Fora Remains

KENYA   KOOBI FORA

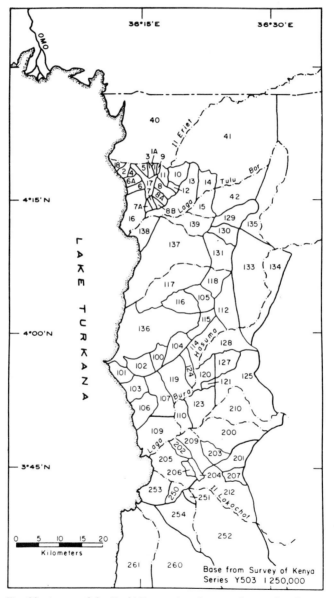

Fig. 68. A map of the Koobi Fora region showing the numbered areas in which finds have been made. *Courtesy of Professor F. H. Brown and C. S. Feibel.*

Synonyms and other names	*Australopithecus cf. boisei* (Leakey, 1970); *Australopithecus sp.* (Leakey, 1971); *Homo sp.* (Leakey, 1971); *Homo ergaster* (Groves and Mazák, 1975); *Homo erectus* (Leakey, 1976).
Site	In north-east Kenya to the east of Lake Turkana. The area was formerly known as East Rudolf but is now called the Koobi Fora region. The research area extends from Ileret in the north to Allia Bay in the south, and from the shores of the lake in the.west to the Miocene volcanic hills in the east; a total of 1,000 sq kms. The research area has been subdivided into numbered areas each corresponding to an area of exposure of fossiliferous sediments.
Found by	The East Rudolf Research Project, after 1975 renamed the Koobi Fora Research Project, led by R. E. F. Leakey and the late G. L. Isaac.
Geology	The basin of Lake Turkana appears to be of great antiquity and basement rocks are exposed only in the extreme north-east portion of the study area. On these there rests a long succession of Miocene to early Pliocene volcanics and sediments, some of which are fossiliferous. Downwarping along the axis now occupied by the lake led to the deposition of a long series of late Pliocene to early Pleistocene sedimentary beds which are interspersed with volcanic tuffs. At the basin margins these sediments lap against unwarped hills formed by rocks of the earlier volcanic series. A series of papers devoted to the geology of the Turkana basin is to be found in Bishop (1978).
	The lithostratigraphic nomenclature of the Koobi Fora region has been revised recently. As redefined the Koobi Fora Formation encompasses the entire Plio-Pleistocene sedimentary sequence and is subdivided into eight members. These members are defined using volcanic tuff horizons that have been identified chemically and often correlated with tuff horizons such as those known from the Shungura Formation in the Omo region (*q.v.*) or from West Turkana (*q.v.*) within the Lake Turkana basin. Correlations with more distant tuffaceous deposits have also been made, such as those from Hadar (*q.v.*) and deep sea cores from the Gulf of Aden (Brown *et al.*, 1985; Brown and Feibel, in press).
	The new nomenclature seems likely to supersede that formerly used since it corrects errors in previous correlations.
	The sedimentary sequence at Koobi Fora attains an aggregate thickness of 560 m and spans a period from about 4·3 to 0·6 m.y. B.P. The members of the Koobi Fora Formation are defined as those sediments between the base of one designated tuff and the base of the next. Each member takes its name from the tuff at its base.
Associated finds	Stone tools are known from several sites within the research area. A series of core tools, cobbles and flakes identified as belonging to

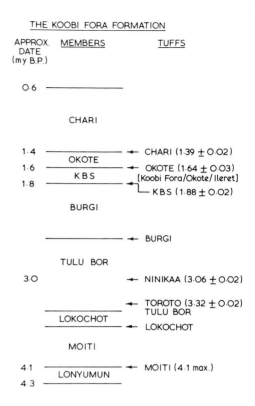

Fig. 69. The Koobi Fora Formation including the names of its members, their approximate time ranges and the dates that are known for its tuffs (*After Brown & Feibel, In Press*).

the Oldowan industry have been recovered from the KBS tuff itself and another industry known as the Karari Industry has also been described from the area (Leakey, 1970; Isaac *et al.*, 1971; Isaac, 1976a; Isaac *et al.*, 1976; Harris and Isaac, 1976).

One archaeological excavation has revealed an occupation site beside a water course with evidence of butchery from cut marks on bones; conjoined flakes and conjoined animal bone fragments suggest meat-eating and food transport. The site is dated to 1·5–1·6 m.y. B.P. (Bunn *et al.*, 1980).

The fossil ungulates, proboscidea, perissodactyla and the suids have been described in detail (Harris, 1983). The cercopithecoid monkeys and other faunae of the Turkana Basin document possible palaeoenvironmental changes (Leakey, M., 1980; Harris, 1983) whilst the mollusc fauna of the same area has made a contribution to the debate concerning the gradualism versus punctuated equilibrium model of biological evolution (Williamson, 1981). The ancient flora of the region has been studied through pollen analysis; the vegetation of the palaeoenvironment of the past 4·5 m.y. B.P. has been reconstructed (Bonnefille, 1976; Bonnefille and Vincens, 1977, 1980).

Fig. 70. The KNM–ER 406 cranium (left lateral view).

Dating   The dating of the site is based upon stratigraphic, faunal, palaeomagnetic and radiometric data. The sequence of deposits from the
oldest to the youngest is nowhere complete, but sections of the
sequence can be correlated by the tuffs (Brown and Cerling, 1982;
Brown *et al.*, 1985) and the fossils contained in the sediments
between these layers (Harris, 1983). The ages of the tuffs between
the sedimentary units are gradually being determined. One, the KBS
tuff, was the subject of controversy (Fitch and Miller, 1970, 1976;
Curtis *et al.*, 1975; Cerling *et al.*, 1979). Work has continued on
the stratigraphy at Koobi Fora and its correlation with the layers in
the Lower Omo Valley. It corrects previous identification and mapping errors at Koobi Fora (Brown and Cerling, 1982; Cerling and
Brown, 1982). This work accounts for much of the 'missing' sediment from a previously published stratigraphic column (Fitch, Findlater, Watkins and Miller, 1974).

Dated Tuffs at Koobi Fora

Names	Millions of years B.P.
CHARI	$1·39 \pm 0·02$
KOOBI FORA/OKOTE/ILERET	$1·64 \pm 0·03$
MALBE	$1·86 \pm 0·02$
KBS	$1·88 \pm 0·02$
BURGI	—
INGUMWAI	—
HASUMA	—

NINIKAA	3.06 ± 0.03
ALLIA	—
TOROTO	3.32 ± 0.02
TULU BOR	—
LOKOCHOT	—
MOITI	4.1 (max)

After McDougall (1985); McDougall *et al.* (1985)

It is of interest to note perhaps (for those who put faith only in chemical or physical dating methods) that it was faunal discrepancies between the two sites (the Omo and Koobi Fora) that alerted geochronologists to the problem of the dating of the KBS tuff (Howell and Petter, 1976; Cooke, 1976; White and Harris, 1977). On the other hand it is modern chemical analysis, including trace element profiles, that has shown previous field identifications and correlations to be in error.

The magnetostratigraphy of the lower part of the Koobi Fora

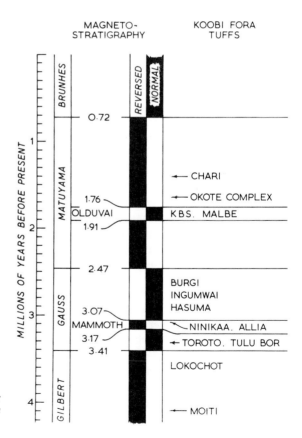

Fig. 71. The Koobi Fora tuffs and their magnetostratigraphy (*After Hillhouse et al; in press*)

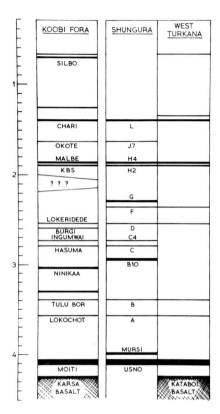

Fig. 72. The Koobi Fora, Shungura (Omo) and West Turkana tuff correlations within the Lake Turkana Basin (*After
Brown et al.;* 1985).

Formation (Hillhouse *et al.*, in press) coupled with the radiometric
dates (McDougall, 1985; McDougall *et al.*, 1985) and the correlations obtained between the Koobi Fora and Shungura Formations
(Brown *et al.*, 1978; Brown *et al.*, 1985) permits the construction
of a dated sequence that will date securely the fauna, the tools and
the hominids from the site.

It is apparent, therefore, that the majority of the fossils from Koobi
Fora come from three members; the Chari, the Okote and the KBS
members dated at < 1·4, < 1·6 and < 1·8 m.y. B.P. respectively.

Morphology   *KNM–ER 406*

A virtually complete cranium lacking teeth recovered from the
Upper Member of the Koobi Fora Formation (Area 10). The cranium
is heavily built with a large face and a small neurocranium. The
facial buttresses are robust with a stout brow ridge and broad
zygomata. The cranial capacity must be small and there is considerable postorbital constriction. The cranium possesses a sagittal crest
as well as occipital and supramastoid crests which were probably
associated with a heavy mandible and powerful muscles of masti-

catation (Leakey, 1970; Leakey, Mungai and Walker, 1971; Holloway, 1973).

KNM–ER 729

A robust mandible with teeth recovered from the Upper Member of the Koobi Fora Formation (Area 8). The body of the mandible is virtually intact but the ramus on the left is badly eroded and the condyloid process on the right is missing. The body is deep and stout bearing a marked *prominentia lateralis* but no chin. The ramus on the right is tall and buttressed internally by a *crista pharyngea*. The teeth that are present include the central incisors, the canines, the left PM_1, both PM_2 teeth, the right M_1 and the M_2 and M_3 of both sides. The dentition shows marked anteroposterior disproportion and a considerable molarization of the premolars (Leakey, 1971; Leakey, Mungai and Walker, 1972).

KNM–ER 730

Part of a mandibular body recovered from the Upper Member of the Koobi Fora Formation (Area 103), including the right side, the symphysial region and a smaller part of the left side. The crowns of the left molar teeth are retained but heavily worn. The mandible bears a slight chin, a *planum alveolare* and evidence of periodontal disease (Leakey, 1971; Day and Leakey, 1973). More of this skull has been recovered recently including most of the occipital bone, part of the left parietal, and a part of the left maxilla (Leakey and Walker, 1985).

KNM–ER 732A

A gracile demicranium including the right maxilla, much of the frontal and parietals and the right temporal bone recovered from the Upper Member of the Koobi Fora Formation (Area 10). The vault bones are thin, the maxilla broad and the temporal bone rugged in construction. The supramastoid crest is prominent but the temporal lines are weakly imprinted and do not fuse to form a crest. The only dental remains that are preserved are the roots of the molars and part of the crown of the right P^4 (Leakey, 1971; Leakey, Mungai and Walker, 1972; Holloway, 1973).

KNM–ER 736

The shaft of a massive left femur from the Upper Member of the Koobi Fora Formation (Area 103). Superiorly the head, neck and greater trochanter are missing and the lesser trochanter is mostly eroded away; inferiorly the bone is broken across just proximal to the development of the supracondylar lines. The gluteus maximus impression is extensive and includes an hypotrochanteric fossa

7
6
5
4
3
2
1
C M
1
2
3
4
5
6

Fig. 73. The KNM–ER 732A demicranium (cast).

whilst the *linea aspera* is well defined. The medial border of the bone is convex medially and the narrowest point on the shaft is low (Leakey, 1971; Leakey, Mungai and Walker, 1972; Day, 1978).

KNM–ER 737

The shaft of a left femur from the Upper Member of the Koobi Fora Formation (Area 103). The head and part of the neck are missing, as well as the greater and lesser trochanters, and the bone is broken across distally through the popliteal surface. The bone is characterized by its flatness or platymeria, by the low position of its narrowest point and by the convexity of its medial border (Leakey, 1971; Day and Leakey, 1973; Day, 1978).

KNM–ER 739

The shaft and lower end of a large right humerus from the Upper Member of the Koobi Fora Formation (Area 1). The shaft is marked by a large deltoid impression and a deep groove for the long head of biceps. Distally the lower end is expanded and bears a rounded capitulum and a trochlear surface surmounted by trochlear and capitular fossae. Posteriorly, the olecranon fossa is deep while the medial epicondyle is very pronounced. The lateral border of the shaft distally shows a marked brachioradialis flange (Leakey, 1971; Leakey, Mungai and Walker, 1972; Day, 1978). A metrical analysis of the lower end of this humerus was ambiguous but discounted knuckle-walking as the locomotor mode of its owner (McHenry, 1976).

KNM–ER 803

A partial skeleton recovered from the Upper Member of the Koobi Fora Formation (Area 8). It includes parts of the shafts of a femur, a tibia, an ulna, fibulae, phalanges, a metatarsal and many other fragments from both left and right sides. The femoral fragment is flattened and tapers distally and shows a pronounced *linea aspera* but no pilaster (Leakey, 1972; Day and Leakey, 1974).

KNM–ER 813

A right talus and part of the shaft of a tibia or a femur from the Upper Member of the Koobi Fora Formation (Area 104). The talus is a little eroded and shows little horizontal angulation of the neck but considerable torsion of the neck (Leakey, 1972; Leakey and Wood, 1973; Wood, 1973; Day, 1978).

KNM–ER 820

A juvenile mandible from the Ileret Member of the Koobi Fora Formation (Area 1) with an almost complete dentition. This pretty little jaw contains elements of both the deciduous and permanent dentitions. The deciduous teeth that are present include the left canine and all four deciduous molars but in addition all four permanent incisors are present as well as both first permanent molars. The incisor teeth are large and spatulate and the first permanent molars show the basic Y5 cusp morphology (Leakey, 1972; Leakey and Wood, 1973).

KNM–ER 992

The two halves of a mandibular body and parts of both rami of a jaw recovered from the Upper Member of the Koobi Fora Formation (Area 1). The mandible contains all of the molars and premolars as well as parts of both canines and a left incisor. The mandible is broken through the symphysial region. The body of the mandible is relatively gracile and its upper and lower borders are parallel. The tooth row shows a pronounced curve of Spee with no canine projection (Leakey, 1972; Leakey and Wood, 1973).

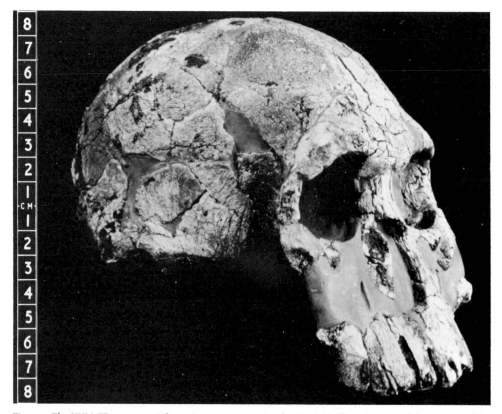

Fig. 74. The KNM–ER 1470 partial cranium; reconstruction by Dr A. Walker. *Courtesy of the Director of the National Museums of Kenya and Anglia Television Ltd.*

KNM–ER 1470

A partial cranium from the Lower Member of the Koobi Fora Formation (Area 131). The calvaria has suffered some distortion but with retention of the alignment of midline structures; it is long and ovoid with moderate postorbital construction. The vault bones are thin but the endocranial surface has suffered some loss of the inner cortical bone. The face is moderately well preserved being broad but with no strong development of the supraorbital ridge and with little or no subnasal prognathism. The palate is broad and the alveolar processes stout; erosion of these processes gives a false impression of the shallowness of the palate. The maxillary air sinuses are well developed and project down between the molar roots; the development of these sinuses as well as that of the mastoid air cells suggest that the cranium is that of an adult (Leakey, 1973; Day, Leakey, Walker and Wood, 1974).

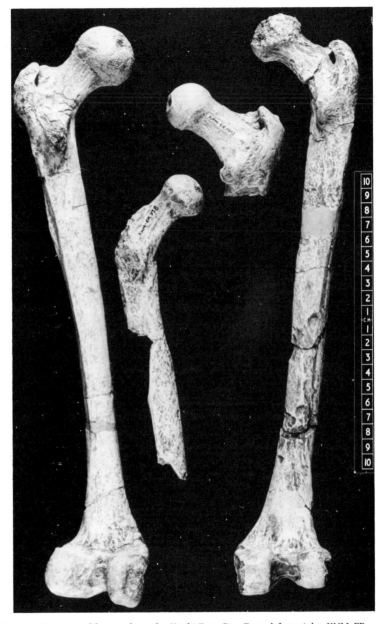

Fig. 75. A group of femora from the Koobi Fora Site. From left to right. KNM–ER 1481, KNM–ER 738, KNM–ER 1503 and KNM–ER 1475 Posterior views. *Courtesy of the Director of the National Museums of Kenya and Professor B. A. Wood.*

KNM–ER 1477

The body of a juvenile mandible with dentition, from the Upper Member of the Koobi Fora Formation (Area 105). The specimen contains part of the deciduous dentition, the first permanent molar germs in open crypts and other tooth germs visible in the mandibular body where its external surface is broken away. The symphysial region shows a distinct post-incisive *planum alveolar* bounded below by a stout superior transverse torus below which are paired genial pits. The first permanent molar germs of both sides are large and possess five main cusps, a Y-fissure pattern and both anterior and posterior foveae (Leakey, 1973; Day, Leakey, Walker and Wood, 1976).

KNM–ER 1481

An associated group of leg bones from the Lower Member of the Koobi Fora Formation (Area 131), including a left femur, proximal and distal left tibial fragments and a distal fibular fragment. The femur is virtually complete and has a large head, a rounded neck, a flared greater trochanter, a prominent lesser trochanter, a well marked *linea aspera* and some degree of shaft flattening. The gluteus maximus impression is present as a *fossa hypotrochanterica* with some lateral swelling of the shaft. The narrow point of the shaft appears to be distally placed (Leakey, 1973; Day, Leakey, Walker and Wood, 1974; Day, 1978). It has been contended that this femur shows sufficient features to ally it to *Homo erectus* (Kennedy, 1983); it has also been attributed to *Homo habilis* (Trinkaus, 1984).

KNM–ER 1500

An associated skeleton from the Lower Member of the Koobi Fora Formation (Area 130), including parts of a femur, a tibia, a radius, an ulna, a humerus and a metatarsal as well as many other fragments. The skeleton is that of a small individual whose femur is characterized by marked anteroposterior compression of the neck (Leakey, 1973; Day, Leakey, Walker and Wood, 1976; Day, 1978).

KNM–ER 1503

An almost perfect proximal end of a right femur from the Koobi Fora Formation (Area 123). The head of the bone is small and the neck long and flattened anteroposteriorly. There is no *linea intertrochanterica* marking the attachment of the vertical fibres of the iliofemoral ligament, but there is a prominent femoral tubercle. The posterior aspect of the neck is marked by a broad shallow groove for the obturator externus tendon (Leakey, 1973; Day, Leakey, Walker and Wood, 1976).

KNM–ER 1590

A partial cranium with a juvenile dentition recovered from the Lower Member of the Koobi Fora Formation just below the KBS tuff (Area 12). It consists of both parietals and fragments of frontal of an immature skull associated with deciduous and permanent teeth. The cranial vault is thin but suggests that the cranial volume was large. The teeth are well preserved and include a permanent left first incisor, the left deciduous canine and second deciduous molar, both unerupted canines and premolars, the erupted left and right first molars and the left second molar (Leakey, 1974; Day, Leakey, Walker and Wood, 1976).

KNM–ER 1802

A beautifully preserved body of an adult mandible from the Lower Member of the Koobi Fora Formation (Area 133). The body is preserved from the distal end of the second molar on the left through the symphysia to the inter-alveolar septum between the second and third molars on the right. The symphysis is thick, but there are no superior or inferior transverse tori. The first molar teeth of both sides are present and show six cusps arranged in a Y pattern; the second molars are also present and are larger than the first molars. No significant curve of Spee has developed (Leakey, 1974; Day, Leakey, Walker and Wood, 1976).

KNM–ER 1805

A cranium and mandible recovered from the Upper Member of the Koobi Fora Formation (Area 130). The cranium is almost complete, heavily built and possesses a distinct sagittal crest and a marked supramastoid crest on the left. The face is represented by the maxillae and nasal bones and the palate is almost complete although somewhat splayed and contains an almost complete dentition. The body of the mandible is moderately robust and contains the right second and third molar teeth and the roots of many others. The rami are missing (Leakey, 1974; Day, Leakey, Walker and Wood, 1976).

KNM–ER 1808

A partial skeleton was located in the Upper Member of the Koobi Fora Formation at Area 103 in 1973, and work over a number of years has resulted in the recovery of much of the skull and mandible and many parts of the postcranial skeleton. It has been attributed to *Homo erectus* despite the recognition of extensive bone pathology. The condition has been alleged to have been caused by hypervitaminosis A due to an excessive dietary intake of carnivore liver

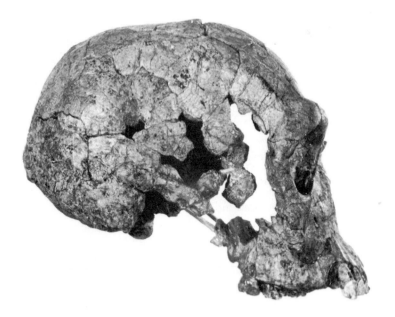

Fig. 76. The KNM–ER 1813 cranium (right lateral view). *Courtesy of the Director of the National Museums of Kenya.*

Fig. 77. The KNM–ER 1813 palate and dentition. *Courtesy of the Director of the National Museums of Kenya.*

(Walker, Zimmerman and Leakey, 1982; Leakey and Walker, 1985).

KNM–ER 1813

A cranium recovered from the Koobi Fora Formation (Area 123). The cranium is virtually complete, missing only part of the base, the left zygomatic region and part of the left orbit. The dentition includes the left canine, both left premolars and all three molars on the left as well as the right incisors, canine and second and third molars. The skull is small, lightly built and with no cranial cresting. The supraorbital ridges are modest and the face shows a small degree of nasal prominence (Leakey, 1974; Day, Leakey, Walker and Wood, 1976).

KNM–ER 3228

A right hip bone (*os coxa*) from the Lower Member of the Koobi Fora Formation (Area 102). The bone is almost complete missing only the pubic portion. The bone is robustly constructed with a broad iliac flange, an acute sciatic notch, an hyper-robust iliac pillar and a medially rotated ischium. The acetabular fossa is large, indicating a large femoral head (Leakey, 1976). The similarities of this hip bone to those known from Olduvai (OH 28), Arago (Arago XLIV) and Koobi Fora (KNM–ER 1808) were noted (Day, 1982) and later confirmed when the bone was fully described (Rose, 1984).

KNM–ER 3733

A remarkably preserved cranium from the Upper Member of the Koobi Fora Formation (Area 104). The vault is complete and undistorted and much of the facial skeleton is present as well as examples of the premolar and molar teeth. The cranial capacity is 848 cc (Holloway, 1983). The preliminary description of the specimen (Leakey, 1976) makes it clear that there is little doubt that this skull must be attributed to *Homo erectus*. Its similarities to the Peking skulls are striking (Leakey, 1976; Leakey and Walker, 1985). The contemporaneous occurrence of this cranium and that of a robust australopithecine (KNM–ER 406) was a telling blow to the 'single species hypothesis' of hominid evolution (Leakey and Walker, 1976).

Recently a number of new finds have been described (Leakey and Walker, 1985) that include teeth, mandibles, calvariae and postcranial bones too numerous to describe in detail. Of these the KNM–ER 3883 calvaria is the best preserved. Brief details are given in the table of the Koobi Fora hominids. Details of all the fossil hominids found at Koobi Fora 1968–1974 have been given in

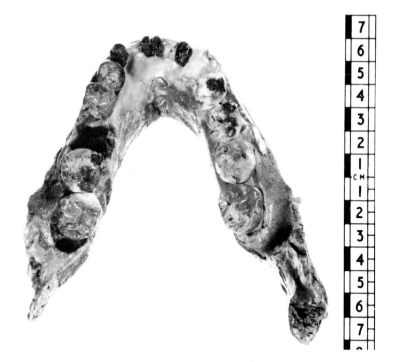

Fig. 78. The KNM–ER 729 mandible (occlusal view—cast).

Volume I of the monographs documenting the Koobi Fora Research Project (Leakey and Leakey, 1978).

Dimensions   The dimensions of the East Rudolf hominid material described in this section are to be found in the descriptive publications referred to in relation to each specimen.

Affinities   At the present time all of the material from this site has been placed in the family Hominidae; of this some has been placed in the genus *Australopithecus*, some into the genus *Homo* and the remainder left *incertae sedis* (see table below). As a matter of policy, the hominid group of the Koobi Fora Research Project has usually refrained from making considered specific allocations or erecting new taxa until the material has been published in detail to avoid the confusions that can arise from premature systematic assertions, whilst ensuring the publication of new finds as rapidly as possible. Naturally this policy relies heavily on the co-operation of scholars the world over, co-operation that has for the most part been given readily. This self-imposed convention was breached in relation to the attribution of KNM–ER 3733 to *Homo erectus* on the grounds of its importance as evidence for the refutation of the 'single species hypothesis' of hominid evolution (Leakey and Walker, 1976).

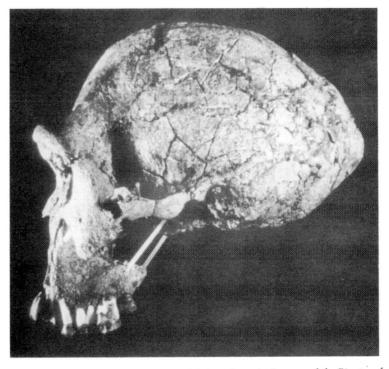

Fig. 79. The KNM–ER 3733 cranium (left lateral view). *Courtesy of the Director of the National Museums of Kenya.*

Table 6   *Koobi Fora Hominids*

KNM–ER No.	Year	Area	Specimen	Stratigraphic Position	Published Taxonomic Status
164A, B & C	1969/71	104	Parietal frag., 2 phalanges 2 vertebrae	Upper Memb. K.F. formation above KBS tuff	Homo
403	1968	103	Rt. ½ mandibular body	Upper Memb. K.F. formation below Okote tuff complex	*Australopithecus*
404	1968	7A	Rt. ½ mandibular body	Upper Memb. K.F. formation below Chari tuff	*Australopithecus*
405	1968	105	Palate lacking teeth	Upper Memb. K.F. formation above post-KBS erosional surface	Australopithecus
406	1969	10	Cranium lacking teeth	Upper Memb. K.F. formation below Okote tuff complex	*Australopithecus*
407	1969	10	Partial calvaria lacking face	Upper Memb. K.F. formation below Okote tuff complex	cf. *Australopithecus*
417	1968	129	Parietal frag.	Upper Memb. K.F. formation below KBS tuff	*Australopithecus*
725	1970	1	Lt. ½ mandibular body	Upper Memb. K.F. formation just above Okote tuff complex	*Australopithecus*
726	1970	10	Lt. ½ mandibular body	Upper Memb. K.F. formation just above Okote tuff complex	*Australopithecus*
727	1970	6A	Frag. rt. ½ mandibular body	Upper Memb. K.F. formation just below Okote tuff complex	*Australopithecus*
728	1970	1	Rt. ½ mandibular body	Upper Memb. K.F. formation just above Okote tuff complex	*Australopithecus*

Table 6 *Koobi Fora Hominids (continued)*

KNM– ER No.	Year	Area	Specimen	Stratigraphic Position	Published Taxonomic Status
729	1970	8	Mandible with dentition	Upper Memb. K.F. formation lower part of Okote tuff complex	*Australopithecus*
730	1970/80	103	Mandible lacking rt. side post. to P₄, lt. M₁–M₃ Cranial and maxillary frags	Upper Memb. K.F. formation just below Okote tuff complex	cf. *Homo erectus*
731	1970	6A	Lt. ½ mandibular body lacking teeth	Upper Memb. K.F. formation below Chari tuff	*Homo*
732A	1970	10	Demi-cranium	Upper Memb. K.F. formation below Okote tuff complex	*Australopithecus*
733	1970	8	Rt. ½ mandibular body, lt. maxilla, cranial frags.	Upper Memb. K.F. formation in Okote tuff complex	*Australopithecus*
734	1970	103	Parietal frag.	Upper Memb. K.F. formation just below Okote tuff complex	*Incertae sedis*
736	1970	103	Lt. femoral shaft	Upper Memb. K.F. formation below projected level of Okote tuff complex	*Australopithecus* or early *Homo*
737	1970	103	Lt. femoral shaft	Upper Memb. K.F. formation in base of Koobi Fora tuff	*Homo*
738	1970	105	Prox. end lt. femur	Upper Memb. K.F. formation above post KBS erosional surface	*Australopithecus*
739	1970	1	Rt. humerus	Upper Memb. K.F. formation just above Okote tuff complex	*Australopithecus*
740	1970	1	Frag. distal end lt. humerus	Upper Memb. K.F. formation just above Okote tuff complex	*Australopithecus*
741	1970	1	Prox. end rt. tibia	Upper Memb. K.F. formation above Okote tuff complex	*Australopithecus* or early *Homo*
801	1971	6A	Rt. ½ mandibular body and assoc. isolated teeth	Upper Memb. K.F. formation below Okote tuff complex	*Australopithecus*
802	1971	6A	Isolated upper and lower teeth	Upper Memb. K.F. formation below Okote tuff complex	*Australopithecus*
803	1971	8	Associated skeletal elements	Upper Memb. K.F. formation in Okote tuff complex	*Homo*
805	1971	1	Frag. lt. ½ mandibular body	Upper Memb. K.F. formation above Okote tuff complex	*Australopithecus*
806	1971	8	Isolated teeth	Upper Memb. K.F. formation in Okote tuff complex	*Homo*
807A	1971/73	8A	Frag. rt. maxilla, M³ part M² Frag. rt. maxilla, M¹	Upper Memb. K.F. formation in Okote tuff complex	*Homo*
808	1971	8	Isolated juvenile teeth	Upper Memb. K.F. formation in Okote tuff complex	*Homo*
809	1971	8	Isolated teeth	Upper Memb. K.F. formation in Okote tuff complex	*Homo*
810	1971	104	Lt. ½ mandibular body, small part of rt. side, M₃	Upper Memb. K.F. formation above KBS tuff	*Australopithecus*
811	1971	104	Parietal frag.	K.F. formation, probably below KBS tuff	*Homo*
812	1971	104	Frag. lt. ½ juvenile mandible	Upper Memb. K.F. formation above KBS tuff	*Australopithecus*
813	1971	104	Rt. talus and frag. distal end rt. tibia	Upper Memb. K.F. formation above KBS tuff	*Homo*
814	1971	104	Cranial frags.	Upper Memb. K.F. formation above KBS tuff	*Australopithecus*
815	1971	10	Frag. prox. end lt. femur	Upper Memb. K.F. formation below Okote tuff complex	*Australopithecus*
816	1971	104	Lt. upper canine and molar frags.	Upper Memb. K.F. formation above KBS tuff	*Australopithecus*
817	1971	124	Frags. lt. ½ mandibular body	Upper Memb. Koobi Fora formation, above KBS tuff	*Homo*
818	1971	6A	Lt. ½ mandibular body, P₃–M₃	Upper Memb. K.F. formation within Okote tuff complex	*Australopithecus*
819	1971	1	Lt. ½ mandibular body	Upper Memb. K.F. formation just below Okote tuff complex	*Australopithecus*

Table 6 *Koobi Fora Hominids (continued)*

KNM–ER No.	Year	Area	Specimen	Stratigraphic Position	Published Taxonomic Status
820	1971	1	Juvenile mandible with dentition	Upper Memb. K.F. formation in lower part of Okote tuff complex	*Homo*
992	1971	1	Mandible with dentition	Upper Memb. K.F. formation above Okote tuff complex	*Homo*
993	1971	1	Distal ¾ rt. femur	Upper Memb. K.F. formation just above Okote tuff complex	*Australopithecus*
997	1971	104	Prox. end lt. metatarsal III	Upper Memb. K.F. formation above KBS tuff	*Australopithecus*
998	1971	104	Rt. I²	Upper Memb. K.F. formation above KBS tuff	*Australopithecus*
999	1971	6A	Lt. femur, frag. femoral condyle, isolated frags.	Upper Memb. K.F. formation	*Homo*
1170	1971	6A	Cranial frags.	Upper Memb. K.F. formation below Okote tuff complex	*Australopithecus*
1171	1971	6A	Isolated juvenile teeth	Upper Memb. K.F. formation below Okote tuff complex	*Australopithecus*
1462	1972	130	Isolated lt. M₃	Lower Memb. K.F. formation below KBS tuff	*Homo*
1463	1972	1	Rt. femoral shaft	Upper Memb. K.F. formation in Okote tuff complex	*Australopithecus*
1464	1972	6A	Rt. talus	Upper Memb. K.F. formation below Okote tuff complex	*Australopithecus* or early *Homo*
1465	1972	11	Frag. prox. end lt. femur	Upper Memb. K.F. formation below Chari tuff	*Australopithecus*
1466	1972	6	Fronto-parietal frag.	Upper Memb. K.F. formation above Okote tuff complex	*Homo*
1467	1972	3	Isolated lt. M₃	Upper Memb. K.F. formation above Okote tuff complex	*Australopithecus*
1468	1972	11	Rt. ½ mandibular body	Upper Memb. K.F. formation just in or above Okote tuff complex	*Australopithecus*
1469	1972	131	Lt. ½ mandibular body, M₂–M₃	Lower Memb. K.F. formation below KBS tuff	*Australopithecus*
1470	1972	131	Cranium	Lower Memb. K.F. formation below KBS tuff	*Homo*
1471	1972	131	Prox. ½ rt. tibia	Lower Memb. K.F. formation below KBS tuff	*Australopithecus* or early *Homo*
1472	1972	131	Rt. femur	Lower Memb. K.F. formation below KBS tuff	*Homo*
1473	1972	131	Prox. end rt. humerus	Lower Memb. K.F. formation below KBS tuff	*Incertae sedis*
1474	1972	131	Parietal frag.	Lower Memb. K.F. formation below KBS tuff	*Incertae sedis*
1475	1972	131	Prox. end rt. femur	Lower Memb. K.F. formation below KBS tuff	*Homo*
1476	1972	105	Lt. talus, prox. end lt. tibia, frag. shaft rt. tibia	Upper Memb. K.F. formation above post KBS erosional surface	*Australopithecus*
1477	1972	105	Juv. mandible with dentition	Upper Memb. K.F. formation above post KBS erosional surface	*Australopithecus*
1478	1972	105	Cranial frags.	Upper Memb. K.F. formation above post KBS erosional surface	*Australopithecus*
1479	1972	105	Isolated tooth frags.	Upper Memb. K.F. formation above post KBS erosional surface	*Australopithecus*
1480	1972	105	Isolated rt. M₃	Upper Memb. K.F. formation above post KBS erosional surface	*Homo*
1481	1972	131	Lt. femur, prox and dist. ends lt. tibia, dist. end lt. fibula	Lower Memb. K.F. formation below KBS tuff	*Homo*
1482	1972	131	Mandible, and isolated teeth	Lower Memb. K.F. formation below KBS tuff	*Incertae sedis*
1483	1972	131	Mandibular frags.	Lower Memb. K.F. formation below KBS tuff	*Homo*

Table 6   *Koobi Fora Hominids (continued)*

KNM–ER No.	Year	Area	Specimen	Stratigraphic Position	Published Taxonomic Status
1500	1972	130	Associated skeletal elements	Lower Memb. K.F. formation just below KBS tuff	*Australopithecus*
1501	1972	123	Rt. $\frac{1}{2}$ mandibular body	Upper Memb. (provisional) K.F. formation	*Homo*
1502	1972	123	Frag. rt. $\frac{1}{2}$ mandibular body, M$_1$	Upper Memb. (provisional) K.F. formation	*Homo*
1503	1972	123	Prox. end rt. femur	Upper Memb. (provisional) K.F. formation	*Australopithecus*
1504	1972	123	Frag. dist. end rt. humerus	Upper Memb. (provisional) K.F. formation	*Australopithecus*
1505	1972	123	Prox. end lt. femur, frag. dist. end lt. femoral shaft	Upper Memb. (provisional) K.F. formation	*Australopithecus*
1506	1972	121	Frag. rt. $\frac{1}{2}$ mandibular body, M$_1$, M$_2$, isolated P^3, P^4	Upper Memb. (provisional) K.F. formation	*Australopithecus*
1507	1972	127	Lt. $\frac{1}{2}$ juvenile mandibular body	Upper Memb. K.F. formation below Okote tuff complex	*Homo*
1508	1972	127	Isolated rt. molar	Upper Memb. K.F. formation below Okote tuff complex	*Homo*
1509	1972	119	Isolated teeth C–M$_3$	Upper Memb. K.F. formation below Okote tuff complex	*Australopithecus*
1515	1972	103	Isolated rt. I^2	Upper Memb. K.F. formation below Okote tuff complex	*Incertae sedis*
1590	1972	12	Partial juvenile cranium with dentition	Lower Memb. K.F. formation below KBS tuff	*Homo*
1591	1972	12	Rt. humerus lacking head	Upper Memb. K.F. formation above KBS tuff	*Homo*
1592	1972	12	Dist. $\frac{1}{2}$ rt. femur	Upper Memb. K.F. formation above KBS tuff	*Australopithecus*
1593	1972	12	Parietal and mandibular frags.	At base of Upper Memb. K.F. formation at projected level of KBS tuff	*Homo*
1648	1971	105	Parietal frag.	Upper Memb. K.F. formation below Okote tuff complex	*Incertae sedis*
1800	1973	130	Cranial frags.	Lower Memb. K.F. formation below KBS tuff	*Incertae sedis*
1801	1973	131	Lt. $\frac{1}{2}$ mandibular body, P$_4$, M$_1$, M$_3$	Lower Memb. K.F. formation below KBS tuff	cf. *Homo*
1802	1973	131	Mandible, tooth frags.	Lower Memb. K.F. formation below KBS tuff	cf. *Homo*
1803	1973	131	Frag. rt. $\frac{1}{2}$ mandibular body	Lower Memb. K.F. formation below KBS tuff	*Incertae sedis*
1804	1973	104	Frag. rt. maxilla, P^3–M^2	Upper Memb. K.F. formation above KBS tuff	*Incertae sedis*
1805	1973	130	Cranium and mandible with dentition	Upper Memb. K.F. formation below Okote tuff complex	*Incertae sedis*
1806	1973	130	Mandible, no teeth	Upper Memb. K.F. formation below Okote tuff complex	cf. *Australopithecus*
1807	1973	103	Dist. $\frac{2}{3}$ femoral shaft	Upper Memb. K.F. formation above Okote tuff complex	*Incertae sedis*
1808	1973	103	Associated skeletal and cranial elements	Upper Memb. K.F. formation below Okote tuff complex	cf. *Homo erectus*
1809	1973	121	Rt. femoral shaft	Upper Memb. K.F. formation (provisional)	*Incertae sedis*
1810	1973	123	Prox. end lt. tibia	Upper Memb. (provisional) K.F. formation	*Incertae sedis*
1811	1973	123	Mandibular frags.	Upper Memb. (provisional) K.F. formation	*Incertae sedis*
1812	1973	123	Frag. rt. $\frac{1}{2}$ mandibular body isolated lt. I$_1$, M, head of radius	Upper Memb. (provisional) K.F. formation	*Incertae sedis*

Table 6   *Koobi Fora Hominids (continued)*

KNM–ER No.	Year	Area	Specimen	Stratigraphic Position	Published Taxonomic Status
1813	1973	123	Cranium, dentition	Upper Memb. (provisional) K.F. formation	cf. *Australopithecus*
1814	1973	127	Associated elements of a lower dentition	Upper Memb. (provisional) K.F. formation	*Incertae sedis*
1816	1973	6A	Frags. juv. mandible	Upper Memb. K.F. formation below Okote tuff complex	*Incertae sedis*
1817	1973	1	Lt. ½ mandibular body	Upper Memb. K.F. formation in or just below Okote tuff complex	*Incertae sedis*
1818	1973	6A	Isolated lt. I^1	Upper Memb. K.F. formation below Okote tuff complex	*Incertae sedis*
1819	1973	3	Isolated lt. M$_3$ crown	Upper Memb. K.F. formation below Okote tuff complex	*Incertae sedis*
1820	1973	103	Frag. lt. ½ mandibular body dm$_2$ and M$_1$	Upper Memb. K.F. formation below Okote tuff complex	*Incertae sedis*
1821	1972	123	Parietal frag.	Upper Memb. (provisional) K.F. formation	*Incertae sedis*
1822	1973	123	Frag. femoral shaft	Upper Memb. (provisional) K.F. formation	*Incertae sedis*
1823	1971	6A	Prox. end metatarsal	Upper Memb. K.F. formation below Okote tuff complex	*Incertae sedis*
1824	1971	6A	Dist. end rt. humerus frag.	Upper Memb. K.F. formation below Okote tuff complex	*Incertae sedis*
1825	1971	6A	Frag. atlas	Upper Memb. K.F. formation below Okote tuff complex	*Incertae sedis*
2592	1974	6	Parietal frag.	Upper Memb. K.F. formation probably below Okote tuff complex	—
2593	1974	6	Molar frag.	Upper Memb. K.F. formation in or above Okote tuff complex	—
2594	1974	6A	Prox. tibia and shaft	Upper Memb. K.F. formation below Chari tuff	—
2595	1974	1A	Parietal frag.	Upper Memb. K.F. formation probably below Okote tuff complex	—
2596	1974	15	Dist. end lt. tibia	Upper Memb. K.F. formation above KBS tuff	—
2597	1974	15	Lower lt. molar (M$_2$ or M$_3$)	K.F. formation approx. level KBS tuff	—
2598	1974	15	Occipital frag.	K.F. formation approx. level KBS tuff	—
2599	1974	15	Frag. lt. P$_4$	K.F. formation approx. level KBS tuff	—
2600	1974	130	Half lower molar	Lower Memb. K.F. formation below KBS tuff	—
2601	1974	130	Crown, rt. lower molar	Lower Memb. K.F. formation below KBS tuff	—
2602	1974	117	Cranial frags.	Lower Memb. K.F. formation just above Tulu Bor tuff	—
2603	1974	117	Tooth frag.	Lower Memb. K.F. formation below Tulu Bor tuff	—
2604	1974	117	Tooth frag.	Lower Memb. K.F. formation just above Tulu Bor tuff	—
2605	1974	117	Tooth frag.	Lower Memb. K.F. formation below Tulu Bor tuff	—
2606	1974	117	Tooth frag.	Lower Memb. K.F. formation below Tulu Bor tuff	—
2607	1972	105	Molar frag.	Upper Memb. K.F. formation above KBS tuff	*Homo* (first published as KNM–ER 1480B)
3228	1975	102	Rt. innominate	Lower Memb. K.F. formation below KBS tuff	—
3229	1975	103	Lt. & Rt. Mandibular isolated Lt. & Rt. P$_4$	Upper Memb. K.F. formation below Okote tuff complex	—
3230	1974	130	Mandible with dentition	Upper Memb. K.F. formation in Okote tuff complex	—

Table 6   *Koobi Fora Hominids (continued)*

KNM–ER No.	Year	Area	Specimen	Stratigraphic Position	Published Taxonomic Status
3728	1975	100	Shaft and neck of right femur	Lower Memb. K.F. formation below KBS tuff	—
3729	1975	102	Body of left mandible, partial roots C–M₃	Upper Memb. K.F. formation above KBS tuff	—
3731	1975	105	Body of left mandible, partial roots I–M₃	Lower Memb. K.F. formation below KBS tuff	—
3732	1975	105	Partial cranium	Lower Memb. K.F. formation below KBS tuff	—
3733	1975	104	Cranium with partial dentition	Upper Memb. K.F. formation below Okote tuff complex	*Homo erectus*
3734	1975	105	Body of left mandible, C–M₂, frag. of M₃	Lower Memb. K.F. formation below KBS tuff	—
3735	1975	116	Associated skeletal frags.	Lower Memb. K.F. formation below KBS tuff	—
3736	1975	105	Proximal ⅔ of a radius	Upper Memb. K.F. formation above KBS tuff	—
3737	1971	6A	Frags. rt. M₃ and M₁	Upper Memb. K.F. formation below Okote tuff complex	*Australopithecus* (first published as KNM–ER 802)
3883	1976	1	Calvaria	Upper Memb. K.F. formation above Okote tuff complex	—
3884	1976	5	Cranium	Upper Memb. K.F. formation	—
3885	1976	104	Isolated rt. P₄	Upper Memb. K.F. formation above KBS tuff	—
3886	1976	104	Isolated lt. dM²	Upper Memb. K.F. formation above KBS tuff	—
3887	1976	1	Isolated rt. M³ frag.	Upper Memb. K.F. formation above Okote tuff complex	—
3888	1976	1	Prox. rt. radius	Upper Memb. K.F. formation above Okote tuff complex	—
3889	1976	1	Ant. mandibular body	Upper Memb. K.F. formation above Okote tuff complex	—
3890	1976	6A	Isolated M₁ or M₂	Upper Memb. K.F. formation below Okote tuff complex	—
3891	1976	105	Associated cranial frags.	Upper Memb. K.F. formation above post-KBS erosion surface	—
3892	1976	103	Lt. frontal frag.	Upper Memb. K.F. formation below Okote tuff complex	—
3950	1977	121	Mandibular frag.	Upper Memb. K.F. formation above KBS tuff	—
3951	1977	131	Distal lt. femur	Lower Memb. K.F. formation level of KBS tuff	—
3952	1977	105	Lower tooth frags.	Upper Memb. K.F. formation above KBS tuff	—
3953	1977	105	Rt. M₃ crown	Lower Memb. K.F. formation level of KBS tuff	—
3954	1977	121	Mandibular corpus	Upper Memb. K.F. formation below Okote tuff complex	—
3956	1977	106	Lt. radius, ulna and humeral frags.	Upper Memb. K.F. formation below Okote tuff complex	—
5428	1978	119	Rt. talus	Upper Memb. K.F. formation in Okote tuff complex	—
5429	1978	119	Rt. mandibular frag.	Lower Memb. K.F. formation level of KBS tuff	—
5431	1978	203	Isolated lower teeth	Lower Memb. K.F. formation between Tulu Bor and Burgi tuffs	—
5877	1980	3	Rt. mandibular frag.	Upper Memb. K.F. formation below Chari tuff	—
5879	1980	123	Parietal frags	K.F. formation approx. level of KBS tuff	—

Table 6 *Koobi Fora Hominids (continued)*

KNM– ER No.	Year	Area	Specimen	Stratigraphic Position	Published Taxonomic Status
5880	1980	119	Rt. femoral frags	Upper Memb. K.F. formation above KBS tuff	—
5881	1980	105	Rt. femoral shaft frag.	Upper Memb. K.F. formation above KBS tuff	—
5882	1980	105	Distal rt. femoral shaft	Upper Memb. K.F. formation above KBS tuff	—
5884	1980	105	Lower decid. incisor crown	Upper Memb. K.F. formation above KBS tuff	—
6020	1980	1	Distal lt. humerus	Upper Memb. K.F. formation above KBS tuff	—
6080	1979	8A	Lower molar germ	Upper Memb. K.F. formation in Okote tuff complex	—
6081	1979	1A	Molar crown frag.	Upper Memb. K.F. formation in Okote tuff complex	—
6082	1979	8A	Lt. P_4 germ frag.	Upper Memb. K.F. formation in Okote tuff complex	—
7330	1981	119	Rt. maxill. frag. P^3, $\frac{1}{2} P^4$	Upper Memb. K.F. formation above KBS tuff	—
7727	1982	S. of Allia Bay	Lt. M^2 crown	Lower Memb. K.F. formation below Allia tuff	—

Originals The National Museum of Kenya, Nairobi, Kenya.

Casts The Supervisor, Casting Department, National Museums of Kenya, P.O. Box 40658, Nairobi, Kenya.

References Fitch, F. J. and Miller, J. A. (1970) Radioisotopic age discriminations of Lake Rudolf artefact site. *Nature 226*, 226–228.

Leakey, R. E. F. (1970) New Hominid remains and early artefacts from Northern Kenya. *Nature 226*, 223–224.

Isaac, G. I., Leakey, R. E. F. and Behrensmeyer, A. K. (1971) Archaeological traces of early hominid activities, east of Lake Rudolf, Kenya. *Science N.Y. 173*, 245–248.

Leakey, R. E. F. (1971) Further evidence of Lower Pleistocene hominids from East Rudolf, North Kenya. *Nature 231*, 241–245.

Leakey, R. E. F., Mungai, J. M. and Walker, A. C. (1971) New australopithecines from East Rudolf, Kenya. *Am. J. phys. Anthrop. 35*, 175–186.

Leakey, R. E. F. (1972) Further evidence of Lower Pleistocene hominids from East Rudolf, North Kenya 1971. *Nature 237*, 264–269.

Leakey, R. E. F., Mungai, J. M. and Walker, A. C. (1972) New australopithecines from East Rudolf, Kenya (11). *Am. J. phys. Anthrop. 36*, 235–251.

Leakey, R. E. F. (1973) Further evidence of Lower Pleistocene hominids from East Rudolf, North Kenya 1972. *Nature 242*, 170–173.

Day, M. H. and Leakey, R. E. F. (1973) New evidence for the genus *Homo* from East Rudolf, Kenya. 1. *Am. J. phys. Anthrop. 39*, 341–354.

Leakey, R. E. F. and Wood, B. A. (1973) New evidence for the genus *Homo* from East Rudolf, Kenya 11. *Am. J. phys. Anthrop. 39*, 355–368.

Holloway, R. L. (1973) New endocranial values for the East African early hominids. *Nature 243*, 97–99.

Wood, B. A. (1973) Locomotor affinities of hominoid tali from Kenya. *Nature 246*, 45–46.

Day, M. H. and Leakey, R. E. F. (1974) New evidence for the genus *Homo* from East Rudolf, Kenya 111. *Am. phys. Anthrop. 41*, 367–380.

Day, M. H., Leakey, R. E. F., Walker, A. C. and Wood, B. A. (1974) New hominids from East Rudolf, Kenya, 1. *Am. J. Phys. Anthrop. 42*, 461–476.

Fitch, F. J., Findlater, I. C., Watkins, R. T. and Miller, J. A. (1974) Dating of the rock succession containing fossil hominids at East Rudolf, Kenya. *Nature 251*, 213–215.

Leakey, R. E. F. (1974) Further evidence of Lower Pleistocene hominids from East Rudolf, North Kenya, 1973. *Nature 248*, 653–656.

Curtis, G. H., Drake, T., Cerling and Hampel [*sic*] (1975) Age of KBS tuff in Koobi Fora Formation, East Rudolf, Kenya. *Nature 258*, 395–398.

Groves, C. P. and Mazák, V. (1975) An approach to the taxonomy of the Hominidae: gracile Villafranchian hominids of Africa. *Cas. Miner. Geol. 20*, 225–247.

Day, M. H., Leakey, R. E. F., Walker, A. C. and Wood, B. A. (1976) New hominids from East Turkana, Kenya. *Am. J. phys. Anthrop. 45*, 369–436

Bonnefille, R. (1976) Implications of pollen assemblages from the Koobi Fora Formation, East Rudolf, Kenya. *Nature 264*, 403–407.

Cooke, H. B. S. (1976) Suidae from Plio-Pleistocene Strata of the Rudolf Basin. In *Earliest Man and Environments in the Lake Rudolf Basin*, 251–263. Eds. Y. Coppens, F. Clark Howell, G. Ll Isaac and R. E. F. Leakey. Chicago: University of Chicago Press.

Fitch, F. J. and Miller, J. A. (1976) Conventional Potassium-Argon and Argon-40/Argon-39 dating of the volcanic rocks from East Rudolf. *Ibid.*

Fitch, F. J. and Vondra, C. F. (1976) 'Tectonic Framework'. *Ibid.*

Harris, J. W. K. and Isaac, G. Ll. (1976) The Karari industry: early Pleistocene archaeological evidence from the terrain east of Lake Turkana, Kenya. *Nature 262*. 102–107.

Howell, F. C. and Petter, G. (1976) Carnivora from Omo Group Formations, Southern Ethiopia. *Ibid*, 314–331.

Isaac, G. Ll. (1976a) Plio-Pleistocene artefact assemblages from East Rudolf, Kenya. In *Earliest Man and Environments in the Lake Rudolf Basin*. Eds. Y. Coppens, F. C. Howell, G. Ll. Isaac and R. E. F. Leakey, Chicago: Chicago University Press.

Isaac, G. Ll. (1976b) The activities of early African hominids: a review of archaeological evidence from the time span two and half to one million years ago. In *Human Origins*, 483–514. Eds. G. Ll. Isaac and E. R. McCown. Menlo Park, California: W. A. Benjamin, Inc.

Isaac, G. L., Harris, J. W. K. and Crader, D. (1976) Archaeological evidence from the Koobi Fora formation. *Ibid.*

Leakey, R. E. F. (1976) New hominid fossils from the Koobi Fora formation in Northern Kenya. *Nature 261*, 574–576.

Leakey, R. E. and Walker, A. C. (1976) *Australopithecus*, *Homo erectus* and the single species hypothesis. *Nature 261*, 572–574.

McHenry, H. M. (1976) Multivariate analysis of early hominid humeri. In *The Measures of Man*, 338–371. Eds. E. Giles and J. S. Friedlaender. Harvard: Peabody Museum Press.

Bonnefille, R. and Vincens, A. (1977) Representation pollinique d'environnements arides a l'Est du lac Turkana (Kenya). *Bull. Assoc. Fr. Étude Quaternaire*, *(INQUA, 1977) 50*, 235–347.

White, T. D. and Harris, J. M. (1977) Suid evolution and correlation of African hominid localities. *Science 198*, 13–21.

Bishop, W.W. (Ed.) (1978) *Background to Evolution in Africa*. Edinburgh: Scottish Academic Press. 585 pp.

Brown, F.H., Clark Howell, F. and G.G. Eck (1978) Observations on problems of correlation of late Cenozoic hominid-bearing formations in the North Lake Turkana Basin. In *Geological Background to Fossil Man*, 473–498.

Day, M.H. (1978) Functional interpretations of the morphology of postcranial remains of early African hominids. In *Early Hominids of Africa*, 311–345. Ed. C. Jolly. London: Duckworth.

Leakey, M.G. and Leakey, R.E. Eds. (1978) *Koobi Fora Research Project. Vol. 1: The Fossil Hominids and an Introduction to their Context 1968–1974*. Oxford: Clarendon Press.

Cerling, T.E., Brown, F.H., Cerling, B.W., Curtis, G.H. and Drake, R.E. (1979) Preliminary correlations between the Koobi Fora and Shungura Formations, East Africa. *Nature 279*, 118–121.

Bunn, H., Harris, J.W.K., Isaac, G., Kaufulu, Z., Kroll, E., Schick, K., Toth, N. and Behrensmeyer, A.K. (1980) FxJj 50: an early Pleistocene site in northern Kenya. *Wld. Archaeol 12*, 109–136.

Leakey, M.G. (1980) Evidence of palaeoenvironmental changes in the Turkana Basin from some extinct Cercopithecoidea. *Proc. Afr. Cong. Prehist. quaternary Stud., 8. Nairobi. Sept. 1977*, 118–122.

Williamson, P.G. (1981) Palaeontological documentation of speciation in Cenozoic molluscs from Turkana Basin. *Nature 293*, 437–443.

Brown, F.H. and Cerling, T.E. (1982) Stratigraphical significance of the Tulu Bor tuff of the Koobi Fora Formation. *Nature 299*, 212–215.

Cerling, T.E. and Brown, F.H. (1982) Tuffaceous marker horizons in the Koobi Fora region and the Lower Omo Valley. *Nature 299*, 216–221.

Day, M.H. (1982) The *Homo erectus* pelvis: Punctuation or Gradualism? *Cong. Inter. Paleont. Hum., 1, Nice, 1982*. Prètirage, 411–421.

Walker, A., Zimmerman, M.R. and Leakey, R.E.F. (1982) A possible case of hypervitaminosis A in *Homo erectus*. *Nature 296*, 248–250.

Harris, J.M. Ed. (1983) *Koobi Fora Research Project. Vol. 2: The Fossil Ungulates: Proboscidea, Perissodactyla and Suidae*. Oxford: Clarendon Press.

Holloway, R.L. (1983) Human palaeontological evidence relevant to language and behaviour. *Hum. Neurobiol. 2*, 105–114.

Kennedy, G.E. (1983) A morphometric and taxonomic assessment of a hominine femur from the Lower Member, Koobi Fora, Lake Turkana. *Am. J. phys. Anthrop. 61*, 429–436.

Rose, M.D. (1984) A hominine hip bone, KNM—ER 3228, from East Lake Turkana, Kenya. *Am. J. phys. Anthrop. 63*, 371–378.

Trinkaus, E. (1984) Does KNM—ER 1481 establish *Homo erectus* at 2·0 m.y. B.P.? *A. J. phys. Anthrop. 64*, 137–139.

Brown, F.H., McDougall, I., Davies, T. and Maier, R. (1985) An integrated Plio-Pleistocene chronology for the Turkana Basin. In *Ancestors*, 82–90. Ed. E. Delson. New York: Alan R. Liss.

Leakey, R.E.F. and Walker, A.C. (1985) Further hominids from the Plio-Pleistocene of Koobi Fora, Kenya. *Am. J. phys. Anthrop. 67*, 135–163.

McDougall, I. (1985) K–Ar and $^{40}Ar/^{39}Ar$ dating of the hominid-bearing Pliocene-Pleistocene sequence at Koobi Fora, Lake Turkana, northern Kenya. *Geol. Soc. Am. Bull. 96*, 159–175.

McDougall, I., Davies, T., Maier, R. and Rudowski, R. (1985) Age of the Okote Tuff Complex at Koobi Fora, Kenya. *Nature 316*, 792–794.

Brown, F. H. and Feibel, C. S. (in press) Revision of lithostratigraphic nomenclature in the Koobi Fora Region, Kenya.

Hillhouse, J. W., Cerling, T. E. and Brown, F. H. (in press) Magnetostratigraphy of the lower part of the Koobi Fora Formation, Lake Turkana.

The Baringo Remains

Fig. 80. The KNM–BK 67 mandible (occlusal view). *Courtesy of the Director of the National Museums of Kenya.*

Synonyms and other names   1. Family: Hominidae, Gen. and *sp.* indet. (Bishop and Chapman, 1970); The Ngorora tooth.

2. Family: Hominidae, Gen. and *sp.* indet. (Pickford, 1975); The Lukeino tooth.

3. (a) Family: Hominidae, Gen. and *sp.* indet. (Tobias, 1967); The Chemeron temporal fragment.

(b) Superfamily: Hominoidea, Family, Gen and *sp.* indet. (Pickford *et al.*, 1983); The Chemeron humeral fragment.

4. (a) *Homo cf. erectus* (M. Leakey *et al.*, 1969); The Kapthurin mandible (KNM–BK 67) and upper limb remains.

(b) *cf. Homo erectus* or *Homo habilis* (Van Noten, 1983); *Homo sp.* indet. (aff. *erectus*) (Wood and Van Noten, 1986); The Kapthurin mandible (KNM–BK 8518).

5. (a) *A. boisei* (Gowlett *et al.*, 1981); The Chemoigut australopithecine.

(b) *cf. A. robustus/A. boisei* (Carney *et al.*, 1971); The Chesowanja australopithecines.

Site   All of the sites are in the vicinity of Lake Baringo, Northern Rift Valley, Kenya.

Found by   1. A field assistant (Kiptalam Cheboi) to G. R. Chapman, a member of the East African Geological Research Unit (EAGRU), Bedford College, University of London, February 1968 (Ngorora tooth).

2. M. Pickford, 1973. (Lukeino tooth).

3. (a) A field assistant (John Kimengich) to J. E. Martyn (EAGRU), October 1965 (The Chemeron temporal fragment).

(b) M. Pickford, 1973 [The specimen initially identified as hominid but later rejected; in 1980, subsequent to the find of AL 288-1 in Ethiopia, the specimen was recognized as hominid by the finder] (The Chemeron humeral fragment).

4. (a) A field assistant (Edward Kandini) to Mary D. Leakey, 7th February 1966 (The Kapthurin mandible and upper limb bones).

(b) A field assistant (John Kimengich) to F. van Noten, leader of the Belgian Expedition to Kenya of the Royal Museum for Central Africa at Tervuren, 4th August 1983 (The second Kapthurin mandible).

5. (a) Field assistants (Bernard Ngeneo and Wambua Mangao) to John Gowlett, 1978 (The Chemoigut australopithecine).

(b) J. Carney (EAGRU), 1970 (The Chesowanja australopithecine).

Geology   The geology of the Lake Baringo Basin has been the subject of study for over 90 years, but litho-stratigraphical units were first established by McCall, Baker and Walsh (1967) in accordance with normal stratigraphic principles and named in accordance with the recommendations reported in Bishop (1967). The East African Geological Research Unit of Bedford College, University of London, under the direction of B. C. King, began work in 1965 and was responsible for mapping the area. During the course of this project the full stratigraphic succession was established and many of the fossil hominids reported here were found. The Lake Baringo Basin lies in the floor of the Rift Valley between the faulted anticline of the Kamasia range (Tugen Hills) to the west and the Laikipia escarpment to the east. Twelve different fossiliferous units have been described ranging in time from 14 m.y. B.P. to the Holocene Period (Bishop *et al.* 1971, 1978). Of these, six formations have produced hominid fossils. They are the Ngorora, the Lukeino, the Chemeron, the Chemoigut, the Chesowanja, and the Kapthurin sedimentary formations from older to younger.

Associated finds   1. An extensive invertebrate and vertebrate fauna has been reported from the Ngorora Formation (Bishop and Chapman, 1970; Bishop *et al.*, 1971; Bishop and Pickford, 1975; Pickford, 1978). The fauna includes molluscs, arthropods, fish, reptiles, birds and mammals. The large mammals include a gomphothere (*Gomphotherium ngorora*), a deinothere (*Deinotherium bozasi*), an equid (*Hipparion primigenium*), a giraffid (*Palaeotragus sp.*), a new suid as well as several bovids (Gentry, 1978) and the oldest hippopotamids known (Coryndon, 1978). The palaeoenvironment suggested includes a freshwater lake with oscillatory lake levels (Bishop and Pickford, 1975).

2. The Lukeino Formation has yielded an extensive invertebrate and vertebrate fauna (Bishop *et al.*, 1971, Pickford, 1975). This fauna includes proboscidians (*Anancus sp.*, *Deinotherium sp.*, *Primelephas*), an equid (*Hipparion*), artiodactyls including giraffids, antelopes, pigs and hippopotami, carnivores such as canids, viverrids and hyaenids. A full list is given by Pickford (1978). The palaeoenvironment seems to have been associated with the presence of a large freshwater lake.

3. The Chemeron Formation is subdivided into five members in the Chemeron basin (Martyn, 1967; Bishop *et al.*, 1971). Member 1 (Basal Beds), 2 (Lower Fish Beds) and 4 (Upper Fish Beds) have produced fossils. Sediments in the Kipcherere tectonic basin and its northern extension have yielded a vertebrate fauna similar to that from certain of the sites in Member 1. Faunal lists referring to both basins have been given by Bishop *et al.*, (1971) and by Pickford *et al.*, (1983). These lists include invertebrates and vertebrates, most of which are lake or lake marginal species such as fish, molluscs and crocodiles. The mammalian fauna includes proboscideans (*Anancus sp.*, *Deinotherium bozasi*; *Mammuthus subplanifrons*; *Loxodonta adaurora*, *Elephas recki*), an equid (aff. *Hipparion*), a rhinocerotid (*Ceratotherium simum*), pigs (several *spp.*), hippopotami (2 *spp.*), giraffids, bovids, rodent (*cf. Xenohystrix crassidens*), a colobus monkey (*Paracolobus chemeroni*) and a baboon (*Papio baringensis*) (Bishop *et al.*, 1971).

4. Numerous stone tools and flakes were found, both on the surface and *in situ*, at what has been termed a 'living site'. The artefacts recovered include both flake and core tools of Acheulean type (M. D. Leakey *et al.* 1969; Gowlett, 1981).

The Kapthurin Formation has yielded an extensive fauna which is essentially modern; similar to that living in open bushland in the area today (Tallon, 1978). This fauna also contains lake, marginal lake, and marsh dwelling forms such as fish (*Tilapia sp.*), molluscs (*Melanoides sp.*), crocodiles (*Crocodylus sp.*). The mammals recovered include elephant (*Loxodonta* sp.), rhinoceros (*Ceratotherium sp.*), pigs (*Mesochoerus sp., Notochoerus sp., Potamochoerus sp., Phacochoerus sp.*), hippopotamus (*Hippopotomus amphibius*), as well as antelopes and some rodents (Bishop *et al.*, 1971; Coryndon, 1978; Gentry 1978; Tallon, 1978).

5. (a) The Chemoigut Formation has produced several archaeological sites that have together produced over 1,000 artefacts *in situ*. They have been assigned to the Oldowan industrial complex equivalent to those from Olduvai Bed I and Lower Bed II. It has been termed the Chemoigut Industry (Bishop and Pickford, 1975; Gowlett *et al.*, 1981); Harris and Gowlett, 1981).

Faunal remains from the site are numerous and include molluscs, fish, reptiles and mammals such as elephants (*Elephas cf. recki*), a deinothere (*Deinotherium bozasi*), equids (*Equus sp.*), bovids, suids, giraffids, hippopotami (*Hippopotamus amphibius*), and a rhinoceros (*Ceratotherium simum*) (Carney *et al.*, 1971; Bishop *et al.*, 1971; Bishop and Pickford, 1975; Gowlett *et al.*, 1981).

5. (b) The Chesowanja Formation has also produced artefacts of small size made of lava. They have been attributed to the Developed Oldowan industry. Numbers of bifaces are certainly associated with this assemblage. A subset of this industry made of welded tuff has been termed the Losokweta Industry and is regarded as cf. Developed Oldowan in character (Gowlett *et al.*, 1981; Harris and Gowlett, 1981).

The presence of fire at the site has been claimed from the evidence of burnt clay. Magnetic studies indicate that the fire was of low temperature and thus, perhaps, a small, controlled fire used by hominids (Gowlett *et al.*, 1981). It seems that better evidence than this will be needed to establish fire use by hominids at a date as early as that usually given for the Chesowanja Formation.

The fauna from the Chesowanja Formation seems in essence the same as that known from the Chemoigut Formation; both have been sampled at Chesowanja (Carney *et al.*, 1971; Bishop *et al.*, 1971).

Dating   *1. The Ngorora Formation*

Preliminary K–Ar dates given for this formation indicated an age of 9–12 m.y. B.P. (Bishop and Chapman, 1970). Stratigraphic studies accompanied by faunal studies and further K–Ar dates confirmed the age (Bishop *et al.*, 1971; Bishop and Pickford, 1975). More recent studies have provided a series of K–Ar dates through the type-section from 12·83 m.y. at the base to 10·50 about two-thirds of the way up the sequence (Hill *et al.*, in press). Faunal evidence suggests that exposures of the formation in the south of the discontinuous outcrop may reveal sequences younger than the type section.

2. *The Lukeino Formation*

The same preliminary studies that established the stratigraphy and faunal contents and initial dating of the Ngorora Formation (see above) also suggested that the date of the Lukeino Formation was about 6·5 m.y. B.P. (Pickford, 1975). Recent studies with new K–Ar dates indicate that the formation is dated at between 5·5 and 6·0 m.y. B.P. (Hill *et al.*, in press).

3. (*a*) *The Chemeron Formation*

Five members are recognized in the Chemeron of the Chemeron basin (Martyn, 1967). It is believed that Member 4 (Upper Fish Beds) was the source of the hominid temporal yet it does not contain a good mammalian fauna for direct faunal dating. Member 1 (Basal Beds) contains locally abundant mammalian fossils, most of which indicate an age of between 4 and 5 m.y., but at one site in this member there are much younger faunal elements (*E. recki*, *C. simum*) that suggest an age of 2·0–2·5 m.y. B.P. and 'young' taxa also occur nearby in Member 2 (Lower Fish Beds) (Bishop *et al.*, 1971). This problem is yet to be resolved. Isotopic dates (K–Ar) for lavas that overlie, or are intercalated in the top of the formation in the Chemeron basin are 1·57 m.y. and 2·13 m.y. B.P. The temporal fragment was found in the same near-continuous river section that yielded the younger 'Basal Beds' fauna (Bishop, 1972) and probably should thus be dated at between 1·5 and 2·5 m.y. B.P.

(*b*) The humeral fragment was recovered from sediments correlated with those in the Kipcherere tectonic basin; these were originally referred to as Kipcherere Beds and were broadly correlated with the Chemeron Formation (Bishop, 1972, Bishop *et al.*, 1971). Fossiliferous horizons in these sediments overlie a lapilli-tuff that has been isotopically (K–Ar) dated at 5·1 m.y. B.P. (Pickford *et al.*, 1983). This is consistent with an age of 5·5 m.y. (recalculated with new constants) from the underlying Kaparaina basalts formation given by Chapman and Brook (1978). The fauna in these sediments, especially the suids, indicate an age of a little older than 4·0 m.y. (Pickford *et al.*, 1983) or 4·15 m.y. (Hill *et al.*, in press). The humeral fragment thus appears to be dated at between 4 and 5 m.y. B.P.

4. (*a*) When the Kapthurin (KNM–BK 67) mandible was recovered

from the Kapthurin Formation it was believed on faunal grounds that the site was of late Middle Pleistocene age (M. Leakey *et al.*, 1969). Later a single K–Ar determination suggested an age of 230,000 years B.P. (Bishop *et al.*, 1971); other K–Ar dates from the Kapthurin Beds range between 230,000 years B.P. and 870,000 years B.P. (Tallon, 1978). A series of papers on the Lake Baringo Basin is to be found in Bishop (1978), including several on the stratigraphy and dating of the area.

(*b*) Correlation of the Grey Tuffs in the Kapthurin Formation may indicate that the Kapthurin (KNM–BK 8518) mandible and the Kapthurin (KNM–BK 67) mandible are of the same age (Wood and Van Noten, 1986).

5. (*a*) The Chesowanja Basalt which immediately overlies the Chemoigut Formation has been dated to 1.42 ± 0.07 m.y. B.P. by K–Ar dating (Hooker and Miller, 1979).

(*b*) The date originally given for the Chesowanja australopithecine site was 1.13 ± 0.06 m.y. B.P. (Carney *et al.*, 1971). Later, after further geological study and faunal analysis, a minimum age of 1.34 m.y. B.P. has been given for this site (Bishop *et al.*, 1975).

Morphology   1. *The Ngorora tooth (KNM–BN 1378).*

This is the crown of a left upper molar from which the roots have broken away. There are contact facets both medially and distally of the nature of those between molars, thus it may be a left upper second molar. The crown is low, almost unworn and with a good cusp and fissure pattern; there is no cingulum (L. S. B. Leakey in Bishop and Chapman, 1970).

2. *The Lukeino tooth (KNM–LU 335).*

This is a left lower molar crown that was probably unerupted; there is no sign of root development. The crown is short and broad with low and rounded cusps showing good relief and a dryopithecine Y-fissure pattern. There is secondary enamel wrinkling and thick enamel (Andrews, in Pickford, 1975).

3. (*a*) *The Chemeron temporal fragment (KNM–BC 1).*

The specimen comprises most of the right temporal bone including the mandibular fossa, the tympanic bone and the bony acoustic meatus; part of the mastoid process and most of the petrous portion of the bone. The squamous portion is broken away. The mandibular fossa is large, anteroposteriorly 'uncompressed' and with a three-
fold curvature. The postglenoid process is small and the mastoid process projects strongly on the side of the base of the skull (Tobias, 1967).

(b) The Chemeron humeral fragment (KNM–BC 1745).

The specimen is from the left side and comprises parts of the head, the greater tuberosity, the lesser tuberosity, the neck and the upper shaft. The intertubercular groove is broad and shallow. The specimen is subadult according to the state of epiphyseal development. The attachments of pectoralis major and subscapularis are discernible. The head is elliptical (Pickford *et al.*, 1983).

4. (a) The Kapthurin Upper Limb Bones and Mandible
(KNM–BK 63–67).

The mandible is almost complete, lacking only small parts of the angles of the jaw and the coronoid processes. The anterior teeth and a small part of the adjacent alveolar process of bone are missing. The crowns of the right second premolar and the three molars are present as well as the left second and third molars and the stumps of several other teeth. The third molars are fully erupted and bear some occlusal attrition. The jaw as a whole is a little warped but its principal morphological features are easily seen. It has a sloping symphysis menti, a well defined planum alveolare, a superior and an inferior transverse torus and parallel upper and lower borders to the body. The ramus is remarkably broad.

The ulna is in three pieces that fit together. It is long, thin, curved and has a relatively small upper end with a broad rather shallow (articular) notch. The head of the bone is missing. There are also two phalanges and a metatarsal from the site that were recovered *in situ*.

(b) The Second Kapthurin Mandible (KNM–BK 8518).

This adult mandible was found in four pieces. The body is cracked and warped but essentially intact. The teeth are heavily and asymmetrically worn and the dental arcade has been distorted post-mortem. The body bears a well marked *incisura submentalis* but no chin. The outer aspect of the body bears a torus parallel to the alveolar border, there are also some signs of periodontal disease.

The upper and lower borders of the body are parallel and the digastric fossae face posteroinferiorly. There is also a well marked planum alveolare. The left ramus bears a stout crista endocoronoidea. The molar teeth are so heavily worn that almost no cusp and fissure morphology is distinguishable. The third molar teeth are bigger than the first and second molars which are themselves about equal in size.

5. (a) The Chemoigut Australopithecine (KNM–CH 304).

This fragmentary cranium comprises five cranial vault fragments. One includes lambda, inion and most of the left side of the bone including asterion, others include the left parietal, the left squamous temporal and a small piece of right parietal. The bones bear prominent ectocranial crests and the occipital is grooved for a prominent occipital venous sinus (Gowlett *et al.*, 1981).

(b) The Chesowanja Australopithecine (KNM–CH 1; KNM–CH 302).

The specimen comprises most of the face, some of the base and some of the vault of a robust cranium. The upper teeth on the right side are preserved. The teeth are very large with molarization of the premolars and a relatively small canine. The specimen is the subject of some crushing and deformation so that details of its anatomy are obscured but it is possible to see that it had a broad dished face, with well developed frontal air sinuses (Carney *et al.*, 1971).

Further remains from the same site (KNM–CH 302) came to light in 1973, they consist of fragmentary upper molar teeth that may have come from the first cranium to be found at the site and described above (Bishop and Pickford, 1975).

Dimensions   *1. The Ngorora tooth (KNM–BN 1378)*

Mesiodistal length	12·35
Buccolingual breadth	14·00

(Bishop and Chapman, 1970)

2. The Lukeino tooth (KNM–LU 335)

Mesiodistal length	11·4
Buccolingual breadth	10·6

(Pickford, 1975)

3. (a) The Chemeron temporal fragment (KNM–BC 1)

Mandibular fossa:

Length	26·7
Breadth	35·7
Depth	10·6

(Tobias, 1967)

3. (b) The Chemeron humeral fragment (KNM–BC 1745)

Cortical thickness:

At midpoint of intertubercular groove	2·5
At lateral edge of intertubercular groove	4·3
Diameter of medullary cavity at break point	12

(Pickford *et al.*, 1975)

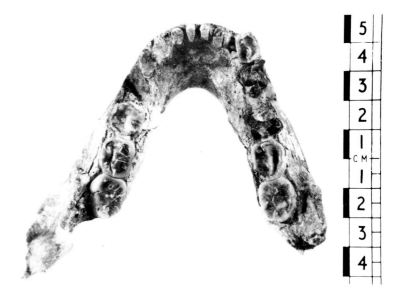

Fig. 81. The KNM–BK 8518 mandible (occlusal view). *Courtesy of the Director of the National Museums of Kenya.*

4. (a) *The Kapthurin mandible (KNM–BK 67)*

Thickness of mandibular corpus:

	At 2nd Premolar	At M_1	At M_3
Left	17·1	—	—
Right	16·4	17·3	19·8

(Tobias, in Leakey *et al.*, 1969)

4. (b) *The Kapthurin mandible (KNM–BK 8518)*

Symphyseal height   30
Thickness of mandibular corpus:

	At 2nd Premolar	At M_1	At M_2	At M_3
Left	18·5	21·0	23·0	22·0
Right	19·0	20·5	22·0	21·5

(Wood and Van Noten, 1986)

5. (a) *The Chemoigut australopithecine (KNM–CH 304)*

Parietal
    Sagital chord   75
    Thickness at bregma   5·3
    Thickness at asterion   2·3
Occipital
    Inion—left asterion chord   52
    Lambda—Inion chord   37

Thickness at lambda   10
Thickness at asterion   14·5

(B. A. Wood in Gowlett et al., 1981)

5. (b) *The Chesowanja australopithecine (KNM–CH 1)*

		I^1	I^2	C	PM^1	PM^2	M^1	M^2	M^3
				Upper Teeth (Crown Dimensions)					
Left	l	—	—	—	—	—	—	—	—
Side	b	—	—	—	—	—	—	—	—
Right	l	—	—	8·2	10·0	11·7	14·4	15·5	17·2
Side	b	—	—	8·4	13·7	15·5	14·8	16·0	16·5

(Carney et al., 1971)

Affinities   1. *The Ngorora tooth (KNM–BN 1378)*

At between 9–12 m.y. B.P. this tooth may be the oldest example of a hominid from anywhere in the world should its attribution to the Hominidae be substantiated by other finds and more diagnostic material.

2. *The Lukeino tooth (KNM–LU 335)*

At 6·5 m.y. B.P. this tooth is also one of the older examples of hominids from East Africa and its attribution to the Hominidae also needs substantiation by new finds and more diagnostic remains.

3. (a) *The Chemeron temporal fragment (KNM–BC 1)*

This specimen has been referred to the Hominidae, Gen. et sp. indet., yet it is admitted that most of its features suggest that it belonged to an australopithecine (Tobias, 1967). In my view there is sufficient evidence to allow its attribution to *Australopithecus cf. boisei.*

(b) *The Chemeron humeral fragment (KNM–BC 1745)*

This specimen has been cautiously referred to the Superfamily Hominoidea whilst hinting at its hominid affinities by drawing attention to its similarities to AL 288-1r from Hadar (q.v.), a specimen attributed to *Australopithecus afarensis* (Pickford *et al.*, 1975). This would seem as far as it is safe to go on such scanty evidence.

4. (a) *The Kapthurin upper limb bones and mandible*
(*KNM–BK 63–67*)

This Kapthurin mandible has been attributed to the genus *Homo* cf. *erectus* on the basis of its similarities to the mandibles known from Ternifine in North Africa (q.v.). It is said to 'fit comfortably' within the ranges of features shown by these mandibles attributed to *Homo erectus*. Caution has prevented a full attribution however, since the remains are insufficient for confidence (Tobias, 1967). To my eye the specimen has sufficient evidence for a clear attribution to *Homo erectus*.

(b) The Kapthurin mandible (KNM–BL 8518)

From personal examination, and from the published description, this mandible has many similarities to those of *Homo erectus*, as well as to the previous mandible found in the same deposits. There are, however, sufficient doubts in the minds of its describers to take a cautious view until other material from East Africa is fully described, cf. Tobias (in Leakey *et al.*, 1969) with the KNM–BK 67 mandible. It is clear, however, that it is not regarded as australopithecine and that both mandibles from the Kapthurin Formation would fit comfortably in the same taxon. The Kapthurin mandible (KNM–BK 8518) has been placed in *Homo* sp. indet. (aff. *erectus*).

5. (a) The Chemoigut australopithecine (KNM–CH 304)

These skull fragments have been confidently attributed to *Australopithecus boisei* on the grounds of their similarity to both KNM–ER 406 and Olduvai Hominid 5 (*q.v.*) (Gowlett *et al.*, 1981).

(b) The Chesowanja australopithecine (KNM–CH 1 and KNM–CH 302)

The larger specimen has been attributed to cf. *A. robustus/A. boisei* of 'late' type whose more gross features have been refined (Carney *et al.*, 1971). This view has not been substantiated by other finds such as the previous Chemoigut australopithecine (Gowlett *et al.*, 1981).

The principal interest of this specimen, the Chesowanja australopithecine, is that at 1·4 m.y. B.P. it is probably one of the latest sites to produce a robust australopithecine fossil since their extinction must be presumed soon after this date.

Originals The National Museum of Kenya, Nairobi.

Casts The Supervisor, Casting Department, National Museum of Kenya, P.O. Box 40658, Nairobi, Kenya.

References Bishop, W. W. (1967) Stratigraphical nomenclature in the Baringo area of the northern Kenya Rift Valley. *Proc. pan-Afr. Cong. Prehist. Dakar 1967*, 332–333.

Martyn, J. E. (1967) Pleistocene deposits and new fossil localities in Kenya. *Nature* 215, 476–480.

McCall, G. J. H., Baker, B. H. and Walsh, J. (1967) Late Tertiary and Quaternary sediments of the Kenya Rift Valley. In *Background to Evolution in Africa*, 191–220. Eds. W. W. Bishop and J. D. Clark. Chicago: University of Chicago Press.

Tobias, P. V. (1967) *Ibid*, 479–480.

Leakey, M., Tobias, P. V., Martyn, J. E. and Leakey, R. E. F. (1969) An Acheulean Industry with prepared core technique and the discovery of a contemporary hominid mandible at Lake Baringo, Kenya. *Proc. prehist. Soc. XXXV*, 48–76.

Bishop, W. W. and Chapman, G. R. (1970) Early Pliocene sediments and fossils from the northern Kenya Rift Valley. *Nature 226*. 914–918.

Bishop, W. W., Chapman, G. R., Hill, A. and Miller, J. A. (1971) Succession of Cainozoic vertebrate assemblages from the northern Kenya Rift Valley. *Nature 233*, 389–394.

Carney, J., Hill, A., Miller, J. A., Walker, A. (1971) Late Australopithecine from Baringo. *Nature 230*, 509–514.

Bishop, W. W. (1972) Stratigraphic succession 'versus' calibration in East Africa. In *Calibration of Hominoid Evolution*, 219–246. Eds. W. W. Bishop and J. A. Miller. Edinburgh: Scottish Academic Press.

Bishop, W. W. and Pickford, M. (1975) Geology, fauna and palaeoenvironments of the Ngorora Formation, Kenya Rift Valley. *Nature 254*, 185–192.

Bishop, W. W., Pickford, M. and Hill, A. (1975) New evidence regarding the Quaternary geology, archaeology and hominids of Chesowanja, Kenya. *Nature 258*, 204–208.

Pickford, M. (1975) Late Miocene sediments and fossils from the northern Kenya Rift Valley. *Nature 256*, 279–284.

Bishop, W. W. Ed. (1978) *Geological Background to Fossil Man*. Edinburgh: Scottish Academic Press.

Chapman, G. R. and Brook, M. (1978) Chronostratigraphy of the Baringo Basin, Kenya. *Ibid*, 207–223.

Coryndon, S. C. (1978) Fossil Hippopotamidae from the Baringo Basin and relationships within the Gregory Rift, Kenya. *Ibid*, 279–292.

Dagley, P., Mussett, A. E. and Palmer, H. C. (1978) Preliminary observations on the palaeomagnetic stratigraphy of the area west of Lake Baringo, Kenya. *Ibid*, 225–235.

Gentry, A. W. (1978) Fossil Bovidae of the Baringo Area, Kenya. *Ibid*, 293–308.

Pickford, M. H. L. (1978) Geology, palaeoenvironments and vertebrate faunas of the mid-Miocene Ngorora Formation, Kenya. *Ibid*, 237–267.

Pickford, M. H. L. (1978) Stratigraphy and mammalian palaeontology of the late-Miocene Lukeino Formation, Kenya. *Ibid*, 263–278.

Tallon, P. W. J. (1978) Geological setting of the hominid fossils and Acheulian artifacts from the Kapthurin Formation, Baringo District, Kenya. *Ibid*, 361–373.

Hooker, P. J. and Miller, J. A. (1979) K–Ar dating of the Pleistocene fossil hominid site at Chesowanja, north Kenya. *Nature 282*, 710–712.

Gowlett, J. A. J. (1981) Acheulean sites in the central Rift Valley, Kenya. *Proc. pan.-Afr. Cong. Prehist. Nairobi 1977*, 213–217.

Gowlett, J. A. J., Harris, J. W. K., Walton, D. and Wood, B. A. (1981) Early archaeological sites, hominid remains and traces of fire from Chesowanja, Kenya. *Nature 294*, 125–129.

Harris, J. W. K. and Gowlett, J. A. J. (1981) Evidence of early stone industries at Chesowanja, Kenya. *Proc. pan-Afr. Cong. Prehist. Nairobi 1977*, 208–212.

Pickford, M., Johanson, D.C., Lovejoy, C.C., White, T.D. and Aronson, J.L. (1983) A hominoid humeral fragment from the Pliocene of Kenya. *Am. J. phys. Anthrop.* 60, 337–346.

Van Noten, F. (1983) News from Kenya. *Antiquity* July 1983, 139–140.

Hill, A., Curtis, G. and Drake, R. (in press) Sedimentary stratigraphy of the Tugen Hills, Baringo, Kenya. In *Sedimentation in the African Rift System*. Eds. L.E. Frostick, R. Renaut, I. Reid and J. Tiercelin. Oxford: Blackwells.

Wood, B.A. and Van Noten, F.L. (1986) Preliminary observations on the BK 8518 mandible from Baringo, Kenya. *Am. J. phys. Anthrop.* 69. 117–127.

The West Turkana Skeleton

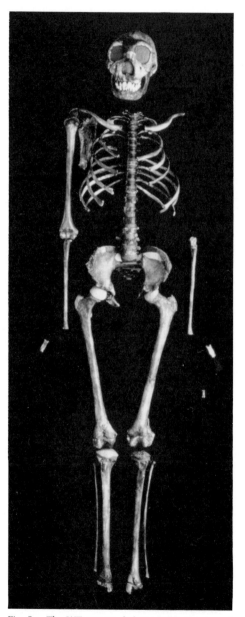

Fig. 82. The WT 15000 skeleton NYP. *Courtesy of the Director of the National Museums of Kenya.*

Synonyms and other names	*Homo erectus* (Brown *et al.*, 1985a); KNM–WT 15000.
Site	Nariokotome III, on the south bank of the Nariokotome river; this ephemeral river drains into the west side of Lake Turkana, northern Kenya.
Found by	Bw Kamoya Kimeu of the hominid research group of the National Museum of Kenya, directed by R. E. Leakey.
Geology	Ancient sediments of Lake Turkana are interspersed volcanic tuffs that have resulted from previous volcanic eruptions. Several of these tuffs have been correlated with tuffs elsewhere in the Turkana Basin. The hominid skeleton derives from a siltstone that immediately overlies a tuff identified as a component ash of the Okote Tuff complex of the Koobi Fora Formation (*q.v.*).
	A site plan of the excavation shows that the bones of the skeleton were dispersed before final sedimentary burial, their alignment in the deposit suggests only minor water transport; the majority of the bones were recovered from an area of about 20 m² (215 ft²).
Associated finds	There are no stone tools directly associated with the skeleton.
	The vertebrate faunal remains closely associated with the skeleton are mostly small and large fish, suggesting that the skeleton was deposited in or near the margin of the lake. Several other vertebrate fossil sites were found near that which yielded the hominid. These sites produced the following species from both sides of the lake at horizons below the Okote Tuff: proboscidians (*Deinotherium bozasi*, *Elephas recki ileretensis*), rhinoceros (*Diceros bicornis*), a suid (*Metridiochoerus andrewsi*) and a bovid (*Gazella janenschi*). Another suid was found only at a horizon above the Okote Tuff (*Metridiochoerus compactus*). So far only one bovid (*Tragelaphus scriptus*) is known from the west side of the lake that is not also represented on the east side.
Dating	The skeleton was found in lake sediments that immediately overlie a tuff identified as a component ash of the Okote Tuff complex of the Koobi Fora Formation. The age of the Okote Tuff complex has been given as approximately 1·65 m.y. B.P. (McDougall *et al.*, 1985; Brown and Feibel, 1985). Another ash that correlates with Tuff L of the Shungura Formation of the Omo region (*q.v.*) and the Chari Tuff of the Koobi Fora Formation (*q.v.*) lies 34 m above the hominid level. These tuffs have been dated at 1·39 m.y. B.P. (McDougall, 1985; Brown *et al.*, 1985b) and an unnamed tuff at 46 m above the hominid site has been dated at 1·33 m.y. (Brown *et al.*, 1985b). The faunal evidence is in conformity with these suggested dates, so the hominid can be dated at very close to 1·6 m.y. B.P. with some confidence.

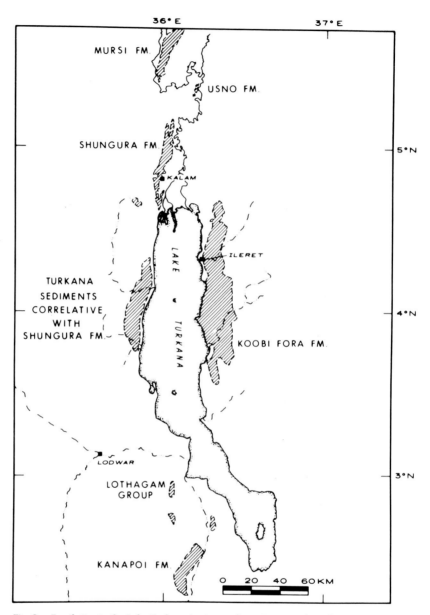

Fig. 83. Fossil sites in the Lake Turkana basin, northern Kenya and southern Ethiopia.
Courtsey of F. H. Brown.

Morphology   The hominid skeleton is virtually complete and comprises the cranium and mandible, 19 vertebrae from all parts of the vertebrate column (even the coccyx), 16 ribs, both clavicles and scapulae and the right humerus, the pelvis, both femora, both tibiae and both

Table 7   *Skeletal parts of KNM–WT 15000*

Cranium (A)	Right rib 5 fragment (BJ)
Mandible (B)	Right rib 6 (AL)
Cervical vertebra 7 (R)	Left rib 7 (AP)
Thoracic vertebra 1 (S)	Right rib 7 (AK)
Thoracic vertebra 2 (T)	Left rib 8 (AU)
Thoracic vertebra 3 (U)	Right rib 8 (AM)
Thoracic vertebra 6 or 7 spine or laminae (BI)	Left rib 9 (AO)
Thoracic vertebra 8 (V)	Right rib 9 (AS)
Thoracic vertebra 9 (W)	Right rib 10 (AJ)
Thoracic vertebra 10 (X)	Left rib 11 (AN)
Thoracic vertebra 11 (Y)	Left clavicle (C)
Lumbar vertebra 1, body and right lamina and inferior facet (AR, BA)	Right clavicle (D)
Lumbar vertebra 2 (AA, AV)	Left scapula, spine and axillary border (BK, BL)
Lumbar vertebra 3, pedicle laminae and spine (Z)	Right scapula (E)
Lumbar vertebra 4 (AB)	Right humerus (F)
Lumbar vertebra 5 (AC)	Left ilium (L, BF, BG)
Sacral vertebra 1 (AD)	Left ilium (L, BF, BG)
Sacral vertebra 3, laminae and spine (BB)	Left ischium (Q)
Sacral vertebra, right half (BC)	Right ilium (O)
Sacral vertebra 5 (AE)	Right ischium (P)
Coccygeal vertebra 1 (AF)	Right pubic fragments (AW, AX)
Left rib 1 (AG)	Left femur (G)
Right rib 1 (AY, AZ)	Right femur (H, M)
Left rib 2 (AQ)	Left tibia (I)
Right rib 2 (AH)	Right tibia (J)
Left rib 3 (AT)	Left fibular (K, BH)
Right rib 4 (AI, BD, BE)	Right fibula (L)

(After Brown *et al.*, 1985)

fibulae. Further remains recovered in 1985 included both ulnae, another lumber vertebra, several more partial ribs, some hand bones, and all the missing teeth including the deciduous upper canines (R. E. Leakey, pers. comm.). Excavations are continuing and there are hopes that the remaining omissions will be remedied. It is without doubt the most complete and remarkable find of a hominid of this age from anywhere in the world.

There are no signs of carnivore or scavenger damage nor serious bone pathology. Damage is limited to some breakage and crushing of cancellous bone which might have resulted from trampling by large mammals at the water's edge.

The skeleton is immature as shown by the dentition and the state of the skeletal development; all the epiphyses are unfused. On the basis of modern human comparison an age of 12 ± 1 year would be appropriate.

The Skull

The cranium has been reconstructed from 70 pieces and is large, considering that it is immature. It lacks robust tori and strong temporal markings yet its palate is broader, its facial skeleton larger and its tori thicker than those of KNM–ER 3733 from Koobi Fora (*q.v.*), a skull attributed to *Homo erectus* of the same geological age and presumed to be female. This may mean that sexual dimorphism was considerable in these hominids. The mandible is chinless and has a broad ramus.

The Teeth

The teeth recovered (see below) are close in size to the means of those from the Peking *Homo erectus* sample but the incisors are larger.

The Postcranial Bones

The postcranial bones are of immense importance since they are clearly associated with the skull and dentition. The range of the skeletal parts is such that it has been possible to estimate stature on the basis of regression formulae (1·68 m/5′7″ white males; 1·64 m/5′3½″ black males). It will also be possible to determine brain/body ratios when the cranial capacity is known. Of particular interest is the similarity of the hip bones to those of OH 28 from Olduvai (*q.v.*) and KNM–ER 3228 from Koobi Fora (*q.v.*).

Several of the features described for these specimens (Day, 1971; Rose, 1984) and suggested as characteristic of *Homo erectus* (Day 1971, 1982, 1984) have been noted. The acetabulo-cristal buttress is not yet fully developed in this immature individual, but the femoral head diameter is similar to that of modern man and quite unlike that of contemporary australopithecines.

Dimensions   *Skull*

Not available at present.

Teeth

KNM–WT 15000	I¹	I²	C	Upper Teeth (Crown Dimensions) PM¹	PM²	M¹	M²	M³
Left l	—	7·9	—	—	—	11·1	13·3	—
Side b	—	8·3	—	—	—	11·8	11·7	—
Right l	—	7·9	—	8·3	8·2	12·2	12·5	—
Side b	—	8·5	11·5	11·5	11·8	11·8	12·6	—

	I_1	I_2	C	Lower Teeth (Crown Dimensions) PM_1	PM_2	M_1	M_2	M_3
Left l	—	—	8·6	8·5	9·0	12·2	12·2	—
Side b	—	—	9·4	10·1	9·5	10·9	11·5	—
Right l	—	—	8·8	9·0	—	11·9	12·4	—
Side b	—	—	9·0	10·1	—	11·1	11·4	—

Postcranial Bones

Diameter of head of femur 44
Neck—shaft angle of femur 110°

Affinities There is clearly no doubt in the minds of those who described this skeleton that it should be attributed to *Homo erectus*; a decision based upon cranial, dental and postcranial evidence not all of which has been published as yet.

Described as 'human-like' in many respects, some anatomical differences from *Homo sapiens* have been noted, and indeed some are apparent from the illustrations. These include recession of the forehead and chin, dental features and features of the vertebral column and pelvis. The skeleton is regarded as male on pelvic evidence. It can be expected that further study will contribute significantly to the debate that currently surrounds the status of the taxon *Homo erectus*; the relationships between its African and Asian examples, its ancestral relationship (or not) to modern *Homo sapiens* and its validity as a taxon in the light of phylogenetic analysis. (See also The *Homo erectus* question, this volume.)

Originals The National Museum of Kenya, Nairobi, Republic of Kenya.

Casts Not available at present.

References Day, M. H. (1971) Postcranial remains of *Homo erectus* from Bed IV, Olduvai Gorge, Tanzania. *Nature 232*, 383–387.

Day, M. H. (1982) The *Homo erectus* pelvis: punctuation or gradualism? In *L'Homo erectus et la place de l'homme de Tautavel parmi les hominids fossiles.* Cong. Int. Paléont. hum. Nice 1982. Prétirage, 411–421.

Day, M. H. (1984) The postcranial remains of *Homo erectus* from Africa, Asia and possibly Europe. *Cour. Forsch. Inst. Senck. 69*, 113–121.

Rose, M. D. (1984) A hominine hip bone, KNM–ER 3228, from East Turkana, Kenya, *Am. J. phys. Anthrop. 63*, 371–387.

Brown, F., Harris, J. R., Leakey, E. and Walker, A. (1985) Early *Homo erectus* skeleton from west Lake Turkana, Kenya. *Nature 316*, 788–792.

Brown, F. H., McDougall, I., Davis, T. and Maier, R. (1985) An integrated Plio-Pleistocene chronology for the Turkana Basin. In *Ancestors*, 82–90. Ed. E. Delson. New York: Alan R. Liss.

Brown, F. H. and Feibel, C. S. (1985) Stratigraphical notes on the Okote Tuff Complex at Koobi Fora, Kenya. *Nature 316*, 794–797.

McDougall, I. (1985) K–Ar and ^{40}Ar/^{39}Ar dating of the hominid bearing Plio-Pleistocene sequence at Koobi Fora, Lake Turkana, northern Kenya. *Bull. geol. Soc. Am. 96*, 159–175.

McDougall, I. Davies, T., Maier, R. and Rudowski, R. (1985) Age of the Okote Tuff Complex at Koobi Fora, Kenya. *Nature 316*, 792–794.

The Omo Remains

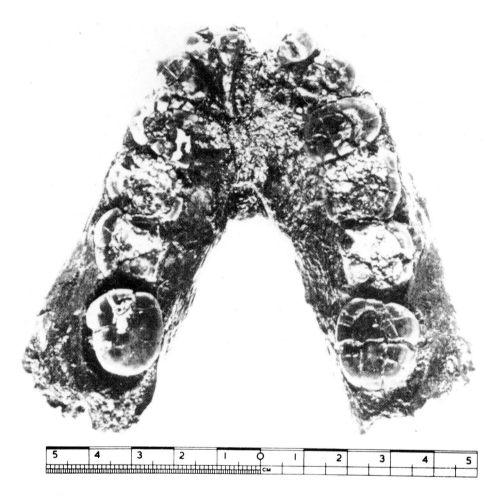

Fig. 84. The Omo SL7A–125 mandible and dentition (occlusal view). *Courtesy of F. Clark Howell.*

Synonyms and other names   (1) *Paraustralopithecus aethiopicus* (Arambourg and Coppens, 1967)
(2) *Australopithecus cf. africanus* (Howell, 1969)
  Australopithecus aff. *africanus* (Howell, 1978)
  Australopithecus sp. (Howell, 1978)
  Australopithecus cf. boisei (Howell, 1969)
  Australopithecus boisei (Howell and Wood, 1974)
  Australopithecus boisei (Howell, 1978)

        cf. Homo habilis (Howell, 1978)
        Homo erectus (Howell, 1978)
(3) *Homo sapiens* (Day, 1969)

Site The lower basin of the Omo river, southwest Ethiopia.

Found by The International Palaeontological Research Expedition to the Omo Valley. (1) Material recovered by the French team. (2) Material recovered by the American team. (3) Material recovered by the Kenyan team, 1967.

Geology Five sedimentary formations have been formally recognized within the lower Omo basin, a tectonic depression that forms the northern part of the Lake Turkana trough. The Mursi, Nkalabong, Usno and Shungura Formations comprise the Omo group and are primarily fluvial deposits consisting of cross-bedded sands, silts and clays, interspersed with several pebble gravel lenses. Throughout each formation the fluvial deposits grade both laterally and stratigraphically into sediments of deltaic and lacustrine origin. The depositional environment of these deposits was probably not unlike that of the present day in relation to the Omo River, its delta and Lake Turkana into which it extends. Interbedded within these sediments are well over 100 tuffaceous beds. In the Shungura Formation, the most extensive formation within the basin, thirteen principal tuffs (designated A–M upwards) have been recognized. In addition to containing elements capable of being dated by the potassium-argon technique, these tuffs provide a useful series of marker beds for further dividing the sequence into members which are named according to their underlying tuff. The last of the five formations is the much younger Kibish Formation which unconformably overlies the older formations in all regions of the basin. It is upon this formation that the present-day land surface is formed. The French and American teams recovered hominids from the Usno Formation at Brown Sands and White Sands as well as from Members B, C, D, E, F, G, H, K and L of the Shungura Formation. The Kenyan team worked only in 1967 in more recent deposits in the Kibish Formation which is divided into four Members (I–IV); hominid fossils were recovered from the oldest of these Members, Member I.

Associated finds Both the American and French teams recovered stone artefacts from their respective areas, many made of quartz and all small flake fragments and angular fragments some of which show signs of utilization and retouch. No large tools were found that compare with those from Olduvai Gorge (*q.v.*).
The Kenyan team recovered very few tools from the Kibish hominid sites, all of which were surface finds except for a few flakes that

were found *in situ*. (Merrick, de Heinzelin, Haesaerts and Howell, 1973; Coppens, Chavaillon and Beden, 1973).

Over 40,000 specimens of fossil mammals have been recovered from the Omo region including elephants, pigs, bovids, cercopithecoid primates, hippopotami, rhinoceroses and carnivores (Arambourg, Chavaillon and Coppens, 1967; Howell and Coppens 1974; Howell, Fichter and Eck, 1969; Coppens, 1978; Howell, 1978).

Fossil mammals recovered from the Kibish Formation include buffalo, rhinoceros, elephant and cercopithecoid primates.

Dating   The lower Omo valley contains a long sequence of sedimentary and pyroclastic deposits of Plio/Pleistocene age (Brown, 1972) as well as deposits of later Pleistocene and Holocene age (Butzer, 1971). The Omo deposits have yielded a fossil vertebrate assemblage from a long sequence of deposits which affords many opportunities for both radiometric dating and palaeomagnetic correlation.

The Mursi and Nkalabong Formations span the early half of the Pliocene epoch. The basaltic lava flow at the top of the Mursi Formation has a potassium-argon age of c. 4·05 m.y. B.P., and within Member II of the Nkalabong Formation are a series of tuffs which have been radiometrically dated at c. 3·95 m.y. B.P. The basalt Member of the Usno Formation has been dated at 3·31 m.y. B.P. Both the faunal and radiometric dating indicate that the Usno Formation spans the later half of the Pliocene and is contemporary with deposits in the Shungura Formation. The Usno Formation has been divided into 20 units (U1–U20) from below upwards correlative with the Shungura Formation Basal Member up to B-10 of Member B (Howell, 1978).

The Shungura Formation has produced a substantial number of vertebrate fossils, most of them coming from fluviatile Members B to the lower Member G. The revised potassium-argon dating (Brown, *et al.*, 1985) places the age for Tuff B in the lower part of the section at 3·35 m.y. B.P. and Tuff L (the youngest dated tuff) at 1·4 m.y. B.P. The palaeomagnetic evidence from this formation is in agreement with the potassium-argon age estimates for the various tuffs and inclusive members (see figs. 71 and 72).

Mursi Formation	4·1 m.y. B.P.
Nkalabong Formation	3·95 m.y. B.P.
Usno Formation	2·97–3·3 m.y. B.P.
Shungura Formation	1·34–3·3 m.y. B.P.
	(Howell, 1978; Chavaillon, 1982)

The Kibish Formation has been dated to between 3,100–130,000 years B.P. (Butzer, 1971).

Morphology   A résumé of the hominids from the Omo has been given by Howell and Coppens (1976). (1) A mandibular body containing tooth roots that indicate small incisors and canines but large molars and premolars. The rami of the mandible are missing and the body is extremely robust. The *planum alveolare* is small and the genioglossal fossae are deep; the symphysis is very thick as are the right and left sides of the body in the region of the molar teeth.

(2) L7A–125

The body of a robust mandible containing all of the teeth except three incisors. The mandibular body is massive with no chin and a deep and stout symphysis. The dentition displays marked anteroposterior disproportion with heavy molarization of the premolars and reduction of the canines and incisors.

L74A–21

The right side of a mandibular body containing the canine and the P_4 as well as the roots of the P_3 and the first molar. The body of the mandible is comparatively slender but deep; the ramus is missing other than a small part of its root. The second premolar shows some degree of molarization but heavy attrition has removed much of the cusp detail.

L40–19

An almost complete right ulna that is long and attenuated with shaft curvature that is marked and convex posteriorly. Features that depart from the human condition include its length and curvature, its cross-sectional shaft profile, and some features of the head of the bone and of the muscle attachment pattern. Overall these features seem to point to an elongated forearm with some adaptions not unlike those seen in modern knuckle-walkers; however, features that are unlike those of knuckle-walkers are the 'set' of the articular surface of the upper end and the lack of buttressing of the coronoid process. A metrical analysis of the Omo ulna showed it to be unique in shape among extant hominoids although most similar to *Pan* and *Homo* (McHenry *et al.*, 1976). A fragmentary gracile hominid cranium has been described from Upper Member G of the Shungura Formation. Its reconstruction is somewhat speculative since few of the fragments have contacts (Boaz and Howell, 1977).

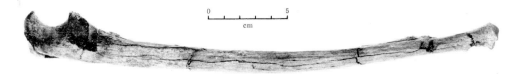

Fig. 85. The Omo L40–19 right ulna (lateral view). *Courtesy of Professor B. A. Wood.*

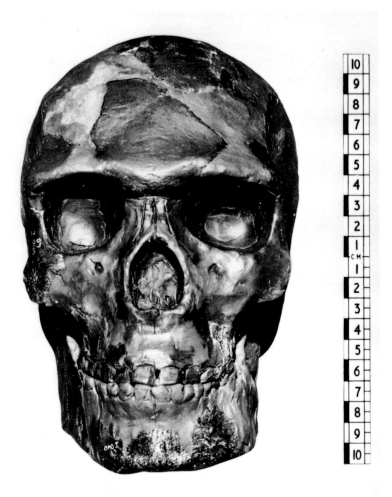

Fig. 86. The Omo I skull reconstructed by Professor M. H. Day and Dr C. B. Stringer.

(3) *Omo 1*

Site KHS produced a partial skeleton that was found partly *in situ* from the level of a minor unconformity within Member I of the Kibish Formation. It consists of an incomplete vault, parts of the mandible and both maxillae and two tooth crowns (a right upper canine and a left lower first molar). The postcranial remains are extensive and include parts of the skeleton of the upper limb girdle, the arm, forearm and hand as well as parts of the vertebral column. The lower limb remains include parts of the right femur, both tibiae, the right fibula and the right foot.

The skull is robust in construction with a rounded vault, an ex-

panded parietal region and a restricted nuchal plane. The mandibular and maxillary fragments show a rounded dental arcade while
the symphysial portion of the mandible has a well marked chin.
The teeth are robust but worn. The postcranial skeleton is essentially sapient in its general morphology (Kennedy, 1984).

Omo II

This calvaria was recovered from Site PHS as a surface find and it
is an almost intact cranial vault with much of the base retained.
The skull is heavily built with stout parietes. The form of the vault
is dolichocephalic with a receding forehead, a striking occipital
torus and an extensive flattened nuchal plane. In frontal view the
low vault is marked by a sessile keel with parasagittal flattenings
and the maximum breadth of the vault is low on the mastoid
portion of the temporal bone. The mastoid processes are large and
downturned whilst the articular fossae are deep.

Omo III

This specimen consists of a glabellar fragment and a frontoparietal
vault fragment. The glabellar fragment is heavily built with some
evidence of a broad brow and frontal recession.

Dimensions   (*1*) *Mandible*
Arambourg and Coppens (1968)

Total length of fragment	75
Height of body at M_2	33
Thickness of body at M_2	26
Symphysial height	35

(*2*) *L7A–125*

Mandible

Howell (1969)
No mandibular dimensions were given in the original description.

Teeth

		I_2	I_2	C	Lower Teeth (Crown Dimensions)				
					PM_1	PM_2	M_1	M_2	M_3
Left	l	—	—	7·8	10·4	11·7*	c. 18·7*	c. 16·2*	c. 18·2*
Side	b	—	—	9·6	c. 17·5*	c. 18·9*	c. 16·8*	18·0*	14.8*
Right	l	—	?	?	11·2	?	c. 18·7*	c. 16·2*	c. 18·2*
Side	b	—	?	?	c. 17·5*	c. 18·9*	c. 16·8*	18·0*	14·8*

* Details of side are not given for these teeth thus the dimensions may refer to either
or both sides.

L74A–21

Mandibular Fragment

No mandibular dimensions were given in the original description.

Teeth

				Lower Teeth (Crown Dimensions)				
	I_1	I_2	C	PM_1	PM_2	M_1	M_2	M_3
Right l	—	—	8·8	c. 12·8	13·0	—	—	—
Side b	—	—	9·7	—	13·75	—	—	—

L40–19

Ulna

Howell and Wood (1974)		McHenry, Corrucini and Howell (1976)	
Maximum length	315	Maximum length	313
		Midshaft A/P diameter	14·2

(3) *Omo 1*

Day (1969)

Skull

Maximum length	210
Maximum breadth	144*
Cranial index	68·5

Reconstructed Teeth

Right upper canine	Length	8·9
	Breadth	8·1
Left lower first molar	Length	—
	Breadth	11·5

Postcranial Bones

Provisionally the dimensions are within the range of modern man.

Omo II

Skull

Maximum length	215	Cranial capacity 1,435 ± 20
Maximum breadth	145	
Cranial index	67·5	

Omo III

No dimensions of value are available.

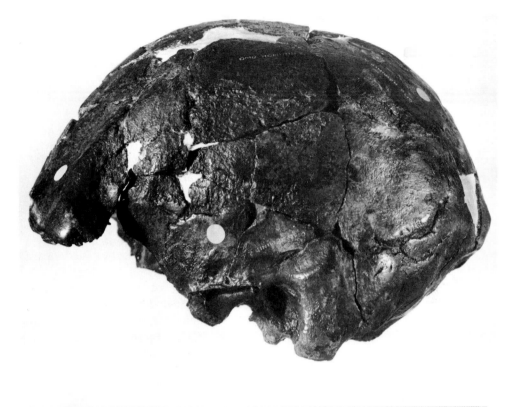

Fig. 87. The Omo II calvaria (left lateral view).

Affinities   (1) and (2) The hominids recovered from Members B, C, D, E and F and the lower units of G of the Shungura Formation have been attributed to *Australopithecus* and affined to the species *africanus*. Clearly this was not an easy determination since the remains tend to be small and fragmentary. Specimens from Members E, F, G and possibly L of the Shungura Formation have been attributed to *A. boisei* with more confidence. Some teeth and the partial cranium L. 894–1 have been attributed to *cf. Homo habilis*. These specimens derive from Members G, H and perhaps L of the Shungura Formation. From the uppermost part of Member K some cranial fragments are claimed to be diagnostic of *Homo erectus* (Howell, 1978).

The principal significance of the Omo Pliocene and earlier Pleistocene sites in the lower Omo basin resides in the fact that this region preserves and exposes the thickest, most continuous fossiliferous record of deposits of this age from anywhere in East Africa. The

Plio-Pleistocene succession in the lower Omo has an aggregate thickness of over one kilometre (1,093 m). Numerous tuffs are interspersed with lake sediments, and an unrivalled palaeomagnetic sequence has been recorded. Sadly, the depositional conditions seem to have resulted in the destruction of many of the hominid fossils so that the hominids recovered are disappointing in quantity and quality.

(3) In the original description and discussions of the Omo I and II calvariae (Day, 1969, 1971 and 1973) it was concluded that whilst they showed anatomical differences, these differences could be accommodated within the range of variability known for *Homo sapiens*, albeit of an archaic type. The relatively anatomically modern form of Omo I and the erectus-like features of Omo II have led to speculation that the date of the two specimens is not the same. The original dating of these skulls, suggesting their contemporaneity, is indeed unconfirmed and no other evidence seems likely to be forthcoming. The suggestion that they are closely related forms has been supported by Rightmire (1976, 1980, 1981, 1984) and Bräuer (1984) but following a new reconstruction of the Omo I calvaria, Day and Stringer (1982) have aligned Omo I with anatomically modern *Homo sapiens* and Omo II with *Homo erectus*. This study stops short of attributing Omo II to *Homo erectus*.

Originals   National Museum of Ethiopia, Addis Ababa, Ethiopia

Casts   Not available at present

References   Arambourg, C. and Coppens, Y. (1967) Sur la découverte dans le Pléistocène Inferieur de la vallée de l'Omo (Éthiopie) d'une mandibule d'australopithécien. *C..r. Acad. Sci. Paris 265*, 589–590.

Arambourg, C., Chavaillon, J. and Coppens, Y., (1967) Expédition internationale de recherche paléontologiques dans la vallée de l'Omo (Éthiopie) en 1967. *Actes 6è Cong. pan.Afr. Préhist. d'Études Q., Dakar*, 135–140.

Arambourg, C. and Coppens, Y. (1968) Découverte d'un australopithécien nouveau dans les gisements de l'Omo (Éthiopie). *S. Afr. J. Sci. 64*, 58–59.

Day, M. H. (1969) Omo human skeletal remains. *Nature 222*, 1135–1138.

Howell, F. C. (1969) Remains of Hominidae from Pliocene/Pleistocene formations in the lower Omo basin, Ethiopia. *Nature 223*, 1234–1239.

Howell, F. C., Fichter, L. S. and Eck, G. (1969) Vertebrate assemblages from the Usno Formation, White Sands and Brown Sands localities, lower Omo basin; Ethiopia. *Quaternaria 11*, 65–88.

Brown, F. H. (1972) Radiometric dating of sedimentary formations in the lower Omo valley, southern Ethiopia. In *Calibration of Hominoid Evolution*, Eds. W. W. Bishop and J. A. Miller. Edinburgh; Scottish Academic Press.

Butzer, K. W. (1971) *Recent history of an Ethiopian delta*. Chicago: Department of Geography; Chicago University.

Day, M. H. (1971) The Omo human skeletal remains. In *The Origin of Homo sapiens*. (Ecology and Conservation, 3) UNESCO, 31–35.

Coppens, Y., Chavaillon, J. and Beden, M. (1973) Résultats de la nouvelle mission de l'Omo (campagne 1972)—Découverte de restes d'Hominidés et d'une industrie sur éclats. *C. Acad. Sci. Paris 276*, 161–164.

Day, M. H. (1973) The development of *Homo sapiens*. In *Darwin Centenary Symposium on the Origin of Man*, 87–95. Rome: Accademia Nazionale dei Lincei.

Howell, F. C. and Coppens, Y. (1974) Les faunes de mammifères fossiles de formations Plio/Plèistocènes de l'Omo en Éthiopie. *C.r. Acad. Sci. Paris 278*, 2275–2278.

Merrick, H. V., Haesaerts, P., de Heinzelin, J. and Howell, F. C. (1973) Artefactual occurrences associated with the Pliocene/Pleistocene Shungura Formation, southern Ethiopia. *Nature 242*, 572–575.

Howell, F. C. and Wood, B. A. (1974) Early hominid ulna from the Omo basin, Ethiopia. *Nature 249*, 174–176.

Howell, F. C. and Coppens, Y. (1976) An overview of Hominidae from the Omo Succession, Ethiopia. In *Earliest Man and Environments in the Lake Rudolf Basin*, 522–532. Eds. Y. Coppens, F. C. Howell, G.Ll. Isaac and R. E. F. Leakey. Chicago: University of Chicago Press.

McHenry, H. M., Corruccini, R. S. and Howell, F. C. (1976) Analysis of an early hominid ulna from the Omo Basin, Ethiopia. *Am. J. phys. Anthrop. 44*, 295–304.

Rightmire, G. P. (1976) Relationships of Middle and Upper Pleistocene hominids from sub-Saharan Africa. *Nature 260*, 238–240.

Boaz, N. T. and Howell, F. C. (1977) A gracile hominid cranium from Upper Member G of the Shungura Formation, Ethiopia. *Am. J. phys. Anthrop. 46*, 93–108.

Coppens, Y. (1978) Evolution of the hominids and of their environment during the Plio /Pleistocene in the lower Omo Valley, Ethiopia. In *Geological Background to Fossil Man*, 499–506. Ed. W. W. Bishop. Edinburgh: Scottish Academic Press.

Howell, F. C. (1978) Overview of the Pliocene and earlier Pleistocene of the lower Omo Basin, southern Ethiopia. In *Early Hominids of Africa*, 85–130. Ed. C. Jolly. London: Duckworth.

Rightmire, G. P. (1980) *Homo erectus* and human evolution in the African Middle Pleistocene. In *Current Argument on Early Man*, 70–85. Ed. L.-K. Konigsson. Oxford: Pergamon.

Rightmire, G. P. (1981) Later Pleistocene hominids of eastern and southern Africa. *Anthropologie (Brno). 19*, 15–26.

Chavaillon, J. (1982) Position chronologique des hominidés fossiles d'Éthiopie. *Cong. Int. Paléont. hum.* 1, Nice Prétirage, 766–797.

Day, M. H. and Stringer. C. B. (1982) A reconsideration of the Omo Kibish remains and the erectus-sapiens transition. *Cong. Int. Paléont. hum.* 1, Nice Prétirage, 814–846.

Bräuer, G. (1984) The 'Afro-European *sapiens*-hypothesis', and hominid evolution in East Asia during the late Middle and Upper Pleistocene. *Cour. Forsch. Inst. Senckenberg 69*, 145–165.

Kennedy, G. E. (1984) The emergence of *Homo sapiens*: the post cranial evidence. *Man 19*, 94–100.

Rightmire, G. P. (1984) Comparisons of *Homo erectus* from Africa and southeast Asia. *Cour. Forsch Inst. Senckenberg 69*, 83–98.

Brown, F. H., McDougall, I., Davies, T. and Maier, R. (1985) An integrated Plio-Pleistocene chronology for the Turkana Basin. In *Ancestors*, 82–90. Ed. E. Delson. New York: Alan R. Liss.

The Hadar Remains

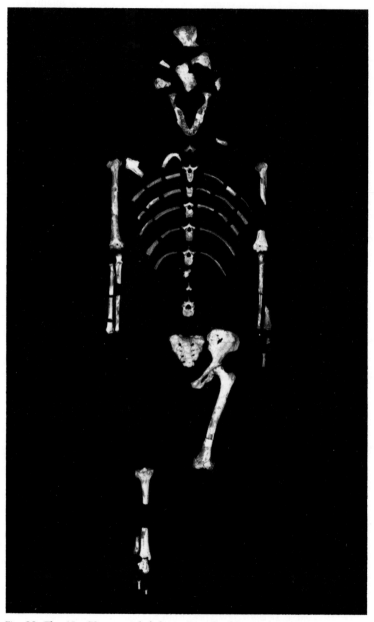

Fig. 88. The AL 288–1 partial skeleton. Length of femur *c.* 280 mm. *Courtesy of Dr D. C. Johanson.*

Synonyms and other names	1. aff. *Australopithecus robustus* (Johanson *et al.*, 1978); *Paranthropus africanus* (Olson, 1981) 2. aff. *Australopithecus africanus* (sensu stricto) (Johanson *et al.*, 1978); *Homo africanus aethiopicus* (Olson, 1985) 3. aff. *Homo sp.* (Johanson and Taieb, 1976). 1,2,3. *Australopithecus afarensis* (Hinrichsen, 1978); *Homo antiquus* (Ferguson, 1984)

Site   The Hadar site is located in the Afar depression in the west central Afar sedimentary basin, near the Awash river about 300 km north-east of Addis Ababa, Ethiopia.

Found by   The International Afar Research Expedition led by D. C. Johanson and M. Taieb, on 30th October, 1973. Further finds were made later that season and also in 1974, 1975 and 1976.

Geology   The Afar region is at the northern end of the East African rift valley and contains a Plio-Pleistocene sedimentary basin capped unconformably by an uppermost unit of Pleistocene gravels and sands. The Plio-Pleistocene strata have been termed the Central Afar Group and include a number of sequences, one of which has been referred to as the Hadar Formation. This Formation contains four members named, from below upwards, the Basal Member, the Sidi Hakoma Member, the Denen Dora Member and the Kada Hadar Member totalling some 180–280 m of deposits. Four sedimentary units can be discerned in the Sidi Hakoma Member (SH 1–4), three in the Denen Dora Member (DD 1–3) and four in the Kada Hadar Member (KH 1–4). The sediments represent lacustrine, lake margin and associated fluvial deposits interspersed with volcanic tuffs and a single basalt flow. The hominid finds are in two principal groups, one about 40 m above the basalt in the Sidi Hakoma Member and one extending to about 40 m below the basalt (Taieb, Johanson, Coppens and Aronson, 1976; Johanson *et al.*, 1978; Taieb and Tiercelin, 1980; Johanson, Taieb and Coppens, 1982).

Associated finds   Artefacts of many types have been recovered from the area, often in mixed assemblages although none from the hominid-bearing deposits. A few sites contained assemblages of an homogeneous character including Acheulean sites. The artefacts found in the area have been placed in five categories; (1) choppers, polyhedral and modified pebbles, crude flakes and protohandaxes; (2) bifaces and flakes of Middle Acheulean type; (3) flakes and cores of a Middle Stone Age Industry; (4) flakes, cores and waste of a Late Stone Age industry; (5) flakes, cores and waste from subrecent to recent industries (Corvinus, 1975, 1976; Corvinus and Roche, 1980). Some evidence has been found at Hadar (Sites 72 and 73) of an industry the absolute date of which is uncertain. In its form, however, it is close to the Oldowan from Olduvai, to Gomboré I from Melka Kunturé, to the KBS industry from Koobi Fora and to similar artefacts from the Omo (Johanson *et al.*, 1978; Taieb *et al.*, 1978; Roche and Tiercelin, 1980).

Numerous fossil mammalian bones have been recovered from the site including proboscidians, hippopotamids, suids, giraffids, bovids, rodents, carnivores and primates, as well as numerous fossil reptilian and avian remains. Three faunal units have been suggested; a lower unit including Elephantidae associated with *Notochoerus euilus, Nyanzachoerus pattersoni, Tragelaphus cf. nakuae, Aepyceros sp.* and cercopithecines; a middle unit containing *N. euilus, T. cf. nakuae, Aepyceros sp.* and *Kobus sp.*; and an upper unit containing *N. euilus, T. cf. nakuae, Kobus sp.*, Alcephalini and Elephantidae (Taieb, Johanson, Coppens and Aronson, 1976).

A study of the suids revealed that *Nyanzachoerus pattersoni* is plentiful in the Sidi Hakoma Member; that *Notochoerus euilus* is found throughout the deposits as is a new species of suid, *Kolpochoerus afarensis*. Correlations of the suid fauna with those from the Lower Shungura Formation and the Usno Formation from the Omo site (*q.v.*) suggest a date of 3·0–3·5 m.y. B.P. (Cooke, 1978).

The fauna recovered from the site of Hadar now totals over 6,000 specimens from 73 species, many of which have been listed and compared with those from other Plio-Pleistocene sites in East Africa. It was concluded that, had the site not been dated in other ways than by the fauna, it would be between 2·5 and 3·5 m.y. B.P. (Coppens *et al.*, 1980). A recent study of the fauna, from the viewpoint of biostratigraphy, has favoured an even older date of 3·6 m.y. B.P. (White *et al.* 1984).

Other aspects of the Hadar fauna have been studied by Beden (1980) [proboscidians] and palaeoenvironmental evidence has been considered by Gray *et al.* (1980). The latter authors concluded that fluctuating conditions from closed to open woodland, characterized the environment during the period represented by the Hadar sequence.

Dating   The dating of the Hadar site is based upon stratigraphic, faunal, radiometric and palaeomagnetic data. The faunal correlation that seemed to fit most closely was that with the Omo I Zone (Usno Formation and the Basal Member and Members A and B of the Shungura Formation). The time span given to this sequence in the Omo is c. 2·6–3·1 m.y. B.P. Potassium argon results based on basalt and tuffs are in agreement at 2·9–3·0 m.y. B.P. with an experimental error of 200,000 years either way. The geomagnetic results show that the polarity of the basalt is reversed while the hominid fossil bearing sediments both above and below are normally polarized. It is suggested that the reversed sample represents the Kaena or the Mammoth event within the Gauss Normal Epoch (Taieb *et* *al.*, 1976); a conclusion confirmed by Schmitt *et al.* (1980) and Schmitt and Nairn (1984).

New K/Ar results on the date of the 'hominid-bearing Hadar Formation' very slightly widened the range of dates for the site to 2·6–3·1 m.y. (Aronson *et al.*, 1977; Aronson *et al.*, 1980). Revised K/Ar dates were given later and the range shifted dramatically to 2·9–3·6 m.y. (Walter and Aronson, 1982). This revision was criticized on faunal grounds (Boaz *et al.*, 1982) and on the grounds of the correlation of the Tulu Bor tuff from Koobi Fora with the Sidi Hakoma tuff at Hadar, a correlation made by microprobe analysis and trace element profiles (Brown, 1982) (see Day, 1982 for a review). The debate continued (Aronson *et al.*, 1983; Brown, 1983) until some remarkable work correlated tuffs from sites in the Turkana Basin, Kenya, Hadar, Ethiopia and from deep-sea cores from the Gulf of Aden (Sarna-Wojcicki, *et al.*, 1985). This work showed that volcanic activity in East Africa in the Plio-Pleistocene had widespread effects that could be traced and correlated geochemically and dated at each site. This evidence coupled with the magnetostratigraphy seems a powerful case for dating the Sidi Hakoma tuff from Hadar at 3·3 m.y. B.P. rather than 3·6 m.y. B.P. as proposed in the revision by Walter and Aronson (1982). Subsequently Brown's work extended to other sites in the Turkana Basin (Brown *et al.*, 1985) with similar results.

Morphology   (*1*) *AL 211–1*

The proximal end of a right femoral shaft lacking the head and part of the neck. The cross section of the neck is flattened and oval, the trochanteric fossa is well marked and the muscular markings are prominent.

AL 166–9

A temporal fragment.

(*2*) *AL 288–1*

An associated partial skeleton including a mandible, some cranial fragments, vertebrae, ribs, humeri, a right scapular fragment, ulnae, parts of radii, some hand and foot bones, a sacrum, a left hip bone, a left femur, a right tibia and part of a fibula and a right talus. The pelvic remains suggest that the skeleton belonged to a female. The bones are remarkable for their small size, despite the fact that there is no evidence of immaturity; this indicates that the stature of this individual was diminutive.

Comparisons show similarities to material from the Sterkfontein site in the Transvaal.

Fig. 89. A composite reconstruction of the skull of the Hadar hominids by T. D. White and W. H. Kimbel.

AL 128–1, AL 129–1a–c, AL 128–23

A group of material believed to be associated consisting of two proximal femoral fragments of opposite sides and a right distal femoral fragment as well as a right proximal tibial fragment. All of these remains resemble their counterparts in AL 288–1 (Johanson and Coppens, 1976).

(3) AL 199–1

A right maxillary fragment containing teeth that include the lateral incisor root, the canine, both premolars and the molars. This adult half-palate is shallow and has well developed alveolar prognathism. The maxillary sinus is large and the zygomatic root takes off above the distal portion of the first molar.

AL 200–1a and b

A complete and undistorted palate with a full dentition. The tooth rows are sub-parallel with a broad anterior portion of the dental arcade to accommodate the spatulate central incisors. Marked dias-

Fig. 90. The A.L. 200–1a palate and upper dentition. *Courtesy of Dr D.C. Johanson.*

temata are present between the lateral incisors and the canines. The palate is shallow with pronounced alveolar prognathism and the maxillary sinuses are large. The zygomatic roots are situated above the first molars. Marked similarities exist between the previous half-palate and this specimen, but the former specimen is smaller in its general dimensions. This has led to the speculation that these two specimens represent male and female counterparts.

AL 266–1

A mandibular fragment consisting of the right side of the body, the symphysial region and part of the left side of the body containing the premolars and molars on the right but only the premolars and first two molars on the left. The dental arcade is rounded anteriorly and the tooth rows are straight diverging a little posteriorly. There is a moderately developed *planum alveolare* (Johanson and Taieb, 1976).

Locality AL 333/333W has produced the most remarkable material from Hadar including a total of no fewer than 200 hominid specimens from a minimum of 13 individuals, nine of whom are adult and four are immature. Excavations in 1976/77 produced 18 hominid specimens *in situ* that are regarded as a catastrophic death assemblage but without simultaneous burial. None of these remains shows carnivore damage (Johanson *et al.*, 1982). The sheer volume of these finds precludes description of them all here. They have been described in detail, with all the other Plio-Pleistocene hominids recovered from the site between 1974 and 1977, in a series of papers that occupy the whole of Volume 57, Number 4 of the *American Journal of Physical Anthropology* (pp. 373–719) to which the reader is referred. In general terms the remains are those of primitive hominids of australopithecine type with small brains, evidence of the ability to stand and walk upright, some primitive dental and cranial features and (if the sample from Hadar is drawn from one species, a matter of current debate) a very wide range of sexual dimorphism.

Some other debates are in progress concerning the morphology and functional anatomy of the Hadar hominids. One such is the contention that the cerebral endocast pattern of sulci and gyri shows an advance in organization ahead of expansion in volume (Holloway, 1983); a suggestion challenged after a different interpretation of the same material (Falk, 1985).

The postcranial skeleton of the Hadar hominids has also provoked debate after the suggestion that the hind limbs of AL 288 (the partial skeleton that permits measurement of limb lengths) were relatively short and thus less efficient in bipedal locomotion (Jungers, 1982). This contention was subsequently denied (Wolpoff, 1983a, b). Similarly, it has been held that the Hadar hominids have in their locomotor skeletons significant adaptations for arboreal locomotion that are not simply retained archaic features but evidence of arboreal ability combined with bipedalism in their locomotor repertoire (Stern and Susman, 1983; Susman, Stern and Jungers, 1984, 1985). This conclusion is supported in part by the work of Senut and Tardieu (1985) who see two forms of locomotor anatomy present from the examination of knees and elbows. One is more arboreally adapted and the other more bipedally adapted. This they do not accept as possible in a widely sexually dimorphic single species, thus they favour specific or even generic separation of the Hadar remains into two groups. A comparative study of the capitate bones from Hadar and from Sterkfontein (*q.v.*) shows them to be almost identical, and both are closer to those of man than to the chimpanzee (McHenry, 1983).

Dimensions   The anatomical descriptions published in the *American Journal of Physical Anthropology* Volume 57, Number 4 (1982) contain numerous dimensions taken from the Hadar hominids.

Affinities   The material from the Hadar site was announced (Taieb *et al.*, 1972, 1974 and 1975) and briefly described (Johanson and Taieb, 1976), and the conclusions put forward were preliminary and subject to revision following detailed study. With this in mind it was suggested that there are the remains of three groups of hominids present at this site, one affined to the robust australopithecine material from Olduvai, Swartkrans and East Rudolf, one to the gracile australopithecine material from Sterkfontein and one to hominine material from Java and East Rudolf. This view changed radically following further study and led to all of the Hadar hominids being placed within a new species of the genus *Australopithecus*, the name given being *Australopithecus afarensis*. This was orally announced at the 41st Nobel Symposium, Karlskoga, Sweden, and reported in Hinrichsen (1978). It has produced nomenclatural and taxonomic difficulties since the name was made available in that publication but no holotype was designated. Thus Laetoli Hominid 4 should have been designated as the *lectotype* in (Johanson, White and Coppens, 1978), a paper in which other material was included, that should have been termed a *paralectotype*, namely *Meganthropus africanus* (Day *et al.*, 1980; Logan *et al.*, 1983). Nomenclatural and procedural difficulties aside, however, the essence of the new systematic assessment of the Hadar hominids contends that *A. afarensis* is a single hominid species from which all subsequently known hominids arose; *A. africanus* is a side branch that gave rise to the robust australopithecines and *A. afarensis* gave rise to *Homo habilis*, *Homo erectus* and *Homo sapiens* (Johanson and White, 1979). This contention has provoked a continuing debate outlined elsewhere (see The Australopithecine Problem).

Originals   The National Museum of Ethiopia, Addis Ababa.

Casts   Not available at present.

References
Taieb, M., Coppens, Y., Johanson, D.C. and Kalb, J. (1972) Dépôts sédimentaires et faunes du Plio-Pléistocène de la basse vallée de l'Awash (Afar central, Ethiopia). *C.r. Acad. Sci. Paris 275*, 819–822.

Taieb, M., Johanson, D.C., Coppens, Y., Bonnefille, R. and Kalb, J. (1974) Découverte d'Hominidés dans les séries Plio-Pléistocènes d'Hadar (Bassin de l'Awash; Afar, Ethiopia). *C.r. Acad. Sci. Paris 279*, 735–738.

Corvinus, G. (1975) Palaeolithic remains at the Hadar in the Afar region. *Nature 256*, 468–471.

Taieb, M., Johanson, D.C. and Coppen, Y. (1975) Expédition internationale de l'Afar, Éthiopie (3e campagne 1974); découverte d'Hominidés Plio-Pléistocènes à Hadar. *C.r. Acad. Sci. Paris 281*, 1297–1300.

Taieb, M., Johanson, D.C., Coppens, Y. and Aronson, J.L. (1976) Geological and palaeontological background of Hadar hominid site, Afar, Ethiopia. *Nature 260*, 289–293.

Johanson, D. C. and Taieb, M. (1976) A preliminary anatomical diagnosis of the first Plio-Pleistocene hominid discovered in the Central Afar, Ethiopia. *Am. J. phys. Anthrop.* 45, 217–233.

Corvinus, G. (1976) Prehistoric exploration at Hadar, Ethiopia. *Nature*, 261, 571–572.

Aronson, J. L., Schmitt, T. J., Walter, R. C., Taieb, M., Tiercelin, J.-J., Johanson, D. C., Naeser, C. W. and Nairn, A. E. M. (1977) New geochronologic and paleomagnetic data for the hominid-bearing Hadar Formation, Ethiopia. *Nature*, 267, 323–327.

Cooke, H. B. S. (1978) Pliocene-Pleistocene Suidae from Hadar, Ethiopia. *Kirtlandia*, 29.

Hinrichsen, D. (1978) How old are our ancestors? *New Scientist* 78, 571.

Johanson, D. C., Taieb, M., Gray, B. T. and Coppens, Y. (1978) Geological framework of the Pliocene Hadar Formation (Afar, Ethiopia), with notes on paleontology including hominids. In *Geological Background to Fossil Man*, 549–564. Ed. W. W. Bishop. Edinburgh: Scottish Academic Press.

Johanson, D. C., Taieb, M., Coppens, Y. and Roche, H. (1978) Expedition internationale de l'Afar, Éthiopie (4ème et 5 ème Campagne 1975–1977): Nouvelles découvertes d'hominidés et découvertes d'industries lithiques pliocène à Hadar. *C.r. Acad. Sci. (Paris)* D 287, 237–240.

Taieb, M., Johanson, D. C., Coppens, Y. and Tiercelin, J.-J. (1978) Expedition internationale de l'Afar, Éthiopie (4 ème et 5 ème Campagne 1975–1977): Chronostratigraphie des gisements a hominidés pliocène de l'Hadar et corrélations avec les sites préhistoriques du Kada Gona. *C.r. Acad. Sci. (Paris)* D 287, 459–461.

Johanson, D. C. and White, T. D. (1979) A systematic assessment of early African hominids. *Science* 202, 321–330.

Aronson, J. L., Walter, R. C., Taieb, M. and Naeser, C. W. (1980) New geochronological information for the Hadar Formation and the adjacent central Afar. *Proc. pan-Afr. Cong. Prehist. Quaternary Stud.* 8. 47–52.

Beden, M. (1980) Données recentes sur l'evolution des Proboscidiens pendant le plio-pléistocène en Afrique orientale. *Proc. pan-Afr. Cong. Prehist. Quaternary Stud.*, 8. 72–76.

Coppens, Y, Gray, B. T. and Johanson, D. C. with the collaboration of Beden, M., Eisenmann, V. and Guerin, C. (1980) Biostratigraphie d'Hadar et comparison avec d'autres sites plio/pléistocène. *Proc. pan-Afr. Cong. Prehist. Quaternary Stud.*, 8. 56–57.

Corvinus, G. and Roche, H. (1980) Prehistoric exploration at Hadar in the Afar/Ethiopia in 1973, 1974 and 1976. *Proc. pan-Afr. Cong. Prehist. Quaternary Stud.* 8. 186–188.

Gray, B. T., Beden, M., Guerin, C. Taieb, M., Tiercelin, J.-J. and Page, N. (1980) Environmental indications provided by the Hadar Formation (Afar, Ethiopia) fauna and correlation with geological evidence. *Proc. pan-afr. Cong. Prehist. Quaternary Stud.*, 8. 115–117.

Johanson, D. C. (1980) Early African hominid phylogenesis. A re-evaluation. In *Current Argument on Early Man*. Eds. L.-K. Konigsson and S. Sundstrom. Oxford: Pergamon Press.

Roche, H. and Tiercelin, J.-J. (1980) Industries lithiques de la formation plio-pléistocène d'Hadar: campagne 1976. *Proc. pan-Afr. Cong. Prehist. Quaternary Stud.*, 8. 194–199.

Schmitt, T. J., Walter, R. C., Taieb, M., Tiercelin, J.-J. and Page, N. (1980) Magnetostratigraphy of the Hadar Formation of Ethiopia. *Proc. pan-Afr. Cong. Prehist. Quaternary Stud.*, 8. 53–55.

Taieb, M. and Tiercelin, J.-J. (1980) La stratigraphie et paléoenvironnements sédimentaires de la formation d'Hadar, dépression de l'Afar, Ethiopie. *Proc. pan-Afr. Cong. Prehist. Quarternary Stud.*, 8. 109–114.

Day, M. H., Leakey, M. D. and Olson, T. R. (1980) On the status of *Australopithecus afarensis. Science 207*, 1102–1103.

Olson, T. R. (1981) Basicranial morphology of the extant hominoids and Pliocene hominids: The new material from the Hadar Formation, Ethiopia, and its significance in early human evolution and taxonomy. In *Aspects of Human Evolution*, 99–128. Ed. C. B. Stringer. London: Taylor and Francis.

Boaz, N. T., Howell, F. C. and McCrossin, M. L. (1982) Faunal age of the Usno, Shungura B and Hadar Formations, Ethiopia. *Nature 300*, 633–635.

Brown, F. H. (1982) Tulu Bor Tuff at Koobi Fora correlated with the Sidi Hakoma Tuff at Hadar. *Nature 300*, 631–633.

Day, M. H. (1982) 'Lucy' jilted? *Nature 300*, 574.

Jungers, W. L. (1982) Lucy's limbs: skeletal allometry and locomotion in *Australopithecus afarensis. Nature 297*, 678–696.

Walter, R. C. and Aronson, J. L. (1982) Revisions of K/Ar ages for the Hadar hominid site, Ethiopia. *Nature 296*, 122–127.

Johanson, D. C., Taieb, M. and Coppens, Y. (1982) Pliocene hominids from the Hadar Formation (1973–1977): Stratigraphic, chronologic and paleoenvironmental contexts, with notes on hominid morphology and systematics. In Pliocene Hominid Fossils from Hadar, Ethiopia. *Am. J. phys. Anthrop. 57*, 373–402.

Johanson, D. C., Lovejoy, C. O., Kimbel, W. H., White, T. D., Ward, S. C., Bush, M. E., Latimer, B. M. and Coppens, Y. (1982) Morphology of the Pliocene partial hominid skeleton (A. L. 288–1) from the Hadar Formation, Ethiopia. *Ibid*, 403–452.

Kimbel, W. H., Johanson, D. C. and Coppens, Y. (1982) Pliocene hominid cranial remains from the Hadar Formation, Ethiopia. *Ibid*, 452–500.

White, T. D. and Johanson, D. C. (1982) Pliocene hominid mandibles from the Hadar Formation, Ethiopia: 1974–1977 Collections. *Ibid*, 501–544.

Johanson, D. C., White, T. D. and Coppens, Y. (1982) Dental remains from the Hadar Formation, Ethiopia: 1974–1977 Collections. *Ibid*, 545–604.

Ward, S. C., Johanson, D. C. and Coppens, Y. (1982) Morphology and alveolar process relationships of hominid gnathic elements from the Hadar Formation: 1974–1977 Collections. *Ibid*, 605–630.

Lovejoy, C. O., Johanson, D. C. and Coppens, Y. (1982) Elements of the axial skeleton recovered from the Hadar Formation: 1974–1977 Collections. *Ibid*, 637–650.

Bush, M. E., Lovejoy, C. O., Johanson, D. C. and Coppens, Y. (1982) Hominid carpal, metacarpal, and phalangeal bones recovered from the Hadar Formation: 1974–1977 Collections. *Ibid*, 651–678.

Lovejoy, C. O., Johanson, D. C. and Coppens, Y. (1982) Hominid upper limbs recovered from the Hadar Formation: 1974–1977 Collections. *Ibid.*, 637–650.

Lovejoy, C. O., Johanson, D. C. and Coppens, Y. (1982) Hominid lower limb bones recovered from the Hadar Formation: 1974–1977 Collections. *Ibid*, 679–700.

Latimer, B. M., Lovejoy, C. O., Johanson, D. C. and Coppens, Y. (1982) Hominid tarsal, metatarsal, and phalangeal bones recovered from the Hadar Formation: 1974–1977 Collections. *Ibid*, 701–720.

Aronson, J. L., Walter, R. C. and Taieb, M. (1983) Correlation of Tulu Bor Tuff at Koobi Fora with the Sidi Hakoma Tuff at Hadar. *Nature 306,* 209–210.

Brown, F. H. (1983) Comment. *Ibid,* 310.

Holloway, R. G. (1983) Cerebral brain endocast pattern of *Australopithecus afarensis* hominid. *Nature 303,* 420–422.

Logan, T. R., Lucas, S. G. and Sobus, J. C. (1983) The taxonomic status of *Australopithecus afarensis.* Johanson in Hinrichsen 1978 (Mammalia, Primates). *UNM Contr. Anthrop. 2,* 122–127.

McHenry, H. M. (1983) The capitate of *Australopithecus afarensis* and *A. africanus. Am. J. phys. Anthrop. 62,* 187–198.

Stern, J. T. and Susman, R. L. (1983) The locomotor anatomy of *Australopithecus afarensis. Am. J. phys. Anthrop. 60,* 279–317.

Wolpoff, M. H. (1983a) Lucy's little legs. *J. hum. Evol. 12,* 443–453.

Wolpoff, M. H. (1983b) Lucy's lower limbs: long enough for Lucy to be fully bipedal? *Nature 304,* 59–61.

Ferguson, W. W. (1984) Revision of fossil hominid jaws from the Plio/Pleistocene of Hadar, in Ethiopia, including a new species of the genus *Homo* (Hominoidea: Homininae. *Primates 25* 519–529.

Schmitt, T. J. and Nairn, A. E. M. (1984) Interpretations of the magnetostratigraphy of the Hadar hominid site, Ethiopia. *Nature 309,* 704–706.

Susman, R. L., Stern, J. T., Jnr. and Jungers, W. L. (1984) Arboreality and bipedality in the Hadar hominids. *Folia primatol. 43,* 113–156.

White, T. D., Moore, R. V. and Suwa, G. (1984) Hadar biostratigraphy and hominid evolution. *J. vert. Paleont. 4,* 575–583.

Brown, F. H., McDougall, I., Davies, T. and Maier, R. (1985) An integrated Plio/Pleistocene chronology for the Turkana Basin. In *Ancestors,* 82–90. Ed. E. Delson. New York: Alan R. Liss.

Falk, D. (1985) Hadar AL 162–28 endocast as evidence that brain enlargement preceded cortical reorganization in hominid evolution. *Nature 313,* 45–46.

Olson, T. R. (1985) Cranial morphology and systematics of the Hadar Formation hominids and 'Australopithecus' africanus. In *Ancestors,* 102–119. Ed. E. Delson. New York: Alan R. Liss.

Sarna-Wojcici, A. M., Meyer, C. E., Roth, P. H. and Brown, F. H. (1985) Ages of tuff beds at East African early hominid sites and sediments in the Gulf of Aden. *Nature 313,* 306–308.

Senut, B. and Tardieu, C. (1985) Functional aspects of Plio-Pleistocene hominid limb bones: Implications for taxonomy and phylogeny. In *Ancestors,* 193–201. Ed. E. Delson. New York: Alan R. Liss.

Susman, R. L., Stern, J. T. Jnr. and Jungers, W. L. (1985) Locomotor adaptations in the Hadar hominids. In *Ancestors,* 184–192. Ed. E. Delson. New York: Alan R. Liss.

The Middle Awash Remains

Fig. 91. The Middle Awash remains. *Courtesy of T. D. White.*

Synonyms and other names	*Australopithecus sp.* (Clark *et al.*, 1984); The Maka femur; The Belohdelie frontal.
Site	The west central Afar basin, Ethiopia, along the Awash River between Hadar in the north and Gewane in the south. The area boundaries within the study area are defined by modern catchment areas that drain into the Awash. Two of these areas to the east of the Awash are adjacent, Maka to the north and Belohdelie to the south, and each has provided hominid remains.
Found by	The Maka femur (MAK–VP–1/1) was found by T. D. White, 25 November, 1981. The Belohdelie frontal (BEL–VP–1/1) was found by L. Krishtalka, 4 December, 1981.
Geology	Earlier expeditions to the Middle Awash Valley, Ethiopia (Kalb, *et al.*, 1982a and b), and to Hadar (*q.v.*) to the north, have disclosed

a sedimentary sequence that relates to the Afar triple junction that is over 1 km in thickness. In the Middle Awash area that produced the femur and the frontal fragment, there is a succession of Middle to Lower Pliocene silts, clays, diatomites, sands, gravels, limestones and volcanic ashes. The sequence contains five to seven tuffaceous units and has a composite thickness of over 70 m. Among the marker horizons that outcrop is a tuff, termed the Cindery Tuff: a grey ashfall tuff that contains pumice clasts, glass shards, zircons and feldspars. The femur fragment was found 7 m above the Cindery Tuff horizon whilst the frontal fragment was found 700 m to the north east, 11 m below the Cindery Tuff. Both are surface finds but apparently freshly exposed.

Associated finds   Numerous stone tools have been recovered from a number of sites in the Middle Awash area including Oldowan and Acheulean artefacts (Kalb, 1982b; Clark *et al.*, 1984) but none was recovered in direct association with the Pliocene hominid remains.

Fossil mammalian remains recovered from the Maka hominid layer include primitive suids (*Notochoerus euilus, Nyanzachoerus kanamensis*), a proboscidian (*Elephas recki brumpti*), a primitive theropithecine (*Theropithecus sp.*), bovids (*Ugandax sp., Praedamalis deturi*) and a rhinoceros (*Ceratotherium praecox*) (Clark *et al.*, 1984).

Dating   The fauna shows that the deposit containing the Maka femoral fragment is at least as old as the Sidi Hakoma Member of the Hadar site (*q.v.*) to the north and the Laetolil Beds (*q.v.*) in Tanzania. The age of the Sidi Hakoma Member is still in doubt (Boaz *et al.*, 1982; Brown, 1982; White *et al.*, 1984) whilst the Laetolil Beds are well dated to c. 3·7 m.y. B.P. (Leakey and Hay, 1979). The Maka femoral fragment is therefore believed to be dated to 3·5–4 m.y. B.P. (White, 1984). The Cindery Tuff has been dated by means of $^{40}Ar/^{39}Ar$ ratios and fission track analysis of zircons and has indicated an age of 3·8–4·0 m.y. B.P. The Cindery Tuff lies between the femoral fragment and the frontal fragment thus the frontal fragment is at least of this age (Hall *et al.*, 1984).

Morphology   *The Maka femoral fragment (MAK–VP–1/1) consists of the upper end of the shaft, the greater and lesser trochanters and the neck of a sub-adult left femur. The head of the bone is missing but the sub-epiphyseal surface is partly intact. The epiphysis for the greater trochanter is fused. The upper end of the shaft is flattened, has a thick cortex and bears a hypotrochanteric crest for the attachment of gluteus maximus muscle. The greater trochanter lacks flare and the lesser trochanter is posteriorly placed. The neck of the bone is relatively long, flattened and deeply webbed and does not bear a well defined intertrochanteric line. There is a well marked obturator externus groove on the posterior aspect of the neck and a well* marked attachment and groove for ilio-psoas tendon on the front of the neck. These features are typically those of femora attributed to *Australopithecus* (Napier, 1964; Day, 1969; Walker 1973; White, 1984).

The Belohdelie frontal fragment (BEL–VP–1/1) consists of a number of smaller fragments some of which articulate. It appears to be adult since the section of the coronal suture present is closed but not obliterated. Parts of the temporal lines can be traced on both sides. The orbital margin is intact on the right as is part of the temporal fossa on that side, but the bone is a little warped in the region of the right half of the coronal suture. The postorbital constriction seems to be moderate in amount, and in general terms the frontal seems short but the glabella is missing. It compares well in size with a sample of modern common chimpanzees. The tight vault curvature seems to indicate a small vault size (White, 1984).

Dimensions White (1984)
Vault thickness (10 mm in front of bregma)–8·4

Affinities The affinities of the Middle Awash remains will be discussed with the remainder of the australopithecine material. It is worthy of note, however, that these remains are the earliest evidence of *Australopithecus* from anywhere in the world and the earliest evidence of hominid bipedalism yet discovered.

Originals The National Museum of Ethiopia, Addis Ababa.

Casts Not available at present.

References
Napier, J.R. (1964) The evolution of bipedal walking in the hominids. *Arch. Biol.* (Liège) *75*, Suppt., 673–708.

Day, M.H. (1969) Femoral fragment of a robust australopithecine from Olduvai Gorge, Tanzania. *Nature 221*, 230–233.

Walker, A. (1973) New *Australopithecus* femora from E. Rudolf, Kenya, *J. hum. Evol. 2*, 545–555.

Kalb, J.E., Oswald, E.B., Tebedge, S., Mebrate, A., Tola, E. and Peak, D. (1982a) Geology and stratigraphy of Neogene deposits, Middle Awash Valley, Ethiopia. *Nature 298*, 17–25.

Kalb, J.E., Jolly, C.J., Mebrate, A., Tebedge, S., Smart, C., Oswald, E.B., Cramer, D., Whitehead, P., Wood, C.B., Conroy, G.C., Adefris, T., Sperling, L. and Kana, B. (1982b) Fossil mammals and artefacts from the Middle Awash Valley, Ethiopia. *Nature 298*, 25–29.

Clark, J.D., Asfaw, B., Assefa, G., Harris, J.W.K., Kurashina, H., Walter, R.C., White, T.D. and Williams, M.A.J. (1984) Palaeoanthropological discoveries in the Middle Awash Valley, Ethiopia. *Nature 307*, 423–428.

Hall, C.M., Walter, R.C., Westgate, J.A. and York, D. (1984) Geochronology, stratigraphy and geochemistry of Cindery Tuff in Pliocene hominid-bearing sediments of the Middle Awash, Ethiopia. *Nature 308*, 26–31.

White, T.D. (1984) Pliocene hominids from the Middle Awash, Ethiopia. In *Cour. Forsch. Inst. Senckenberg*, 69, 57–68.

White, T.D., Moore, R.V. and Suwa, G. (1984) Hadar biostratigraphy and hominid evolution. *J. vert. Paleont.* 4, 575–583.

Southern Africa

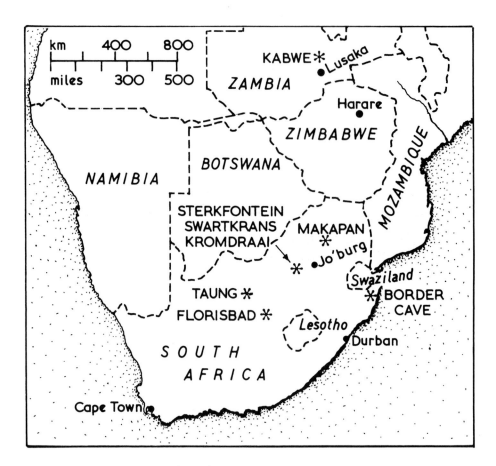

Fig. 92. Hominid fossil sites in southern Africa.

The Kabwe (Rhodesian) Remains

ZAMBIA   KABWE

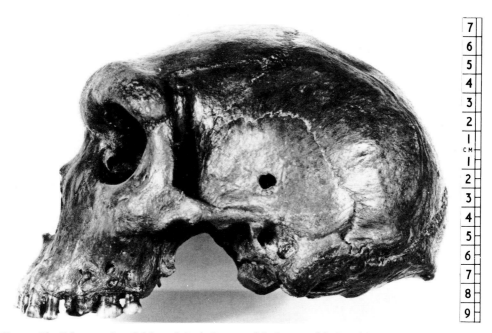

Fig. 93. The Kabwe cranium (left lateral view). *Courtesy of the Trustees of the British Museum.*

Synonyms and other names *Homo rhodesiensis* (Woodward, 1921); *Cyphanthropus rhodesiensis* (Pycraft, 1928); *Homo sapiens rhodesiensis* (Campbell, 1964) Rhodesian man; Broken Hill man.

Site The Broken Hill Mine, Kabwe, Zambia.

Found by T. Zwigelaar, 17th June, 1921, cranium; other remains found by A. S. Armstrong, 1921, A. W. Whittington, 1921 and H. Hrdlička, 1925.

Geology The mine included two kopjes or small hills of dolomitic limestone which contained lead and zinc ore. One of the hills was tunnelled at its base by a cave filled with fossilized and mineralized bones. During the clearance of this cavern the skull was found at its farthest and deepest point about 60 feet below ground level. Subsequent excavations produced the rest of the remains, but continued mining has destroyed the original cave.

Associated finds   With the hominid bones, although not associated on a living floor, were some quartz and chert stone tools. These implements belong to African flake cultures known as the Stillbay and Proto-Stillbay of the Middle Stone Age. In addition there were several supposed bolas stones and a few bone tools.

The associated fauna included fossil birds, reptiles and mammals many of which belong to living species. A mammalian faunal list for the Kabwe site has been given by Cooke (1964); forms identified include a large primate (*?Simopithecus sp.*), mongoose (*Herpestes ichneumon*), large carnivores (*Panthera leo, Panthera pardus*), an extinct carnivore (*Leptailurus hintoni*), African elephant (*Loxodonta africana*), zebra (*Equus burchelli*), black rhinoceros (*Diceros bicornis*) and several artiodactyls including an extinct buffalo (*Homoioceras bainii*).

Dating   Initially it was believed that the skull and the other bones may be of differing ages because of variations in the mineral content of the specimens. Oakley (1947) suggested that these differences might be due to local variations in the mineral constituents of the soil at the site of burial. Further chemical and radiometric investigations indicate that the skull and the other bones are ancient and of the same age (Oakley, 1957, 1958). A new excavation at Kabwe has produced more stone implements of a similar type to those found with the skeletal remains. The new finds have been attributed to the early Middle Stone Age (Upper Pleistocene) after comparison with the tools from another Kabwe site which contains an established sequence (Clark, 1947, 1959). Thus on faunal, archaeological and chemical grounds it was believed that Rhodesian man lived during the Upper Pleistocene, possibly about 40,000 years B.P.

However, it has been suggested that the dating of the Kabwe site should be revised on the grounds of a revaluation of the artefacts and the fauna. The new date has given a minimum age of 125,000 years B.P. (Klein, 1973).

A reappraisal of the Kabwe site, remains and associated fauns has led Partridge (1982) and Vrba (1982) to support the view that the skull is older than originally suspected and probably of late Middle Pleistocene antiquity.

Morphology   The remains belong to at least three and possibly four individuals and consist of a skull, a parietal, a maxilla, a humerus, a sacrum, two ilia, several femoral fragments and some tibial remains.

The Skull

The cranium is heavily built with massive brow ridges, a retreating forehead and a flattened vault; the occipital region is rounded above the occipital torus but flattened beneath. The foramen magnum is placed well forward and faces downward, indicating an erect head carriage. The mastoid process is of moderate size but the supra-mastoid crest is prominent. The greatest diameter of the cranium is situated very low.

The face is very long with inflated, but flat, maxillae having no canine fossae; the lateral walls of the nose pass smoothly on to the face but there is a nasal spine at the apex of two ridges which lead back to join the lateral wall half-way up the nasal opening. The alveolar processes of the maxillae are very deep and the bony palate is extremely large both in width and length.

The separate maxilla was re-examined by Wells (1947) who found that it differs in several respects from the corresponding bone in the skull. It is a smaller bone with a transversely arranged zygomatic process and a canine fossa 'modelling essentially as in modern human skulls'. However, he concluded that the maxilla and the skull belonged to a single type, perhaps not even specifically distinct from *Homo sapiens*.

The Teeth

The teeth are large and set in a horseshoe-shaped arcade. All the teeth are considerably worn and most are affected by caries. The crowns are generally of modern form and the third molar is reduced in size.

The Postcranial Bones

These bones have few features which lie outside the range of normal variation of modern man. The limb bones are stout and long, in-dicating tall stature, whilst the lower limb bones have no features which are incompatible with an upright stance and a bipedal strid-ing gait. In a new study, however, Kennedy has suggested that femoral features contribute to the designation of Kabwe man as an example of the subspecies *Homo sapiens rhodesiensis* (Kennedy, 1984).

A new femoral shaft fragment has come to light after being in private possession for many years (Clark *et al.*, 1968). The new fragment does not fit with any of the previously known femoral fragments, thus increasing the possible number of individuals found at this site.

Dimensions   *Skull*

Morant (1928)
Max. Length 208·5   Max. Breadth 144·5
Cranial Index 69·3 (Dolichocephalic)
Cranial Capacity 1,280 cc

Postcranial Bones

Pycraft (1928)

Sacrum Length 105   Sacrum Breadth 110

	Right	Left
Femora: Max. Diameter of Heads	52·0	50·0
Ant./Post. Diameter of Shaft	30·0	27·5
Humerus: Ant./Post. Diameter of Shaft	20·0	—

Teeth

Pycraft (1928)

		Upper Teeth (Crown Dimensions)						
	I^1	I^2	C	PM^1	PM^2	M^1	M^2	M^3
Left l	8·0	7·0	10·0	7·5	—	—	13·0	9·0
Side b	8·5	8·0	11·0	11·0	—	—	14·0	12·0
Right l	8·0	—	—	—	—	(14·0)	12·5	—
Side b	8·5	—	—	—	—	13·5	13·5	—

( ) Estimated

Affinities   The Kabwe cranium has several points of similarity with those of European Neandertal man whilst remaining distinct in the structure of the postcranial bones, a situation which raised doubts about the correctness of associating the type skull with the remainder of the skeleton. These doubts were reinforced by the rather unsatisfactory circumstances of the find. However, the chemical and radiometric evidence seems to have established the contemporaneity of the remains.

The resemblances of the Kabwe skeletons to that of Neandertal man did not escape Woodward (1921) but the position of the foramen magnum being much more modern in the Kabwe cranium than in the Neandertalers available to him, he felt obliged to create a new species of man, *Homo rhodesiensis*. Pycraft (1928) was convinced of the peculiarity of the stance and gait of this form and created a new genus, *Cyphanthropus rhodesiensis* or 'Stooping man', a concept which gained little support since Le Gros Clark (1928) explained the error of interpretation which led to this viewpoint.

Morant (1928) has shown that the skull can be distinguished from those of Neandertal man by a number of metrical characteristics and that it tends to resemble *Homo sapiens*; however, he concluded that Kabwe man and Neandertal man seem more closely related to each other than either is to *Homo sapiens* and also that they are equally related to all races of *Homo sapiens*.

Kabwe man was placed near the point of divergence of Neandertal and modern man by von Bonin (1928–1930) on the basis of further comparative skull measurements.

The discovery of the Saldanha calvarium is particularly significant at this point. In its form and dimensions it closely resembles the Kabwe skull, confirming that this is not an isolated or aberrant specimen. Singer (1954) regarded the Kabwe and Saldanha people as African Neandertalians, unlike the European but similar to the Asiatic representatives of this group (Solo man).

Howell (1957) has denied Neandertal penetration 'south of the Sahara' and regards Kabwe man, as well as other related southern African forms, as racially distinct. In a review of the position of Kabwe man, Wells (1957) suggests that the primitive pithecan- thropine stock gave rise to a basic type of *Homo sapiens* which became widely dispersed and underwent regional differentiation into a number of offshoots represented by Broken Hill, Neandertal and Solo man—these three lines becoming extremely specialized and then extinct.

Coon (1963) seeks to show that Kabwe and Saldanha man are both forms of *Homo erectus* leading towards a possible negro evolutionary line, as a part of his general polyphyletic theory of racial origin. This view has received little support and much criticism. An ana- tomical comparison of the Kabwe and Petralona skulls shows that they share some similarities (Murrill, 1975).

It is clear that the principal resemblances of the Kabwe skull are to the Saldanha specimen, but the classification of these remains is still controversial. It would be widely agreed that Kabwe man is a member of the genus *Homo* but the species to which he belongs remains in dispute. However, opinion is growing in favour of clas- sifying Neandertal and Neandertaloid forms a sub-species of *Homo sapiens* (Campbell, 1964).

Rightmire (1976) dismisses the term 'Neandertaloid' in an African context and favours the taxon *Homo sapiens rhodesiensis*, a position maintained in a later publication (Rightmire, 1984). Bräuer (1984), following a comprehensive anatomical and metrical reappraisal of African Middle and Upper Pleistocene hominid skulls, suggested a grade system. In this approach Kabwe is included in the group that is termed early archaic *Homo sapiens* with others such as Saldanha, Bodo, Eyasi, and Ndutu.

The Kabwe skull is central to the debate on the classification of late *Homo erectus*, early *Homo sapiens* and those that are termed *erectus/ sapiens* intermediates. (The problem is discussed elsewhere, see p. 411.) The consensus view would place Kabwe in *Homo sapiens* but the unity of the sample, its dating and its true phylogenetic position are still in doubt.

Originals   British Museum (Natural History), Cromwell Road, South Kensington, London, S.W.7.

Casts   The University Museum, University of Pennsylvania, Philadelphia
4, Pennsylvania, U.S.A.

References   Woodward, A. S. (1921) A new cave man from Rhodesia, South Africa.
Nature 108, 371–372.
Pycraft, W. P. *et al.* (1928) *Rhodesia man and associated remains.* Ed. F. A.
Bather, London: British Museum (Natural History).
Clark, W. E. le Gros (1928) Rhodesian man. *Man 28*, 206–207.
Morant, G. M. (1928) Studies of Paleolithic Man III. The Rhodesian skull
and its relations to Neanderthaloid and modern types. *Ann. Eugen. 3*,
337–360.
Bonin, G. von (1928–1930) Studien zum *Homo rhodesiensis.* Z. Morph.
Anthrop. 2, 347–381.
Clark, J. D. *et al.* (1947) New studies on Rhodesian man. *J. R. anthrop. Inst.*
77, 7–32.
Wells, L. H. (1947) In *New studies on Rhodesian man.* J. D. Clark *et al.* II. A
note on the broken maxillary fragment from the Broken Hill cave. *J.R.
anthrop. Inst. 77*, 11–12.
Singer, R. (1954) The Saldanha skull from Hopefield, South Africa. *Am. J.
phys. Anthrop. 12*, 345–362.
Oakley, K. P. (1957) The dating of the Broken Hill, Florisbad and Saldanha
skulls. *Proc. pan-Afr. Cong. Prehist., 3, Livingstone, 1955*, 76–79. Ed. J. D.
Clark. London: Chatto and Windus.
Wells, D. H. (1957) The place of the Broken Hill skull among human types.
Ibid., 172–174.
Oakley, K. P. (1958) The dating of Broken Hill (Rhodesian man). In *Hundert
Jahre Neanderthaler*, 265–266. Ed. G. H. R. von Koenigswald, Utrecht:
Kemink en Zoon.
Clark, J. D. (1959) Further excavations at Broken Hill, Northern Rhodesia.
J. R. anthrop. Inst. 89, 201–231.
Leakey, L. S. B. (1959) A preliminary re-assessment of the fossil fauna from
Broken Hill, N. Rhodesia. *J. R. anthrop. Inst. 89*, 225–231.
Coon, C. S. (1963) *The origin of races*, 621–627. London: Jonathan Cape.
Campbell, B. (1964) Quantitative taxonomy and human evolution. In *Clas-
sification and Human Evolution*, 50–74. Ed. S. L. Washburn. London:
Methuen and Co. Ltd.
Cooke, H. B. S. (1964) Pleistocene mammal faunas of Africa, with particu-
lar reference to Southern Africa. In *African Ecology and Human Evolution*
65–116. Eds. F. C. Howell and F. Bourlière. London: Methuen and Co.
Ltd.
Clark, J. D., Brothwell, D. R., Powers, R. and Oakley, K. P. (1968) Rhodesian
man: notes on a new femur fragment. *Man 3*, 105–111.
Klein, R. G. (1973) Geological antiquity of Rhodesian man. *Nature 244*,
311–312.
Murrill, R. I. (1975) A comparison of the Rhodesian and Petralona upper
jaws in relation to other Pleistocene hominids. *Z. Morph. Anthrop. 66 (2)*,
176–187.
Rightmire, G. P. (1976) Relationships of Middle and Upper Pleistocene hominids from sub-Saharan Africa. *Nature 260*, 238–240.

Partridge, T. C. (1982) The chronological positions of the fossil hominds of Southern Africa. *Cong. Int. Paléont. hum. I. Nice*, Prétirage, 617–675.

Vrba, E. S. (1982) Biostratigraphy and chronology, based particularly on Bovidae, of southern hominid-associated assemblages: Makapansgat, Sterkfontein, Taung, Kromdraai, Swartkrans; also Elandsfontein (Saldanha), Broken Hill (now Kabwe) and Cave of Hearths. *Ibid*, 707–752.

Brauer, G. (1984) A craniological approach to the origin of anatomically modern *Homo sapiens* in Africa and implications for the appearance of modern humans. In *The Origins of Modern Humans*, 327–410. Eds. F. H. Smith and F. Spencer. New York: Alan R. Liss.

Kennedy, G. E. (1984) The emergence of *Homo sapiens*: The post-cranial evidence. *Man 19*, 94–110.

Rightmire, G. P. (1984) *Homo sapiens* in Sub-Saharan Africa. In *The Origins of Modern Humans*, 295–325. Eds. F. H. Smith and F. Spencer. New York: Alan R. Liss.

The Taung Skull

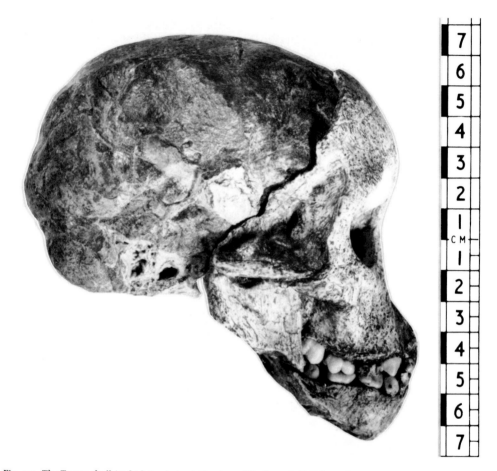

Fig. 94. The Taung skull (right lateral view). *Courtesy of Professor P. V. Tobias, photographed by A. R. Hughes.*

Synonyms and other names	*Australopithecus africanus* (Dart, 1925) *Homo transvaalensis* (Mayr, 1950); *Australopithecus africanus africanus* (Robinson, 1954); *Homo africanus* (Robinson, 1972; Olson, 1978) 'Ape-man'; 'Man-ape'; 'Near-man'
Site	The Buxton Limeworks, Buxton, six miles southwest of Taung, Bophuthatswana, 80 miles north of Kimberley in the northern Cape Province.

Found by A quarryman, M. de Bruyn; recognized by R. A. Dart, November, 1924.

Geology The skull was found in sandy lime which formed the filling of a cave cut into the face of a limestone tufa, just east of the escarpment of the Kaap Plateau. Mining of the tufaceous limestone, for the manufacture of cement, led to the discovery after blasting operations. The Taung cave deposit is believed to have been part of the Thabaseek tufa (Peabody, 1954), although one later investigation has suggested that the skull was associated with the younger Norlim Tufa, in a cave filling intrusive in the Thabaseek Formation. Sedimentological examination of the matrix adhering to the skull suggests its association with a 'wet' depositional phase in contrast to most of the Taung fauna which comes from 'dry-phase' deposits. Most recent analyses have placed it in the Thabaseek tufa, the oldest of four tufas at Buxton (Butzer, 1974, 1980; Partridge, 1982).

Associated finds No artefacts have been recovered from the cave deposit. The fossil mammalian fauna found at the site includes three insectivores (*Elephantulus cf. brachyrhynchus, Mylomygale spiersi, Crocidura taungsensis*), a bat (*Rhinolophus cf. capensis*), several baboons (*Parapapio antiquus, P. jonesi, P. whitei, Papio izodi, P. wellsi*), numerous rodents (*Thallomys debruyni, Gypsorhychus darti, G. minor, Cryptomys robertsi, Pedetes gracile, Dendromus antiquus, Protomys campbelli, Petromus minor*), two hyraces (*Procavia capensis, P. transvaalensis*) and two artiodactyls (*Cephalophus parvus, Oreotragus longiceps*). The bones of neither Carnivora nor Proboscidea have been positively identified in the deposit (Cooke, 1963).

Dating Accurate dating of the remains from Taung has proved difficult since material from this type of deposit is not amenable to the chemical and radiometric techniques that are available at present. Kurtén (1962) attributed the Taung skull to the First Interglacial (Günz-Mindel or Antepenultimate Interglacial) on the grounds of faunal correlation. The balance of evidence from geological and faunal studies suggested that the Taung deposit was laid down early in the sequence of australopithecine sites, during the Upper Villafranchian part of the Lower Pleistocene (Ewer, 1957; Oakley, 1954, 1957, 1964).
Cooke (1970) attempted to correlate some of the South African hominid sites with those that are better dated from East Africa. He concluded that the Sterkfontein and Makapansgat (*q.v.*) sites are 2·5–3·0 million years old. Wells (1967) has expressed doubts, on faunal grounds, that Taung is the oldest of these sites and has been supported by Freedman's (1970) findings in relation to the cercopithecoids.

It has been suggested, on the basis of a geomorphological dating method, that the Taung site might be the youngest of all the southern African cave sites, the date of opening of the Taung cave being given as 0·87 million years B.P. (Partridge, 1973). Whilst accepting that the Taung hominid 'clearly postdates the gracile australopithecines from Sterkfontein and Makapansgat', on the basis of his own studies, Butzer (1974b) does not accept Partridge's attempt at dating the site as valid.

The dating of the site is still problematical after new research (Partridge, 1982). A review of the evidence of baboons from the site has suggested a date of over 2 m.y. B.P. (Delson, 1975), whilst Vogel and Partridge (1984) and Vogel (1985) have proposed, on two new lines of evidence, a date of just over one million years for the Thabaseek carapace. There are now four or five independent lines of evidence pointing to a date nearer to one million years, whilst one line—that of the baboons—suggests a dating twice as great. There seems to be the 'feeling' that the Taung site is probably not as old as had been formerly believed (Tobias, 1978).

Morphology

The Skull

The specimen consists of the greater part of a juvenile skull which contains a remarkable endocast of the brain. The facial skeleton is intact and the dentition complete. Most of the base of the skull is preserved but much of the vault is missing. The lower parts of the body and the angles of the mandible are broken.

The cranium appears to be globular with neither frontal flattening nor supraorbital torus formation, but the glabella is prominent; the sphenoid and parietal bones appear to have been in contact in the temporal fossa. The foramen magnum is set well forward beneath the skull. The face is undistorted, having large rounded orbits, flattened nasal bones and a square nasal opening which runs without interruption on to the maxillae; there is no nasal spine. The nasal flattening gives the face a 'dished' appearance which is accentuated by the degree of sub-nasal prognathism of the maxillae.

The dental arcade is regular and parabolic enclosing a shallow palatal vault marked by an incisive foramen; the palatine foramina are set behind a line drawn posterior to the first permanent molars.

Mandible

This bone is represented by the body and the alveolar processes of bone with the teeth in place. The angles of the mandible and the rami are largely absent. The symphysial region slopes backwards, there being neither chin nor simian shelf present. The body of the mandible is thickened particularly in the region of the erupting first molar.

Teeth

The milk dentition is complete in both upper and lower jaws, and the upper and lower first permanent molars are in process of eruption.

The Upper Deciduous Incisors are heavily worn and damaged. The teeth are well separated one from another, a feature characteristic of other hominids at this stage of dental development.

The Upper Deciduous Canines are also worn and damaged but appear to be small and spatulate.

The Upper First Deciduous Molars are considerably worn particularly on the lingual half of the crowns, but the mesiobuccal angles of the teeth seem exaggerated in their development.

The Upper Second Deciduous Molars are also worn but enough of the crown morphology is discernible to show that they resemble the first milk molars.

The Upper First Permanent Molars are both perfect. The crowns bear four main cusps and show anterior foveae as well as a Carabelli complex of grooves. These features are characteristic of teeth from Sterkfontein.

The Lower Deciduous Incisors are heavily worn and damaged.

The left Lower Deciduous Canine is well preserved and has a distal cusplet. The tooth does not appear to project appreciably above the occlusal line.

The Lower First Deciduous Molars are little damaged and resemble the equivalent teeth from Sterkfontein in some detail: five main cusps are present and the Taung specimens have small sixth cusps.

The Lower Second Deciduous Molars are appreciably worn but the typical dryopithecine cusp pattern can still be defined. Well developed sixth cusps have obliterated the posterior foveae but the anterior foveae are prominent.

The Lower First Permanent Molars are unworn and display five principal cusps, sixth cusps have obliterated the posterior foveae. Deeply incised buccal grooves are present, the anterior ones ending in a distinct pit.

A reappraisal of the deciduous dentition does not support the view that the Taung infant may belong to the 'robust' australopithecine lineage (Grine, 1985). A new study of the skull demonstrated that it has diverged from an ape-like pattern in its remodelling processes (Bromage, 1985) and probably had an age at death of 3·3 years (2·7–3·7). This estimate is based upon a comparison with Sts 24a which is of equivalent dental age to Taung and upon counts of perikymata.

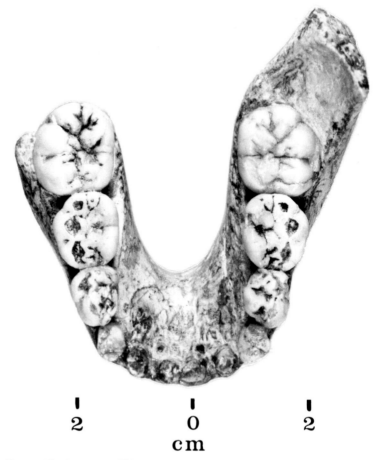

Fig. 95. The Taung mandible (occlusal view). *Courtesy of Professor P. V. Tobias, photographed by A. R. Hughes.*

Dimensions   *Skull*

Max. Length (Glabella/Inion) 127·0   Cranial Index 62·4
Cranial Capacity 405 cc (440 cc adult
value including 8% for growth)

  Holloway (1970)

Teeth

			Upper Dentition (Crown Dimensions)			
		dI¹	dI²	dC	dM¹	dM²	M¹ (Perm.)
Left	l	—*	—*	—*	8·8	—*	12·75
side	b	—*	—*	6·0	10·0	—*	14·0
Right	l	—*	—*	6·8	8·8	10·1	12·75
side	b	—*	—*	5·8	10·0	11·0	14·0

		Lower Dentition (Crown Dimensions)					
		dI_1	dI_2	dC	dM_1	dM_2	M_1 (Perm.)
Left	l	—*	—*	6·5	—*	11·5	14·0
side	b	—*	—*	5·3	—*	10·6	13·5
Right	l	—*	—*	—*	8·7	11·5	14·0
side	b	—*	—*	—*	8·0	10·7	13·5

* Damaged

Affinities The affinities of the Taung skull will be discussed with the rest of the australopithecine remains.

Original The Department of Anatomy, University of the Witwatersrand Medical School, York Road, Parktown, Johannesburg 2193, Republic of South Africa.

Casts The University Museum, University of Pennsylvania, Philadelphia 4, Pennsylvania, U.S.A., and as above.

References Dart, R. A. (1925) *Australopithecus africanus:* the man-ape of South Africa. *Nature* 115, 195–199.

Dart, R. A. (1926) Taungs and its significance. *Nat. Hist.* 3, 315–327.

Dart, R. A. (1934) The dentition of *Australopithecus africanus. Folia anat. jap.* 12, 207–221.

Broom, R., and Schepers, G. W. H. (1946) The South African fossil apemen, the *Australopithecinae. Transv. Mus. Mem.* 2, 1–272.

Mayr, E. (1950) Taxonomic categories in fossil hominids. *Cold Spring Harb. Symp. quant. Biol.* 15, 109–118.

Oakley, K. P. (1954) The dating of the *Australopithecinae* of Africa. *Am. J. phys. Anthrop.* 12, 9–28.

Peabody, F. E. (1954) Travertines and cave deposits of the Kaap escarpment of South Africa and the type locality of *Australopithecus africanus* Dart. *Bull. geol. Soc. Am.* 65, 671–705.

Robinson, J. T. (1956) The dentition of the *Australopithecinae. Transv. Mus. Mem.* 9, 1–179.

Ewer, R. F. (1957) Faunal evidence on the dating of the *Australopithecinae. Proc. pan-Afr. Cong. Prehist.,* 3, Livingstone, 1955, 135–142. Ed. J. D. Clark. London: Chatto and Windus.

Oakley, K. P. (1957) Dating the australopithecines. *Ibid.,* pp. 155–157.

Kurtén, B. (1962) The relative ages of the australopithecines of Transvaal and the pithecanthropines of Java. In *Evolution und Hominisation,* 74–80. Ed. G. Kurth. Stuttgart: Gustav Fischer Verlag.

Cooke, H. B. S. (1964) Pleistocene mammal faunas of Africa, wth particular reference to South Africa. In *African Ecology and Human Evolution,* 65–116. Eds. F. C. Howell and F. Bourlière. London: Methuen and Co. Ltd.

Oakley, K. P. (1964) *Frameworks for dating fossil man.* London: Weidenfeld and Nicolson.

Wells, L. H. (1967) In *Background to Evolution in Africa,* 105–106. Eds. W. W. Bishop, and J. D. Clark. Chicago: Chicago University Press.

Cooke, H. B. S. (1970) Notes from members: Dalhousie University, Halifax, Canada. *News Bull. Soc. vertebra. Palaeont.* 90, 2.

Holloway, R. L. (1970) New endocranial values for the australopithecines. *Nature, 227*, 199–200.

Freedman, L. (1970) A new checklist of fossil Cercopithecoidea of South Africa. *Palaeont. Afr. 13*, 109–110.

Robinson, J. T. (1972) *Early Hominid Posture and Locomotion*. Chicago: Chicago University Press.

Partridge, T. C. (1973) Geomorphological dating of cave openings at Makapansgat, Sterkfontein, Swartkrans and Taung. *Nature 246*, 75–79.

Butzer, K. W. (1974a) Palaeoecology of South African australopithecines: Taung revisited. *Curr. Anthrop. 15*, 367–382.

Butzer, K. W. (1974b) Comment—reply. *Curr. Anthrop. 15*, 413–416.

Delson, E. (1975) Paleoecology and Zoogeography of the Old World monkeys. In *Primate Functional Morphology and Evolution*, 37–66. Ed. R. H. Tuttle. The Hague, Paris: Mouton Publishers.

Olson, T. (1978) Hominid phylogenetics and the existence of *Homo* in Member I of the Swartkrans Formation, South Africa. *J. hum. Evol. 7*, 159–178.

Simons, E. L. and Delson, E. (1978) Cercopithecidae and Parapithecidae. In *Evolution of African Mammals*. Eds. V. J. Maglio and H. B. S. Cooke. Cambridge: Harvard University Press.

Tobias, P. V. (1978) The South African australopithecines in time and hominid phylogeny, with special reference to the dating and affinities of the Taung skull. In *Early Hominids of Africa*, 45–84. Ed. C. Jolly. London: Duckworth.

Butzer, K. W. (1980) The Taung Australopithecine: contextual evidence. *Palaeont. Afr. 23*, 59–60.

Partridge, T. C. (1982) The chronological positions of the fossil hominids of Southern Africa. *Congr. Int. Paleont. hum. 1*. Nice Prétirage, 617–675.

Vrba, E. S. (1982) Biostratigraphy and chronology, based particularly on Bovidae, of southern hominid-associated assemblages: Makapansgat, Sterkfontein, Taung, Kromdraai, Swartkrans; also Elandsfontein (Saldanha), Broken Hill (now Kabwe) and Cave of Hearths. *Congr. Int. Paléont. Hum. 1*. Nice Prétirage, 707–752.

Bromage, T. G. (1985) Taung facial remodelling: a growth and development study. In *Hominid Evolution: Past, Present, and Future*, 239–245. Ed. P. V. Tobias. New York: Alan R. Liss (in press).

Grine, F. (1985) Dental morphology and the systematic affinities of the Taung fossil hominid. *Ibid*, 247–253.

Vogel, J. C. (1985) Further attempts at dating the Taung tufas. *Ibid*, 189–194.

The Sterkfontein Remains

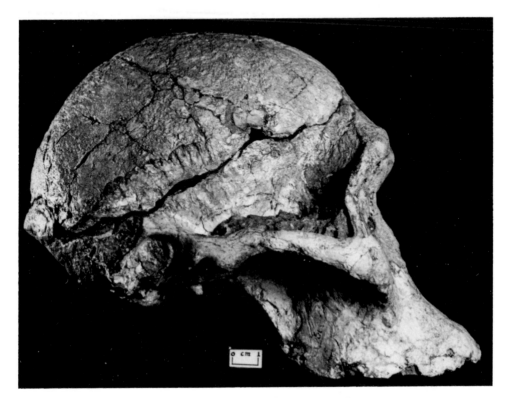

Fig. 96. Sterkfontein skull 5 (right lateral view). *Courtesy of Professor J. T. Robinson.*

Synonyms and other names 1, 2, 3. *Australopithecus transvaalensis* (Broom, 1936); *Plesianthropus transvaalensis* (Broom, 1937); *Homo transvaalensis* (Mayr, 1954); *Australopithecus africanus transvaalensis* (Robinson, 1954); *Homo africanus* (Robinson, 1972); 'Ape-man'; 'Man-ape'; 'Near-man'. 4. *Homo* aff. *habilis* (Hughes and Tobias, 1977)

Site Sterkfontein dolomitic limestone cave deposit, seven miles north-west of Krugersdorp, near Johannesburg, Transvaal, Republic of South Africa.

Found by 1. R. Broom, August, 1936–1939 (Cranial and postcranial bones, teeth).
2. R. Broom and J. T. Robinson, 1947–1949 (Cranial and postcranial bones, teeth).

3. C. K. Brain and J. T. Robinson, 1956–1958 (Artefacts and hominid remains).

4. P. V. Tobias and A. R. Hughes, 1966–the present (Cranial and postcranial bones and teeth).

Geology   At Sterkfontein a number of caves honeycomb a Pre-Cambrian formation of impure dolomitic limestone. The cave fillings consist of calcareous bone breccia that was mined for many years and burned in kilns for lime. The principal site is the remains of a large cavern which communicates with the surface; gradually it had become filled with debris and bones until the cavern floor collapsed into an underlying cavity in the rock. The process then recurred, the new cavern again filling from above. Because of this mode of formation, the breccia is not of uniform character, neither is it regularly stratified. The geology of Sterkfontein has been investigated in detail (Brain, 1957, 1958; Robinson and Mason, 1962) and further work has been reported more recently (Tobias and Hughes, 1969; Tobias, 1973); Partridge, 1978; Stiles and Partridge, 1979; Tobias, 1979). This work has shown that there is an earlier 'bone-bearing' breccia under the travertine that was formerly believed to be the floor of the main deposit (Wilkinson, 1985). It has also shown that there is a sequence of six superimposed members in the deposit numbered from below upwards. All the discoveries of *Australopithecus africanus* came from Member 4. Member 5 contains the remains attributed to *Homo habilis* and probably also some attributed to *A. robustus*. Member 6 is relatively recent (Upper Pleistocene) and contains bovids of the Middle Stone Age faunal zone.

Associated finds   A number of stone tools have been recovered from the breccia of Member 5 exposed in what was called the Extension Site (Robinson, 1957; Brain, 1958; Robinson and Mason, 1962). They comprise many hand-axes, choppers, flakes, irregular artefacts and a spheroid. The tools are made of diabase, quartzite or chert. The culture has been described as Late Oldowan or Early African Acheulean in character and was originally attributed to later pithecanthropines thought to have occupied the site (Robinson and Mason, 1962).

More recent work has shown that many foreign stones and artefacts occur in Member 5 and are associated with remains of *Homo habilis*. No stone artefacts are known from Member 4, the gracile australopithecine-bearing member.

The fossil mammalian fauna recovered from Sterkfontein Type Site include insectivores (*Chlorotalpa spelea, Elephantulus langi, Crocidura cf. bicolor, Suncus cf. etruscus, Myosorex robinsoni*), primates (*Parapapio jonesi, P. broomi, P. whitei, Cercopithecoides williamsi*), numerous rodents, some carnivores (*Canis mesomelas pappos, Canis brevirostris, Lycyaena silberbergi, Therailurus barlowi, Megantereon gra-*

cile), hyraces (*Procavia antiqua, P. transvaalensis*) and some artio-dactyls ('*Tapinochoerus' meadowsi, Hippotragus broomi, Gazella wellsi*) (Cooke, 1964).

Numerous other mammalian faunal remains have since been re-covered from the site including bovids, a chalicothere, hyenas, jack-als, monkeys and the three-toed horse (*Hipparion*) (Tobias, 1985). Cooke (1970) has attempted to correlate the Sterkfontein site on faunal grounds with those that are better dated in East Africa. He concluded that the Sterkfontein site should be dated at 2·5–3·0 million years B.P., about twice as old as had been formerly believed. Vrba (1974, 1975, 1976, 1982, 1985a, 1985b) has studied bovid material from Sterkfontein and other sites in South and East Africa. She concludes that bovids can be both chronological and palaeo-ecological indicators. A habitat change from bush and tree cover to more open grassland was envisaged at between 2 and 3 m.y. B.P. (Vrba, 1980, 1985a), which may have led to a 'speciation pulse' in a number of mammalian groups, possibly even in the hominids. Preliminary pollen analysis of material from Member 5 suggests that at that time the climate was dry and the environment one of open grassland (Horowitz, 1975). This supports the faunal analysis. The best estimate for the date of the australopithecine-bearing de-posit (Member 4) is 2·4–2·8 m.y. B.P. and for the *Homo habilis*-bearing deposit (Member 5) is 1·5–1·8 m.y. B.P.

Dating   The same difficulties arise in dating the Sterkfontein sites as were encountered at the other australopithecine sites; the problem has been discussed by a number of authors (Howell, 1955; Ewer, 1957; Oakley, 1954, 1957; Brain, 1958; Robinson and Mason, 1962 and Kurtén, 1962). The faunal evidence for the dating of the site (see above) has been added to by an attempt to date the opening of the Sterkfontein caves by a geomorphological method (Partridge, 1973). The conclusion of this study was that the Sterkfontein cave opened as early as 3·26 million years B.P. and began to collect the lower three members below the hominid-bearing Member 4. The validity of this method was seriously questioned (Butzer, 1974).

No radiometric methods or biochemical dating techniques have proved possible at Sterkfontein, but the position has been reviewed recently (Partridge, 1982).

Morphology   The early Phase 1 excavation produced a broken cranium, maxil-lary, zygomatic and nasal bones, some mandibular fragments, sock-eted and isolated teeth, the lower end of a left femur and a capitate. The Phase 2 excavation was rewarded by an almost complete cran-ium, several other damaged and incomplete crania, a nearly com plete mandible, parts of other mandibles, several maxillae, numer-ous socketed and isolated teeth, and a partial skeleton (Sts 14).

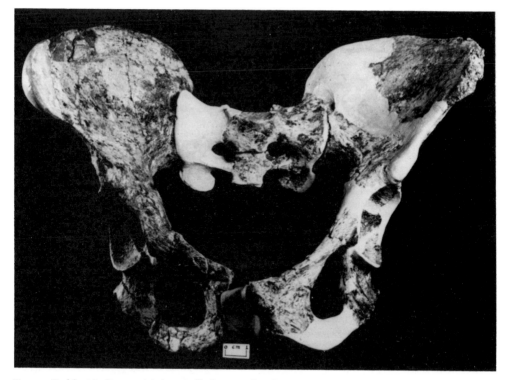

Fig. 97. Sterkfontein Sts 14 pelvis (restored). *Courtesy of Professor J. T. Robinson.*

Later still Phase 3 excavations continued to be productive, but since 1966 (Phase 4) the site has produced 21 isolated teeth, four adult articulated lumbar vertebrae (StW/8), an adult cranium (StW/12, 13 and 17), a young adult mandible with eight teeth (StW/14) and an adolescent right maxilla with five teeth (StW/18a, b and c) (Tobias, 1973). To present the continuing work produced 320 hominid specimens from Members 4 and 5 and from the dumps derived from them. The specimens are both cranial and postcranial. Perhaps the most important new specimen is StW 53 from Member 5 (Hughes and Tobias, 1977). Numerous new fossil hominid remains have been recovered from Sterkfontein recently but are as yet unpublished; these include parts of femora, ulnae, radii, tali as well as cranial remains and numerous teeth (Tobias, pers. comm.).

Skull

Sts 5 is that of a mature female widely known colloquially as 'Mrs Ples'; it is virtually complete, lacking only the upper teeth. The vault is rounded and marked anteriorly by a modest supraorbital ridge and some prominence of the glabella. The occipital crest is

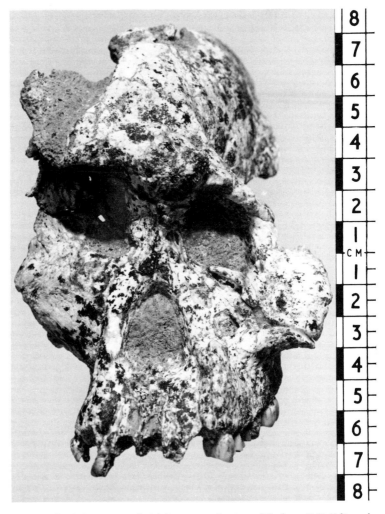

Fig. 98. The StW 13 craniofacial fragments. *Courtesy of Professor P. V. Tobias, photographed by A. R. Hughes.*

weak and the nuchal plane low. The foramen magnum is set well beneath the cranium and the mastoid processes are small. The greatest breadth of the cranium is bitemporal.

StW 53 consists of much of the cranium including occipital, frontal, parietal and temporal fragments as well as much of the face and palate and all five cheek teeth of the right side. It has been termed 'mesati-cephalic' suggesting a brain size intermediate between that of *Australopithecus africanus* and *Homo erectus* (Tobias, 1978).

Mandible

The most complete of the mandibles (Sts 52b) is rather crushed, particularly on the right side; most of the teeth are preserved but they are heavily worn. The jaw is large and robust, the symphysial region is well preserved and there is neither chin nor simian shelf. The body of the mandible is stout and the rami are tall.

Permanent Teeth

About 470 permanent teeth are known from Sterkfontein, 263 are maxillary and 207 are mandibular teeth.

The Upper Incisors are broad (I^1), small (I^2) and moderately shovelled, having marginal ridges on their lingual faces.

The Upper Canines are symmetrical and pointed, projecting a little beyond the adjacent teeth; the lingual faces of these teeth have parallel grooves whilst several specimens have small lingual tubercles.

The Upper First Premolars are bicuspid and have well defined buccal grooves. Two are 3 rooted, four are 2 rooted and one has a single root.

The Upper Second Premolars resemble the first premolars in having the same occlusal features and buccal grooves. The roots tend to be narrow.

The Upper First Molars are rhomboid in shape, having a simple quadrituberculate cusp pattern. A Carabelli complex seems to be a constant feature of these teeth.

The Upper Second Molars are similar to the first molars but slightly larger. Characteristically a well developed cingulum is present running from the lingual groove to the lingual end of the mesial face. An extra cusp is often found distally.

The Upper Third Molars are essentially the same size and shape as the second molars, having a lingual groove and part of a Carabelli complex. The fissure pattern of the occlusal surface is complicated.

*   *   *

The Lower Incisors tend to be shovelled and have horizontal incisal margins. Both central and lateral specimens have five well developed mamelons.

The Lower Canines differ considerably from the upper in that the crown is always asymmetrical; the apex of the tooth is distal to its midline and the cingulum reaches higher up the mesial face than the distal face. The cingulum on the distal face forms a distinct cusplet.

The Lower First and Second Premolar crowns are bicuspid and asymmetrical. The lingual cusp is smaller than the buccal cusp, and the anterior and posterior foveae are well defined.

The Lower First Molars are rectangular having five cusps and a larger anterior fovea.

The Lower Second Molars have six cusps and a moderate anterior fovea.

The Lower Third Molars tend to be triangular; they usually have six cusps and a distinct anterior fovea.

Deciduous Teeth

The Upper First Molar is asymmetrical due to the large mesiobuccal angle of its crown; a fifth cusp is present.

The Upper Second Molar is similar in form to the first permanent molar and has a distinct Carabelli cusp.

*   *   *

The Lower Incisors are either damaged or worn.

The Lower Canine has a moderately high crown with distal and mesial cusplets.

The Lower First Molar has five cusps and a large anterior fovea.

The Lower Second Molar has a similar cusp arrangement to the first permanent molar.

The Postcranial Bones

The Scapula (Sts 7) is a little crushed and has lost its lower and inner half. The neck of the bone is not clearly defined and there is no scapular notch.

A new study of the scapula suggests that the Sterkfontein australopithecines were not knuckle-walkers (Vrba, 1979).

The Humerus (Sts 7) belongs to the same individual as the scapula and has the head and upper end of the shaft in good condition. The remainder of the shaft is badly crushed, and the lower end is missing. The head of the bone is very like that of modern man, having greater and lesser tuberosities separated by an intertubercular groove and a well rounded articular surface.

Of the two *Hip Bones* (Sts 14) the right one is almost complete, lacking only its anterior superior iliac spine. The ilium is broad and similar to that of man but its ischium and pubis are badly crushed. The iliac pillar, which in man extends from the acetabulum to the tubercle of the crest, is feeble and runs forward to the anterior superior iliac spine. The sacral articulation is small, as is the roughened region above for the sacro-iliac ligaments. The ischial tuberosity, which is irregular, and flattened, is set well away from the edge of the acetabulum to produce a strikingly long pelvic ischial segment. The orientation of the pelvis is distinctive; in man the iliac crests are mainly directed forwards, but in this form they were mainly directed laterally. The left hip bone is badly damaged and has been much repaired. Some doubts have been cast on the

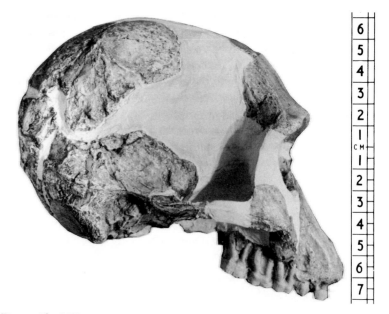

Fig. 99. The StW 53 cranium. *Courtesy of Professor P. V. Tobias, photographed by P. Faugust.*

correctness of its reconstruction (Day, 1974). An attempt has been made to calculate the stature and weight of Sts 14 from the hip bone (Reed and Falk, 1977).

Closely associated with the pelvis was part of a left *Femur*. The specimen is almost valueless since it lacks a head and the shaft consists of irregularly glued fragments that are barely diagnostic. Two other fragments, the lower ends of right and left femora, are very similar in size and shape. They closely resemble the femur of man but differ in the relative depth and forward extension of their intercondylar grooves.

The Capitate Bone (TM 1526) and a *Phalangeal Fragment* were recovered during the early excavation. The capitate is small and similar to that of man in its essential features. The postcranial material from this site has been analysed and conclusions reached concerning posture and locomotion (Robinson, 1972).

The remaining postcranial bones have not yet been described.

Dimensions   *Skull Sts 5*

Broom, Robinson and Schepers (1950)
Max. Length 146·8   Max. Breadth 99·0
Cranial Index 67·5   Cranial Capacity 482 cc
                                    485 cc (Holloway, 1970)

Mandible StS 52b

Body Thickness at M1 24·0   Body Depth at M₁ 37·0
Coronoid Height 86·5   Minimum Ramus Breadth *c.* 60·0

Teeth

Robinson (1956)

					Upper Permanent Teeth (Crown Dimensions)			
Sts 52a		I¹	I²	C	PM¹	PM²	M¹	M²	M³
Left	l	9·5	7·3	9·8	8·7	9·1	12·3	13·2	—
Side	b	8·2	7·0	9·9	12·8	(13·2)	14·0	15·2	—
Right	l	9·3	6·8	9·9	8·6	9·3	12·2	13·3	12·5
Side	b	8·3	7·0	9·7	12·8	13·3	14·1	15·2	14·6

Sts 52b					*Lower Permanant Teeth (Crown Dimensions)*				
Left	l	—	—	—	—	—	13·4	14·8	13·5
Side	b	—	—	—	—	—	—	13·3	12·9
Right	l	5·9	7·1	9·1	9·0	9·8	13·0	14·4	13·7
Side	b	8·1	8·1	10·0	11·7	11·7	12·9	13·4	12·7

		Upper Deciduous Teeth (Crown Dimensions)				
Sts 2		dI¹	dI²	dC	dM¹	dM²
Left	l	—	—	—	—	
Side	b	—	—	—	—	—
Right	l	—	—	—	9·9	11·2
Side	b	—	—	—	9·6	11·3

Sts 24		*Lower Deciduous Teeth (Crown Dimensions)*				
Left	l	4·2	—	6·4	—	—
Side	b	—	—	5·6	—	—
Right	l	—	—	6·3	8·2	10·7
Side	b	—	—	5·6	6·9	9·0

Postcranial Bones

Scapula: Glenoid Cavity Max. Length *c.* 33
                    Max. Breadth 20
Humerus: Diameter of Head *c.* 40
                    Length Between 290 and 310
Innominate Bone: Ant. Sup. Spine-Post. Sup. Spine *c.* 115
                    Sacral articulation, Max. Length 29
Femur: Max. Length *c.* 310

Affinities   The affinities of the Sterkfontein remains will be discussed with the rest of the australopithecine material.

Originals   Specimens from Phases 1–3: The Transvaal Museum, Pretoria, Republic of South Africa. Specimens from Phase 4: address as below.

Casts   Department of Anatomy, University of the Witwatersrand Medical School, York Road, Parktown, Johannesburg 2193, Republic of South Africa.

References   Broom, R. (1936) A new fossil anthropoid skull from South Africa. *Nature* *138*, 486–488.

Broom, R. (1937) The Sterkfontein ape. *Nature 139*, 326.

Broom, R. and Schepers, G. W. H. (1946) The South African fossil ape-men, the Australopithecinae. *Transv. Mus. Mem. 2*, 1–272.

Kern, H. M. and Straus, W. L. (1949) The femur of *Plesianthropus transvaalensis*. *Am. J. phys. Anthrop. 7*, 53–77.

Broom, R., Robinson, J. T., and Schepers, G. W. H. (1950) Sterkfontein ape-man, *Plesianthropus*. *Transv. Mus. Mem. 4*, 1–117.

Mayr, E. (1950) Taxonomic categories in fossil hominids. *Cold Spring Harb. Symp. Quant. Biol. 15*, 109–118.

Oakley, K. P. (1954) Dating the australopithecines of Africa. *Am. J. phys. Anthrop. 12*, 9–23.

Robinson, J. T. (1954) The genera and species of the Australopithecinae. *Am. J. phys. Anthrop. 12*, 181–200.

Howell, F. C. (1955) The age of the australopithecines of Southern Africa. *Am. J. phys. Anthrop. 13*, 635–662.

Robinson, J. T. (1956) The dentition of the Australopithecinae. *Transv. Mus. Mem. 9*, 1–179.

Brain, C. K. (1957) New evidence for the correlation of the Transvaal ape-man bearing cave deposits. *Proc. pan-Afr. Cong. Prehist. 3*, *Livingstone, 1955*, 143–148. Ed. J. D. Clark. London: Chatto and Windus.

Ewer, R. F. (1957) Faunal evidence on the dating of the Australopithecinae. *Ibid.*, 135–142.

Oakley, K. P. (1957) Dating the australopithecines. *Ibid.*, 155–157.

Robinson, J. T., and Mason, R. J. (1957) Occurrence of stone artefacts with *Australopithecus* at Sterkfontein. *Nature 180*, 521–524.

Brain, C. K. (1958) The Transvaal ape-man bearing cave eposits. *Trans. Mus. Mem. 11*, 1–125.

Robinson, J. T., (1958) The Sterkfontein tool-maker. *The Leech (Johannesburg) 28*, 94–100.

Robinson, J. T. and Mason, R. J. (1962) Australopithecines and artefacts at Sterkfontein. *S. Afr. arch. Bull. 17*, 87–125.

Kurtén, B. (1962) The relative ages of the australopithecines of Transvaal and the pithecanthropines of Java. In *Evolution und Hominisation*, 74–80. Ed. G. Kurth. Stuttgart: Gustav Fischer Verlag.

Cooke, H. B. S. (1964) Pleistocene mammal faunas of Africa, with particular reference to South Africa. In *African Ecology and Human Evolution*, 65–116. Eds. F. C. Howell and F. Boulière. London: Methuen and Co. Ltd.

Tobias, P. V., and Hughes, A. R. (1969) The new Witwatersrand University excavation at Sterkfontein. *S. Afr. arch. Bull. 24*, 158–169.

Cooke, H. B. S. (1970) Notes from members: Dalhousie University, Halifax, Canada. *Bull. Soc. vertebra. Paleont. 90*, 2.

Holloway, R. L. (1970) New endocranial values for the australopithecines. *Nature 227*, 199–200.

Robinson, J. T. (1972) *Early Hominid Posture and Locomotion*. Chicago: Chicago University Press.

Day, M. H. (1973) Locomotor features of the lower limb in hominids. *Symp. zool. Soc. Lond. 33*, 29–51.

Partridge, T. (1973) Geomorphological dating of cave openings at Makapansgat, Sterkfontein, Swartkrans and Taung. *Nature, 246*, 75–79.

Tobias, P. V. (1973) A new chapter in the history of the Sterkfontein early hominid site. *J. S. Afr. biol. Soc. 14*, 30–44.

Butzer, K. W. (1974) Curr. Anthrop. Comment. Reply. *Curr. Anthrop. 15*, 413–416.

Vrba, E. S. (1974) Chronological and ecological implications of the fossil Bovidae at the Sterkfontein australopithecine site. *Nature 250*, 19–23.

Vrba, E. S. (1975) Some evidence of chronology and palaeoecology of Sterkfontein, Swartkrans and Kromdraai from the fossil Bovidae. *Nature 254*, 301–304.

Horowitz, A. (1975) Preliminary palaeoenvironmental implications of pollen analysis of Middle Breccia from Sterkfontein. *Nature 258*, 417–418.

Vrba, E. S. (1976) The fossil Bovidae of Sterkfontein, Swartkrans and Kromdraai. *Transv. Mus. Mem. 27*, 1–166.

Hughes, A. R. and Tobias, P. V. (1977) A fossil skull probably of the genus *Homo* from Sterkfontein, Transvaal. *Nature 265*, 310–312.

Reed, C. A. and Falk, D. (1977) The stature and weight of Sterkfontein 14, a gracile Australopithecine from Transvaal, as determined from the innominate bone. *Fieldiana 33*, 423–440.

Partridge, T. C. (1978) Re-appraisal of lithostratigraphy of Sterkfontein hominid site. *Nature 275*, 282–287.

Tobias, P. V. (1978) The earliest Transvaal members of the genus *Homo* with another look at some problems of hominid taxonomy and systematics. *Z. Morph. Anthrop. 69*, 225–265.

Stiles, D. N. and Partridge, T. C. (1979) Results of recent archaeological and palaeoenvironmental studies at the Sterkfontein Extension Site. *S. Afr. J. Sci, 75*, 346–352.

Tobias, P. V. (1979) The Silberberg Grotto, Sterkfontein, Transvaal, and its importance in palaeoanthropological researches. *S. Afr. J. Sci. 75*, 161–164.

Vrba, E. S. (1979) A new study of the scapula of *Australopithecus africanus* from Sterkfontein. *Am. J. phys. Anthrop. 51*, 117–129.

Vrba, E. S. (1980) The significance of bovid remains as indicators of environment and predation patterns. In *Fossils in the Making*, 247–271. Eds. A. K. Behrensmeyer and A. P. Hill. Chicago: Chicago University Press.

Partridge, T. C. (1982) The chronological positions of the fossil hominids of Southern Africa. *Cong. Int. Paléont. Hum. 1*, Nice Prétirage, 617–675.

Vrba, E. S. (1982) Biostratigraphy and chronology, based particularly on Bovidae, of southern hominid-associated assemblages: Makapansgat, Sterkfontein, Taung. Kromdraai, Swartkrans; also Elandsfontein (Saldanha), Broken Hill (now Kabwe) and Cave of Hearths. *Cong. Int. Paléont. hum. 1*, Nice. Prétirage, 707–752.

Tobias, P. V. (1985) Sterkfontein. In *Excursion Booklet*. University of Witwatersrand and University of Mmabatho: Taung '60 Symposium.

Tobias, P. V. (1985) Pers. Comm.

Vrba, E. S. (1985a) Ethological and adaptive changes associated with early hominid evolution. In *Ancestors*, 63–71. Ed. E. Delson. New York: Alan R. Liss.

Vrba, E. S. (1985b) Early hominids in Southern Africa: Updated observations on chronological and evolutionary background. In *Hominid Evolution: Past, Present, and Future*, 195–200. Ed. P. V. Tobias. New York: Alan R. Liss.

Wilkinson, M. J. (1985) Lower-lying and possibly older fossiliferous deposits at Sterkfontein. In *Hominid Evolution: Past, Present and Future*, 165–170. Ed. P. V. Tobias. New York: Alan R. Liss.

The Kromdraai Remains

Fig. 100. The TM 1517 craniofacial fragment (left lateral view). *Courtesy of the Director of the Transvaal Museum, photographed by D. C. Panagos.*

Synonyms and other names *Paranthropus robustus* (Broom, 1938); *Homo transvaalensis* (Mayr, 1950); *Paranthropus robustus robustus* (Robinson, 1954); *Australopithecus robustus* (Oakley, 1954); *Australopithecus robustus robustus* (Campbell, 1964)
'Near-man'; 'Ape-man'; 'Man-ape'.

Site Kromdraai, two miles east of Sterkfontein, nine miles northwest of Krugersdorp, near Johannesburg, Transvaal, Republic of South Africa.

Found by (*a*) G. Terblanche, June, 1938; recognized by R. Broom. Cranial and postcranial bones.
(*b*) R. Broom, February, 1941. Juvenile mandible.
(*c*) E. S. Vrba, 1977–1980. Teeth

Geology   The bones were found in a block of stony breccia loose on the surface of the hillside at a point later named Kromdraai B. Excavation showed that this block was derived from the filling of a cave, formed in Pre-Cambrian dolomitic limestone, whose roof had completely weathered away. A similar cave filling nearby, Kromdraai A, has yielded quantities of mammalian fossil bones but no hominid material. The geology of the site has been investigated in detail (Brain, 1957, 1958).

New excavations have added greatly to knowledge of the geology and stratigraphy of the site. Kromdraai B has been divided into two formations, Kromdraai B East and Kromdraai B West. The former has been subdivided into Members 1–5 and the latter Members 1–3. Member 3 of the Kromdraai B East Formation has produced dental remains of australopithecines, the first *in situ* specimens from the site (Vrba, 1981).

Associated finds   One unquestionable chert artefact has been claimed from Kromdraai B and four other specimens from the same site regarded as less convincing stone tools (Brain, 1958). Until more evidence is available it would be unwise to classify these implements as a recognizable culture. Recent excavations have not produced any further stone tools.

Fossil mammalian bones recovered from Kromdraai A include insectivores (*Proamblysomus antiquus, Elephantulus langi, Crocidura cf. bicolor, Suncus cf. etruscus*), primates (*Gorgopithecus major, Parapapio jonesi, Papio angusticeps, Papio robinsoni*), a number of extinct rodents, several large and small carnivores (*Nyctereutes terblanchei, Herpestes mesotes, Crocuta crocuta, Panthera pardus, Panthera leo*), elephant (*Loxodonta atlantica*), hyraces (*Procavia antiqua, P. transvaalensis*), equids (*Stylohipparion steytleri, Equus plicatus, Equus helmei*) and a pig (*Potamochoerus antiquus*) (Cooke, 1964; Turner, 1984a, b, in press; Ficcarelli, Torre and Turner, 1985).

The latest excavation has added to the fauna known from the site and includes a colobus monkey (*Cercopithecoides williamsi*), a large carnivore (*Megantereon cf. gracile*), a hippopotamus (*Hippopotamus sp.* aff. *protamphibius*), a buffalo (*Syncerus cf. acoelotus*) and a tortoise (*cf. Testudo sp.*) (Vrba, 1981).

Dating   The fossil bones recovered from Kromdraai cannot at present be dated by radiometric or fission track methods since they were preserved in limestone; assessments of their age must rely therefore on geological and faunal evidence. Kromdraai was formerly commonly regarded as one of the most recent of the Transvaal australopithecine sites and attributed to the Basal Middle Pleistocene (Oakley, 1954, 1964). This conclusion was supported by a study of the bovid remains from the site (Vrba, 1975) which showed Kromdraai

B, the hominid fossil-bearing formation, to be younger than Kromdraai A. This work has now been entirely discounted in the light of new studies revealing possible temporal heterogeneity within the two Kromdraai deposits (Vrba, 1981, 1982). New attempts to date Kromdraai B East Member 3 (the hominid-bearing layer) by new faunal assessments have been frustrated by the recovery of chronologically uninformative taxa and attempts to determine the palaeomagnetic status have also failed. The best estimate of the age of KBE Member 3 as between 1–2 m.y. B.P. would fit the presently known facts (Vrba, 1981). Partridge agrees with this view and places Kromdraai B East Member 3 at 1–1·2 m.y. B.P. (Partridge, 1982).

Morphology The fossil hominid bones recovered from Kromdraai B comprise the left half of a cranium including the left maxilla and zygomatic bones, part of the left sphenoid, the left temporal, a fragmentary right maxilla, the right half of the body of a mandible, three isolated molars and four premolars. In addition some postcranial bones were found including the distal end of a right humerus, the proximal end of a right ulna, and a broken talus. Doubts have been cast on the correctness of the hominid identification of a metacarpal and a number of phalanges recovered from the site (Day and Scheuer, 1973; Day, 1978; Day and Thornton, 1985). Later (1941) a juvenile mandible was found containing most of the deciduous teeth and the right first permanent molar (TM 1536) and a second juvenile mandibular dentition was recovered in 1978/79 (KB 5223).

Skull (TM 1517a)

The skull is heavily built, having a relatively large face and a small cranium; the infratemporal fossa is deep, suggesting marked postorbital constriction. The brow ridges are absent but it seems likely that they were prominent, rather than exaggerated.

The position of the foramen magnum is well beneath the skull, and the mastoid process is small. The glenoid fossa is broad and shallow, bounded in front by an articular eminence and behind by a modest postglenoid tubercle. This arrangement suggests a temporomandibular mechanism of human character, a concept borne out by the nature of the wear of the teeth. The tympanic bone is broad and flat, forming the posterior wall of the articular fossa.

The maxilla is broad and flat, bearing a single infra-orbital foramen; there is no sign of a maxillopremaxillary suture on the anterior aspect of the maxilla which is moderately prognathic.

The mandible TM 1517b is represented by the anterior two-thirds of the body on the right side; this is very stout and bears the premolar and molar teeth. There is neither pronounced mandibular torus nor chin and the mental foramina are multiple.

Permanent Teeth

The Upper Incisors and Canines are lost but the second incisor and canine sockets are small.

The First Upper Premolars are large and have two rounded cusps separated by a fissure; there is a well marked posterior fovea. The socketed specimen has two buccal roots and a lingual root.

The Second Upper Premolars are similar to the first premolars but a little larger; they also have three roots.

The Upper First Molar is irregularly rhomboidal in shape, has four cusps and no trace of a Carabelli complex.

The Upper Second Molars are four-cusped and similar in shape to the first molars.

The Upper Third Molars are basically four-cusped: the arrangement of the cusps is somewhat simplified.

*   *   *

The Lower Incisor and Canine Teeth are missing but their sockets in a symphysial fragment are remarkably small.

The Lower First Premolars are large with two main cusps which are low and rounded. The anterior fovea is deep and there is no cingulum.

The Lower Second Premolars are large and bicuspid, perhaps tending to be molariform.

The Lower First Molars are represented by a worn specimen in the type jaw, and an incompletely erupted specimen in the juvenile mandible. The worn specimen has five cusps and a small sixth cusp, whereas the other tooth is small and has no sixth cusp.

The Lower Second Molar is broken but appears to be larger than the first molar; the cusps show evidence of flat wear.

The Lower Third Molar is in the mandible and is well preserved; it has six cusps and is larger than the other two molars.

Deciduous Teeth

These teeth are known from the mandible of a juvenile whose dental age has been estimated at about three to four years.

The First Lower Deciduous Incisor is absent.

The Second Lower Deciduous Incisor is small and very like the corresponding human tooth.

The Lower Deciduous Canine has a very small crown with a moderately well defined cingulum, and mesial and distal cusplets.

The First Deciduous Molars are both present and unworn. They appear to be remarkably human in their shape and cusp pattern.

The Second Deciduous Molar is rather elongated mesiodistally, has five main cusps and a rudimentary sixth cusp.

The second mandiblular dentition known from Kromdraai (KB 5223) is from a subadult and is said to be conspecific with the other Kromdraai australopithecines known from the site (Grine, 1982).

Postcranial Bones

The Lower Extremity of the Right Humerus (TM 1517g) is well preserved and remarkably human in its general shape. The capitulum
is rounded but set a little farther back than is usual in modern
man. The medial epicondyle is rather pointed but is marked for the
attachment of the flexor muscles of the forearm. The lateral epicondyle is similarly marked for the extensor muscles. According to Le
Gros Clark (1947) the humerus has none of the distinctive features
found in the recent anthropoid apes; however, this view is not
shared by Straus (1948) who suggests that this humerus is 'no
more hominid than anthropoid' and believes that its principal affinities are with man *and* chimpanzee. The mixed features of this bone
have been confirmed by Patterson and Howells (1967) and
McHenry and Corruccini (1974).

The Ulnar Fragment (TM 1517e) was found near the end of the
humerus and almost certainly belongs with it; it resembles that of
modern man. The olecranon process is small, suggesting that the
range of elbow extension was full.

The Talus (TM 1517d) lacks the lower part of the body and head. It
is a small bone with a narrow superior articular surface but a broad
head and short neck. The horizontal angle of the neck is high by
comparison with modern man.

The assemblage of extremity bones said to form part of the type
specimen of *Paranthropus robustus* TM 1517h–o (Broom and Schepers, 1946) have been re-examined recently. All save one have
been referred to species of baboon, several of which are known from
the site. The exception is a hominid hallucial terminal phalanx that
shows bipedal features (Day and Thornton, 1985).

Dimensions

Skull

Broom and Schepers (1946)
Cranial Capacity 650 cc (estimated)

Mandible

Body Thickness (PM2) 23·4

Teeth

Robinson (1956)

		I¹	I²	C	PM¹	PM²	M¹	M²	M³
					Upper Permanent Teeth (Crown Dimensions)				
Left	l	—	—	—	10·0	10·3	13·7	13·8	14·4
side	b	—	—	—	13·7	15·2	14·6	15·9	16·2
Right	l	—	—	—	10·2	—	—	13·8	14·2
side	b	—	—	—	—	—	—	15·9	16·1

| | | Lower Permanent Teeth (Crown Dimensions) | | | | | | | |
		I_1	I_2	C	PM_1	PM_2	M_1	M_2	M_3
Left	l	—	—	—	10·0	11·1	—	—	—
side	b	—	—	—	12·2	13·0	—	—	—
Right	l	—	—	—	—	11·0	14·4	—	16·4
side	b	—	—	—	—	13·1	13·0	—	14·0

| | | Lower Deciduous Teeth (Crown Dimensions) | | | | | |
		DI_1	DI_2	DC	DM_1	DM_2	M_1 (Perm.)
Left	l	—	—	—	9·7	12·5*	—
side	b	—	—	—	8·1	10·0	—
Right	l	—	4·6	5·2	9·7	11·6	12·7
side	b	—	3·7	4·9	8·1	9·7	11·5

* Damaged

Postcranial Bones

Broom and Schepers (1946)
Humerus Bicondylar Width 54·0
　　　　　Max. Width of Articular Surface 40·0
Talus (taken from a cast)
　Length 34·5
　Breadth 28·5
　Length/Breadth Index 82·6
　Horizontal Angle of Neck 30°
　Torsion of Neck approx. 30°
Humerus Straus (1948; from a cast)
　Bicondylar Width 54·0
　Width of the Trochlear 20·0
　Depth of the Trochlear 23·0
　Width of the Capitulum 16·0
　Max. Width of Articular Surface 40·0

Affinities The affinities of the Kromdraai remains will be discussed with the rest of the australopithecine material.

Originals The Transvaal Museum, Pretoria, Republic of South Africa.

Casts The University Museum, University of Pennsylvania, Philadelphia 4, Pennsylvania, U.S.A.

References Broom, R. (1938) The Pleistocene anthropoid apes of South Africa. *Nature* 142, 377–379.
Broom, R. and Schepers, G. W. H. (1946) The South African fossil ape-men, the Australopithecinae. *Transv. Mus. Mem. 2*, 1–272.
Clark, W. E. le Gros (1947) Observations on the anatomy of the fossil Australopithecinae. *J. Anat. (Lond.) 81*, 300–333.

Straus, W. L. jnr. (1948) The humerus of *Paranthropus robustus. Am. J. phys. Anthrop. 6*, 285–311.

Mayr, E. (1950) Taxonomic categories in fossil hominids. *Cold Spring Harb. Symp. Quant. Biol. 15*, 109–118.

Oakley, K. P. (1954) Dating the australopithecines of Africa. *Am. J. phys. Anthrop. 12*, 9–23.

Robinson, J. T. (1954) The genera and species of the Australopithecinae. *Am. J. phys. Anthrop. 12*, 181–200.

Robinson, J. T. (1956) The dentition of the Australopithecinae. *Transv. Mus. Mem. 9*, 1–179.

Brain, C. K. (1957) New evidence for the correlation of the Transvaal ape-man bearing cave deposits. *Proc. pan-Afr. Cong. Prehist. 3, Livingstone,* 1955, 143–148. Ed. J. D. Clark. London: Chatto and Windus.

Brain, C. K. (1958) The Transvaal ape-man bearing cave deposits. *Trans. Mus. Mem. 11*, 1–125.

Oakley, K. P. (1964) *Frameworks for Dating Fossil Man*, 291. London: Weidenfeld and Nicolson.

Campbell, B. (1964) Quantitative taxonomy and human evolution. In *Classification and Human Evolution*, 50–74. Ed. S. L. Washburn. London: Methuen and Co. Ltd.

Cooke, H. B. S. (1964) Pleistocene mammal faunas of Africa, with particular reference to South Africa. In *African Ecology and Human Evolution*, 65–116. Eds. F. C. Howell and F. Bourlière. London: Methuen and Co. Ltd.

Patterson, B., and Howells, W. W. (1967) Hominid humeral fragment from Early Pleistocene of northwestern Kenya. *Science, 156*, 64–66.

Day, M. H. and Scheuer, J. L. (1973) SKW 14147: a new hominid metacarpal from Swartkrans. *J. hum. Evol. 2*, 429–438.

McHenry, H. and Corruccini, R. S. (1974) Distal humerus in hominid evolution. *Folia Primatologia*, 227–244.

Vrba, E. S. (1975) Some evidence of chronology and palaeoecology of Sterkfontein, Swartkrans and Kromdraai from the fossil Bovidae. *Nature 254*, 301–304.

Day, M. H. (1978) Functional interpretations of the morphology of postcranial remains of early African hominids. In *Early Hominids of Africa*, 311–345. Ed. C. Jolly. London: Duckworth.

Vrba, E. S. (1981) The Kromdraai australopithicine site revisited in 1980: Recent investigations and results. *Annls Trans. Mus. 33*, 17–60.

Grine, F. E. (1982) A new juvenile hominid (Mammalia: Primates) from Member 3, Kromdraai Formation, Transvaal, South Africa. *Annls Trans. Mus. 33*, 165–239.

Partridge, T. C. (1982) The chronological positions of the fossil hominids of Southern Africa. *Cong. Int. Paléont. hum. 1*. Prétirage, 617–675.

Vrba, E. S. (1982) Biostratigraphy and chronology, based particularly on Bovidae, of southern hominid-associated assemblages: Makapansgat, Sterkfontein, Taung, Kromdraai, Swartkrans; also Elandsfontein (Saldanha), Broken Hill (now Kabwe) and Cave of Hearths. *Cong. Internat. Paléont. hum. 1*. Prétirage, 707–752.

Turner, A. (1984a) The interpretation of variation in fossil specimens of spotted hyaena (*Crocuta crocuta*) (Erxleben, 1977) from Sterkfontein Valley sites (Mammalia: Carnivora) *Annls Trans. Mus. 33*, 399–418.

Turner, A. (1984b) *Panthera crassidens* Broom, 1948. The cat that never was? *S. Afr. J. Sci. 80*, 227–233.

Ficcarelli, G., Torre, D. and Turner, A. (1985) First evidence for a species of raccoon dog, *Nycterentes* Temminck, 1838, in South African Plio-

Pleistocene deposits. *Boll. Soc. Pal. Italiana 23*, 125–130.

Day, M.H. and Thornton, C. (1986) The extremity bones of *Paranthropus robustus* from Kromdraai B, East Formation Member 3, Republic of South Africa—A Reappraisal. *Anthropos* (BRNO) 23: 91–99.

Turner, A. Miscellaneous carnivore remains from Plio-Pleistocene deposits in the Sterkfontein Valley (Mammalia: Carnivora). *Annls Trans. Mus.* (in press).

The Swartkrans Remains

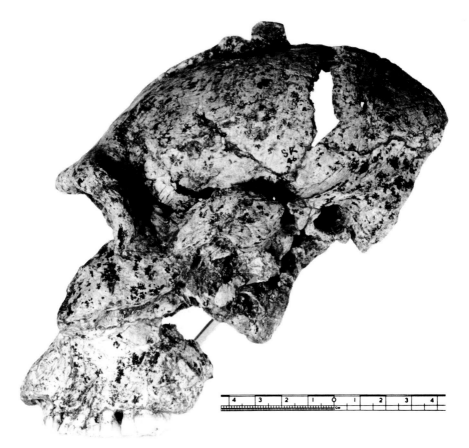

Fig. 101. The SK 46 cranium (left lateral view). *Courtesy of the Director of the Transvaal Museum, photographed by D. C. Panagos.*

Synonyms and other names	1. *Paranthropus crassidens* (Broom, 1949); *Homo transvaalensis* (Mayr, 1950); *Australopithecus (Paranthropus) crassidens* (Oakley, 1954); *Paranthropus robustus crassidens* (Robinson, 1954); *Australopithecus robustus crassidens* (Campbell, 1964); *Paranthropus robustus* (Brain, 1970); 'Ape-man'; 'Man-ape'; 'Near-man'

2. *Telanthropus capensis* (Broom and Robinson, 1949); *Pithecanthropus capensis* (Simonetta, 1957); *Homo erectus* (Robinson, 1961); *Australopithecus capensis* (Oakley, 1964); *Homo sp. indet.* (Clarke, Clark Howell and Brain, 1970).

3. Hominidae, genus and species indet. (Day and Scheuer, 1973).

Site   Swartkrans, six miles northwest of Krugersdorp, near Johannesburg, Republic of South Africa.

Found by   R. Broom, November, 1948–1951; J. T. Robinson, 1948–1952; J. T. Robinson, April 1949; C. K. Brain, 1966, 1967 and 1968 *et seq.*

Geology   The Swartkrans site is situated near to the Sterkfontein and Kromdraai excavations and consists of the remains of a cavern in Pre-Cambrian dolomitic limestone. The roof of the Outer Cave has been removed by erosion but the Inner Cave is still protected by a thick layer of dolomite. The cavern appears to have originated from subsidence of the deposit into an underlying solution cavity or Lower Cave.

The geology of the site has been investigated in detail (Brain, 1958, 1970, 1976; Butzer, 1976). Initially two major breccias, the pink and the brown, were recognized; the older unstratified pink breccia containing nearly all of the hominid fossils overlain by the stratified brown breccia. Following detailed sedimentological studies, Butzer (1976) designated the older and younger deposits as Members 1 and 2 of the Swartkrans Formation. Member 1 consists of a massive block of calcified sediment adherent to the north wall of the cave and undercut by an erosional surface. It has been termed the 'Hanging Remnant' of Member 1. The original Member 1 is made up of the Hanging Remnant and the Lower Bank which rests on the floor of the cave. All of the robust australopithecine remains derive from Member 1. Also the SK 846/847/80 composite cranium attributed to *Homo sp.* is derived from Member 2.

Associated finds   At first several quartzite artefacts were recovered from the dumps of breccia which surrounded the excavation. They appeared to be of Oldowan type but too few were recovered to allow a definite cultural assessment.

Recently a new assemblage of stone tools has been recovered associated with hominid remains (Brain, 1970). The new assemblage has been studied and the following tool types identified; side and end choppers, bifaces, discoids, subspheroids, scrapers and picks. All are in sharp condition. By comparison with Oldowan tools from Olduvai they are relatively large, but otherwise they show a number of similarities (Leakey, 1970).

Worn bone fragments recovered from the Lower Bank of Member 1 have been interpreted as digging tools used for obtaining edible bulbs (Brain, 1982, 1985).

The fossil mammalian bones that were found include those of insectivores (*Chlorotalpa spelea, Elephantulus langi, Elephantulus cf. brachyrhynchus, Suncus cf. etruscus*), primates (*Simopithecus danieli, Parapapio jonesi, Papio robinsoni, Dinopithecus ingens, Cercopithecoides williamsi*), rodents (*Dasymys bolti, Palaeotomys gracilis, Cryptomys robertsi*), several carnivores (*Canis mesomelas pappos, Cynictis penicillata, Lycyaena silberbergi, Lycyaena nitidula, Leecyaena forfex, Crocuta crocuta angella, Crocuta venustula, Hyaena brunnea, H. brunnea dispar, Panthera* aff. *leo, P. pardus incurva, Megantereon eurynodon*), hyraces (*Procavia antiqua, P. transvaalensis*) and two suids ('*Tapinochoerus*' *meadowsi, Potamochoerus antiquus*) (Cooke, 1964). A new and extended faunal list has been given that includes the minimum numbers of individual animals (Brain, 1976).

Dating The dating problem has been discussed by a number of authors (Howell, 1955; Ewer, 1957; Oakley, 1954, 1957; Brain, 1958). It has been suggested that the opening of the Swartkrans cave should be dated at 2·57 million years B.P. on the basis of a geomorphological method (Partridge, 1973). The method has been criticized and is not universally accepted as a valid technique (Butzer, 1974). On the basis of the fossil antelopes from the site Vrba has suggested that Member 1 may be referred to as the Swartkrans Faunal Span within the 1·5–2 m.y. B.P. range. Member 2 and channel-fill sediment can be regarded as covering a longer range from the late Cornelia Span, less than 0·5 m.y. B.P. up to the present day (Vrba, 1975; Brain, 1976).

No radiometric, fission track or biochemical methods have proved usable at Swartkrans. Attempts to determine the palaeomagnetic status of the deposits were unsuccessful (Brock *et al.*, 1977).

Morphology The remains from Swartkrans include:
1. An almost complete cranium, the left half of a cranium with both maxillae, a juvenile cranium, an adolescent cranium and several other crania which have been crushed during fossilization. A number of specimens of maxillae, with most of the upper dentition, were recovered as well as three adult mandibles. Several other mandibles were found, both adult and juvenile, and about 100 isolated teeth. The postcranial bones include the crushed lower end of a humerus, a left thumb metacarpal, an incomplete innominate bone and the proximal ends of two right femora. An infant mandible containing deciduous molars (SK 3978), a natural endocast of a hominid skull (SK 1585), a thoracic vertebra (T_{12}) and a lumbar vertebra (L_5) (SK 3981). In addition to these specimens there have been recovered a number of mandibular and cranial fragments as well as a dozen isolated teeth (Brain, 1970).

Newly recognized or newly described material includes SK 3155b, a right innominate fragment (McHenry, 1975), SK 858/883/861 a robust composite mandible recognized from the articulation of three separate specimens (White, 1976) and a group of juvenile

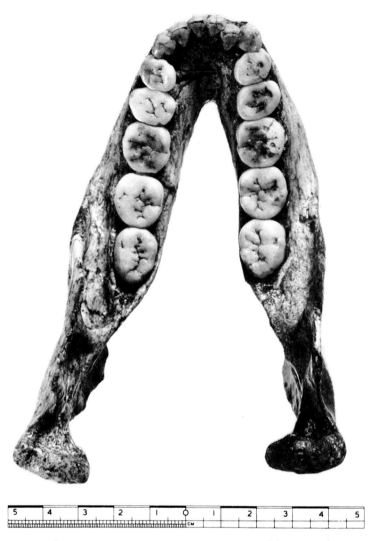

Fig. 102. The SK 23 mandible. *Courtesy of the Director of the Transvaal Museum, photographed by D. C. Panagos.*

dental and mandibular specimens, SK 839/852, 1595 and 2147 (Grine, 1981).

2. A mandible (SK 15), a mandibular fragment (SK 45) containing two molar teeth, a maxillary fragment (SK 80), an isolated lower third premolar (SK 18a), the proximal end of a radius (SK 18b) and the distal end of a fourth left metacarpal (SK 85). Following a recent examination of the Swartkrans remains (Clarke, Clark Howell and Brain, 1970), one of these authors (R. J. Clarke) was able to associ-

ate parts of a skull (SK 847) and much of a left temporal bone (SK 846b), both formerly attributed to *A. robustus*, with the previously known maxillary fragment (SK 80). The specimen comprises most of the left side of the face, the infratemporal fossa and the left temporal region. The whole unit is now termed SK 847.

A juvenile cranium formerly regarded as an aberrant robust australopithecine, SK 27, has been reclassified as a member of the genus *Homo* (Clarke, 1977).

3. Subsequently an adult left fifth metacarpal (SKW 14147) was recovered from a block of breccia (Day and Scheuer, 1973).

1. Skull

The best cranium (SK 48) obtained from Swartkrans is probably that of a female; it is somewhat crushed and was broken during excavation. The supraorbital ridge is well marked, particularly in the midline, showing a prominent glabella; the forehead is concave and restricted by the union of the temporal lines forming a sagittal crest. The brain case is small in relation to the size of the facial skeleton, and constricted behind the orbits. Posteriorly the occipital region is damaged but the occipital crest is well defined. The glenoid fossa is deep and bounded posteriorly by the tympanic bone.

The maxillae are robust and flat, separated by a broad nasal opening, but the premaxillary region is shortened giving the dental arcade a 'squared-off' appearance. The palate is large and bounded by stout alveolar processes of bone bearing three molars on the left side and the first premolar and canine on the right.

Mandible

The best-preserved mandible (SK 23) is a fine specimen, virtually complete, with an almost perfect adult dentition. The only damage it has sustained is some crushing of the body which has resulted in fracture of the symphysial region and narrowing of the dental arcade. This specimen is probably female since two other jaws from Swartkrans are similar in their general features but are even more massive.

The body of the female mandible is stout; the ramus is very tall and buttressed internally by paired ridges running to the coronoid and condyloid processes from the *crista pharyngea*, a crest which runs upwards from the lingual side of the third molar. The symphysial region, although broken, shows that there is neither chin nor true simian shelf, but there is a genioglossal fossa internally in the midline below the flattened alveolar plane. The internal mandibular torus is of moderate size; externally the anterior border of the coronoid process runs down on to the body as a ridge which passes below the molar teeth and fades away beneath the single mental foramen.

Permanent Teeth

About 300 permanent teeth are known from Swartkrans.

The Upper Incisors are relatively small and shovel-shaped with raised marginal ridges. The lateral incisors tend to be smaller than the central incisors.

The Upper Canines are small-crowned and stout-rooted; they are symmetrical and have blunt points. The lingual faces of these teeth have characteristic grooves.

The Upper First Premolars are bicuspid and asymmetrical in occlusal view; the primary fissure is usually deeply cut.

The Upper Second Premolars resemble the first premolars in cusp pattern but usually have a distinct talon.

The Upper First Molars are characteristically trapezoidal in shape and the crown pattern is simple and four-cusped.

The Upper Second Molars are also skewed in occlusal view and several examples have some of the Carabelli complex.

The Upper Third Molars resemble the second molars in some respects but tend to be even more irregular in shape.

*   *   *

The Lower Incisors are relatively simple having horizontal cutting edges; the lateral specimens are slightly shovel-shaped.

The Lower Canines are asymmetrical having a distal cusplet formed by the remnants of the cingulum.

The Lower First Premolars are robust, bicuspid and asymmetrical. The buccal cusp is the larger and it is commonly joined to the lingual cusp by a ridge which separates the anterior and posterior foveae.

The Lower Second Premolar is larger than the first and its crown is partially molarized.

The Lower First Molars are typically hominid in shape; five main cusps are present as well as a small sixth cusp. The fissure pattern is normally dryopithecine with some tendency towards the development of the + pattern typical of modern man. There is some wrinkling of the occlusal enamel.

The Lower Second Molars are similar in shape to the first molars but have four main cusps and a small fifth cusp. The fissure pattern is not dryopithecine and there is some secondary enamel wrinkling.

The Lower Third Molars have complex occlusal cusp patterns and crenulated fissure arrangements. The tooth crowns tend to be of irregular shape.

Deciduous Teeth

The Upper Incisors and Canines are not represented well enough for description.

The Upper First Molar is known from a single specimen, a very worn isolated tooth. The crown is asymmetrical and has four cusps.

The Upper Second Molars, though smaller than the first permanent molars, are very like them in the details of their structure and also have four main cusps.

*   *   *

The Lower Incisors are too badly damaged for description.

The Lower Canines have asymmetrical crowns with well marked distal cusplets derived from the cingulum.

The Lower First Molars are well developed and have five cusps separated by the basically dryopithecine fissure system.

The Lower Second Molars are larger than the first and fully molariform. The cusp pattern agrees closely with that of the first molar.

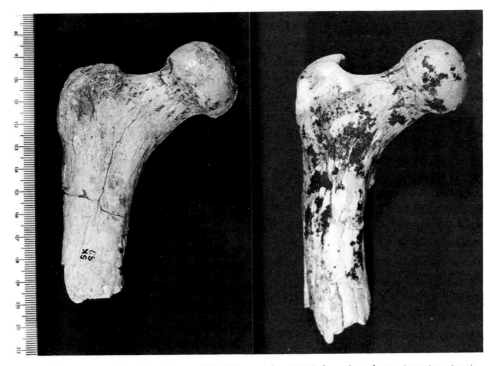

Fig. 103. The upper ends of two femora (left: SK97, right: SK82) from Swartkrans (anterior views). *Photographed by courtesy of the Director of the Transvaal Museum, Pretoria.*

Postcranial Bones

The Left Thumb Metacarpal (SK 84) is robust, curved and strongly impressed by muscular markings. The distal articular surface is asymmetrical and has a beak-like process separating two sesamoid grooves. The proximal articulation is saddle-shaped.

The Innominate Bone (SK 50) belongs to the right side and lacks the iliac crest, the sacral articulation and most of its pubic portion. The acetabulum is complete but crushing has reduced its anteroposterior diameter. The anterior superior iliac spine is prominent and reaches forwards and laterally; although the iliac crest is missing it seems likely that it is less sharply curved than that of man. The ischial segment is long and the ischial tuberosity well separated from the acetabular margin. The distortion and generally poor state of preservation of this fossil hip bone precludes the use of many measurements for comparative purposes.

The Upper Ends of Two Femora (SK 82 and SK 97), both from the right side, are similar in their principal features. The head is small and rounded, bearing a sub-central fovea. The neck, broad at the base, narrows to the articular surface, has an horizontal upper border and a pronounced obturator externus groove indicating clearly that the hip was capable of hyper-extension (Day, 1969). Two vertebrae have been recovered from the Swartkrans cave site (Brain, 1970). It appears that they are derived from a block of breccia similar to that from which the early hominid materials are derived. They have been identified as being a last thoracic vertebra (SK 3981a) and a last lumbar vertebra (SK 3981b).

They both are large and have general resemblances to the australopithecine vertebrae from Sterkfontein (Sts 14); they differ from those of modern man in several respects. In view of this, they have been attributed to *Paranthropus robustus* (Robinson, 1970). In functional terms the most important feature of the last lumbar vertebra may be the disparity between the anterior and posterior depths of the body; this wedging suggests a well developed sacral promontory and marked lumbar lordosis. In turn this supports the view that *Paranthropus robustus* ($\equiv$ *A. robustus*) had habitual upright posture.

Skull (SK 847)

This skull, constructed from materials that were formerly attributed to both *A. robustus* and 'Telanthropus', shows a number of distinctive features. The supraorbital torus is pronounced and quite thick while the postorbital constriction is not marked. The nasal bones are prominent on the face and differ strongly from those of both gracile and robust australopithecines known previously. The position of the articular fossa for the mandibular condyle with relation to the occlusal plane is such that the ramus of the mandible must have been

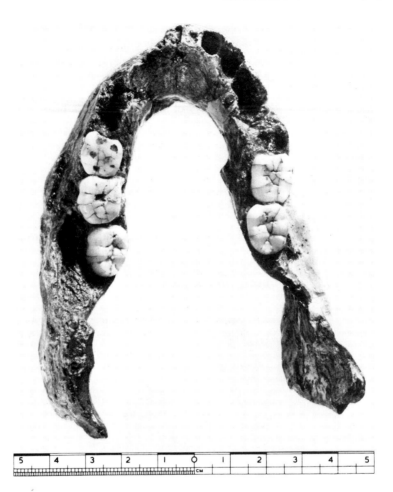

Fig. 104. The SK 15 mandible. *Courtesy of the Director of the Transvaal Museum, photographed by D. C. Panagos.*

squat and quite different in morphology from the tall *A. robustus* mandible (SK 23) known from the same site. In fact the '*Telanthropus*' I mandible (SK 15) 'fits' SK 847 very well although it is dentally not from the same specimen. The other mandibular fragment (SK 45), however, could well represent the same individual.

2. Mandible

In the Swartkrans cave two mandibles were found whose morphology is very different from that of those described in the preceding section. The body of the better specimen (SK 15) is complete and contains five molar teeth, but the ascending rami are broken; the whole jaw is somewhat crushed. The symphysis is almost intact and has neither chin nor simian shelf; internally it is reinforced by a transverse torus below which there is a shallow genioglossal fossa. The body is robust, particularly in the region of the third molar, and the mental foramen on the right side is single.

The second specimen (SK 45) consists of a fragment of the right side of the body of another mandible bearing two molar teeth. An isolated left premolar tooth (SK 18a) was found close to the better mandible.

Teeth

The Premolar is considerably worn but the crown is small and hominid in its general features.

The Left First Molar is intact but worn; however, it is not distinguishable from a modern human lower first molar.

The Second Molars are both worn but it is possible to discern a dryopithecine fissure pattern with six cusps. There seems to be no trace of enamel wrinkling.

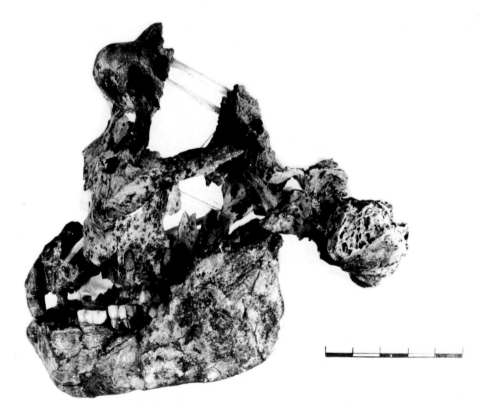

Fig. 105. The Swartkrans (SK847) composite cranium articulated with the SK15 mandible. *Courtesy of R. J. Clarke.*

The Third Molars are intact and little worn, and resemble the second molars. The dryopithecine fissure pattern (Y5) is tending towards the + pattern of modern hominids.

Postcranial Bones

The proximal end of a right *Radius* (SK 18b) was recovered with the better mandible. The distal end of a fourth left *Metacarpal* (SK 85) was found at Swartkrans. It is not particularly robust, nor does it have any of the specializations associated with pongid metacarpals. Apart from its small size it is similar to the corresponding bone of modern man.

3. An adult left fifth metacarpal (Stw 14147) was recovered and later compared with fifth metacarpals from Gorilla, Pan, several baboon species as well as *Homo sapiens*. Whilst clearly different from those of Pan, Gorilla and the baboons, it was not dissimilar to those of modern man (Day and Scheuer, 1977).

Dimensions   *1. Skulls*

None of the crania is sufficiently well preserved to allow reliable measurements of their principal dimensions or cranial capacities.
Natural endocast (SK 1585)—volume 530 cc
Holloway (in Brain, 1970)

Mandible (SK 23)

Robinson (1953)
Max. Length 127·0
Ramus Height 91 (at coronoid); 84 (at condyle)
Ramus Width 52 and 55 (mid-point)
Body Depth (PM2) 39·7
Body Depth (C) 40·0
Body Depth (M2) 35·7
Body Depth (M3) 33·0
Body Width (M2) 25·0

Teeth

Robinson (1956)

		I^1	I^2	C	PM^1	PM^2	M^1	M^2	M^3
				Upper Permanent Teeth (Crown Dimensions)					
Average	l	9·4	7·2	8·7	9·9	10·6	13·8	14·7	15·1
figures	b	7·6	6·8	9·5	14·2	15·4	14·5	15·9	16·9

SK 23				*Lower Permanent Teeth (Crown Dimensions)*					
Left	l	5·6	6·7	7·8	9·4	10·5	14·8	15·2	16·0
side	b	5·9	6·7	7·8	11·4	14·1	14·7	14·8	13·0
Right	l	5·6	6·6	8·1	9·6	10·7	14·7	15·0	17·3
side	b	6·3	6·7	8·0	11·5	13·5	14·6	14·8	14·1

| | | Upper Deciduous Teeth (Crown Dimensions) | | | | |
		dI¹	dI²	dC	dM¹	dM²
Left	l	—	—	—	—	10·2
side	b	—	—	—	—	12·0
Right	l	—	—	—	8·7	—
side	b	—	—	—	9·8	—
Specimen					SK 91	SK 90

| SK 61 | | Lower Deciduous Teeth (Crown Dimensions) | | | | |
		dI1	dI2	dC	dM1	dM2
Left	l	—	—	5·7	10·6	13·3
side	b	—	—	5·3	9·5	11·9
Right	l	3·8	4·9	5·9	11·1	13·4
side	b	—	4·6	5·2	9·5	12·0

Brain (1970)

| SK 3978 | | Lower Deciduous Teeth (Crown Dimensions) | | | | |
		dI₁	dI₂	dC	dM₁	dM₂
Left	l	—	—	—	10·2	13·0
side	b	—	—	—	7·8	10·5
Right	l	—	—	—	9·9	12·9
side	b	—	—	—	8·2	10·7

Postcranial Bones

The Thumb Metacarpal (SK 84) (Napier, 1959)
Max. Length 35·0   Mid-shaft Breadth 7·5 (A.P.), 9·5 (Transverse)
Robusticity Index 24·3
Femur (SK 82)
Length of neck 63·0 (from a cast)
Mean Thickness of shaft 27·5 (below lesser trochanter) (from a cast)
Mean Diameter of head 33·0 (from a cast)

SK 3981a (T₁₂) (Robinson, 1970)

No dimensions available.

SK 3981b (L₅)
Width of neural canal—21·4

Body   Anterior depth—21·3
         Posterior depth—19·0

2. Skull

Clarke, Clark Howell and Brain (1970)

SK 847

Parietal/sagittal chord (damaged) 82·5
Max. thickness (22 mm. anterior to lambda) 7·5
Max. thickness (posterior part of temporal line) 8·5
Distance of temporal line from sagittal suture at lambda 37·0
Max. distance of temporal line from sagittal suture 39·0

Mandibles

Robinson (1953)
Telanthropus I (Restored) (SK 15)
Max. Length 109·0
Body Height (C) 31·5
Body Height (M3) 25·0
Body Width (M2) 22·5
Ramus Height (coronoid) 59·0
Ramus Height (condyle) 55·0
Bicondylar Width 114·0

Teeth

Broom and Robinson (1952)

Lower Permanent Teeth (Crown Dimensions)				
Telanthropus I (SK 15)	PM_1	M_1	M_2	M_3
Left l	8·6	11·9	—	14·3
side b	10·3	11·9	—	12·4
Right l	—	—	13·6	13·9
side b	—	—	13·1	12·3

Postcranial Bones

Fourth Left Metacarpal (SK 85) (Napier, 1959)
Reconstructed Length 50·7
No dimensions are available for the upper end of the radius.

3. SKW 14147 (Day and Scheuer, 1973)

Left fifth metacarpal
Length 47·4
Mean midshaft thickness 7·1

Affinities The affinities of the Swartkrans remains will be discussed with the rest of the australopithecine material.

Originals   The Transvaal Museum, Pretoria, Republic of South Africa.

Casts   The University Museum, University of Pennsylvania, Philadelphia 4, Pennsylvania, U.S.A. 1. Mandible, skull, immature skull, innominate, femora, palate, maxillae. 2. Mandible. 3. Not available at present.

References   Broom, R. (1949) Another new type of fossil ape-man. *Nature 163,* 57.

Broom, R., and Robinson, J. T. (1949) A new type of fossil man. *Nature 164,* 322–323.

Broom, R., and Robinson, J. T. (1950) Man contemporaneous with the Swartkrans ape-man. *Am. J. phys. Anthrop. 8,* 151–156.

Mayr, E. (1950) Taxonomic categories in fossil hominids. *Cold Spring Harb. Symp. Quant. Biol. 15,* 109–118.

Broom, R., and Robinson, J. T. (1952) Swartkrans ape-man. *Paranthropus crassidens. Transv. Mus. Mem. 6,* 1–124.

Robinson, J. T. (1953) *Telanthropus* and its phylogenetic significance. *Am. J. phys. Anthrop. 11,* 445–501.

Oakley, K. P. (1954) Dating the australopithecines of Africa. *Am. J. phys. Anthrop. 12,* 9–23.

Robinson, J. T. (1954) The genera and species of the *Australopithecine. Am. J. phys. Anthrop. 12,* 181–200.

Clark, W. E. le Gros (1955) The *os innominatum* of the recent *Ponginae* with special reference to that of the Australopithecinae. *Am. J. phys. Anthrop. 13,* 19–27.

Dart, R. A. (1955) *Australopithecus prometheus* and *Telanthropus capensis. Am. J. phys. Anthrop. 13,* 67–96.

Howell, F. C. (1955) The age of the australopithecines of Southern Africa. *Am. J. phys. Anthrop. 13,* 635–662.

Robinson, J. T. (1956) The dentition of the Australopithecinae. *Transv. Mus. Mem. 9,* 1–179.

Brain, C. K. (1957) New evidence for the correlation of the Transvaal ape-man bearing cave deposits. *Proc. pan-Afr. Cong. Prehist., 3.* Livingstone, 1955. Ed. J. D. Clark, pp. 143–148. London: Chatto and Windus.

Ewer, R. F. (1957) Faunal evidence for the dating of the Australopithecinae. *Ibid.,* pp. 135–142.

Oakley, K. P. (1957) Dating the australopithecines. *Ibid.,* pp. 155–157.

Simonetta, A. (1957) Catalogo e sinominia annotata degli ominoidi fossili ed attuali (1758–1955). *Atti. Soc. tosc. Sci. Nat. 64,* 53–112.

Brain, C. K. (1958) The Transvaal ape-man bearing cave deposits. *Transv. Mus. Mem. 11,* 1–125.

Napier, J. R. (1959) Fossil metacarpals from Swartkrans. *Fossil Mammals of Africa. No. 17.* London: British Museum (Nat. Hist.)

Robinson, J. T. (1961) The australopithecines and their bearing on the origin of man and of stone tool-making. *S. Afr. J. Sci. 57,* 3–13.

Kurtén, B. (1962) The relative ages of the australopithecines of Transvaal and the pithecanthropines of Java. In *Evolution und Hominisation,* 74–80. Ed. G. Kurth, Stuttgart: Gustav Fischer Verlag.

Campbell, B. (1964) Quantitative taxonomy and human evolution. In *Classification and Human Evolution,* 50–74. Ed. S. L. Washburn. London: Methuen and Co. Ltd.

Cooke, H. B. S. (1964) Pleistocene mammal faunas of Africa, with particular reference to South Africa. In *African Ecology and Human Evolution,*

65–116. Eds. F. C. Howell and F. Bourlière. London: Methuen and Co. Ltd.

Napier, J. R. (1964) The evolution of bipedal walking in the hominids. *Arch. Biol. (Liège) 75*, Supp. 673–708.

Oakley, K. P. (1964) *Frameworks for dating fossil man, 291*. London: Weidenfeld and Nicolson.

Day, M. H. (1969) Femoral fragment of a robust australopithecine from Olduvai Gorge, Tanzania. *Nature 221*, 230–233.

Wolpoff, M. H. (1968) 'Telanthropus' and the single species hypothesis. *Am. Anthrop. 70*, 477–493.

Brain, C. K. (1970) New finds at the Swartkrans site. *Nature 225*, 1112–1119.

Robinson, J. T. (1970) Two new early hominid vertebrae from Swartkrans. *Nature 225*, 1217–1219.

Clarke, R. J., Howell, F. Clark and Brain, C. K. (1970) More evidence of an advanced hominid at Swartkrans. *Nature 225*, 1219–1222.

Leakey, M. D. (1970) Stone artefacts from Swartkrans. *Nature 225*, 1222–1225.

Day, M. H. and Scheuer, J. L. (1973) SKW 14147: a new metacarpal from Swartkrans. *J. hum. Evol. 2*, 429–438.

McHenry, H. M. (1975) A new pelvic fragment from Swartkrans and the relationship between the robust and gracile australopithecines. (SK 3155). *Am. J. phys. Anthrop. 43*, 245–262.

Vrba, E. S. (1975) Some evidence of chronology and palaeoecology of Sterkfontein, Swartkrans and Kromdraai from the fossil Bovidae. *Nature 254*, 301–304.

Brain, C. K. (1976) A re-interpretation of the Swartkrans site and its remains. *S. Afr. J. Sci. 72*, 141–146.

Butzer, K. W. (1976) Lithostratigraphy of the Swartkrans Formation. *S. Afr. J. Sci. 72*, 136–141.

White, T. D. (1976) On a newly associated composite mandible from Swartkrans (Mammalia: Hominidae). *Annls. Transv. Mus. 30*, 97–98.

Brock, A., McFadden, P. L. and Partridge, T. C. (1977) Preliminary palaeomagnetic results from Makapansagat and Swartkrans. *Nature 266*, 249–250.

Clarke, R. J. (1977) A juvenile cranium and some adult teeth of early *Homo* from Swartkrans, Transvaal. *S. Afr. J. Sci. 73*, 46–49.

Grine, F. E. (1981) Description of some juvenile hominid specimens from Swartkrans, Transvaal. *Annls. S. Afr. Mus. 86*, 43–71.

Brain, C. K. (1982) The Swartkrans site: stratigraphy of the fossil hominids and a reconstruction of the environment of early *Homo*. *Cong. Int. Paléont. hum. 1. Nice* Prétirage, 676–706.

Brain, C. K. (1985) Cultural and taphonomic comparisons of hominids from Swartkrans and Sterkfontein. In *Ancestors*, 72–75. Ed. E. Delson. New York: Alan R. Liss.

The Makapansgat Remains

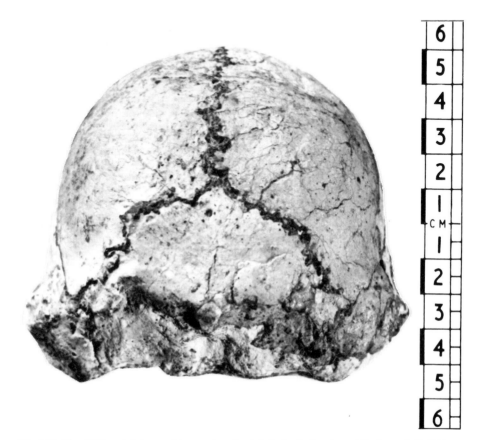

Fig. 106. The MLD 37/38 incomplete cranium (occipital view). *Courtesy of Professor P. V. Tobias, photographed by A. R. Hughes.*

Synonyms and other names	*Australopithecus prometheus* (Dart, 1948a); *Homo transvaalensis* (Mayr, 1950); *Australopithecus africanus transvaalensis* (Robinson, 1954); *Homo africanus* (Robinson, 1972; Olson, 1978) 'Ape-man'; 'Man-ape'; 'Near-man'.
Site	Makapansgat Limeworks Deposit, Makapansgat Farm, 13 miles north-east of Potgieterus, Central Transvaal, Republic of South Africa.
Found by	Professor R. A. Dart, the staff and students of the Department of Anatomy, University of the Witwatersrand, Johannesburg, and

other helpers who included J. Kitching, S. Kitching, B. Kitching, A. R. Hughes, E. L. Boné, R. S. Cunliff and B. Maguire. The majority of finds were made between September 1947 and 1962.

Geology The limeworks site is situated on the south side of the Makapan valley and consists of a large infilled cavern which has formed in the Transvaal dolomitic limestone of the region. The major part of the cave roof has eroded away and exposed the consolidated cave breccia on the surface. The bedrock of the cave is covered by a considerable layer of pure dripstone indicating that the cave did not communicate with the surface at the time of its accumulation. When the cave opened to the surface, breccia was formed. The geology of the site has been studied in detail (King, 1951; Brain, 1958). A reappraisal of the lithostratigraphy of the site has resulted in more detailed information of the geology and a new stratigraphic terminology for the Makapansgat Formation (Partridge, 1979). This identifies five Members, two of which (Members 4 and 5) are divided into Beds A and B, and A–E respectively, from below upwards. Most of the remains of *Australopithecus africanus* derive from Bed 3 (Pink Breccia) whilst one skull (MLD 37/38) derives from Bed B in Member 4. Correlations of the new terminology with previous nomenclature have also been given.

Associated finds Numerous bones, teeth and horns have been claimed as 'shaped' and 'utilized' from the vast accumulation of fossil material from these deposits (Dart, 1957a). Opinion is divided as to whether their appearance is artefactual or natural. A review of the problem of the osteodontokeratic (bone, tooth and horn) culture of the australopithecines (Wolberg, 1970) has given some support to Dart's contentions as to the nature of the bone accumulations and the uses to which they may have been put. The debate continued later (Dart, 1971; Wolberg, 1971) and has been expanded to take in the topic of scavenging as an early hominid activity (Read, Martin and Read, 1975). The accumulation and concentration of bones in the grey breccia has been reconsidered recently and a greater role for carnivores as accumulators is accepted than was hitherto believed (Maguire *et al.*, 1980; Brain, 1981).

The fossil mammalian fauna recovered from this site includes a bat (*Rhinolophus cf. capensis*), primates (*Simopithecus darti, Parapapio jonesi, P. broomi, P. whitei, Cercopithecoides williamsi*), numerous rodents, some carnivores (*Cynictis penicillata brachyodon, Crocuta cf. brevirostris, Hyaena makapani, Therailurus barlowi, Megantereon sp. nov.*), an equid (*Equus helmei*), other perissodactyla (*cf. Ceratotherium simum, cf. Diceros bicornis*) and numerous artiodactyls including antelopes, gazelles, pigs and giraffes (Cooke, 1964).

Work on faunal similarities between the Omo sites (Usno and Shungura) and the Hadar site (*q.v.*) also suggests that similarities in time between Makapansgat and Hadar may be closer than previously suspected (Boaz *et al.*, 1982).

New findings on the bovids indicate that the Makapansgat bovid fauna is the same as that from the Laetoli Beds, Tanzania and the Sidi Hakoma Beds at Hadar (*q.v.*) indicating contemporaneity at about 3 m.y. B.P. (Vrba, 1982, 1985).

Dating   As with the other australopithecine sites in the Transvaal, accurate dating has proved difficult because of the nature of the deposits; the problem has been discussed by several authors (Howell, 1955; Ewer, 1957; Oakley, 1954, 1957; Brain, 1958). Later the Makapansgat site was attributed to the First Interglacial (Günz-Mindel or Antepenultimate Interglacial) on the grounds of faunal correlation (Kurtén, 1962). A reappraisal of the fauna (Cooke, 1970), in the light of East African evidence, has led to the suggestion that this site should be dated to a period 2·5–3·00 million years B.P. Partridge (1973), using a geomorphological method, dates the opening of the Makapansgat cave to an even earlier date, approximately 3·67 million years B.P. Butzer (1974) following a reappraisal of the Taung site concludes that Makapansgat clearly antedates the Taung remains, while not accepting the validity of Partridge's geomorphological dating method.

The Makapansgat site still remains refractory to radiometric and fission track dating methods but palaeomagnetic determinations have been carried out successfully (Brock *et al.*, 1977; McFadden *et al.*, 1979). The pattern of normal and reversed polarities obtained from the site indicates that Member 2, underlying Member 3, is within that part of the Gauss Normal Epoch that predates the Mammoth event and has age limits of 3·06–3·32 m.y. B.P. Member 3, from which most of the hominid specimens have come, appears to have an age greater than 2·90 m.y. B.P. and possibly greater than 3·06 m.y. B.P. but less than 3·32 m.y. B.P. These new dates confirm the faunal findings noted above.

Morphology   The hominid remains recovered from the excavation include a cranium, parts of other crania, a cranio-facial fragment, parts of a number of mandibles, teeth, parts of maxillae, two left ilia, a right ischium and fragments of humerus, radius, clavicle and femur.

Skull

The best cranium (MLD 37 and MLD 38) (Dart, 1962a) was found split in half in a divided block of Upper Phase I pink breccia (Member 4, Bed B). Subsequent search was rewarded by the recovery of the other half. When the specimens were developed from the matrix

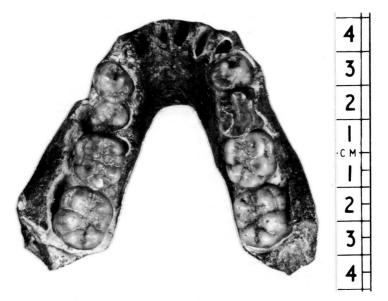

Fig. 107. A juvenile mandible (MLD 2) from Makapansgat. *Courtesy of Professor P. V. Tobias, photographed by A. R. Hughes.*

and restored they were found to constitute the major part of the brain-case, the base of the skull and part of the palate. The remainder of the facial skeleton and the frontal region is missing. The cranium has a remarkable resemblance to the best Sterkfontein skull (Sts 5) (*q.v.*), only differing in minor respects such as lack of an occipital torus, reduction of the postglenoid process and in details of the cranial dimensions. The absence of an occipital torus has led to the suggestion that this specimen is probably female. The craniofacial fragment discloses that the degree of prognathism was not large.

Mandibles

A range of specimens is available from this site displaying most of the mandibular morphology from infancy to senility. One of the best specimens is half an adult mandible (MLD 40) which contains the canine, premolar and molar teeth. The body of the mandible is stout and on these grounds it is believed to be male. The symphysial region is damaged but the mental foramen is single. The ramus is short by comparison with the large australopithecine from Swartkrans, but comparable with those known from Sterkfontein.

Teeth

The principal morphological features of the teeth fall within the range of variation of those previously described from Sterkfontein.

Postcranial Bones

The Ischium (MLD 8) resembles the one that forms part of the Sterkfontein innominate, but differs markedly from the ischia of recent apes and from that of the Swartkrans australopithecine. It is a small bone with a moderate ischial tuberosity separated from the remains of the acetabular margin by a groove. This groove is narrower than that shown on the Sterkfontein pelvis and in this respect more nearly resembles the condition found in modern man.

The Ilia are adolescent, small and believed to be of opposite sex, the first specimen male (MLD 7) and the second female (MLD 25). The blade of the ilium is broad and twisted into an S-shape when viewed from above. The anterior superior spine is prominent and reaches well forward, recalling the shape of the Swartkrans pelvis. The iliac pillar, which runs upwards from the acetabulum to the tuberosity of the iliac crest, is absent, but some thickening of the cortical bone in this region was disclosed when one specimen was accidentally broken.

Although these pelvic fragments differ in a number of respects from their modern human counterparts they differ even more widely from the pelvic bones of modern apes. It is difficult to escape the conclusion that these australopithecines were habitually erect and bipedal in their form of locomotion.

The shaft of the *Humerus* is robust and well marked by the attachment of muscles. It is not unlike that of modern man (Boné, 1955). The remaining postcranial bones are fragmentary.

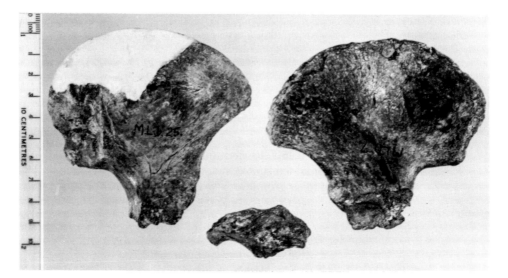

Fig. 108. Two juvenile ilia (MLD7 and MLD25) and an ischial fragment from Makapansgat. *Courtesy of Professor P. V. Tobias, photographed by A. R. Hughes.*

Dimensions   *Skull*

Dart (1962a)   Holloway (1970)
Max. Cranial Breadth 106   Cranial Capacity 435 cc

Mandible (MLD 40)

Dart (1962b)
Max. Length 123·5 (damaged)
Body Height (M1) 36·0
Body Thickness (M1) 23·5
Max. Ramus Width 45·5
Max. Ramus Height (coronoid) 62·5

Teeth
Robinson (1956), Dart (1962b)

		I¹	I²	C	PM¹	PM²	M¹	M²	M³
		Upper Permanent Teeth (Crown Dimensions)							
Average	l	—	—	—	8·8	9·4	12·5	13·9	—
figures	b	—	—	—	12·0	12·6	12·8	15·7	—

MLD 40		*Lower Permanent Teeth (Crown Dimensions)*							
Left	l	—	—	8·3*	10·0	10·0	12·8	15·0	15·0
side	b	—	—	9·5*	11·0	14·0	12·3	14·3	14·0

* Damaged

Affinities   The affinities of the Makapansgat remains will be discussed with the rest of the australopithecine material.

Originals   The Department of Anatomy, University of the Witwatersrand Medical School, York Road, Parktown, Johannesburg 2193, Republic of South Africa.

Casts   The Department of Anatomy, University of the Witwatersrand Medical School, York Road, Parktown, Johannesburg 2193, Republic of South Africa.

References
Dart, R. A. (1948a) The Makapansgat proto-human *Australopithecus prometheus*. Am. J. phys. Anthrop. 6, 259–284.
Dart, R. A. (1948b) The adolescent mandible of *Australopithecus prometheus*. Ibid., 6, 391–412.
Dart, R. A. (1949a) The cranio-facial fragment of *Australopithecus prometheus*. Ibid., 7, 187–214.
Dart, R. A. (1949b) Innominate fragments of *Australopithecus prometheus*. Ibid., 7, 301–333.

Dart, R. A. (1949c) A second adult palate of *Australopithecus prometheus.* *Ibid.,* 7, 335–338.

Mayr, E. (1950) Taxonomic categories in fossil hominids. *Cold Spring Harb. Symp. quant. Biol.* 15, 109–118.

King, L. C. (1951) The geology of Makapan and other caves. *Trans. R. Soc. S. Afr.* 33, 121–151.

Dart, R. A. (1954) The second or adult female mandible of *Australopithecus prometheus. Am. J. phys. Anthrop.* 12, 313–343.

Oakley, K. P. (1954) Dating the australopithecines of Africa. *Ibid.,* 12, 9–23.

Robinson, J. T. (1954) The genera and species of the *Australopithecinae. Ibid.,* 12, 181–200.

Boné, E. L., and Dart, R. A. (1955) A catalogue of australopithecine fossils found at the Limeworks, Makapansgat. *Ibid.,* 13, 621–624.

Dart, R. A. (1955) *Australopithecus prometheus* and *Telanthropus capensis. Ibid.,* 13, 67–96.

Howell, F. C. (1955) The age of the australopithecines of Southern Africa. *Ibid.,* 13, 635–662.

Robinson, J. T. (1956) The dentition of the Australopithecinae. *Transv. Mus. Mem.* 9, 1–179.

Brain, C. K. (1957) New evidence for the correlation of the Transvaal ape-man bearing cave deposits. *Proc. Pan-African Cong. Prehist.,* 3. *Livingstone,* 1955, 143–148. Ed. J. D. Clark. London: Chatto and Windus.

Dart, R. A. (1957a) The osteodontokeratic culture of *Australopithecus prometheus. Transv. Mus. Mem.* 10, 1–105.

Dart, R. A. (1957b) The second adolescent (female) ilium of *Australopithecus prometheus. J. palaeont. Soc. India* 2, 73–82.

Ewer, R. F. (1957) Faunal evidence on the dating of the Australopithecinae. *Proc. pan-Afr. Cong. Prehist.,* 3. *Livingstone,* 1955, 135–142. Ed. J. D. Clark. London: Chatto and Windus.

Oakley, K. P. (1957) Dating the australopithecines. *Ibid.,* 155–157.

Brain, C. K. (1958) The Transvaal ape-man bearing cave deposits. *Transv. Mus. Mem.* 11, 1–125.

Dart, R. A. (1958) A further adolescent australopithecine ilium from Makapansgat. *Am. J. phys. Anthrop.* 16, 473–480.

Dart, R. A. (1959) The first australopithecine cranium from the pink breccia at Makapansgat. *Ibid.,* 17, 77–82.

Dart, R. A. (1962a) The Makapansgat pink breccia australopithecine skull. *Ibid.,* 20, 119–126.

Dart, R. A. (1962b) A cleft adult mandible and nine other lower jaw fragments from Makapansgat. *Ibid.,* 20, 267–286.

Kurtén, B., (1962) The relative ages of the australopithecines of Transvaal and the pithecanthropines of Java. In *Evolution und Hominisation,* 74–80. Ed. G. Kurth. Stuttgart: Gustav Fischer Verlag.

Cooke, H. B. S. (1964) Pleistocene mammal faunas of Africa, with particular reference to South Africa. In *African Ecology and Human Evolution,* 65–116. Eds. F. C. Howell and F. Bourlière. London: Methuen and Co. Ltd.

Cooke, H. B. S. (1970) Notes from Members: Dalhousie University, Halifax, Canada. *News Bull. Soc. vertebr. Paleont.* 90, 2.

Holloway, R. L. (1970) New endocranial values for the australopithecines. *Nature* 227, 199–200.

Wolberg, D. L. (1970) The hypothesized osteodontokeratic culture of the Australopithecinae: a look at the evidence and the opinions. *Curr. Anthrop.* 11, 23–30.

Dart, R. A. (1971) On the osteodontokeratic culture of the Australopithecinae. *Curr. Anthrop. 12*, 233–235.

Wolberg, D. L. (1971) Curr. Anthrop. Comment. Reply. *Curr. Anthrop. 12*, 235–236.

Robinson, J. T. (1972) *Early Hominid Posture and Locomotion.* Chicago: Chicago University Press.

Partridge, T. C. (1973) Geomorphological dating of cave openings at Makapansgat, Sterkfontein, Swartkrans and Taung. *Nature 246*, 75–79.

Butzer, K. W. (1974) Curr. Anthrop. Comment. Reply. *Curr. Anthrop. 15*, 413–416.

Brock, A., McFadden, P. L. and Partridge, T. C. (1977) Preliminary palaeomagnetic results from Makapansgat and Swartkrans. *Nature 266*, 249–250.

Olson, T. R. (1978) Hominid phylogenetics and the existence of *Homo* in Member I of the Swartkrans Formation, South Africa. *J. hum. Evol. 7*, 159–178.

McFadden, P. L., Brock, A. and Partridge, T. C. (1979) Palaeomagnetism and the age of the Makapansgat hominid site. *Earth Planet. Sci. Let. 44*, 373–382.

Partridge, T. C. (1979) Reappraisal of lithostratigraphy of Makapansgat Limeworks hominid site. *Nature 279*, 484–488.

Maguire, J. M. Pemberton, D. and Collett, M. H. (1980) The Makapansgat Limeworks Grey Breccia: Hominids, hyaenas, hystricids or hillwash? *Palaeont. Afr. 23*, 75–98.

Brain, C. K. (1981) *The Hunters or the Hunted?* Chicago: University of Chicago Press.

Boaz, N. T., Howell, F. C. and McCrossin, M. L. (1982) Faunal age of the Usno, Shungura B and Hadar Formations, Ethiopia. *Nature 300*, 633–635.

Vrba, E. S. (1982) Biostratigraphy and chronology, based particularly on Bovidae, of southern hominid-associated assemblages: Makapansgat, Sterkfontein, Taung, Kromdraai, Swartkrans; also Elandsfontein (Saldanha), Broken Hill (now Kabwe) and Cave of Hearths. *Cong. Int. Paléont. hum.* 1. Prétirage, 707–752.

Vrba, E. S. (1985) Early hominids in Southern Africa: Updated observations on chronological and evolutionary background. In *Hominid Evolution: Past, Present, and Future.* Ed. P. V. Tobias. New York: Alan R. Liss.

The Florisbad Skull

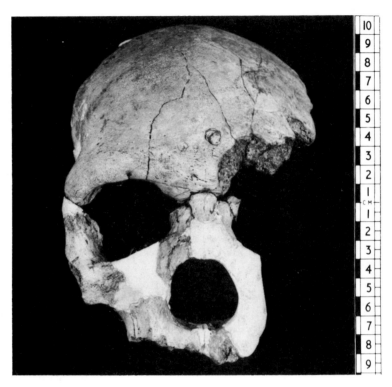

Fig. 109. The Florisbad craniofacial fragment (frontal view) reconstructed and photographed by R. J. Clarke.

Synonyms and other names	*Homo (Africanthropus) helmei* (Dreyer, 1935); *Homo florisbadensis (helmei)* (Drennan, 1935); *Homo sapiens* (Rightmire, 1978).
Found by	T. F. Dreyer, 1932.
Site	Florisbad, 30 miles north northwest of Bloemfontein, Orange Free State, Republic of South Africa.
Geology	The deposits are on the southern slope of the Hagenstad salt-pan which is near a medicinal watering place. The area is marked by numerous springs, many of which have become choked with accumulated debris; when this occurs a new spring eye opens near by. The debris consists of sand containing stone artefacts, broken bones and teeth. The heavier sand is ilmenite with garnets and

diopside, whilst above this layer there is a cap of pure white quartz sand (Dreyer, 1935).

Investigation of the site has disclosed a profile of eleven strata including a basal layer and four other layers of 'peat'. These 'peat' layers are in fact dark coloured sand and clay containing little organic matter.

The skull was found at the side of the eye of a spring about 18 feet from the surface.

Associated finds   Dreyer reported the occurrence of stone tools of African Middle Stone Age culture. The available evidence suggests that tools of this culture are present throughout the section below 'Peat III'; later stone implements occur above this level (Partridge, 1982).

The fossil mammalian fauna that was found includes several living rodents and carnivores as well as extinct species such as giant buffalo (*Connochaetes antiquus, Alcelaphus helmei*) and two equids (*Equus helmei, Equus burchelli*) (Cooke, 1964). It is essentially an Upper Pleistocene fauna with no Middle Pleistocene elements (Ewer, 1957; Klein, 1975).

Dating   The stratigraphy of this specimen is confusing from the point of view of establishing its age. However, the implements suggest that the deposits belong to the Upper Pleistocene or even the Holocene. A pollen investigation (van Zinderen Bakker, 1957) suggests that the oldest parts of the profile were probably formed at the beginning of the Upper Pleistocene during a dry phase or interpluvial. The radiocarbon dates of 41,000 years B.P. given for the 'Dark Layer I' by Libby (1954) and of 37,000 years B.P. (quoted by van Zinderen Bakker, 1957) have been considered too high because the Pleistocene plant material in that layer is probably contaminated by 'dead carbon' carried up by the spring from underlying Palaeozoic coal measures (Oakley, 1957).

Carbon 14 dating of this skull has been given as between 38–39,000 years B.P. (Protsch, 1975) whilst Vogel (1970) quotes results that are beyond Carbon 14 range.

Morphology   The skull fragment consists of part of the face and vault including the right orbital margin and part of the maxilla; the base of the skull and the mandible are missing.

The cranium is large but rather flattened with no parietal, and feeble frontal, bosses. The superciliary ridges are as those found in modern man, there being no evidence of a supraorbital torus. The face is moderately prognathic. The palate is incomplete and the only tooth present is the right upper third molar which is very worn. A new reconstruction has been made recently (Clarke, 1985) (see figure. 109).

Dimensions   Max. Length approx. 200   Max. Breadth approx. 150

Affinities   In the original description of this skull Dreyer (1935) named the specimen *Homo (Africanthropus) helmei* thus asserting that this form was sub-generically distinct from other members of the genus *Homo*. However, in the same publication Kappers, who had studied the endocranial cast, emphasized its likeness to *Homo sapiens fossilis*. Drennan (1935, 1937) urged the Neandertal characters of this skull and endocast on metrical grounds, and proposed the name *Homo florisbadensis (helmei)* as being more appropriate. This view was opposed by Galloway (1937, 1938) who emphasized that the non-metrical features of the Florisbad skull linked it with *Homo sapiens*, and moreover with the Australoid variety of this species. Several authors have written in favour of its affinity with the Saldanha skull and the Kabwe skull (q.v.) (Singer, 1956, 1958; Tobias, 1968; Rightmire, 1978). Most recently Clarke (1985) has related it to two East African crania dated to the beginning of the Upper Pleistocene, Ngaloba of Tanzania and Omo II of Ethiopia (q.v.).

Original   National Museum, Bloemfontein, Orange Free State, Republic of South Africa.

Casts   The University Museum, University of Pennsylvania, Philadelphia 4, Pennsylvania, U.S.A.

References   Dreyer, T.F. (1935) A human skull from Florisbad. *Proc. Acad. Sci. Amst.* *38*, 119–128.
Drennan, M.R. (1935) The Florisbad skull. *S. Afr. J. Sci. 32*, 601–602.
Dreyer, T.F. (1936) The endocranial cast of the Florisbad skull—a correction. *Soöl. Navors. nas. Mus. Bloemfontein 1*, 21–23.
Drennan, M.R. (1937) The Florisbad skull and brain cast. *Trans. R. Soc. S. Afr. 25*, 103–114.
Galloway, A. (1937) Man in Africa in the light of recent discoveries. *S. Afr. J. Sci. 34*, 89–120.
Galloway, A. (1938) The nature and status of the Florisbad skull as revealed by its non-metrical features. *Am. J. phys. Anthrop. 23*, 1–16.
Libby, W.F. (1954) Chicago radiocarbon dates, V. *Science 120*, 733–742.
Singer, R. (1956) Man and mammals in South Africa (with special reference to Saldanha Man). *J. Palaeont. Soc. India, Lucknow 1*, 122–130.
Bakker, E.M. Van Zinderen (1957) A pollen analytical investigation of the Florisbad deposits (South Africa). *Proc. pan-Afr. Cong. Prehist., 3, Livingstone, 1955*, 56–57. Ed. J.D. Clark. London: Chatto and Windus.
Ewer, R.F. (1957) The fossil pigs of Florisbad. *Res. Nat. Mus. Bloem. 1*, 239–257.
Oakley, K.P. (1957) The dating of the Broken Hill, Florisbad and Saldanha skulls. *Ibid.*, 76–79.
Boule, M., and Vallois, H.V. (1957) *Fossil man*, 4th Ed., 462. London: Thames and Hudson.
Singer, R. (1958) The Rhodesian, Florisbad and Saldanha skulls. In *Hundert*

Jahre Neanderthaler, 52–62. Ed. G. H. R. von Koenigswald. Utrecht: Kemink en Zoon.

Cooke, H. B. S. (1964) Pleistocene mammal faunas of Africa, with particular reference to Southern Africa. In *African Ecology and Human Evolution*, 65–116. Eds. F. C. Howell and F. Bourlière. London: Methuen and Co. Ltd.

Tobias, P. V. (1968) Middle and early Upper Pleistocene members of the genus *Homo* in Africa. In *Evolution and Hominization* 2nd ed., 176–194. Ed. G. Kurth. Stuttgart: Gustav Fischer Verlag.

Vogel, J. C. (1970) Groningen radiocarbon dates IX. *Radiocarbon 12*, 444–471.

Protsch, R. (1973) The dating of Upper Pleistocene subsaharan fossil hominids and their place in human evolution: the morphological and archaeological implications. *Ph.D. thesis, University of California, L.A.*

Klein, R. G. (1975) Middle Stone Age man-animal relationships in Southern Africa: evidence from Die Kelders and Klasies River Mouth. *Science 190*, 265–267.

Protsch, R. (1975) The absolute dating of Upper Pleistocene sub-Saharan fossil hominids and their place in human evolution. *J. hum. Evol. 4*, 297–322.

Rightmire, G. P. (1978) Florisbad and human population succession in Southern Africa. *Am. J. phys. Anthrop. 48*, 475–486.

Partridge, T. C. (1982) The chronological positions of the fossil hominids of Southern Africa. *Cong. Int. Paléont. hum. 1 Nice*. Prétirage, 617–675.

Rightmire, G. P. (1984) *Homo sapiens* in Sub-Saharan Africa. In *The Origins of Modern Humans*, 295–325. Eds. F. H. Smith and F. Spencer. New York: Alan R. Liss.

Clarke, R. J. (1985) A new reconstruction of the Florisbad cranium, with notes on the site. In *Ancestors*, 301–305. Ed. E. Delson. New York: Alan R. Liss.

The Border Cave Remains

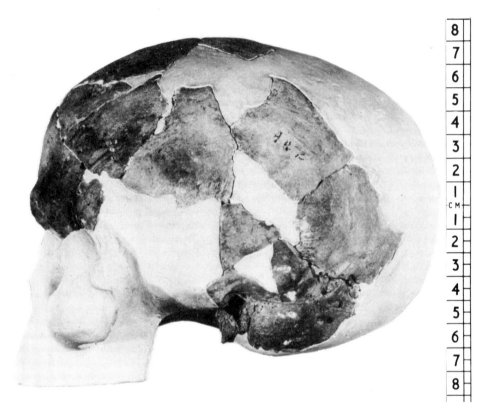

Fig. 110. The Border Cave 1 cranial reconstruction (left lateral view). *Courtesy of Professor P. V. Tobias, photographed by A. R. Hughes.*

Synonyms and other names	*Homo sapiens afer* (Wells, 1969); *Homo sapiens sapiens* (Beaumont and Boshier, 1972); Border Cave 1–5; Ingwavuma 1–5.
Site	Border Cave, as its name implies, is found almost on the international boundary between northern KwaZulu and Swaziland high on the western scarp flank of the Lebombo Mountains; it is about 2 km north of the Ngwavuma river gorge.
Found by	1940 W. E. Horton (frontal, tibial and femoral fragments).
	1941 T. R. Jones (parietal fragment).
	1941 and 1942 H. B. S. Cooke, B. D. Malan and L. H. Wells (further fragments including parietal, temporal and occipital parts as well as

a mandible. An infant skeleton was also recovered from a shallow grave). The cranial fragments have been collectively designated Border Cave 1, the adult mandible Border Cave 2 and the infant skeleton Border Cave 3.

1970/71 P. Beaumont (a contracted Iron-Age burial designated Border Cave 4).

10 April 1974 C. Powell and P. Beaumont (mandible designated Border Cave 5).

Geology   The cave extends for about 50 m in width and 30 m in depth and 2–7 m in height at an elevation of about 600 m just below the escarpment rim. It is accessible from above by a narrow ledge or from below up a long steep talus slope—an ideal sheltered habitation that would have been easy to defend. The bedrock of the Lebombo Mountains consists of rhyolites under- and overlain by basalts that relate to the uppermost Stormberg series of the Karroo system.

The cave deposits have been studied in detail and fifteen sedimentary units (with several sub-units) have been described (Butzer, Beaumont and Vogel, 1978). The provenance and context of the hominids seems to be as follows:

Border Cave 1 and 2

From Horton's 'guano pit'; matrix adherent equivalent to Level 10 (Butzer *et al.*, 1978). Middle Stone Age deposits.

Border Cave 3

Excavated by Cooke *et al.* (1945) equivalent to Levels 9–10 (Butzer *et al.*, 1978). Middle Stone Age deposits.

Border Cave 4
Iron Age burial.

Border Cave 5
Removed directly from Level 8 (Butzer *et al.*, 1978).

Associated finds   Stone tools associated with the remains were made from local trachytic lavas and quartzite, also from the gravels of the Ngwavuma river and from chalcedony and quartz. All the tools are of Levallois type and have been ascribed to the Middle Stone Age of Africa. Superimposed industries range from basal 'Pietersburg' with retouched points, through 'Howieson's Poort' typified by backed blades, to terminal Middle Stone Age assemblages that include ground warthog tusk 'daggers' (Cooke *et al.*, 1945; Beaumont *et al.*, 1978).

The mammalian faunal remains recovered from the cave deposits nearly all relate to the modern lowveld fauna including hippopotamus, bushpig, warthog, Cape buffalo, roan or sable antelope, kudu, waterbuck, wildebeest, impala, reedbuck, duiker and steenbok, common zebra, hyrax and baboon. Extinct forms comprise *Equus capensis* and *Antidorcas bondi* (Klein, 1977). The mammalian microfauna has also been published (Avery, 1982).

Comparative studies on the sedimentological sequences of southern Africa, including Border Cave, suggest that repeated and significant changes occurred to the environment during the late Quaternary (Butzer, 1984).

Dating   The dating of Border Cave initially depended upon the correlation of Middle Stone Age sites in that continent but later Carbon 14 studies indicated an age of not less than 46,300 yr B.P. for that complex at Border Cave (Vogel and Beaumont, 1972a; Beaumont and Vogel, 1972b). Further studies in the same year and the next year (Beaumont, 1972, 1973) revealed the age of the Middle Stone Age layers from Border Cave to be greater than 48,700 yr B.P. This date was confirmed as a minimum using the amino-acid racemization technique (Protsch, 1975). Later, new data allowed a revised chronology of modern man in sub-Saharan Africa prior to 49,000 yr B.P. and this placed the age of the Border Cave Middle Stone Age deposits at a minimum of 49,000 yr B.P. and a maximum of 130,000 yr B.P. (Beaumont *et al.*, 1978). This work was confirmed by Butzer *et al.* (1978) who dated Border Cave 1, 2, and 3 at 115,000 yr B.P. and Border Cave 5 at 90,000 yr B.P. In a résumé given by Beaumont (1980) Border Cave Hominids 1, 2 and 3 are given as of Middle Stone Age Phases 1 and 2 and are dated to between 90–110,000 yr B.P. The most recent reappraisals are based upon the climatic and cultural correlations of evidence derived from other sites in South Africa, inferred oxygen isotope stages and the generalized palaeotemperature curve.

Morphology   The remains were first described by Cooke *et al.* (1945) and later illustrated by Wells (1950).

Border Cave 1

This specimen is a fragmentary adult cranium consisting of frontal, parietal, temporal and occipital parts. The face is represented solely by a partial right zygomatic arch. The sutures of the vault are open and the general features of the vault have led to its allocation to a male individual.

The forehead is steep and there is no supraorbital torus; the frontal region is broad with moderate bossing, the parietal eminences are

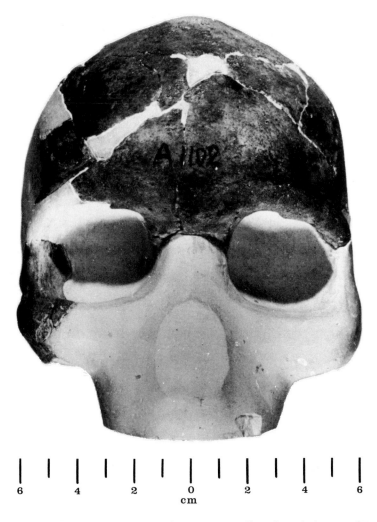

Fig. 111. The Border Cave 1 cranial reconstruction (frontal view). *Courtesy of Professor P. V. Tobias, photographed by A. R. Hughes.*

marked and the occipital bone is rounded in profile. The features of the cranium do not appear to depart from those known for anatomically modern *Homo sapiens*.

Border Cave 2

This specimen includes most of the body of an isolated adult mandible without teeth. It is of an adult and of moderate height and robusticity. It has a single mental foramen. It is too small to articulate with Border Cave 1 and may have belonged to a female.

Border Cave 3

The partial skeleton of an infant whose age at death was between four and six months on the grounds of limb length and dental development (de Villiers, 1973).

Border Cave 4

An Iron Age skeleton *c.* 38–45 years of age (Beaumont, 1980).

Border Cave 5

A second isolated adult mandible was recovered in 1974 that comprises the major part of the body and some worn teeth (de Villiers, 1976).

Dimensions   de Villiers (1973)

Border Cave 1

Vault thickness 5–9 mm
Max. length (194)
Auricular height (115)
Max. Breadth (141)
Cranial Index (72·6)
Cranial Capacity 1507 cc (formula estimate)
(   ) Estimated

Border Cave 2

Symphysial height 30
Symphysial thickness 14·5
Symphysial Index 48·3

Affinities   The importance of the Border Cave site rests upon general agreement that the remains are those of anatomically modern members of the species *Homo sapiens* (de Villiers, 1973, 1976; Rightmire, 1979). (The use of subspecific designations for modern human geographic races is seldom, if ever, used today.) Secondly, its rests upon the supposed antiquity of the site and the recovery of the remains (Border Cave 1, 2 and 3) from identifiable layers within the deposit (Border Cave 5 was recovered *in situ*).

The dating evidence has improved in recent years with new investigations but doubts about the provenance will always remain. The early dating of the site led Beaumont and Boshier (1972) to regard this site as evidence of southern Africa being the cradle of anatomically modern man, a view supported by the evidence of de Villiers (1973, 1976) and Beaumont *et al.* (1978). In an important paper Rightmire (1979) contended that Border Cave need not mark the only or necessarily the earliest appearance of fully modern man in the African Upper Pleistocene. He went on to show that the Border Cave remains can be linked with recent African local populations on morphometric grounds. This paper drew comments and criticisms of the statistical conclusions (Campbell, 1980) which were answered (Rightmire, 1981). Bräuer (1982, 1984) has set out an 'Afro-European *sapiens* hypothesis' which concerns the evolution from archaic to anatomically modern *Homo sapiens* in eastern and southern Africa, a process in which the evidence from Border Cave has a part to play subject to the correctness of the dating and the provenance of the material.

Rightmire (1984a,b) has restated his view that the Border Cave findings suggest strongly that some Middle Stone Age populations of southern Africa were anatomically modern at an early date if the stratigraphic provenance can be shown to be correct. If that is so, people very much like the San or the negroes (de Villiers and Fatti, 1982) have been living in southern Africa for a very long time. Even if this is the case, however, it is too soon to base sweeping generalizations concerning the origins of modern humans on this evidence. On the other hand it is my view that the evidence of Border Cave cannot simply be discounted by those who would argue for a late and/or Eurocentric origin for modern man.

Originals   Department of Anatomy, University of the Witwatersrand Medical School, York Road, Parktown, Johannesburg 2193, Republic of South Africa.

Casts   Department of Anatomy, University of the Witwatersrand Medical School, York Road, Parktown, Johannesburg 2193, Republic of South Africa.

References   Cooke, H. B. S., Malan, B. D. and Wells, L. H. (1945) Fossil Man in the Lebombo Mountains, South Africa: The 'Border Cave', Ingwavuma District, Zululand. *Man 45*, 6–13.

Wells, L. H. (1950) The Border Cave skull, Ingwavuma District, Zululand. *Am. J. phys. Anthrop. 8*, 241–243.

Wells, L. H. (1969) *Homo sapiens afer* Linn.: Content and earliest representatives. *S. Afr. archaeol. Bull. 24*, 172–173.

Beaumont, P. B. and Boshier, A. K. (1972) Some comments on recent findings at Border Cave, Northern Natal. *S. Afr. J. Sci. 68*, 22–24.

Beaumont, P. B. (1973) Border Cave—A progress report. *S. Afr. J. Sci. 69*, 41–46.

Beaumont, P. B. and Vogel, J. C. (1972) On a new radiocarbon chronology for Africa south of the Equator. *Afr. Stud. 31*, 65–89 and 155–182.

Vogel, J. C. and Beaumont, P. B. (1972) Revised radiocarbon chronology for the Stone Age in South Africa. *Nature 237*, 50–51.

de Villiers, H. (1973) Human skeletal remains from Border Cave, Ingwavuma District, KwaZulu, South Africa. *Ann. Transv. Mus. 28*, 229–256.

Protsch, R. (1975) The absolute dating of Upper Pleistocene Sub-Saharan fossil hominids and their place in human evolution. *J. hum. Evol. 4*, 297–322.

de Villiers, H. (1976) A second adult human mandible from Border Cave, Ingwavuma District, KwaZulu, South Africa. *S. Afr. J. Sci. 72*, 212–215.

Klein, R. G. (1977) The mammalian fauna from the Middle and Later Stone Age (Upper Pleistocene) levels of Border Cave, Natal Province, South Africa. *S. Afr. Archaeol. Bull. 32*, 14–27.

Beaumont, P. B., de Villiers, H. and Vogel, J. C. (1978) Modern man in sub-Saharan Africa prior to 49,000 years B.P.: A review and evaluation with particular reference to Border Cave. *S. Afr. J. Sci. 74*, 409–419.

Butzer, K. W., Beaumont, P. B. and Vogel, J. C. (1978) Lithostratigraphy of Border Cave, KwaZulu, South Africa: a Middle Stone Age sequence beginning c. 195,000 B.P. *J. Archaeol. Sci. 5*, 317–341.

Rightmire, G. P. (1979) Implications of Border Cave skeletal remains for later Pleistocene human evolution. *Curr. Anthrop. 20*, 23–35.

Beaumont, P. B. (1980) On the age of Border Cave hominids 1–5. *Palaeont. Afr. 23*, 21–33.

Campbell, N. A. (1980) On the study of the Border Cave remains: Statistical comments. *Curr. Anthrop. 21*, 532–535.

Rightmire, G. P. (1981) More on the study of the Border Cave remains. *Curr. Anthrop. 22*, 199–200.

Avery, D. M. (1982) The micromammalian fauna from Border Cave, KwaZulu, South Africa. *J. Archaeol. Sci. 9*, 187–204.

de Villiers, H. and Fatti, L. P. (1982) The antiquity of the negro. *S. Afr. J. Sci. 78*, 212–215.

Bräuer, G. (1984) A craniological approach to the origin of anatomically modern *Homo sapiens* in Africa and implications for the appearance of modern Europeans. In *The Origins of Modern Humans*, 327–410. Eds. F. H. Smith and F. Spencer. New York: Alan R. Liss.

Butzer, K. W. (1984) Late Quaternary environments in South Africa. In *Late Cainozoic palaeoclimates of the Southern Hemisphere*, 235–264. Ed. J. C. Vogel. Rotterdam: A. A. Balkema.

Rightmire, G. P. (1984a) *Homo sapiens* in Sub-Saharan Africa. In *The Origins of Modern Humans*, 295–325. Eds. F. H. Smith and F. Spencer. New York: Alan R. Liss.

Rightmire, G. P. (1984b) The fossil evidence for hominid evolution in southern Africa. In *Southern African Prehistory and Paleoenvironments*, 147–168. Rotterdam: A. A. Balkema.

The Far East

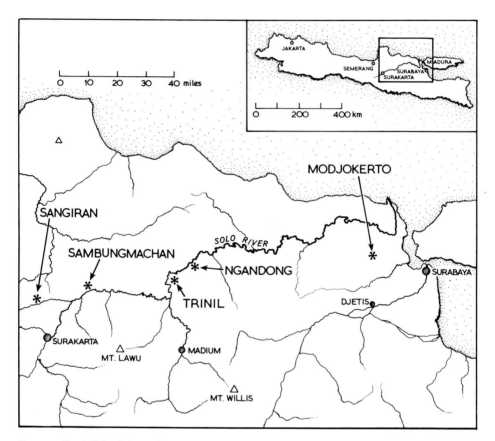

Fig. 112. Hominid fossil sites in Java.

The Trinil Remains

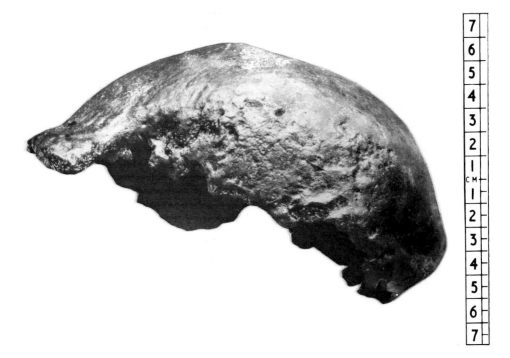

Fig. 113. The Trinil calotte (Pithecanthropus I) (left lateral view). *Courtesy of the late Professor J. S. Weiner and Dr D. A. Hooijer.*

Synonyms and other names	*Anthropopithecus erectus* (Dubois, 1892); *Pithecanthropus erectus* (Dubois, 1894); Pithecanthropus I (von Koenigswald and Weidenreich, 1939); *Homo erectus javensis* (Weidenreich, 1940); *Homo erectus* (Mayr, 1950); *Homo erectus erectus* (Dobzhansky, 1944; Campbell, 1964); Trinil 1–9 (Oakley, Campbell and Molleson, 1975); Java man.
Site	Trinil, approximately 20 miles northwest of Madium, six miles west of Ngawi, Central Java, Indonesia.
Found by	Eugene Dubois, 1891–1898; G. Kriele, 1900.
Geology	Trinil lies at the foot of a volcano, Lawu, whose lavas and cinders have spilled over a wide area. Elevated Pleistocene deposits include the Kabuh beds which overlie the Pucangan beds. The Trinil hominid remains were believed to have been found in the Kabuh beds

which consist of fresh-water sandstones and conglomerates containing volcanic material, within a few yards of the waters of the river Solo. The femur was uncovered 15 metres upstream.

For many years there have been doubts about the methods used by Dubois in his collection of fossils (purchase from villagers, poor stratigraphic control); these criticisms have recently been contested (de Vos and Sondaar, 1982). New work on the sedimentary geology, stratigraphy, prehistory and faunal remains of the deposits from Trinil, however, asserts that the fossil remains found in the Solo meander near Trinil come from two stratigraphic units and that the so-called 'Trinil fauna' is not a distinct entity. It is claimed that Dubois and the later Selenka excavation dug through both overlying High Terrace deposits and the underlying Kabuh deposits and that the faunal assemblage therefore is mixed (Bartstra, 1982a). Serious doubts arise from this as to the provenance of both the Pithecanthropus I calotte and the Trinil I femur. The provenance of Trinil femora II–VI has always been a matter of doubt (Day and Molleson, 1973).

Further doubts have been cast on the provenance of the Trinil I femur following new analytical studies on the Javan Trinil remains (Day, 1984).

Associated finds   No artefacts were found in association with the remains but some have been found since in the Kabuh layer that would be termed the tools of *Homo erectus* (Bartstra, 1982a). Numerous fossil mammalian bones have been recovered from the site. Amongst these were the remains of stegodont elephant (*Stegodon*), rhinoceros (*Rhinoceros sondaicus*), carnivores (*Felis*), and some ungulates including axis deer (*Axis leydekkeri*) and a small antelope (*Duboisia kroesenii*) (Selenka and Blanckenhorn, 1911). This fauna is known as the Trinil fauna.

In a reinterpretation of the fauna from Trinil it is now claimed that the fauna of the type locality is older than the Jetis fauna and the fauna of Kedung Brubus, the latter two faunae being regarded as similar (de Vos et al., 1982). This proposed reversal provoked a vigorous debate with confusing consequences since the Kedung Brubus deposits usually overlie the Kabuh layers (Bartstra, 1983b; Hooijer, 1983; Sondaar et al., 1983; Hooijer, 1984; de Vos, 1985).

Dating   According to von Koenigswald (1934, 1949), three series of deposits succeeded each other in Central Java; the Jetis (Lower Pleistocene), the Trinil (Mid-Pleistocene) and the Ngandong (Upper Pleistocene) with a more recent fauna. Hooijer (1951, 1956, 1957, 1962) has accepted the Trinil bed as Mid-Pleistocene, but has denied a faunal distinction between the Jetis and Trinil layers and claims that they are probably both Middle Pleistocene. Estimations of the fluorine content of the Trinil calotte and femur was claimed to have established their contemporeneity both with each other and with their associated fauna (Bergman and Karsten, 1952). In an attempt to correlate the dating of European, African and Asian fossils Kurtén (1962) has equated *Pithecanthropus erectus* of Java with *Paranthropus* from South Africa, and assigned to them both a Middle Pleistocene date (Mindel or Antepenultimate Glaciation). Later by the use of the radiometric potassium–argon dating on tektites and basalt found in deposits which are said to correspond with those at Trinil, von Koenigswald *et al.* (1962) have claimed a chronological age of 550,000 years B.P. for *Pithecanthropus erectus*, within the First Glaciation (Günz or Early Glaciation). Subsequently a potassium–argon date of approximately 500,000 years B.P. was obtained from Trinil deposits related to the Muriah volcano and a date of over 700,000 years B.P. from tektites recovered from Kabuh Beds (Trinil fauna) at Sangiran (von Koegnigswald, 1968). Analytical studies on Trinil fossils neither confirmed nor denied the Middle Pleistocene antiquity of the material although it was thought to confirm the provenance of the calotte and femora I–V (Trinil 3, 6, 7, 8 and 9) (Day and Molleson, 1973).

More recent microanalytical studies, conducted after it was shown that the Trinil fauna is probably mixed, have indicated that the Trinil I femur differs in its composition from the calotte and the other femora (Day, 1984; Day, 1986).

An attempt to date the hominid-bearing beds in Java has been made by taking account of published dates in conjunction with work on planktonic diatom assemblages from marine intercalations in the lowermost hominid-bearing beds. From this the base of the Pucangan Beds is put at 1·9–2·0 m.y. B.P. whilst the base of the Kabuh Beds is put at about 1·3 m.y. B.P. (Ninkovich and Burckle, 1978). Other dates given for the Kabuh Beds include K/Ar of 0·83 m.y. B.P. (Jacob, 1975), 0·6 m.y. B.P. (Van Heekeren, 1972), fission track dates of 0·7 m.y. B.P. (Suzuki and Wikarno, 1982) and 0·67 m.y. B.P. (Nishimura *et al.*, 1980). In a recent review of all the Asian hominids Pope and Cronin (1984) do not accept an age of greater than 1·0–1·3 m.y. B.P. for any Asian hominid site.

In a new review the date of the Trinil fauna has been placed at 1 m.y. B.P. by comparison with other sites (Leinders *et al.*, 1985). Whilst the dating of the Trinil remains from the Kabuh Beds is still uncertain it seems that a date of 0·5–0·75 m.y. B.P. is as good a working estimate as is available at present.

Morphology   The finds include a calotte made up of parts of the frontal, parietal and occipital bones with little or no sign of suture lines. It is thick,

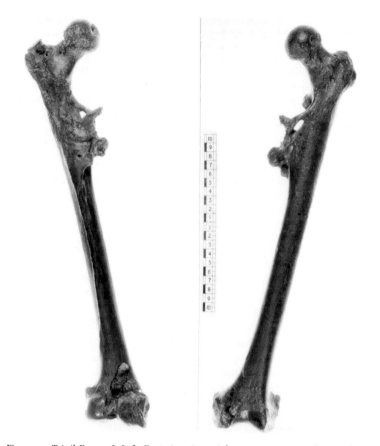

Fig. 114. Trinil Femur I. Left: Posterior view; right: anterior view. *Photographed by courtesy of the Director of the Rijksmuseum von Natuurlijke Historie, Netherlands.*

undistorted and heavily mineralized. The frontal region of the vault is markedly flattened in profile, leading forwards to a heavy supra-orbital torus which is hollowed by paired frontal air sinuses. Behind the brow ridge the frontal region is sharply constricted producing a postorbital waist, whilst in the midline the bone is heaped into a sessile ridge or keel. The temporal lines are well shown but widely separated. Internally the calotte is moulded by the cerebral convolutions and grooved by the meningeal blood vessels.

In addition to the calotte some femoral remains were recovered. They include one complete femur and four femoral fragments. A sixth femoral fragment recovered from Kedung Brubus has been discounted (Day and Molleson, 1973) but after a new study Jourdan (1984) concludes that it is indeed human.

The complete femur is remarkable in its general resemblance to that of modern man. The shaft is straight and has a prominent linea aspera, but in its upper third the specimen is marred by a pathological outgrowth. The head of the bone is rounded, the neck stout and angulated to the shaft, whilst the greater and lesser trochanters are well developed indicating the attachment of powerful muscles around the hip joint.

The features of this femur, in particular the 'weight-carrying-angle' between the shaft and the condyles, suggest strongly that Java man was capable of standing and walking erectly. A study of the Trinil femora (Day and Molleson, 1973) concludes that the gross, radiological and microscopical anatomy of these bones does not distinguish them from modern human femora.

In a review of *Homo erectus* femora from Africa (OH 28; KNM–ER 1481, 1422, 737, 1808), Europe (Arago 44) and Asia (Peking I and IV; Trinil I–VI) it has been noted that the Javan femora form a group distinct from the others with more sapient morphological characters (Lamy, 1984).

Dimensions   *Calotte (Trinil 2)*

Length 183   Breadth 134
Cephalic Index 70 (Dolichocephalic)
Cranial capacity 900 cc (Dubois, 1924)
             914 cc (von Koenigswald and Weidenreich, 1939)
             850 cc (Boule and Vallois, 1957)
             940 cc (Ashley Montagu, 1960)
             940 cc (Holloway, 1981)

Femur 1 (Trinil 3)

Length 455   Mean mid-shaft diameter 28·6
Bicondylar breadth 77   Mean diameter of head 44·8
Angle of neck 122°   Femoro-condylar angle 100°

Affinities   These were the first significant finds in the search for fossil man in the Far East. Despite the opposition of Dubois, subsequent finds at Sangiran (*q.v*) and Modjokerto confirmed that the Trinil specimens are representative of a group of hominids who occupied Java in the Middle Pleistocene. Further finds in China (Peking man) suggested that hominids of this grade were widely distributed in the Far East, for the morphological differences between the two groups indicate only racial variation (Weidenreich, 1938, 1940). Java man is widely classified as *Homo erectus erectus*, only subspecifically distinct from *Homo erectus pekinensis* (Dobzhansky, 1944; Campbell, 1964). The species *Homo erectus* was reviewed in some detail by Howells (1980) and it formed the focus of the von Koenigswald Memorial Symposium (1984). At this meeting Rightmire compared the African and Southeast Asian examples of the taxon and emphasized their overall similarity. He concluded that there is no need to define this extinct species of man by arbitrary dates or gaps in the fossil record. Andrews (1984), however, in questioning the existence of *Homo erectus* as a taxon in Europe or in Africa, suggests that such similarities as there are between Asian and supposed European and African examples of the species are shared characters of common inheritance and thus, in a cladistic analysis, should be disregarded. It is fair to say that this viewpoint was not generally accepted and the problem remained unresolved.

Originals Collection Dubois, Rijksmuseum von Natuurlijke Historie, Leiden, Netherlands.

Casts 1. Rijksmuseum von Natuurlijke Historie, Leiden, Netherlands.
2. The University Museum, University of Pennsylvania, Philadelphia 4, Pennsylvania U.S.A.

References Dubois, E. (1892) Palaeontologische anderzoekingen op Java. *Versl. Mijnw. Batavia* 3, 10–14.
Dubois, E. (1894) Pithecanthropus erectus, *eine menschenaehnliche Ubergangsform aus Java*. Batavia: Landesdruckerei.
Dubois, E. (1985) *Pithecanthropus erectus du Pliocene de Java*. P. V. Bull. Soc. belge Geol. 9, 151–160.
Selenka, M.L., and Blanckenhorn, M. (1911) Die Pithecanthropus— *Schichten auf Java*. Leipzig: Verlag von Wilhelm Engelmann.
Dubois, E. (1924) On the principal characters of the cranium and the brain, the mandible and the teeth of *Pithecanthropus erectus*. Proc. Acad. Sci. Amst. 27, 265–278.
Dubois, E. (1926) On the principal characters of the femur of *Pithecanthropus erectus*. Proc. Acad. Sci. Amst. 29, 730–743.
Weinert, H. (1928) Pithecanthropus erectus. Z. ges. Anat. 87, 429–547.
Koenigswald, G.H.R. von (1934) Zur Stratigraphie des javanischen Pleistocän. Ing. Ned. Ind. 1, 185–201.
Weidenreich, F. (1938) *Pithecanthropus* and *Sinanthropus*. Nature 141, 378–379.
Weidenreich, F. (1940) Some problems dealing with ancient man. Am. Anthrop. 42, 375–383.
Dobzhansky, T. (1944) On the species and races of living and fossil men. Am. J. phys. Anthrop. 2, 251–265.
Koenigswald, G.H.R. von (1949) The discovery of early man in Java and Southern China. In *Early Man in the Far East*. Ed. W.W. Howells; Philadelphia. Stud. Phys. Anthrop. 1, 83–98.
Mayr, E. (1950) Taxonomic categories in fossil hominids. Cold Spring Harb. Symp. Quant. Biol. 15, 109–118.
Hooijer, D.A. (1951) The geological age of *Pithecanthropus, Meganthropus* and *Gigantopithecus*. Am. J. phys. Anthrop. 9, 265–281.
Bergman, R.A.M., and Karsten, P. (1952) The fluorine content of *Pithecanthropus* and other specimens from the Trinil fauna. Proc. Acad. Sci. Amst. B. 55, 1, 150–152.
Hooijer, D.A. (1956) The lower boundary of the Pleistocene in Java and the age of *Pithecanthropus*. Quaternaria 3, 1, 5–10.
Hooijer, D.A. (1957) The correlation of fossil mammalian faunas and the

Plio-Pleistocene boundary in Java. *Proc. Acad. Sci. Amst. B. 690*, 1–10.

Hooijer, D. A. (1962) The Middle Pleistocene fauna of Java. In *Evolution und Hominisation*, 108–111. Ed. G. Kurth. Stuttgart: Gustav Fischer Verlag.

Kurtén, B. (1962) The australopithecines of Transvaal and the pithecanthropines of Java. *Ibid.*, 74–80.

Koenigswald, G. H. R. von (1962) Das absolute Alter des *Pithecanthropus erectus* Dubois. *Ibid.*, 112–119.

Van Heekeren, H. R. (1972) The stone age of Indonesia. *Verhandeligen van het Koninklijk Instituut voor Taal-, Land- en Volkenkunde 61*, 1–247.

Day, M. H. and Molleson, T. I. (1973) The Trinil Femora. In *Human Evolution* Symp. S.S.H.B. Vol. 11, 127–154. Ed. M. H. Day. London: Taylor and Francis Ltd.

Jacob, T. (1975) Morphology and paleoecology of early man in Java. In *Paleoanthropology, Morphology and Paleoecology*, 311–326. Ed. R. H. Tuttle. The Hague: Mouton.

Oakley, K. P., Campbell, B. G. and Molleson, T. I. (1975) *Catalogue of Fossil Hominids Part III: Americas, Asia, Australasia*. London: Trustees of the British Museum (Natural History).

Ninkovich, D. and Burckle, L. H. (1978) Absolute age of the base of the hominid-bearing beds in Eastern Java. *Nature 275*, 306–307.

Howells, W. W. (1980) *Homo erectus*: Who, When and Where: A Survey. *Yearbk. phys. Anthrop. 23*, 1–23.

Nishimura, S. T., Thio, K. H. and Hehuwat, F. (1980) Fission-track ages of the tuffs of the Pucangan and Kabuh formations, and the tektite at Sangiran, Central Java. In *Physical Geology of Indonesian Island Arcs*, 72–80. Ed. S. Nishimura. Kyoto: Kyoto University.

Barstra, G.-J. (1982a) The river-laid strata near Trinil, site of *Homo erectus erectus*, Java, Indonesia. *Mod. quat. Res. S.E. Asia, 7*, 97–130.

Barstra, G.-J. (1982b) *Homo erectus erectus*: The search for his artifacts. *Curr. Anthrop. 23*, 318–320.

de Vos, J., and Sondaar, P. Y. (1982) The importance of the 'Dubois Collection' reconsidered. *Mod. quat. Res. S.E. Asia, 7*, 35–63.

de Vos, J., Sartono, S., Harkja-Sasmita, S. and Sondaar, P. Y. (1982) The fauna from Trinil, type locality of *Homo erectus*; a reinterpretation. *Geologie en Mijnbouw 61*, 207–211.

Suzuki, M. and Wikarno (1982) Fission track ages of pumice tuffs, tuff layers and javites of hominid bearing formations in Sangiran, Central Java. *Comm. xi Cong. 11, INQUA, Moscou 1982*, res. comm., II, 322.

Bartstra, G.-J. (1983a) Some remarks upon: Fossil man from Java, his age, and his tools. *Bydragen to de Taal-, Land- and Volkenkunde, 139*, 421–434.

Barstra, G.-J. (1983b) The fauna from Trinil, type locality of *Homo erectus*: a reinterpretation. (Comment II.) *Geologie en Mijnbouw 62*, 329–336.

Hooijer, D. (1983) *Ibid* (Comment I), 337–338.

Sondaar, P. Y., de Vos, J. and Leinders, J. J. M. (1983) *Ibid* (Reply), 339–343.

Andrews, P. (1984) On the characters that define *Homo erectus*. *Cour. Forsch. Inst. Senckenberg 69*, 167–175.

Day, M. H. (1984) The postcranial remains of *Homo erectus* from Africa, Asia and possibly Europe. *Ibid*, 113–121.

Hooijer, D. A. (1984) The mammalian faunas of Trinil and Kedungbrubus in Java once more. *Mod. quat. Res. S.E. Asia 8*, 95–102.

Jourdan, L. (1984) Le femur 6 de Trinil. In *L'homme fossile et son environment à Java*, 53–58. Paris: Muséum National d'Histoire Naturelle.

Lamy, P. (1984) Les femurs des *Homo erectus* d'apres les découvertes faites a Java. *Ibid*, 49–52.

Pope, G. G. and Cronin J. E., (1984) The Asian Hominidae. *J. hum. Evol.* 13, 377–396.

Rightmire, G. P. (1984) Comparisons of *Homo erectus* from Africa and Southeast Asia. *Cour. Forsch. Inst. Senckenberg* 69, 83–98.

de Vos, J. (1985) Faunal stratigraphy and correlation of the Indonesian hominid sites. In *Ancestors*, 215–220. New York: Alan R. Liss.

Leinders, J. J. M., Aziz, F., Sondaar, P. Y. and de Vos, J. (1985) The age of the hominid-bearing deposits of Java: state of the art. *Geol. en Mijnbouw* 64, 167–173.

The Sangiran Remains

Fig. 115. The first Sangiran calvaria (Pithecanthropus II) (left lateral view). *Courtesy of the late Profesor J. S. Weiner.*

(In this section it is proposed that only the four most significant finds from this important site will be discussed. For a full list of the remains, and their various designations, see table, page 356).

Synonyms and other names

(1) *Sangiran 2 Pithecanthropus* (von Koenigswald, 1938); Pithecanthropus II (von Koenigswald and Weidenreich, 1939); *Homo erectus* (Mayr, 1950); *Homo erectus erectus* (Campbell, 1964); *P. erectus* (Jacob, 1975); *Homo erectus trinilensis* (Sartono, 1981).

(2) *Sangiran 4* Pithecanthropus IV (von Koenigswald and Weidenreich, 1939); *Pithecanthropus* (von Koenigswald, 1942); *Pithecanthropus robustus* (Weidenreich, 1945); *Pithecanthropus modjokertensis* (von Koenigswald, 1950); *Homo erectus* (Mayr, 1950); *Pithecanthropus erectus* (Piveteau, 1957); *Homo erectus erectus* (Dobzhansky, 1944; Campbell, 1964); *Homo soloensis* (Dubois, 1940); *Homo modjokertensis* (von Koenigswald, 1975); *Homo erectus modjokertensis* (von Koenigswald, 1973); *Homo palaeojavanicus modjokertensis* (Sartono, 1981); *Homo palaeojavanicus robustus* (Sartono, 1982).

(3) *Sangiran 17* Pithecanthropus VIII (Sartono, 1971); *Homo erectus ngandongensis* (Sartono, 1981, 1982); *Pithecanthropus soloensis* (Jacob, 1978).

(4) *Sangiran 6 Meganthropus palaeojavanicus* (Weidenreich, 1945a); Meganthropus I (Robinson, 1953); *Paranthropus palaeojavanicus* (Robinson, 1954); *Pithecanthropus palaeojavanicus* (Piveteau, 1957); *Homo palaeojavanicus sangiranensis* (Sartono, 1981); Meganthropus A (1941 and 1950 specimens).

Sangiran 8 Meganthropus (Marks, 1953); Meganthropus II (Robinson, 1953); *Paranthropus palaeojavanicus* (Robinson, 1954); *Pithecanthropus palaeojavanicus* (Piveteau, 1957); *Homo palaeojavanicus mojokertensis* (Sartono, 1981); *Homo palaeojavanicus robustus* (Sartono, 1982); *Homo erectus* (Lovejoy, 1970); Meganthropus B (1952 specimen).

Site   Sangiran, by the river Tjemoro, a tributary of the Solo about 40 miles west of Trinil, near Surakarta, Central Java, Indonesia.

Found by   1. G. H. R. von Koenigswald, September 1937.
2. Collectors employed by G. H. R. von Koenigswald, 1938–1939.
3. Mr Towikromo, a collector employed by S. Sartono, 13th September, 1969.
4. G. H. R. von Koenigswald and his assistant, 1941 and 1950; P. Marks, 1952.
The more recent material has been found by S. Sartono and T. Jacob (see table).

Geology   Sangiran lies at the foot of a volcano, Lawu, to the north of Surakarta. Lavas and ashes from this volcano have spilled over a wide area creating deposits that are bedded. The stratigraphy has been divided into four formations, from lowest to highest the Kalibeng, the Pucangan, the Kabuh and the Notopuro. The Grenzbank separates the Pucangan and the Kabuh, the Lower Lahar separates the Kalibeng and the Pucangan, the Upper Lahar separates the Kabuh and the Notopuro, whilst the Uppermost Lahar caps the Notopuro and separates it from Terrace deposits. The Kalibeng has been referred to the Pliocene and the rest to the Lower to Middle Pleistocene. Late Pleistocene Terrace deposits overlie the Kabuh and Notopuro Formations in places and Holocene alluvial deposits are to be found along rivers (Matsu'ura, 1982). The Kabuh deposits consist of conglomerate, volcanic tuffs and sandstones that show evidence of fluviatile deposition. The Pucangan bed consists of black fresh water clay-stones with marine intercalations overlying lower volcanic breccias. The provenance of the individual finds from Sangiran is noted in Table 8. Further details of the geology of the

Sangiran area have been given by Sartono (1968, 1971 and 1972 and 1982).

Associated finds   *Sangiran 2*

1. No artefacts were associated with the find but the fauna from the Kabuh beds is known as the Trinil fauna and includes the remains of stegodont elephant (*Stegodon*), rhinoceros (*Rhinoceros sondaicus*), carnivores (*Felis*) and some ungulates including axis deer (*Axis lydekkeri*) and a small antelope (*Duboisia kroesenii*) (Selenka and Blankenhorn, 1911).

Sangiran 4

2. No artefacts were associated with this find but the fauna from the Pucangan beds is known as the Jetis fauna and includes a primitive horned ox (*Leptobos*) and a sabre-toothed cat (*Epimachairodus*).

Sangiran 17

3. No artefacts were associated with this find which was recovered from the Kabuh beds (Trinil fauna).

Sangiran 6 & 8

4. No artefacts were associated with these finds. The earlier specimens were derived from the Pucangan beds (Jetis fauna) and the most recent from the Kabuh beds (Trinil fauna).

Recent work on the fauna of the Pleistocene of Java has cast doubts on the association of the Kabuh Formation and the Trinil fauna, and the Pucangan Formation and the Jetis fauna since so-called 'guide fossils' occur *in situ* in both formations (Aimi and Aziz, 1983). Trinil faunal elements also occur in the Notopuro of Sangiran whose fauna is the same as that of Kabuh (Van Heekeren, 1972). Faunal correlations between strata at Sangiran and in other parts of Java seem uncertain at present.

Dating   The dating of the remains from Sangiran has been a difficult problem for many years, being part of an even greater problem, that of determining the age of all the Pleistocene deposits in Java. The sequence of deposits in east Java is not generally disputed in that the Kabuh beds, which contain the Trinil fauna are younger than the Pucangan beds containing the Jetis fauna. The Sangiran area reveals both sets of beds at several sites. In the past the Trinil and Jetis faunas have been the subject of contention; Hooijer (1962) accepted the Trinil fauna as Middle Pleistocene and denied a distinction between this fauna and the Jetis fauna, claiming that they are both probably Middle Pleistocene. On the other hand von Koenigswald (1949) always maintained the view that the Jetis fauna is evidence of the Lower Pleistocene age of the layer that contains these fossils. Potassium-argon dating of the Kabuh beds has given dates of 500,000 years B.P and 830,000 years B.P. at differing sites (von Koenigswald, 1964) and at Sangiran a tektite potassium-argon estimation has given 710,000 years B.P. for the same beds.

Whilst there is some evidence that the date of the lower layers of the Pucangan may be as early as 1·7 m.y. B.P. (Semah, 1984) or 1·9–2·1 m.y. B.P. (Ninkovich and Burckle, 1978), two recent reviews would place an upper limit of 1·3 m.y. B.P. for the age of the hominids of Java (Matsu'ura, 1982; Pope and Cronin, 1984).

Morphology 1.   *Sangiran 2*

The calvaria consists of the frontal, parietal, temporal and occipital bones of an adult; both facial skeleton and skull base are missing. The region of the foramen magnum and the right side of the frontal bone are broken away. In general form the specimen strongly resembles the Trinil calotte; the flattening and keeling of the frontal region, the supraorbital torus and the widely separated temporal lines are features common to both. The occipital bone of the Sangiran calvaria shows that the nuchal plane is inclined at an angle intermediate between that of the pongids and modern man; the supramastoid and occipital crests are in continuity and the mastoid processes are very small. The foramen magnum is placed forward, evidence that *Pithecanthropus* was habitually upright in posture. Internally the bones are impressed by the cerebral convolutions and grooved by the larger dural venous sinuses and meningeal vessels.

2.   *Sangiran 4*

The remains consists of the posterior half of a brain case and the lower portion of both maxillae.

Calvaria

The cranium is represented by almost the entire occipital bone, including the foramen magnum and the occipital condyles, the temporal bones and approximately the posterior three-quarters of both parietal bones. The skull is larger than that of Pithecanthropus I or II, but resembles them in that it has a low vault and has its greatest breadth at the base. There is a marked frontal keel, accentuated by parasagittal depressions and a series of 'knob-like' processes leading back from the vertex to the occipital torus—features not seen in any other pithecanthropine. The occipital torus is very large and joins the supramastoid ridges on either side; the nuchal

4
—
3
—
2
—
1
—
C M·
—
1
—
2
—
3

Fig. 116. The Sangiran maxilla (Pithecanthropus IV) (right lateral view). *Courtesy of the late Professor G. H. R. von Koenigswald.*

muscles have left well marked impressions on the occipital bone indicating a powerful neck. The mastoid processes are large and project downwards and inwards, in contrast to the small processes of the first Sangiran calvaria. The external auditory meatus is oval as in modern man, but the tympanic plate is thick; the mandibular fossa is deep and narrow and the articular eminence is absent. Internally the petrous temporal bone is very prominent.

Maxillae

The alveolar processes are complete except for the posterior part of the left side. In addition almost the entire palate, the floor of the nasal cavity and the maxillary sinuses of both sides are preserved. The maxillae were crushed before fossilization, resulting in some distortion. The bony palate is very large and smooth, relieved only by the presence of the palatal groove on the right side which is limited medially by an unusual bony prominence. The incisive canal is double and has a funnel-like opening which is very large and distally placed. The pre-maxillary region is very deep but the pillars of the zygomatic bones arise near the alveolar borders. In lateral view the degree of facial and alveolar prognathism is large but there is no typical nasal spine. The maxillary sinus is large but does not extend back into the maxillary tuberosity.

Teeth

All the teeth are present except the incisors and the left second and third molars. An isolated incisor was found with the previous specimens. The teeth are very little worn. The incisor sockets indicate that the teeth sloped forwards, and that a wide diastema existed between the lateral incisor and the canine. The canines are large by comparison with hominid teeth and their breadths exceed their lengths. The molars decrease in size in the order $M_2 > M_1 > M_3$ and the cusp pattern of their crowns does not differ appreciably from those of Peking man except that the remains of the cingulum are less obvious in the Sangiran molars.

3.   *Sangiran 17*

Pithecanthropus VIII is the most complete skull recovered from this site, indeed the best preserved specimen that has emerged from Java so far. The vault of the skull is almost complete and the face is intact apart from the loss of the left zygomatic region. The base is also well preserved posteriorly but the body of the sphenoid is broken away. The foramen magnum is present but a little broken at its rim. The palate is present in large part and a number of teeth are present including the three molars on the right as well as the canine, while on the left the second premolar is present. The face has suffered some distortion and is displaced posteriorly and rotated under the base.

In lateral view the vault shows a low profile, a well-developed supraorbital torus and a supratoral groove. The inion is high and appears to coincide with the opisthocranion leaving a marked occipital *planum* below, bounded above by an occipital crest that fuses with a strong supramastoid crest. In occipital view the vault profile is broad at its base so that the maximum breadth of the skull is low.

The face is of particular interest since it is the only skull from the lower layers in Java that is at all well preserved in facial morphology. Its most striking features are the breadth of the zygomatic region and the massive nature of the supraorbital tori and the prominence of the glabella.

The teeth are heavily worn but resemble those known from other pithecanthropine specimens. The canine is larger than those of modern man and the molars diminish in length from the first to the third molar (Sartono, 1971, 1972).

Dimensions 1.   Length c. 180 Max. Breadth 140
Cephalic Index 77·8 (Mesocephalic)
Cranial Capacity c. 750 cc (von Koenigswald, 1938)
            850 cc (Weidenreich, 1938)
            775 cc (von Koenigswald, 1949)
            815 cc (Boule and Vallois, 1957)
            813 cc (Holloway 1981)

Comparisons of the dimensions of the sangiran calvaria with those of the Trinil calotte led to the suggestion that the Sangiran specimen was female (von Koenigswald, 1938).

2.   *Calvaria Sangiran 4* Weidenreich (1954)

Max. Length 199   Max. Breadth ?158
Cranial Index ?79·3   Cranial Capacity c. 900 cc
                                                   908 cc
                                                   (Holloway 1981)

		I^1	I^2	C	PM^1	PM^2	M^1	M^2	M^3
				Upper Teeth (Crown Dimensions)					
Left	l	—	—	9·5	8·5	8·5	12·3	—	—
side	b	—	—	11·9	12·4	12·3	13·6	—	—
Right	l	—	10·0	9·5	8·2	8·2	12·1	13·6	10·8
side	b	—	10·4	11·7	12·4	12·1	13·7	15·2	14·0

3.   *Sanigran 17* Sartono (1971)

		I^1	I^2	C	PM^1	PM^2	M^1	M^2	M^3
				Upper Teeth (Crown Dimensions)					
Left	l	—	—	—	—	8·2	—	—	—
side	b	—	—	—	—	10·1	—	—	—
Right	l	—	—	8·9	—	—	10·9	10·7	9·4
side	b	—	—	10·5	—	—	12·9	12·9	13·1

Cranial capacity 1,004cc (Holloway, 1981)

Morphology 4.   *Sangiran 6 Mandible*

The 1941 specimen consists of part of the right side of the body of a massive hominid mandible that extends from the canine socket to the first molar tooth. Three large teeth are *in situ*, the first and second premolars and the first molar. The jaw is remarkable in size, being larger than any known example from modern man, equalled by few modern gorillas and only exceeded by *Gigantopithecus*. The inner aspect of the fragment bears genial tubercles for the attachment of the extrinsic tongue muscles, and shows part of the digastric impression. There is no simian shelf. The mental foramen is placed about midway between the upper and lower borders of the bone.

Sangiran 6 Teeth

The first premolar is bicuspid and asymmetrical in occlusal view, and has two well defined grooves on its buccal surface. The second premolar bears two mesial cusps and a talonid basin. The fused ridges joining the cusps separate the anterior and posterior foveae while the buccal grooves are feebly represented. The first molar is a robust tooth but attrition has exposed the dentine leaving little of the fissural pattern. The occlusal surface is elongated mesiodistally. Despite the extensive wear it is probable that there were six cusps present.

Dimensions   *Mandibles* Weidenreich (1954); Marks (1953)

Specimens	Symphysis	Body height at Mental Foramen	M₂/M₃	Symphysis	Body thickness at Mental Foramen	M₂/M₃
Sangiran 6	47·0	48·0	45·0	25·5	28·0	26·3
Sangiran 8	37·0	42·0	47·0	—	—	—

Affinities 1.   *Sangiran 2*

There is little doubt that the Sangiran 2 calvaria belonged to a hominid of the same type as that of the Trinil calotte; in consequence it was attributed to *Pithecanthropus* by von Koenigswald and Weidenreich (1939). This view was strongly contested by Dubois (1940) who alleged that this skull was really the remains of a Solo man (*Homo soloensis*) said to be synonymous with Wajak man (*Homo wadjakensis*). Despite this controversy it was apparent that Pithecanthropus I and II were almost identical.

   2.   *Sangiran 4*

These remains were examined and described by Weidenreich (1945a), and a tentative reconstruction of the skull was attempted. At first he believed that this calvaria was male and that the previously known specimens must be female. Later he abandoned this idea as he could not reconcile some of the features of the skull with this scheme of interpretation and assumed that it must belong to a different group, *Pithecanthropus robustus*. Von Koenigswald (1950) could not accept this view. Subsequently it has become clear that Pithecanthropus IV is closely allied to the pithecanthropines of the Far East, in particular those of Java, but may well have affinities to remains known from East Africa (Tobias and von Koenigswald, 1964).

   3.   *Sangiran 17*

The new specimen, Pithecanthropus VIII, shows unmistakable similarities to the other pithecanthropines known from Java

Fig. 117. The Meganthropus II mandibular fragment (1941), *Courtesy of the late Professor G. H. R. von Koenigswald.*

although at present detailed comparative studies are not available. Its value will be not only that it increases the sample of hominids from Java but also that the presence of the face is unique.

Sangiran 6 and Sangiran 8

Although the first fragments of this form were found by von Koenigswald in 1941 and 1950, because of wartime difficulties the 1941 fragment was first fully described from casts and named by Weidenreich (1954a). Weidenreich believed that it belonged to a hominid who was ancestral to *Pithecanthropus* and thus to modern man, denying any relationship with the australopithecines. This view was taken up vigorously by Robinson (1953) who suggested that *Meganthropus* is at least equivalent to *Paranthropus*.

Later, in a review of the classification of the australopithecines (Robinson, 1954), *Meganthropus palaeojavanicus* was renamed *Paranthropus palaeojavanicus*. This step was criticized by Remane (1954a and b), rejected by von Koenigswald (1954, 1957), but stoutly defended by Robinson (1955, 1962). Subsequently Tobias and von Koenigswald (1964) have compared the Javan *Meganthro-*

pus jaw fragments and the Olduvai Hominid 7 mandible from Bed I Olduvai Gorge and drawn attention to a number of similarities. The third mandibular fragment, found by Marks in 1952 (Marks, 1953), was considered by von Koenigswald (1968, 1973) who felt that it shows evidence of having been split by a crocodile; yet he agreed with Marks' view that it is a *Meganthropus*. Whilst accepting the hominid nature of this material, von Koenigswald (1973) took the view that *Meganthropus* is a 'terminal form', in contrast to the view expressed by Lovejoy (1970) who cannot detect a discontinuity between the *Meganthropus* specimens and the other *Homo erectus* specimens from similar beds.

In general terms it appears that von Koenigswald believed that the hominid material that is derived from the Putjangan beds (Jetis fauna) should be allocated to *Pithecanthropus modjokertensis* or to *Meganthropus palaeojavanicus* (von Koenigswald, 1973). A more widely held view would place most of the Sangiran hominids into *Homo erectus* (Mayr, 1950; Dobzhansky, 1944; Campbell 1964).

A glance at the section on synonyms and other names gives some idea of the confusion that surrounds the Sangiran hominids, a group solely represented by cranial and dental remains, often in a poor state of preservation and insufficient to allow any real assessment of the range of variability of the sample. I believe, however, that the Sangiran hominids do not provide evidence of australopithecines outside of Africa and that all are the remains of man and should be placed within the genus *Homo* most probably within the species *Homo erectus*.

The debate on the relationship between European and African examples of *Homo erectus* and those from Asia referred to in relation to Trinil (*q.v.*) is also relevant here.

Originals　Projek Penelitin Palaeoantropologi Nasional, Fakultas Kedokteran, Universitas Gadjah Mada, Indonesia.

Table 8　*The Sangiran Remains*

Specimen No. (Jacob, 1973)	Former Designation	Formation	Material	Finder and year of find
Sangiran 1a	Meganthropus	?	Rt. maxilla M_1–M_3	Von Koenigswald pers. comm.
Sangiran 1b	Mandible B	Pucangan	Rt. mandible, P_4–M_3	
Sangiran 2	Pithecanthropus II	Kabuh	Calotte	von Koenigswald, 1937
Sangiran 3	Pithecanthropus III	Kabuh	Parietals, occipital	von Koenigswald, 1938
Sangiran 4	Pithecanthropus IV	Pucangan	Calvaria, maxilla, Lt. C–M^1, Rt. C–M^3	Von Koenigswald, 1938/39
Sangiran 5	(Holotype: *P. robustus*) (Holotype: *P. dubius*)	Pucangan	Rt. mandible, M_1 and M_2	von Koenigswald, 1939

Table 8 *The Sangiran Remains (continued)*

Specimen No. (Jacob, 1973)	Former Designation	Formation	Material	Finder and year of find
Sangiran 6	Meganthropus A (Mandible D) (Holotype: *M. palaeojavanicus*)	Pucangan	Mandible, Rt. P$_3$–M$_1$	von Koenigswald, 1941
Sangiran 7a	—	Pucangan	Isolated teeth	— 1937–41
Sangiran 7b	—	Kabuh	Isolated teeth	— 1937–41
Sangiran 8	Meganthropus B	Kabuh	Mandible, Rt. M$_3$	Marks, 1952
Sangiran 9	Mandible C	Pucangan	Rt. mandible, C, P$_3$ and P$_4$, M$_2$ and M$_3$	Sartono, 1960
Sangiran 10	Pithecanthropus*	Kabuh	Calotte, Lt. zygoma	Jacob, 1963
Sangiran 11	—	Kabuh	Lt. M^3, Rt. I$_1$	Jacob, 1963
Sangiran 12	Pithecanthropus VII	Kabuh	Calotte	Sartono, 1965
Sangiran 13a	—	Kabuh	Calotte fragments	Jacob, 1964
Sangiran 13b	—	Kabuh	Parietal, temporal and sphenoid fragments	Jacob, 1965
Sangiran 14	—	Kabuh	Cranial fragments	Jacob, 1966
Sangiran 15a	—	Pucangan	Lt. maxilla, P^3 and P^4	Sartono, 1969
Sangiran 15b	—	Kabuh	Lt. maxilla, P^3, roots P^4	Jacob, 1969
Sangiran 16	—	Kabuh	Rt. M^2, Lt. p^3 (germ)	Jacob, 1969/70
Sangiran 17	Pithecanthropus VIII	Kabuh	Cranium, Rt. C, M$^{1-3}$, Lt. P^3	Sartono, 1969
Sangiran 18a	—	Kabuh	Calvarial fragments	Jacob, 1970
Sangiran 18b	—	Kabuh	Calvarial fragments	Jacob, 1970
Sangiran 19	—	Kabuh	Occipital	Jacob, 1970
Sangiran 20	—	Kabuh	Calvarial fragments	Jacob, 1970
Sangiran 21	Mandible E	Kabuh	Mandible, M^3	Sartono, 1973
Sangiran 22	Mandible F	Pucangan	Mandible, Lt. I$_2$–M$_1$, Rt. P$_4$–M$_2$ + Lt. M$_{2-3}$. Rt. M$_3$	Sartono, 1974
Sangiran 23	—	Kabuh	Endocast	Jacob, 1975
Sangiran 26	—	Pucangan	—	Jacob, 1978
Sangiran 27	—	Pucangan	Face and cranial fragments	Jacob, 1978
Sangiran 34	—	Kabuh	Temporal endocast	Matsu'ura, 1980
Other finds	Mandible D	Pucangan	Mandibular fragment	Sartono, 1974
	Meganthropus I ?	?	Cranial fragments	Sartono, 1959
	Meganthropus II	Pucangan	Cranial fragments	Sartono, 1979

*Sangiran 10 is listed by Jacob (1966 and 1975) as 'P.V' or 'the sixth skull'.
A further specimen, a fragment of a mandible of *Meganthropus* with Lt. M$_2$ and M$_3$ is mentioned by Tobias and Von Koenigswald

Casts University Museum, University of Pennsylvania, Philadelphia, Pennsylvania 19104, U.S.A. (Sangiran 2 and 4).

References   Selenka, M. L. and Blanckenhorn, M. (1911) *Die Pithecanthropus—Schichten auf Java*. Leipzig: Verlag von Wilhelm Engelmann.

Koenigswald, G. H. R. von (1938) Ein neuer Pithecanthropus-Schädel. *Proc. Acad. Sci. Amst. 41*, 185–192.

Koenigswald, G. H. R. von and Weidenreich, F. (1939) The relationship between Pithecanthropus and Sinanthropus. *Nature. 144*, 926–929.

Dubois, E. (1940) The fossil human remains discovered in Java by Dr G. H. R. von Koenigswald and attributed by him to *Pithecanthropus erectus*, in reality remains of *Homo wadjakensis* (syn. *Homo soloensis*). *Proc. Acad. Sci. Amst. 43*, 494–496, 842–851, 1268–1275.

Koenigswald, G. H. R. von (1942) *The South-African man-apes and Pithecanthropus*. Washington: Carnegie Inst. Publ. No. 530, 205–222.

Dobzhansky, T. (1944) On species and races of living and fossil men. *Am. J. phys. Anthrop. 2*, 251–265.

Weidenreich, F. (1945a) Giant early-man from Java and South China. *Anthrop. Pap. Am. Mus. nat. Hist. 40*, 1–134.

Weidenreich, F. (1945b) *The puzzle of Pithecanthropus. Science and scientists in the Netherlands Indies*. New York: Board for the Netherlands Indies, Surinam and Curaçao.

Koenigswald, G. H. R. von (1949) The discovery of early man in Java and Southern China. In *Early Man in the Far East*. Ed. W. W. Howells. Philadelphia. *Stud. phys. Anthrop. 1*, 83–98.

Koenigswald, G. H. R. von (1950) Fossil hominids from the Lower Pleistocene of Java. *Proc. Int. geol. Cong. 9, London 1948, Sect. 9*, 59–61.

Mayr, E. (1950) Taxonomic categories in fossil hominids. *Cold Spring Harb. Symp. Quant. Biol. 15*, 109–118.

Marks, P. (1953) Preliminary note on the discovery of a new jaw of *Meganthropus*, von Koenigswald, in the Lower Middle Pleistocene of Sangiran, Cental Java. *Indones. J. nat. Sci. 109*, 26–33.

Robinson, J. T. (1953) Meganthropus, australopithecines and hominids. *Am. J. phys. Anthrop. 11*, 1–38.

Koenigswald, G. H. R. von (1954) The Australopithecinae and Pithecanthropus III. *Proc. Acad. Sci. Amst. 57*, 85–91.

Remane, A. (1954a) Structure and relationships of *Meganthropus africanus*. *Am. J. phys. Anthrop. 12*, 123–126.

Remane, A. (1954b) Methodische, probleme der Hominiden—Phylogenie II *Z. Morph. Anthrop. 46*, 225–268.

Robinson, J. T. (1954) The genera and species of the Australopithecinae. *Am. J. phys. Anthrop. 12*, 181–200.

Robinson, J. T. (1955) Further remarks on the relationship between *Meganthropus* and australopithecines. *Am. J. phys. Anthrop. 13*, 429–446.

Koenigswald, G. H. R. von (1957) *Meganthropus* and the Australopithecinae. *Proc. pan-Afr. Cong. Prehist. 3, Livingstone, 1955*, 158–160. Ed. J. D. Clark. London: Chatto and Windus.

Piveteau, J. (1957) *Traité de Paléontologie, VII*. Paris: Masson et Cie.

Sartono, S. (1961) Notes on a new find of a *Pithecanthropus* mandible. *Publikasi Teknik Seri Paleontologi. no. 2*.

Hooijer, D. A. (1962) The Middle Pleistocene fauna of Java. In *Evolution und Hominisation*, 108–111. Ed. G. Kurth. Stuttgart: Gustav Fischer Verlag.

Kurtén, B. (1962) The relative ages of the australopithecines of Transvaal and the pithecanthropines of Java. In *Evolution und Hominisation*, 74–80. Ed. G. Kurth. Stuttgart: Gustav Fischer Verlag.

Robinson, J. T. (1962) The origin and adaptive radiation of the australopithecines. *Ibid.*, 120–140.

Campbell, B. (1964) Quantitative taxonomy and human evolution. In *Classification and Human Evolution*, 50–74. Ed. S. L. Washburn. London: Methuen and Co. Ltd.

Koenigswald, G. H. R. von (1964) Potassium-argon dates and early man: Trinil. *Conf. int. Ass. Quatern. Res. 6. Warsaw 1961*, 325–327.

Tobias, P. V. and Koenigswald, G. H. R. von (1964) A comparison between the Olduvai hominines and those of Java and some implications for hominid phylogeny. *Nature 204*, 515–518.

Jacob, T. (1966) The sixth skull cap of *Pithecanthropus erectus*. *Am. J. phys. Anthrop. 25*, 243–260.

Koenigswald, G. H. R. von (1968) Observations upon two *Pithecanthropus* mandibles from Sangiran Central Java. *Proc. Acad. Sci. Amst. B. 71*, 99–107.

Sartono, S. (1968) Early man in Java: Pithecanthropus skull VII, a male specimen of Pithecanthropus erectus (I). *Proc. Acad. Sci. Amst. B. 71*, 396–422.

Lovejoy, C. O. (1970) The taxonomic status of the 'Meganthropus' mandibular fragments from the Djetis beds of Java. *Man 5*, 228–236.

Sartono, S. (1971) Observations on a new skull of *Pithecanthropus erectus* (Pithecanthropus VIII) from Sangiran, Central Java. *Proc. Acad. Sci. Amst. B. 74*, 185–194.

Sartono, S. (1972) Discovery of another hominid skull at Sangiran, Central Java. *Curr. Anthrop. 13*, 124–126.

Jacob, T. (1972) The absolute date of the Djetis beds at Modjokerto. *Antiquity 46*, 148.

Koenigswald, G. H. R. von (1973) The oldest hominid fossils from Asia and their relation to human evolution. *Proc. of symposium L'origine dell'uomo, Rome 1971*. Quaderno. N. 182, Accademia Nazionale dei Lincei.

Jacob, T. (1975) The Pithecanthropines of Indonesia. *Bull. Mem. Soc. Anthrop. Paris t.2. série XIII*, 243–256.

Oakley, K., Campbell, B., Molleson, T. (1975) *Catalogue of fossil hominids. Part III: Americas, Asia, Australasia*, 108–113. London: Trustees of the British Museum (Natural History).

Van Heekeren, H. R. (1972) The stone age of Indonesia. *Verhandelingen van het Koninklijk Instituut voor Taal-, Land- en Volkenkunde 61*, 1–247.

Koenigswald, von, G. (1975) Early Man in Java: catalogue and problems. In *Paleontology, Morphology and Palaeoecology*, 303–310. Ed. R. Tuttle. The Hague: Mouton.

Sartono, S. and Djubiantono, T. (1982) Note on paleomagnetic age of *Homo modjokertensis*. *Cong. Int. Paléont. hum. 1, Nice*. Prétirage, 534–541.

Sartono, S. (1982) Characteristics and chronology of early men in Java. *Cong. Int. Paléont. hum. 1, Nice*. Prétirage, 491–533.

Jacob, T. (1978) The puzzle of Solo Man. In *Mod. Q. Res. S.E. Asia. 4*, 31–40.

Ninkovich, D. and Burckle, L. H. (1978) Absolute age of the base of the hominid-bearing beds in Eastern Java. *Nature 275*, 306–307.

Matsu'ura, S. (1982) A chronological framing for the Sangiran hominids. *Bull. nat. Sci. Mus. Tokyo 8*, 1–53.

Semah, F. (1984) The Sangiran Dome in the Javanese Plio-Pleistocene chronology. *Cour. Forsch. Inst. Senckenberg 69*, 245–252.

Pope, G. G. and Cronin, J. E. (1984) The Asian Hominidae. *J. hum. Evol. 13*, 377–396.

Aimi, M. and Aziz, F. (1985) Vertebrate fossils from the Sangiran dome, Mojokerto, Trinil and Sambungmacan, Indonesia. *Spec. Pub. No. 4 Geol. Res. Develop. Centre, Indonesia*.

The Ngandong Remains

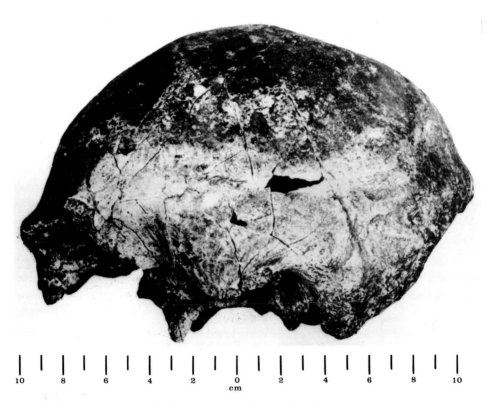

Fig. 118. Ngandong calvaria No. 6. *Courtesy of the late Professor J. S. Weiner.*

Synonyms and other names   *Homo (Javanthropus) soloensis* (Oppenoorth, 1932a); *Homo soloensis* (Oppenoorth, 1932b); *Homo primigenius asiaticus* (Weidenreich, 1933); *Homo neanderthalensis soloensis* (von Koenigswald, 1934); *Homo sapiens soloensis* (Campbell, 1964); *Homo erectus erectus* (Santa Luca, 1980); *Homo (Javanthropus) soloensis* (Sartono, 1982); *Homo erectus* (Pope and Cronin, 1984); Solo man; Ngandong man

Site   Ngandong, six miles north of Ngawi, Central Java, Indonesia.

Found by   C. ter Haar, 1931–1933; G. H. R. von Koenigswald, 1933.

Geology   The valley of the river Solo, north of Ngawi, has three gravel terraces at two m, seven m and 20 m, where the river has cut through the previous fluviatile deposits. It was in the high 20-metre Ngandong terrace, above the Kabuh beds, that the Solo finds were uncovered.

Associated finds A few small stone implements were found with the bones as well as some stone balls, but too few indisputable artefacts were recovered to constitute an industry. Several rayfish spines and deer antlers were found, which may have been used as spearpoints or pickaxes. A large quantity of mammalian bones were associated with the hominid remains, mostly belonging to an axis deer (*Cervus javanicus*) or banteng cattle. Other forms included pigs (*Sus terhaari, Sus macrognathus*), rhinoceros (*Rhinoceros sondaicus*), hippopotamus (*Hexaprotodon ngandongensis*) and primitive elephant (*Stegodon sp.*). The diagnostic fossils for the Ngandong fauna are *Cervus javanicus* and *Sus terhaari*.

Dating Assessment of the stratigraphy and fauna suggest that the dating of the Ngandong deposits is Upper Pleistocene (von Koenigswald, 1949; Bartstra 1983).

Morphology *Calvariae*

In all twelve calvariae and two tibiae were unearthed at this site. Seven were regarded as being adult on grounds of sutural fusion (Weidenreich, 1951) and, of these, two were believed to be male, two female and the remainder of indeterminate sex.

The calvariae are all thick, several showing signs of injury during life. In profile they all possess the same general form which, in combination with similar dimensions, suggests that they represent a homogeneous population. Particular features of the profile are supra-orbital ridges separated by a central depression, sloping foreheads and strongly marked nuchal crests. The glenoid fossae are deep, and the articular eminences and mastoid processes pronounced. The base of No. 11 is complete apart from its anterior portion.

Two further specimens (Ngandong 15) cranial fragments and (Ngandong 16) calotte have been recovered from Ngandong deposits (Jacob, 1982).

Tibiae

Tibia A is broken at both ends, lacking articular surfaces, whereas Tibia B is nearly complete. Both bones are straight and appear modern in form.

Dimensions *Calvariae*

Weidenreich (1951); Von Koenigswald (1958).
Max. Lengths 191–221   Max Breadths 146–159
Cranial Indices 65·2–75·2   Cranial Capacities 1,035–1,255 cc
(Based on the six best-preserved skulls)

TIBIAE	*Length*
Tibia A	300 (broken)
Tibia B	365

*   *   *

Calvariae

Singer (1958)
Measurements taken on the original material.
Max. Lengths 192·5–220·3   Max. Breadths *c.* 144–*c.* 155
Cranial Indices 66·8–76·5

Cranial Lengths, Breadths and Length/Breadth Indices

Skull No.	I	5	6	9	10	11
Length	196·0	220·3	192·5	*c.* 201·0	202·6	200·0
Breadth	*c.* 148·0	*c.* 147·0	*c.* 144·0	*c.* 150·0	*c.* 155·0	*c.* 144·0
Cranial Index*	75·6	66·8	75·3	74·6	76·5	72·0

* Calculated from Singer's figures

Affinities   The calvariae reported by Oppenoorth (1932a) were originally assigned by him to the genus *Homo* and placed in a sub-genus *Javanthropus*. The name was dropped in subsequent publications (Oppenoorth, 1932b, 1937) and the name *Homo soloensis* was proposed. However, Weidenreich (1933) suggested the name *Homo primigenus asiaticus* as part of a wider scheme of hominid classification. Vallois (1935) criticized the creation of a sub-genus for Solo man and suggested that these people were simply a local variety of Neandertal man. Soon after this there followed a protracted controversy between Dubois and von Koenigswald regarding the relationships of all the Javan finds; Dubois (1936) at first proclaimed the 'racial identity' of Solo man, Modjokerto man and Peking man, but later believed that Solo man was identical with Wajak man and thus a form of *Homo sapiens* (Dubois, 1940).

However, von Koenigswald had indicated his belief in the Neandertal affinities of this form by naming it *Homo neanderthalensis soloensis* (von Koenigswald, 1934).

Finally Weidenreich examined all the Solo material in considerable detail and, in an unfinished paper (Weidenreich, 1951), elected not to enter the discussion on nomenclature; he contented himself by stating that 'Ngandong man is not a true Neanderthal type but distinctly more primitive and very close to *Pithecanthropus* and *Sinanthropus*'. None the less, von Koenigswald has adhered to his view that Solo man is a primitive 'tropical Neanderthaler' (von Koenigswald, 1958). In another classification of the Hominidae it has been proposed to include Solo man as a sub-species of *Homo sapiens* (*Homo sapiens soloensis*) distinct from modern man (*H. sap. sapiens*),

Neandertal man (*H. sap. neanderthalensis*) and Kabwe man (*H. sap. rhodesiensis*) (Campbell, 1964).

Jacob has pointed out similarities between *Pithecanthropus erectus, Pithecanthropus pekinensis* and *P. soloensis* (Jacob, 1967, 1982). This seems to suggest that in his terms they indicate a widespread evolutionary series in the Far East.

After an extensive study of the Ngandong fossil hominids Santa Luca (1980) concludes that they all belong to the taxon *Homo erectus erectus*. Pope and Cronin (1984) assign all the Indonesian hominids to *Homo erectus* and include those from Ngandong in this allocation. There remain a number of features of the skulls, such as the cranial capacity, that would persuade some workers of their *erectus/sapiens* transitional status. The late date of the deposits from which they derive would add to that viewpoint.

Originals   The Department of Physical Anthropology, Gadja Mada University, College of Medicine, Yogyakarta, Indonesia.

Casts   Not available at present.

References   Oppenoorth, W. F. F. (1932a) *Homo (Javanthropus) soloensis*, een plistoceene Mensch von Java. *Wet. Meded. Dienst. Mijnb. Ned.-Oast. Indië* 20, 49–75.

Oppenoorth, W. F. F. (1932b) De vondst paleolithische menschelijke schedels op Java. *De Mijningingenieur* 5, 106–116.

Koenigswald, G. H. R. von (1933) Ein neuer Urmensch aus dem Diluvium Javas. *Zbl. Miner., Geol. A und B Paläont.*, 29–42.

Weidenreich, F. (1933) Ueber pithekoide Merkmale bei *Sinanthropus pekinensis* u seine stammesgeschichtliche Beureilung. *Z. Anat. Entw. Gesch.* 99, 212–253.

Koenigswald, G. H. R. von (1934) Zur stratigraphie des javanischen Pleistocän. *Ing. Ned.-Indië.* 1 185–201.

Vallois, H. (1935) Le *Javanthropus. Anthropologie* 45, 71–84.

Dubois, E. (1936) Racial identity of *Homo soloensis*, Oppenoorth (including *Homo modjokertensis*, von Koenigswald) and *Sinanthropus pekinensis*, Davidson Black. *Proc. Acad. Sci. Amst.* 39, 1180–1185.

Oppenoorth, W. F. F. (1937) The place of *Homo soloensis* among fossil men. In *Early Man*, 349–360. Ed. G. G. MacCurdy. Philadelphia and New York: J. B. Lippincott.

Dubois, E. (1940) The fossil human remains discovered by Dr. G. H. R. von Koenigswald and attributed by him to *Pithecanthropus erectus*, in reality remains of *Homo wadjakensis* (syn. *Homo soloensis*). *Proc. Acad. Sci. Amst.* 43, 494–496, 842–851, 1268–1275.

Koenigswald, G. H. R. von (1949) The discovery of early man in Java and Southern China. *Stud. phys. Anthrop.* 1, 83–98.

Weidenreich, F. (1951) Morphology of Solo man. *Anthrop. Pap. Amer. Mus.* 43, 205–290.

Koenigswald, G. H. R. von (1958) Der Solo-Mensch von Java; ein Tropische Neanderthaler. In *Hundert Jahre Neanderthaler*, 21–26. Ed. G. H. R. von Koenigswald. Utrecht: Kemink en Zoon.

Singer, R. (1958) *Ibid.*, p. 22.

Campbell, B. (1964) Quantitative taxonomy and human evolution. In

Classification and Human Evolution, 50–74. Ed. S. L. Washburn. London: Methuen and Co. Ltd.

Jacob, T. (1967) Recent *Pithecanthropus* finds in Indonesia. *Curr. Anthrop.* 8, 501–504.

Santa Luca, A. P. (1980) The Ngandong fossil hominids. *Yale Univ. Publ. Anthrop.* 78, 1–175.

Jacob, T. (1982) Solo Man and Peking Man. In *Homo erectus*. Ed. J. S. Cybulski and B. A. Sigmon. Toronto: University of Toronto Press.

Sartono, S. (1982) Characteristics and chronology of early men in Java. *Cong. Int. Paléont. hum. 1*, Nice. Prétirage, 491–533.

Bartstra, G.-J. (1983) Some remarks upon a fossil man from Java, his age and his tools. *Bijdragen tot de Taal-, Land- en Volkenkunde* 139, 421–434.

Pope, G. C. and Cronin, J. E. (1984) The Asian Hominidae. *J. hum. Evol.* 13, 377–396.

The Sambungmachan Calvaria

Synonyms and other names
P. soloensis (Jacob, 1973); *Homo erectus ngandongensis* (Sartono 1982); Sambungmachan I; SM I

Site
Sambungmachan on the south bank of the Solo river, 12 km east of Sragen, village of Ngadirojo, Central Java, Indonesia.

Found by
T. Jacob, 1973.

Geology
According to Jacob (1976, 1982) it was found *in situ* in a sandstone layer 4·74 m below the surface in the Middle Pleistocene Kabuh Beds. According to Sartono (1979) the geology of the area can be differently interpreted. He suggests that the lowermost limestone bed is the Hitik limestone which, together with dark grey silts and yellow tuffs, belong to the Upper Kalibeng Formation of Upper Pliocene age. He suggests that the Kabuh Formation is not present and that Upper Pleistocene deposits lie unconformably on the Kalibeng Beds. Sartono therefore regards the skull as having come from Upper Pleistocene deposits at the site.

Associated finds
There were no tools associated with the calvaria. The fauna is said to contain both Jetis and Trinil elements including deer (*Cervus zwaani*), and artiodactyl (*Bibos palaeosondaicus*) and stegodont elephant (*Stegodon trigonocephalus*) (Jacob 1973a). Pollen analysis from the site indicates a continental vegetation, similar to rain forest, a result comparable to that obtained from the Kabuh Beds at Trinil (Semah, A.-M., 1982).

Dating
Stratigraphically the date is in some doubt. Jacob (1976) has given a date of 0·9 m.y. B.P. and later Jacob (1978) a date of 0·8 m.y. B.P. Semah (1982) takes the view that there is insufficient data on which to date the site.

Morphology
The specimen consists of a calvaria that is virtually complete, missing only its face and part of the base including the foramen magnum. The vault is low with a sloping forehead, parasagittal flattening, a modest supraorbital ridge and an inflated posterior profile that sets it apart from the Sangiran and Trinil skulls. The mastoid process is large and the occiput is angulated but opisthion and opisthocranium do not appear to coincide. The occipital has a sharp lower border, a triangular prominence and an external occipital crest.

In profile the vault is more rounded frontally and more inflated than those of *Homo erectus*. The specimen is described and illustrated in Jacob (1973b and 1976).

Affinities   It is clear that Jacob believes that almost all the finds from Java belong to the genus *Pithecanthropus* and can be allocated to one of three species, *P. modjokertensis, P. erectus* and *P. soloensis*. Of these he would place Sambungmachan man in *P. soloensis* with the Ngandong remains (*q.v.*) (Jacob, 1982). Orchiston and Siesser (1982) also found marked similarities between the Ngandong and Sambungmachan calvaria and regard them both as belonging to *Homo sapiens soloensis*. Another view of the Javan hominids would place all in *Homo erectus* and that includes the Ngandong hominids (Pope and Cronin, 1984). There seems to be agreement about the general resemblance of the Ngandong and Sambungmachan calvaria; but less about their dating. Should they both prove to be Upper Pleistocene in age then their attribution to *Homo sapiens* would be appropriate.

Stringer suggested that there are similarities between the Ngandong fossils and those of *Homo erectus*, but that some of the Ngandong skulls do differ from the typical *Homo erectus* morphology; it may be that this is also true of Sambungmachan (Stringer, 1984). My view is that the Sambungmachan and Ngandong skulls are similar and that the evidence for a Kabuh Bed age for this specimen or for the Ngandong skulls is not strong. By comparison with the Trinil and Sangiran sample there seems sufficient morphological space to allow the allocation of both Ngandong and Sambungmachan to *Homo sapiens*.

Originals   Projek Penelitian Palaeoantropologi Nasional, Fakultas Kedokteran, Universitas Gadjah Mada, Indonesia.

Casts   Not available at present.

References   Jacob, T. (1973a) New finds of Lower and Middle Pleistocene hominines from Indonesia and their antiquity. *Conf. early Palaeol. E. Asia, Montreal.*
Jacob, T. (1973b) Morphology and paleoecology of early man in Java. *Int. Cong. Anthrop. ethnol. Sci., 9, Chicago.*
Jacob, T. (1973c) Palaeoanthropological discoveries in Indonesia with special reference to the finds of the last two decades. *J. hum. Evol. 2,* 473–485.
Jacob, T. (1976) Early populations in the Indonesian region. In *The Origin of the Australians,* 81–93. Eds. R.L. Kirk and A.G. Thorne. Canberra: Australian Institute of Aboriginal Studies.
Jacob, T. (1978) The puzzle of Solo Man. *Mod. quat. Res. S.E. Asia 4,* 31–40.
Siesser, W.G. and Orchiston, D.W. (1978) Micropalaeontological reassessment of the age of *Pithecanthropus* mandible C from Sangiran, Indonesia. *Mod. quat. Res. S.E. Asia, 4,* 25–30.

Sartono, S. (1979) The age of the vertebrate fossils and artefacts from Cabenge in South Sulawesi, Indonesia. *Mod. Quat. Res. S.E. Asia* 5, 65–81.

Jacob, T. (1982) Solo Man and Peking Man. In *Homo erectus*, 87–104. Eds J. S. Cybulski and B. A. Sigmon. Toronto: University of Toronto Press.

Orchiston, D. W. and Seisser, W. (1982) Chronostratigraphy of the Plio-Pleistocene fossil hominids of Java, *Mod. Quat. Res. SE Asia* 7, 131–149.

Sartono, S. (1982) Characteristics and chronology of early men in Java. *Cong. Int. Paléontol. Hum.* 1, Nice Prétirage, 491–533.

Semah, F. (1982) The Sangiran Dome in the Javanese Plio-Pleistocene chronology. *Cour. Forsch. Inst. Senckenberg* 69, 245–252.

Pope, G. G. and Cronin, J. E. (1984) The Asian Hominidae. *J. hum. Evol.* 13, 377–396.

Stringer, C. B. (1984) The definition of *Homo erectus* and the existence of the species in Africa and Europe. *Cour. Forsch. Inst. Senckenberg* 69, 131–143.

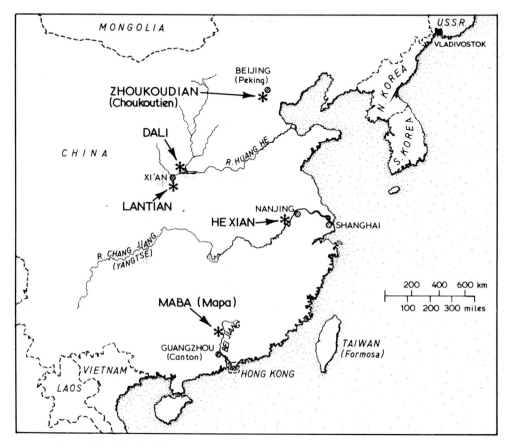

Fig. 119. Hominid fossil sites in China.

The Peking Remains

Fig. 120. The Peking 1966 calvaria. *Courtesy of Professor Wu Rukang (J. K. Woo).*

Synonyms and other names	*Homo sp.* (Zdansky, 1927); *Sinanthropus pekinensis* (Black, 1927); *Pithecanthropus pekinensis* (Boule and Vallois, 1946); *Pithecanthropus sinensis* (Piveteau, 1957); *Homo erectus pekinensis* (Weidenreich, 1940; Campbell, 1964; Wu and Olsen, 1985)
	Pekin man; Peking man; Choukoutien man; Choukou'tien man; Chou-kou-tien man; Zhoukoudian man
Site	The Choukoudian Lower Cave, near the town of Zhoukoudian 25 miles south-west of Peking.
Found by	J. G. Andersson, 1921; O. Zdansky, 1923; B. Bohlin, 1927; W. C. Pei, and the Cenozoic Research Laboratory, 1928–1937; Institute of Vertebrate Palaeontology Team, 1949–1959; J. K. Woo 1959; Institute of Vertebrate Palaeontology and Palaeoanthropology Team, 1966.
Geology	The hills near Zhoukoudian are formed from Ordovician limestone which has been undermined and eroded by percolating ground waters producing caves and fissures. At Locality 1 a huge cavern

roof has collapsed on top of the cave-filing, which is made of red clays and fallen rocks consolidated into a calcareous breccia. The cliff face at the principal site is 150 feet deep and was divided by Davidson Black into 15 sections each of ten feet, lettered A–O from above downwards. It was in this cave-filling, at various levels, that much of the material was found.

Recent studies of the geology have indicated more than 40 m of cave deposits in 17 layers of breccia and non-breccia (sand, silt, clay, travertine and ash) (Liu, 1985).

Climatic changes have been correlated with these layers and cold phases inferred by the breccia layers are identical with those of the glaciation represented by the even numbers of the oxygen isotope curve of deep-sea cores; warm phases are inferred by the interglacial represented by uneven numbers (Liu and Ding, 1984).

Associated finds   The tools found at Locality 1 belong to a crude 'Chopper-tool' industry, and were made from imported coarse-grained quartz and greenstone. They are in the form of a few cores and numerous flakes which were probably utilized. The remains of an extensive mammalian fauna was recovered with Peking man. Amongst the forms recognized were some insectivores, bats and lagomorphs, numerous rodents, some small and large carnivores, a large deer (*Megaloceros pachyosteus*) and rhinoceros. A faunal list has been given by Kahlke (1962). At this site also were found ash and pieces of charcoal; the charcoal, although of no use for radiocarbon dating on account of its age, may provide the first clear evidence of the use of fire by early man.

In a new and extensive review of the archaeology of the Zhoukoudian site it has been suggested that the hominid remains may have been introduced by carnivores, that the 'ash' layers are not hearths and may not even be ash, that the animal bones in the deposit are not evidence of hominid diet and that there is no evidence of 'ritual or economic' cannibalism at the site (Binford and Ho, 1985).

Dating   The usually accepted dating of the Zhoukoudian site, in view of the fauna, is Middle Pleistocene. By a combination of pollen and faunal analysis, Kurtén (1959) suggested that the dating equivalent of the Zhoukoudian deposits should be sought in the European glaciations and not in an interglacial, in his view probably the Second Glaciation (Elster II, Mindel II or the Antepenultimate Glaciation). The age of this glaciation, according to Evernden, Curtis and Kistler (1958) using the potassium–argon method, is 370,000 B.P. (a figure which may be revised to *c*. 400,000 B.P.). This is an appropriate date for the Zhoukoudian deposits but is dependent upon Kurtén's correlation. In a recent assessment of the geology of the cave-filling (Huang, 1960), it has been suggested that the deposits were laid down over a long period as six successive gravel beds; the basal layer during the First Glaciation, the lower two layers during the First Interglacial, and the upper three layers during the Second Glaciation. This correlation is rejected by Kahlke (1962), as were a previous Cromerian correlation and a Mindel-Riss Interglacial correlation proposed on palaeontological grounds.

A recent tentative correlation of early human fossil horizons with loess deep sea core records suggests that the Peking Man fossil layers correspond to loess cycles II–VI which are consistent with terminations III–VIII and oxygen isotope stages 6–15, thus having an age of 128,000–590,000 years B.P., younger than Lantian (*q.v.*) and older than Dali (*q.v.*) (Liu and Ding, 1984). Their older date is consistent with chronometric dates but their younger date is much too young (Wu, 1985). The following table, after Wu (1985), indicates the latest results for the chronometric dating of the Peking Man site.

Table 9 *Some Absolute Dates Obtained on the Peking Man Deposits* (After Wu, 1985)

Layer	Years	Dating Method and Reference
1–3	230,000 $^{+30,000}_{-23,000}$ 256,000 $^{+62,000}_{-40,000}$	Uranium-series[1,2]
4	290,000	Thermoluminescence[3]
6–7	350,000	Uranium-series[2]
7	370–400,000	Palaeomagnetism[4]
8–9	420,000 >400,000 $^{+>180,000;}_{-100,000}$	Uranium-series[1,2]
10	462,000±45,000	Fission track[5]
10	520–620,000	Thermoluminescence[3]
12	>500,000	Uranium-series[2]
13–17	>730,000	Palaeomagnetism[4]

[1] Zhao *et al.*, 1979; [2] Xia, 1982; [3] Pei *et al.*, 1980; [4] Quin *et al.*, 1980; [5] Guo *et al.*, 1980; see also Liu, 1983.

Morphology The hominid remains from Zhoukoudian, which were described in a remarkable series of monographs by Black and Weidenreich, consist of 14 calvariae and 11 mandibles in varying states of preservation, as well as numerous teeth and a few postcranial bones.

A mandible has been attributed to Peking man by Woo and Chao (1959).

New cranial fragments discovered in 1966 were found to fit onto casts of previously known fragments to form a calvaria now known as the '1966 skull'.

Calvariae

The first calvaria to be found, now known as Skull III, was re-covered from Locus E. It is well preserved but the face and base are missing. The braincase is characterized by a flattened but keeled frontal region with a pronounced supraorbital visor, a well marked postorbital constriction and a prominent occipital torus. The man-dibular fossae are deep and narrow. In frontal view the side walls of the cranium slope inwards towards the apex so that the maxi-mum width lies in the region of the temporal bone above the small mastoid process—a feature not found in modern man. This parti-cular skull was described by Black (1931) as being adolescent; later Weidenreich (1943) considered it to be juvenile. The principal morphological features of the remaining calvariae are similar to those of Skull III but tend to be more coarsely represented.

The '1966 Skull' is remarkable in that the newly found fragments articulate with casts of the lost Peking remains to form a new calvaria that underpins the anatomy already known of the Peking skulls from Weidenreich's descriptions and the casts that are avail-able.

The '1966 skull' has a marked frontal visor, in which there are frontal sinuses. There is a huge angular torus on the right parietal bone which is very thick indeed. In lateral view the vault is ovoid, inion and opisthocranion coincide yet the internal and external occipital protuberances are separate. There is a suprainiac depres-sion and a crista on the inner aspect of the vault. The right temporo-occipital fragment and the left temporal fragment derive from the original finds; the frontal fragment (G–1–1) and the right parieto-occipital fragment (G–1–2) derive from the 1966 excavation.

Mandibles

Three of the best-preserved mandibles have been reconstructed by Weidenreich (1936). These show the recession of the symphysial region, the narrow but rounded dental arcade, thickening of the body of the mandible inside the alveolar margin (mandibular torus), the presence of genial tubercles for the tongue muscles and an unusually large bicondylar breadth. A point of detail is the high incidence of multiple mental foramina (cf. Heidelberg jaw). The new mandible (1959) has a narrow alveolar arch, a moderate mandi-bular torus and four mental foramina on the right side.

Teeth

In total 147 teeth were examined by Weidenreich (1937), 83 sock-eted, 64 isolated. Out of the 132 (52 upper and 82 lower identified) permanent teeth present, every tooth was represented but only lower deciduous teeth are known. This collection is believed to come from 32 individuals, 20 of whom were adolescent or adult and 12 children. Five more teeth have been reported, but not described, by Woo (1960).

The most striking feature of the teeth is their variability in size, the range of which has permitted their division into two main groups believed to represent males and females. In general the teeth are robust and characteristically wrinkled. The upper incisors are shovel-shaped and frequently have a well developed basal tubercle with finger-like processes directed toward the free margin of the tooth. The upper canines are large and project beyond the occlusal line whilst the lower canines are smaller and tend to form cutting edges, thus resembling incisors. There is no trace of a diastema and the premolars are non-sectorial. In almost all of the canines, premolars and molars there is a cingulum which in the case of the molars has traces of stylid cusps. The cusp pattern is basically dryopithecine with a tendency towards transformation into the 'plus' pattern by reduction of the metaconid. The first and second permanent molars are of approximately the same size, but the third molar tends to be smaller than either. The permanent molars, premolars and milk molars display a degree of enlargement of the pulp cavity (taurodontism).

The eruption order of the teeth of Peking man differs from that of modern man in that the second permanent molar arises before both premolars and canine.

Postcranial Bones

The limb remains from Zhoukoudian include seven fragments of femoral shaft, none with an articular surface. The femora are unusual in the thickness of the cortical bone, the platymeria of the shaft, the distal positions of the narrowest point of the shaft and the convexity of the medial border of the bone (Weidenreich, 1941). The upper limb remains consist of two fragments of humerus, a lunate bone and a fragment said to be part of a clavicle. (The examination of a cast of the 'clavicular' fragment has raised doubts as to its correct identification.) The humeral fragments have no articular surface, but are thick walled and one has a strong deltoid impression. The lunate belongs to the right side and is small by comparison with those of modern man. The bone is somewhat eroded having lost part of its dorsal surface, part of the semi-lunar facet for the scaphoid and the apex of the ridge joining the radial and triquetral surfaces.

Woo (1960) reported new limb material—'two fragments of humerus and tibia'. The tibial fragment is said to have an even smaller cavity than the femora. No further details of the postcranial bones have been published yet.

Dimensions *Calvariae*

Locus E. Skull III Black (1931)

Length (glabella/occipital) 187·6 Max. Parietal Breadth 133·0

Cranial Index 73·5 (Dolichocephalic) Cranial Capacity 915 cc (Weidenreich)

Crania

Weidenreich (1943)

Max. Length range 188–199

Max. Breadth range 137·2–143

Cranial Index range 71·4–72·6 (Dolichocephalic)

Cranial Capacity (5 skulls) range 915 cc–1,225 cc

Mandibles G1♂ and H1♀

Reconstructed by Weidenreich (1936)

Thickness

No.	Length	Bicondylar Breadth	Symphysial Height	Ramus Height	At Mental Foramen Height	At Mental Foramen Thickness
G1♂	103·0*	164·4*	40·0*	66·7	34·0	16·4
H1♀	94·0*	101·8*	31·5	59·0	26·0	15·4

* Restored.

The differences between these measurements were taken as evidence of sexual dimorphism.

Teeth

widenreich (1937)

Permanent Dentition (Crown Dimension Ranges) Upper Teeth	Length	Breadth
Central Incisors (I^1)	9·8–10·8	7·5– 8·1
Lateral Incisors (I^2)	8·2– 8·3	8·0– 8·2
Canines (C)	8·5–10·5	9·8–10·6
First Premolars (PM^1)	7·4– 9·2	10·5–12·8
Second Premolars (PM^2)	7·2– 8·9	10·3–12·5
First Molars (M^1)	10·0–13·1	11·7–13·7
Second Molars (M^2)	10·2–12·2	12·2–13·4
Third Molars (M^3)	8·7–10·4	10·4–12·5
Lower Teeth	*Length*	*Breadth*
Central Incisors (I_1)	6·0– 6·8	5·8– 6·8
Lateral Incisors (I_2)	6·3– 7·2	6·4– 7·3
Canines (C)	8·1– 9·0	8·2–10·4
First Premolars (PM_1)	7·9– 9·8	9·1–10·8
Second Premolars (PM_2)	8·2– 9·2	8·0–11·1
First Molars (M_1)	9·9–13·6	10·1–12·8
Second Molars (M_2)	11·3–13·1	11·1–12·9
Third Molars (M_3)	10·0–13·8	10·0–12·4

	Deciduous Dentition (Crown Dimensions)	
Lower Teeth	Length	Breadth
Central Incisors (dI1)	4·3	3.6
Lateral Incisors (dI2)	—	—
Canines (dC)	6·1– 6·2	5·2– 5·3
First Molars (dM1)	9·8	8·4–10·1

Postcranial Bones

Weidenreich (1941)
Lunate: Length (prox./dist. diam.) 14·5
Breadth (radio/ulnar diam.) 14·4
Height (dorso/volar) 16·5
Clavicle: Length (145)
Circumference 34 (Mid-point)
Humerus: Angle of Torsion 137°
Length (324)
Femora: Lengths (400–407)
Mid-shaft Widths 29·2–29·7
Mid-shaft Depths 22·8–27·1
( ) Estimated measurement

Affinities   Initially the name *Sinanthropus pekinensis*, conferred by Davidson Black (1927), referred solely to the hominid molar tooth upon which the genus was founded. It was not long before Black's bold step was apparently justified by the subsequent finds, but soon afterwards the resemblances between *Pithecanthropus* and *Sinanthropus* began to become clear (Boule, 1929). Later, when the Zhoukoudian material had been fully studied by Weidenreich, he took the view that the differences between *Pithecanthropus* and *Sinanthropus* were of a racial character only. It has been suggested that Peking man, in company with several other Middle Pleistocene hominids, should be classified under the name of *Homo erectus* (Mayr, 1950) and given the geographic subspecific designation *pekinensis*. This proposal has been incorporated in another classification (Campbell, 1964). Recent studies (Wolpoff *et al.*, 1984; Wolpoff, 1985) have sought to emphasize the possibility of regional continuity from China through East Asia down to Australia as exemplified by the Peking remains and the Mungo remains, and the Sangiran (17) (*q.v.*) and Kow Swamp remains (*q.v.*). This revival of an older idea of polyphyletic evolution has not gained widespread support.

Originals   All of the early material, except one lower premolar and one upper molar, was lost during the 1939–45 war. Fortunately most of the bones had been cast and studied intensively by Weidenreich. The two teeth are at the University of Uppsala, Sweden. The newer material is kept at The Institute of Vertebrate Palaeontology and Palaeoanthropology, Academia Sinica, Beijing, Peoples' Republic of China.

Casts   The University Museum, University of Pennsylvania, Philadelphia 4, Pennsylvania, U.S.A.

References   Zdansky, O. (1927) Preliminary notice on two teeth of a hominid from a cave in Chihli (China). *Bull. geol. Soc. China.* 5, 281–284.

Black, D. (1927) On a lower molar hominid tooth from the Chou Kou Tien deposit. *Palaeont. sin.* Ser. D, 7, 1–29.

Boule, M. (1929) Le *Sinanthropus. Anthropologie* 39, 455–460.

Black, D. (1931) On an adolescent skull of *Sinanthropus pekinensis* in comparison with an adult skull of the same species and with other hominid skulls, recent and fossil. *Palaeont. sin.* Ser. D, 7, II, 1–145.

Weidenreich, F. (1936) The mandibles of *Sinanthropus pekinensis:* a comparative study. *Palaeont. sinica,* Ser. D, 7, III, 1–163.

Weidenreich, F. (1937) The dentition of *Sinanthropus pekinensis:* a comparative odontography of the hominids. *Palaeont. sin.* New Ser. D,1, 1–180, 1–121 (plates).

Weidenreich, F. (1940) Some problems dealing with ancient man. *Am. Anthrop.* 42, 375–383.

Weidenreich, F. (1941) The extremity bones of *Sinanthropus pekinensis. Palaeont. sin.* New Ser. D, 5, 1–150.

Weidenreich, F. (1943) The skull of *Sinanthropus pekinensis*; a comparative study on a primitive hominid skull. *Palaeont. sin.* New Ser. D, 10, 1–291.

Boule, M. and Vallois, H. V. (1946) *Les hommes fossiles.* 3rd Ed., 122. Paris: Masson et Cie.

Mayr, E. (1950) Taxonomic categories in fossil hominids. *Cold Spring Harb. Symp. Quant. Biol.* 15, 109–118.

Piveteau, J. (1957) *Traité de Paléontologie* VII, 384. Paris: Masson et Cie.

Kurtén, B. (1959) New evidence on the age of Pekin man. *Vertebr. Palasiat.* 3, 173–175.

Woo, J. K. and Chao, T. K. (1959) New discovery of *Sinanthropus* mandible from Choukoutien. *Vertebr. Palastiat.* 3, 169–172.

Huang, W. P. (1960) Restudy of the Choukoutien *Sinanthropus* deposits. *Vertebr. Palasiat.* 4, 45–46.

Huang, W. P. (1960) On the age of basal gravel of Choukoutien *Sinanthropus* site and of the 'Upper gravel' and 'Lower gravel' of the Choukoutien region. *Ibid.,* 4, 47–48.

Woo, J. K. (1960) The unbalanced development of the physical features of *Sinanthropus pekinensis* and its interpretation. *Vertebr. Palasiat.* 4, 17–26.

Kahlke, H. D. von (1962) Zur relativen Chronologie ostasiatischer Mittelpleistozän-Faunen und Hominoidea-Funde. In *Evolution und Hominisation,* 84–107. Ed. G. Kurth. Stuttgart: Gustav Fischer Verlag.

Oakley, K. P., Campbell, B. G. and Molleson, T. I. (1975) *Catalogue of Fossil Hominids Part III: Americas, Asia, Australasia.* London: Trustees of the British Museum (Natural History).

Pei, J. *et al.* (1979) Thermoluminescence ages of quartz in ash materials from *Homo erectus pekinensis* site and its geological implications. *Kexue Tongbao* 24, 849.

Zhao, S., Xia, M., Wang, S. *et al.* (1979) Uranium-series dating of Peking Man. *Kexue Tongbao 25*, 447.

Guo, S., Meng, W., Zhang, P., Sun, S., Hao, X, Liu, S., Zhang, F., Hu, R. and Liu, J. (1980) Fission track dating of Peking Man. *Kexue Tongbao 25*, 770–772.

Qian, F. *et al.* (1980) Magnetostratigraphic study on the cave deposits containing fossil Peking Man at Zhoukoudian. *Kexue Tongbao 25*, 359.

Xia, M. (1982) Uranium-series dating of fossil bones from Pekin Man Cave—Mixing Model. *Acta Anthrop. Sin. 1*, 191–196.

Liu, T. (1983) Discussion on the age of 'Yuanmou Man'. *Acta Anthrop. Sin. 2*, 40–48.

Liu, T. and Ding, M. (1984) A tentative chronological correlation of early human fossil horizons in China with the loess-deep sea records. *Acta Anthrop. Sin. 3*, 93–101.

Wolpoff, M., Wu, X.Z. and Thorne, A.G. (1984) Modern *Homo sapiens* origins: A general theory of hominid evolution involving the fossil evidence from East Asia. In *The Origins of Modern Humans*, 411–483. Eds. F.H. Smith and F. Spencer. New York: Alan R. Liss.

Binford, L.R. and Ho, C.K. (1985) Taphonomy at a distance: Zhoukoudian, 'The cave home of Beijing Man'? *Curr. Anthrop. 26*, 413–442.

Liu, Z. (1985) Sequence of sediments at Locality 1 in Zhoukoudian and correlation with loess stratigraphy in northern China and with the chronology of deep-sea cores. *Quat. Res. 23*, 139–153.

Wolpoff, M. (1985) In *Hominid Evolution: Past, Present and Future.* Ed. P.V. Tobias. New York: Alan R. Liss.

Wu, R. (1985) New Chinese *Homo erectus* and recent work at Zhoukoudian. In *Ancestors*, 245–248. Ed. E. Delson. New York: Alan R. Liss, Inc.

Wu, R. and Olsen, J.W. Eds. (1985) *Palaeoanthropology and Palaeolithic Archaeology in the People's Republic of China.* Orlando, Florida and London: Academic Press.

The Lantian Remains

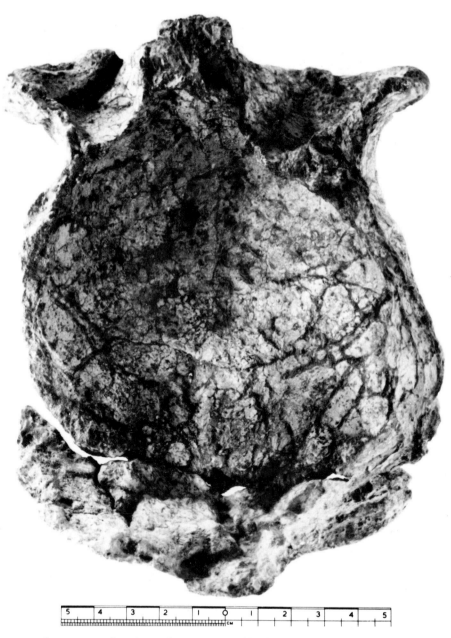

Fig. 121. The Lantian 2 calotte (internal view). *Courtesy of Professor Wu Rukang (J. K. Woo).*

Synonyms and other names	*Sinanthropus lantianensis* (Woo, 1964); *Homo erectus* (Wu, 1982) Lantian man; Lantian 1 and 2 (Oakley *et al.*, 1975).
Site	(i) *Mandible* (Lantian 1). Chenchiawo, Lantian County, Shaanxi Province, northwest China. (ii) *Skull* (Lantian 2). Foothills of the northern slope of the Chinling mountains, Kungwangling Hill (Gongwangling Hill), Lantian County, Shaanxi Province, People's Republic of China.
Found by	J. K. Woo (Wu Rukang) 1963 and 1964; Institute of Vertebrate Palaeontology and Palaeoanthropology Team.
Geology	The Chenchiawo mandible was found in the base of a layer of reddish clay 30 metres thick beneath which there is a layer of gravel one metre thick. The Lantian skull from Gongwangling was found in a block of 'fossil-bearing deposits' sent to the laboratory in Peking.
Associated finds	At both the skull and mandible sites, numerous quartz chopping tools, cores and flakes were recovered (Chia, 1966; Dai, 1966). The mammalian fauna found with the mandible includes red dog (*Cuon cf. alpinus*), tiger (*Felis cf. tigris*), elephant (Elephantidae), boar (*Sus lydekkeri*) and sika deer (*Pseudaxis grayi*) (Chia, 1966). The mammalian fauna found with the skull is predominantly of woodland forms including the sabre-toothed tiger (*Meganteros*), cheetah (*Acinonyx*), lion (*Felis leo*), tapir (*Tapir indicus*) and giant macaque (*Macacus robustus*); most of those forms are poorly represented, but some grassland forms are better preserved (Woo, 1966).
Dating	The dating of the Lantian sites suggests, on stratigraphic grounds, that they are earlier than that of Zhoukoudian and are possibly contemporaneous with the earlier Javan *Homo erectus* sites (Woo, 1966). The Gongwangling locality has been suggested by Ma *et al.* (1978) and Cheng *et al.* (1978) to lie in the Matuyama reversed epoch (750,000–800,000 years B.P.) whilst Chenchiawo may be younger in the early part of the Brunhes normal epoch (650,000 years B.P.). On the basis of correlation with climatic fluctuation (Xu and You, 1982) Gongwangling was given as older than oxygen isotope Stage 22 thus close to 1 m.y. B.P. The Chenchiawo hominid level was given as closer to Stage 16–17 *c.* 590,000–650,000 years B.P. Liu and Ding (1984) gave the Gongwangling calotte an age of 730,000–800,000 years B.P. and the Chenchiawo mandible an age of 500,000–590,00 years B.P.
Morphology	In 1963 a well-preserved mandible was recovered from Chenchiawo, Lantian County in Shaanxi Province. Later, in 1964, a tooth was recovered from Gongwangling Hill at a height of 80 metres. Subsequently from a block recovered nearby a skull was

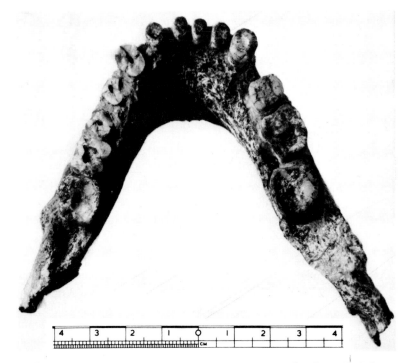

Fig. 122. The Lantian I mandible (occlusal view). *Courtesy of Professor Wu Rukang (J. K. Woo).*

found. It consisted of a calotte with a right temporal bone, parts of the orbits, parts of the nasal bones, parts of the left maxilla, and the right maxilla bearing two teeth. They appear to belong to one individual. The bones are somewhat distorted but the skull has the same general character as other *Homo erectus* skulls from Java and Zhoukoudian. In detail it appears to resemble earlier Javan specimens in terms of postorbital constriction, lowness of the forehead, the size of the supraorbital region and the thickness of the vault bones.

Dimensions   *Calotte Lantian 2.*
Woo (1966)
Cranial capacity 778 cc (Pearson's formula)
775–783 (Tobias' partial endocast method)

Skull thickness

Glabella 24·0
Bregma 16·0
Squamous temporal 11·5

Mandible

(Woo, 1964, 1966)

No.	Height at Mental Foramen	Symphysial Height	Thickness at M1
Lantian 1	27·0	35·0	16·0

Affinities   The Lantian material was at first allocated to a new species of the genus *'Sinanthropus'*, *'Sinanthropus lantianensis'* (Woo, 1965). It seems likely, however, that most anthropologists will regard the new material as further evidence of *Homo erectus* from China (Wu, 1982, Wu and Olsen, 1985).

Originals   The Institute of Vertebrate Palaeontology and Palaeoanthropology, Academia Sinica, Beijing, People's Republic of China.

Casts   Not available as yet.

References

Mayr, E. (1950) Taxonomic categories in fossil hominids. *Cold Spring Harb. Symp. Quant. Biol.* 15, 109–118.

Kurtén, B. (1959) New evidence on the age of Pekin man. *Vert. Palasiat.* 3, 173–175.

Anon (1963) Lantian jaw. *Ill. Lond. News 243*, 742.

Woo, Ju Kang (1964) A newly discovered mandible of the Sinanthropus type—*Sinanthropus lantianensis*. *Scientia Sin.* 13, 891–911.

Woo, Ju Kang (1964) Mandible of *Sinanthropus lantianensis*. *Curr. Anthrop.* 5, 98–99.

Woo, Ju Kang (1965) Preliminary report on a skull of *Sinanthropus lantianensis*, of Lantian, Shensi. *Scienta Sin.* 14.

Woo, Ju Kang (1966) The Skull of Lantian Man. *Curr. Anthrop.* 7, 83–86.

Chia, L. P. (1966) In *Transactions of the Field Conference on the Cenzoic of Lantian, Shensi*, Peking, 151–154 (in Chinese).

Dai, E. J. (1966) The Palaeoliths found at Lantian Man locality of Gongwangling and its vicinity. *Verteb. Palasiat.* 10, 30–34.

Oakley, K. P., Campbell, B. G. and Molleson, T. I. (1975) *Catalogue of fossil hominids Part III: Americas, Asia, Australasia.* London: Trustees of the British Museum (Natural History).

Ma, X., Qian, F., Li, P. and Ju, s. (1978) Paleomagnetic dating of Lantian Man. *Vert. Palasiat.* 16, 238–244.

Cheng, G. *et al.* (1978) Dating of Lantian Man. Symp. Paleoanthrop. Beijing. *Sci. Press*, 151–157.

Wu, R. (1982) Recent Advances of Chinese Palaeoanthropology. *Occ. Pap. Ser. II.* Univ. Hong Kong.

Xu, Q. and You, Y. (1982) Four post-Nihowanian Pleistocene mammalian faunas of North China: Correlation with deep-sea sediments. *Acta Anthrop. Sin.* 1, 180–190.

Liu, T. and Ding, M. (1984) A tentative chronological correlation of early human fossil horizons in China with the loess-deep sea records. *Acta Anthrop. Sin.* 3, 93–101.

Wu, R. and Olsen, J. W. Eds. (1985) *Palaeoanthropology and Palaeolithic Archaeology in the People's Republic of China.* Orlando, Florida and London: Academic Press.

The Hexian Calvaria

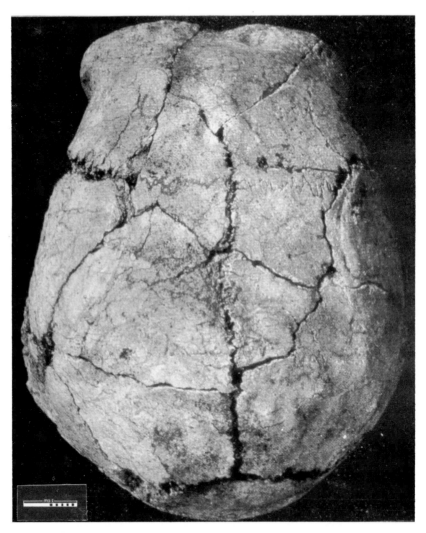

Fig. 123. The Hexian calvaria (vertical view). *Courtesy of Professor Wu Rukang (J. K. Woo).*

Synonyms and other names   *Homo erectus* (Wu and Dong, 1982); Hexian man.

Site
The Hexian fossil site is located on the north slope of Wangjiashan Hill, in the Taodian Commune of Hexian County, in the Province of Anhui, just to the north of the Yangzi River.

Found by
Calvaria, mandibular fragment and four teeth
Huang Wanpo and others from the staff of the Institute for Vertebrate Paleontology and Paleoanthropology, (IVPP), Beijing, 4 November, 1980.
Two cranial fragments and five teeth
Wu Maolin and others from the I.V.P.P., May/June 1981.

Geology
During the construction of a canal, at the side of Wangjiashan Hill which is about 100 m high, a cave was exposed containing fossil bones. Excavation of the site in October and November 1980 brought the remains to light. The fossils derived from a sandy clay that was yellowish brown in colour (Wu, 1985).

Associated finds
Associated with the *Homo erectus* remains were artefacts in the form of worked bones and horns (Jia Lanpo in Wu, 1982). In addition to the artefacts 47 species of associated mammalian fossils have been identified. The assemblage contains several members typical of the 'Ailuropoda—Stegodon' fauna widespread in southern China including the proboscidian (*Stegodon*), Chinese tapir (*Tapirus sinensis*) and the Chinese rhinoceros (*Rhinoceros sinensis*); in addition there are a number of northern members of the Zhoukoudian fauna such as a large beaver (*Trogontherium cuvieri*), large deer (*Megaloceros pachyosteus, Cervus grayi*), and some alpine forms such as shrews (*Anourosorex squamipes; Blarinella quadraticauda*). This would seem to indicate cooler moist conditions similar to those in the southern part of N. China today (Xu, 1984; Wu, 1985). Xu and You (1984) believe that the Hexian fauna could correlate with Layers 3–4 of Locality 1 at Zhoukoudian which produced Peking skull V.

Dating
On faunal grounds the site has been allocated to the Middle Pleistocene (Huang *et al.*, 1981).
Correlation of the Hexian fossil site with loessic and deep-sea data has suggested a date of 150,000–400,000 years B.P. for the site (Liu and Ding, 1984). If the faunal correlation with Zhoukoudian 3–4 published by Xu and You (1984) is correct, then their correlation with oxygen isotope Stage 8 would give an age of 240–280,000 years B.P., a result that may be more likely to be correct (Wu, 1985).

Morphology
Calvaria

The Hexian calvaria consists of frontal, parietal, occipital and temporal bones. It lacks some of the base but much is present, including

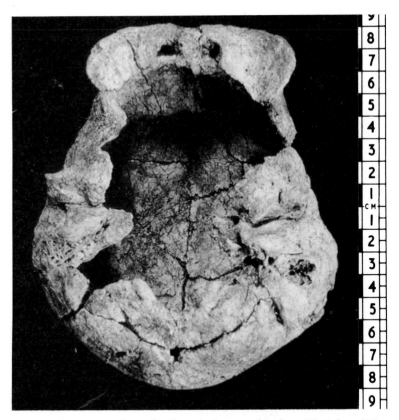

Fig. 124. The Hexian calvaria (basal view). *Courtesy of Professor Wu Rukang (J. K. Woo).*

part of the margin of the foramen magnum posteriorly. The calvaria is large and heavy with pronounced muscular ridges. It appears to be that of a young male since it is a robust calvaria with all its sutures open.

The cranial vault is low with a receding forehead and an ovoid shape. Its opisthion and its opisthocranion coincide. Its maximum breadth is low on the vault between the two supramastoid crests. There is a marked angular torus that is continuous with the supramastoid crest. The temporal squama are low but arched, the mastoid processes are broken but may have been relatively large. The supraorbital torus is heavy and continuous yet there is a slight glabella depression. The supratoral sulcus (ophryonic groove) is present but not as deep as in Peking Man. There is postorbital constriction but, again, not as much as in Peking Man. There is a frontal sagittal keel and a metopic suture that is not obliterated.

The occipital torus is well developed and there is a supratoral sulcus. The occipital bone is sharply angulated. The tympanic plate is thick and almost at right angles to the mid-sagittal line. Internally the Sylvian crest is well developed.

Mandible

The body of the mandible is robust and the crowns and the roots of the socketed teeth are large but M_2 is smaller than M_1.

Teeth

The isolated teeth are worn but some show secondary enamel wrinkling. The incisors are broad and spatulate, shovel-shaped and bear a basal tubercle. The lower molars have a dryopithecine cusp and fissure pattern and also bear a cingulum.

The other cranial fragments include part of the right side of a supraorbital torus and a parietal fragment. Thus there are present the remains of at least three individuals (Wu and Dong, 1982; Wu, 1982; Wu Maolin, 1983; Wu, 1985; Wu and Olsen, 1985).

Dimensions *Calvaria*

Wu and Dong (1982)

Maximum length 190

Maximum breadth 160

Cranial Index 84·2

Cranial Capacity ca. 1,025 cc.

Mandible

Body Thickness 20·7

Body Height 32·0

Robusticity 64·7

Teeth

	Side	M/D Length	B/L Breadth
PA 832 (PM²)	R	9·0	13·4
PA 833 (M²)	L	12·0	14·0
PA 834 (1) (M₁)	L	12·5	13·1
PA 834 (2) (M₂)		13·3	13·6
PA 831 (M₃)	L	11·3	10·7

Teeth

Wu Maolin (1983)

PA 836 (M¹)	—	12·3	13·7
PA 837 (M²)	—	12·5	15·5
PA 838 —	—	13·6	13·9
PA 839 —	—	14·3	13·4

Affinities From the anatomical evidence of the Hexian finds there is no doubt that they belong to *Homo erectus* (Wu and Dong, 1982). The calvaria and the other remains bear marked resemblances to those known from Beijing (*q.v.*). Nevertheless, there are certain advanced or progressive features that have been noted in this calvaria such as the reduced postorbital construction, and the high arched temporal squama by comparison with the Peking skulls. It seems to resemble the later forms of Peking man such as represented by Peking skull V. It is indeed an important find, not least because it is a fine example of *Homo erectus* from China, but also because all the other Peking calvaria have been lost and, because of that, the subject of controversy. The meticulous descriptions of Weidenreich, though never in serious doubt, can now be checked by detailed comparison with this new original specimen, work that is in progress.

Originals

The Institute of Vertebrate Paleontology, Beijing, People's Republic of China.

Casts

Not available at present.

References

Huang, W., Fang, D. and Ye, Y. (1981) Preliminary study on the fossil hominid skull and fauna of Hexian, Anhui. *Vert. Palasiat. 20*, 248–256.

Wu, R. (1982) Recent Advances of Chinese Palaeoanthropology. *Occ. Pap. Ser. II* Univ. Hong Kong.

Wu, R. and Dong, X. (1982) Preliminary study of *Homo erectus* remains from Hexian, Anhui. *Acta Anthrop. Sin. I*, 2–13.

Wu, M. (1983) *Homo erectus* from Hexian, Anhui found in 1981. *Acta Anthrop. Sin. II*, 110–115.

Liu, T. and Ding, M. (1984) A tentative chronological correlation of early human fossil horizons in China with the loess-deep sea records. *Acta Anthrop. Sin. 3*, 93–101.

Xu, Q. and You, Y. (1984) Hexian fauna: Correlation with deep-sea sediments. *Acta Anthrop. Sin. 3*, 62–67.

Wu, R. (1985) New Chinese *Homo erectus* and recent work at Zhoukoudian. In *Ancestors*, 245–248. Ed. E. Delson. New York: Alan R. Liss.

Wu, R. and Olsen, J. W. Eds. (1985) *Palaeoanthropology and Palaeolithic Archaeology in the People's Republic of China*. Orlando, Florida and London: Academic Press.

The Dali Cranium

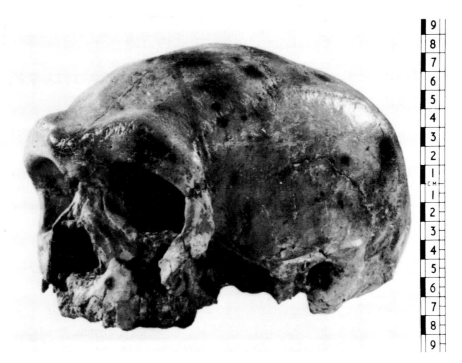

Fig. 125. The Dali cranium. *Courtesy of Professor Wu Rukang (J. K. Woo).*

Synonyms and other names	*Homo erectus* (Wang *et al.*, 1979); *Homo sapiens daliensis* (Wu, 1981); Dali man.
Site	From the village of Jiefang in the western part of Dali County, Shaanxi Province, People's Republic of China.
Found by	Liu Shuntang and others March, 1978.
Geology	The remains were found in a sandy gravel, that may be a secondary accumulation, above which were two palaeosols three metres and two metres thick in the third terrace of the Luo River, a secondary tributary of the Huanghe River. The fossiliferous layer was about one metre thick.
Associated finds	The site initially produced 180 stone tools, mostly small scrapers made from flint and quartzite. There was a small faunal assemblage in which two deer species featured of types slightly different from

those of Zhoudoudian Locality 1 and Dingchun. The large deer (*Megaceros*) was more like that known from Zhoukoudian, Locality 15; another deer (*Pseudaxis sp.*) was like that known from Zhoukoudian Localities 1 and 4 and also found at Dingchun. Other fossil mammals and a bird recovered included proboscidians (*Palaeoloxodon naumanni, Palaeoloxodon sp.*), a horse (*Equus sp.*), a bovid (*Bubalus sp.*), rhinoceros (*Rhinoceros sp.*), beaver (Castoridae) and ostrich (*Struthio anderssoni*) (Wu and You, 1979; Wu, 1981).

New excavations at Dali were made in 1980 and resulted in 384 new artefacts and some new mammalian fossils. In addition two new geological layers were found (Layers 4 and 5) containing cores and flakes as well as fossil remains such as horse (*Equus hemionus*) from Layer 5 and deer (*Cervus canadensis*) from Layer 4 (Zhang and Zhou, 1984).

Dating   From the faunal remains and on the basis of the deer between Zhoukoudian and the later Dingchun site a late Middle Pleistocene date seems most appropriate. Correlation of loessic stages and the oxygen isotope records of deep-sea cores suggests an age of 128,000–250,000 years B.P. for the Dali site (Liu and Ding, 1984). Zhang and Zhou (1984) correlate the Dali man site with Locality 15 at Zhoukoudian.

Morphology   *Cranium*

The Dali cranium is almost complete with only the right posterior portion of the vault and left zygomatic arch missing. The lower part of the face has been crushed upwards.

The cranium is quite large with robust supraorbital ridges, a receding frontal and prominent temporal lines. The sutures of the skull are all visible and it is estimated that the cranium belonged to a male of less than 30 years of age.

The frontal region shows strongly marked vermiculated superciliary ridges, brow ridges that are angulated and not continuous, a distinct frontal keel but no real parasagittal flattening. The mastoid processes are of moderate size. The vault shape from the rear is neither typically tented and erectus-like nor expanded and sapiens-like. The frontozygomatic suture is deeply notched. Despite the crushing of the maxilla the face is low and orthognathic. The occipital torus is modest and occupies half of the width of the cranium only. The occipital bone is angulated and there was an Inca bone present.

Internally the cranium shows a crista galli (absent in Peking man) and a well branched middle meningeal system similar to that known from Zhoukoudian V, one of the latest known Zhoukoudian skulls. The cranium has been described in some detail (Wu, 1981).

Dimensions   Wu (1981); Wu and Olsen, (1985)
Maximum length 207
Maximum breadth 149
Cranial Index 71·9
Cranial Capacity first estimate 1,120 cc
                second estimate 1,200 cc

                                    (Wu, Xinzhi, pers. comm.)

Affinities   After its initial allocation to *Homo erectus* (Wang, 1979) further study revealed a number of features that allied the cranium closer to *Homo sapiens*.

It possesses features of both *Homo erectus* from China as well as a number of more advanced sapient features. This mosaic has led to its allocation to a subspecies *Homo sapiens daliensis* (Wu, 1981).

It seems that this skull has a morphology that is clearly intermediate between *Homo erectus* from China and *Homo sapiens* from the same area and is evidence of evolutionary change of a gradual nature in a continental situation. It is another example of an erectus/sapiens transitional form such as the Ngandong skulls from Java (*q.v.*) and Omo II (*q.v.*) in East Africa.

Originals   Institute of Vertebrate Palaeontology, Beijing (Peking), People's Republic of China.

Casts   Not available as yet.

References   Wang, Y., Xue, X., Yue, L., Zhao, J. and Liu, S. (1979) Discovery of Dali fossil man and its preliminary study. *Sci. Sin.* 24, 303–306.

Wu, X. and You, Y.-Z. (1979) A preliminary observation of Dali man site. *Vert. Palasiat.* 17, 294–303.

Wu, X. (1981) A well-preserved cranium of an archaic type of early *Homo sapiens* from Dali, China. *Sci. Sin.* 241, 530–539.

Liu, T. and Ding, M. (1984) A tentative chronological correlation of early human fossil horizons in China with the loess-deep sea records. *Acta Anthrop. Sin.* 3, 93–101.

Zhang, S. and Zhou, C. (1984) A preliminary study of the second excavation of Dali Man Locality. *Acta Anthrop. Sin.* 3, 19–29.

Wu, R. and Olsen, J. W. Eds. (1985) *Palaeoanthropology and Palaeolithic Archaeology in the People's Republic of China*. Orlando, Florida and London: Academic Press.

The Maba Calotte

Fig. 126. The Maba calotte (right lateral view). *Courtesy of Professor Wu Rukang (J. K. Woo).*

Synonyms and other names	*Homo sapiens* (Wu and Olsen, 1985).
Site	Cave site, Shizi Hill, near Maba village, Shaoquan County, Guangdong Province.
Found by	Farm workers, June, 1958.
Geology	Cave deposits.
Associated finds	The fauna associated with the find was extensive and includes a number of large mammals including proboscidians (*Stegodon sp., Palaeoloxodon namadicus*), tapir (*Tapirus sp.*), rhinoceros (*Rhinoceros sp.*), pig (*Sus sp.*), deer (*Cervus sp.*) and a bovid (*Bos sp.*) (Woo and Peng, 1959).
Dating	The date of the find has been given as late Middle Pleistocene or early Late Pleistocene (Woo and Peng, 1959).
Morphology	The Maba calotte consists of part of the frontal, part of the right parietal, the nasal bones and part of the margin of the right orbit.

The vault is rounded with a modest keel on the frontal which recedes but the forehead is raised behind the brow ridge. The supraorbital torus is divided and angulated but damaged. The nasal bones are broad and angled forward (Wu, 1982).

Dimensions

Frontal chord	115·6	Parietal chord	107·0
Frontal arc	134·0	Parietal arc	114·0

Affinities Whilst the Maba calotte shares some features with *Homo erectus* it also carries some features of *Homo sapiens*. On this basis it is regarded as an early *Homo sapiens* skull of mongoloid type (Wu and Olsen, 1985).

Originals Institute of Vertebrate Palaeontology, Beijing, People's Republic of China.

Casts Not available at present.

References Woo, J.K. and Peng, R.C. (1959) Fossil human skull of Early Palaeoanthropic Stage found at Mapa, Shaoquan, Kwantung Province. *Vert. Palasiat. 3,* 176–182.

Wu, R. (1982) Recent Advances of Chinese Palaeoanthropology. *Occ. Pap. Ser. II* Univ. of Hong Kong.

Wu, R. and Olsen, J.W. Eds. (1985) *Palaeoanthropology and Palaeolithic Archaeology in the People's Republic of China.* Orlando, Florida and London: Academic Press.

Oceania

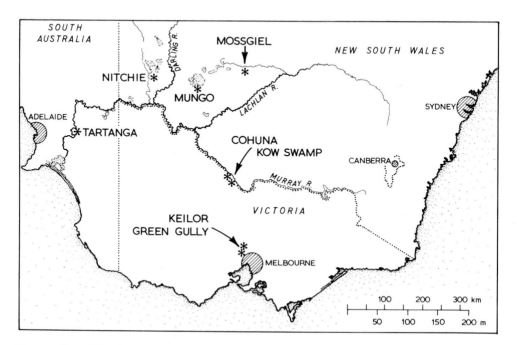

Fig. 127. Hominid fossil sites in Australia.

The Mungo Remains

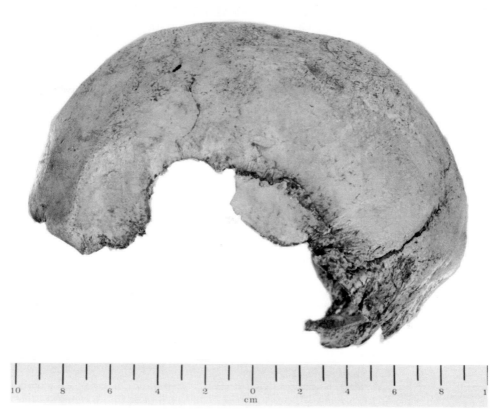

Fig. 128. The Mungo III calotte (left lateral view of a cast).

Synonyms and other names	*Homo sapiens.*
Site	Lake Mungo (now dry) is one of a series of extinct lakes which once formed a terminal drainage system on the Willandra Creek, a distributory stream from the Lachlan River in the Murray–Darling drainage system of western New South Wales.
Found by	*Mungo I and II* (WLH I and II). J. M. Bowler, 5 July, 1968; their human characters were confirmed in March 1969 by H. Allen, R. Jones, C. Ke̱ and D. J. Mulvaney and later confirmed by J. Calaby and A. G. Thorne.

Mungo III (WLH III)

J. M. Bowler, 26 February, 1974; excavated by W. F. Shawcross, S. N. Ragaguru, C. P. Groves, A. Carstairs and A. G. Thorne.

Geology   The lakes of the Willandra system were large in late Quaternary times covering 420 square miles. The lake basins form large level-floored depressions up to 80 feet. below the surrounding plain and have high sand and sandy-clay aeolian transverse dunes, known as lunettes, around their eastern margins. Lake Mungo is the central lake of the system and is bordered on the east by a high dune ridge, known as 'The Walls of China', which has been extensively eroded exposing the stratigraphy over large areas. Three aeolian units are present, from below upwards, the Golgol, Mungo and Zanci sedimentary units. The fragmented human remains were found in the Mungo unit at the south end of the 'Walls of China' lunette, cemented into a fragmented calcrete block (Bowler *et al.*, 1970)

Associated finds   Stone tools were found at the site, 27 *in situ* and some on the surface. Fifteen dark patches containing charcoal were also located in the vicinity; oval or circular and 2–3 feet in diameter they also contained burnt animal and fish bones, skulls and a few artefacts. They were identified as hearths. The tools were made of silcrete, 92 worked and 95 flakes, and derived from a known source some 10 miles to the southwest. They were categorized as 'scrapers' of varying sizes, the majority made from flakes, others were 'horse hoof cores' (Bowler, *et al*, 1970). Faunal remains associated with human occupation include shellfish (*Velesunio ambiguus*) in extensive middens, fish remains, mostly golden perch (*Plectroplites ambiguus*), bird bones and emu egg shell. Mammalian bones included those of rat kangaroo (*Bettongia lesueur*), brown hare wallaby (*Lagorchestes leporides*), western native cat (*Dasyurus geoffroii*), hairy nosed wombat (*Lasiorhinus gillespiei*) and, as a surface find at the site, the Tasmanian tiger (*Thylacinus cynocephalus*) (Bowler, *et al.*, 1970).

Dating   Radiocarbon dating of the site and of the Mungo I skeleton has established that the site was occupied by 32,000 years B.P. and that the Mungo I remains are dated between 24,500–26,500 years B.P. (Bowler *et al.*, 1970; Barbetti and Allen, 1972; Bowler *et al.*, 1972). The Mungo III skeleton has been estimated at between 28,000–32,000 years B.P. (Bowler and Thorne, 1976).

Morphology   Mungo I consists of the cremated remains of a young adult female that is represented by about 25 per cent of the total skeleton. The cranium was reconstructed from 175 fragments of vault and base, the face is not well preserved, much of it is missing or badly fragmented. The mandible is represented by two parts of the body and some ramal fragments. There are three isolated teeth without enamel.

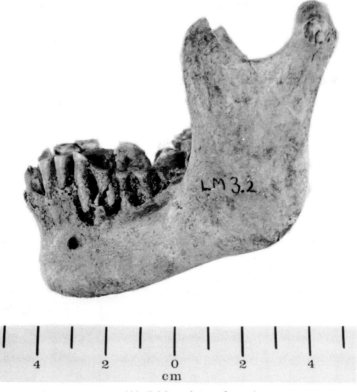

Fig. 129. The Mungo III mandible (left lateral view of a cast).

The postcranial skeleton is widely represented but extensively broken.

Reconstruction discloses that the Lake Mungo I skeleton represents a young female of small stature and gracile build with thin long bones that are not heavily marked by muscle attachments. The basicranium is broad, the vault has no parietal bossing or sagittal keeling. There is some frontal recession and marked postorbital constriction. The foramen ovale is single and the petrotympanic fissure does not lie in the floor of the glenoid fossa.

The Mungo II remains are fragmentary (Bowler *et al.*, 1970).

The Mungo III skeleton is that of an adult male of mature years who suffered from arthritis and dental disease with tooth loss and alveolar resorption. The skeleton is almost complete but was in a fragile state when excavated. There is evidence of red ochre in the staining of the surrounding soil. The general form of the skeleton is less robust than those of modern Australian aboriginals and compares in this with Mungo I (Bowler and Thorne, 1976).

Dimensions   *Mungo I* Thorne (1976)

Cranium

Maximum length (181)
Maximum breadth (130)
    (biparietal)
Cranial Index (71–82)

( ) Approximate

Affinities   The remains from Lake Mungo are of particular interest since they are the oldest dated human remains to be found in Australia. From the beginning, however, there has been little doubt that they are human and attributable to *Homo sapiens* with features that they share with other fossil and modern Australian Aboriginals (Bowler *et al.*, 1970; Thorne, 1971a, b; Bowler *et al.*, 1972; Thorne, 1972). Later analyses have not changed this early view that the Lake Mungo people were gracile in form and belonging to the species *Homo sapiens* (Bowler and Thorne, 1976; Thorne, 1976) yet metrical studies have suggested that a variety of morphological changes have taken place in the Australian (Aboriginal) cranium in the post Pleistocene period (Thorne and Wilson, 1977).

Originals   Australian National University, Canberra, Australia.

Casts   Department of Prehistory, Australian National University, Canberra, Australia.

References   Bowler, J. M., Jones, R., Allen, H. and Thorne, A. G. (1970) Pleistocene human remains from Australia: a living site and human cremation from Lake Mungo, western New South Wales. *Wld Archaeol. 2*, 39–60.

Thorne, A. G. (1971a) The racial affinities and originals of the Australian Aborigines. In *Aboriginal Man and Environment in Australia*, 316–325. Eds. D. J. Mulvaney and J. Golson. Canberra: Australian National University Press.

Thorne, A. G. (1971b) Mungo and Kow Swamp: morphological variation in Pleistocene Australians. *Mankind 8*, 85–89.

Barbetti, M. and Allen, H. (1972) Prehistoric man at Lake Mungo, Australia by 32,000 B.P. *Nature 240*, 46–48.

Bowler, J. M., Thorne, A. G. and Pollach, H. A. (1972) Pleistocene man in Australia: age and significance of the Mungo skeleton. *Nature 240*, 48–50.

Thorne, A. G. (1972) Recent discoveries of fossil man in Australia. *Australian Natural History*, 191–195.

Thorne, A. G. (1976) Morphological contrasts in Pleistocene Australians. In *The Origin of the Australians*, 95–112. Eds. R. L. Kirk and A. G. Thorne. Canberra: Australian Institute of Aboriginal Studies.

Bowler, J. M. and Thorne, A. G. (1976) Human remains from Lake Mungo: discovery and excavation of Lake Mungo III. *Ibid*, 127–138.

Thorne, A. G. and Wilson, S. R. (1977) Pleistocene and Recent Australians: A multivariate comparison. *J. hum. Evol. 6*, 393–402.

The Kow Swamp Remains

AUSTRALIA   VICTORIA

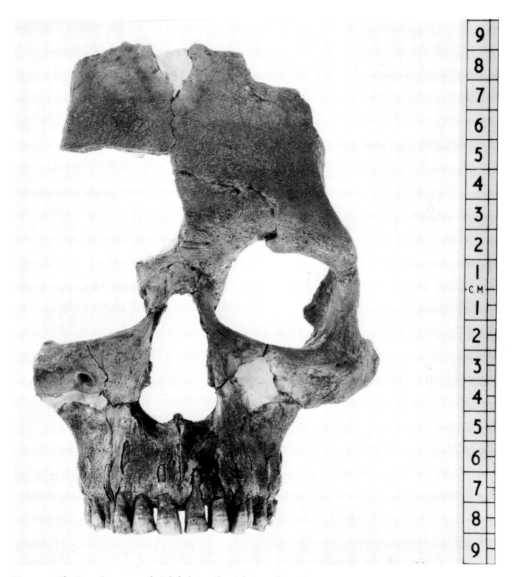

Fig. 130. The Kow Swamp 15 facial skeleton (frontal view of a cast).

Synonyms and other names   *Homo erectus* (Thorne and Macumber, 1972); *Homo sapiens* (Kennedy, 1984); KS–15.

Site   Kow Swamp is situated in northern Victoria within the drainage area of the Murray River system and its tributaries, fed by Gunbower Creek.

Found by   *Kow Swamp I*
A. G. Thorne 1967 in the National Museum of Victoria. In 1968 A. G. Thorne, and P. G. Macumber, recovered the rest of KSI from excavations at the northern end of the swamp.
Later about 40 individuals were located by Mr Gordon Sparks, a local resident. Fifteen of these skeletons are numbered and 11 are primary burials.

Geology   All the burial sites are around the margin of Kow Swamp that lies on the riverine plain in Victoria astride a major flow path of the ancestral Murray River system and its tributaries. The sites fall into two groups, those associated with an old Lake Kow shoreline (KS1–17) and burials in the levees of a former stream system. The Cohuna cranium, found in 1925, comes from the second group. Around the eastern edge of the swamp is a narrow belt of lacustrine silts (Cohuna Silt) in part overlain by the Kow Sand which forms a low crescentic dune (lunette) rising to a height of about four metres above the plain. Skeletal remains have been found in both the Cohuna Silt and the Kow Sand. The Cohuna Silt has produced parts of about 35 individuals from two distinct areas; twelve were recovered from undisturbed graves dug from the present, but eroded, surface. The silts are a shore-line lacustrine deposit on the eastern boundary of the former Lake Kow.
The Kow Sand lunette begins south of Taylor's Creek on the east side of the former Lake Kow and rises to about four metres in height. Skeletal material was recovered from two of three pits dug at random. One revealed the undisturbed KS9 skeleton at a depth of 1·4 m. This grave was deeper than when first dug since continuing dune accretion has occurred. The lunette partly overlies the Cohuna silt with no clear hiatus between the deposits.
The Cohuna Cranium site is near Kow Swamp on levees of the late Pleistocene Mead Stream. The Gunbower and Bourkes Bridge sites are in similar sediments near to Gunbower Creek (Thorne and Macumber, 1972; Thorne, 1972).

Associated finds   There were stone artefacts, ochre, shells and marsupial teeth in some of the graves. There was also evidence of cremation. All the buried objects were coated with carbonate (Thorne and Macumber, 1972).

Dating   Radiocarbon dating on charcoal and bone from the sites indicates that the Kow Swamp shoreline was inhabited from at least 13,000 years B.P. to 9,300 years B.P. (Thorne, 1976).

Morphology   *Crania*

The Kow Swamp crania are large and dolichocephalic with thick vault bone and a number of characters not seen in modern Aboriginal skulls. The most striking feature of several of the crania is marked frontal recession and flattening. A true supraorbital torus is claimed for five of the specimens with postorbital constriction. The occipital bones are stout and in some cases with a prominent occipital torus. The mastoid processes are large and the glenoid fossae wide and deep. The faces are broad and prognathic.

The Mandibles

The mandibles are very large with roughened massetric fossae and in two cases everted gonial angles. There are no mandibular tori and the mental foramina are single. The teeth are heavily worn with little or no enamel left on the crowns. Chronic periodontal disease is common (Thorne, 1971, Thorne and Macumber, 1972). Early doubts concerning the possibility of the extraordinary frontal recession and flattening being due to cultural 'head binding' or 'head pressing' were denied (Larnach, 1974; Thorne, 1976; Larnach, 1978). These doubts were reinforced by Brothwell (1975) and explored in some detail later. Following an extensive comparative study, involving a series of crania from Coobool Crossing that share some of the Kow Swamp features, and a Melanesian series of artificially deformed skulls (the Arawe) and those which were not deformed (Sepik River), it was concluded that KS5 and KS7 showed clear evidence of artificial deformation probably a result of 'head pressing' rather than 'head binding' as shown by the Arawe skulls (Brown, 1981).

Affinities   The initial assessment of the Kow Swamp remains suggested that the cranial features of this group were evidence of the survival of some *Homo erectus* characteristics in Australia until as recently as 10,000 years B.P. The possibility of cultural cranial deformation was not raised at this time (Thorne and Macumber, 1972). The demonstration of head deformation in this population as a cultural practice must modify, if it does not negate, this conclusion (Brown, 1981). It has been suggested that the discovery of the Indonesian *Homo erectus* skull Sangiran 17 (*q.v.*) reveals a group of features shared with the Kow Swamp remains that could indicate regional morphological continuity in Australasia during the Middle and Late Pleistocene (Thorne and Wolpoff, 1981).

A recent study of the femora from Kow Swamp revealed no primitive features and shows that the Kow Swamp femora have close morphometric relationships with samples of *Homo sapiens* femora (Kennedy, 1984). Whilst a final assessment must await the full

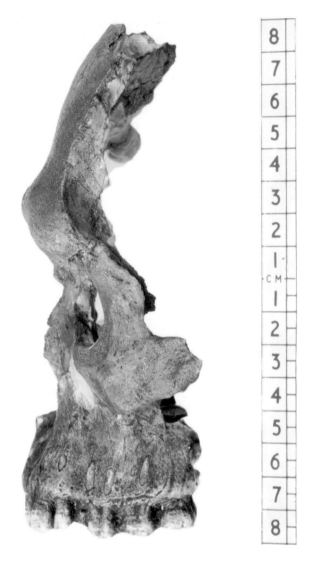

Fig. 131. The Kow Swamp 15 facial skeleton (left lateral view of a cast).

description of these remains it seems clear that cultural deformation of at least some of the Kow Swamp crania has clouded the issues surrounding their taxonomic affinities.

Originals   National Museum of Victoria, Victoria, Australia.

Casts   As above.

References   Thorne, A. G. (1971) Mungo and Kow Swamp: morphological variation in Pleistocene Australians. *Mankind 8*, 85–89.
Thorne, A. G. (1972) Recent discoveries of fossil man in Australia. *Australian Natural History*, 191–195.

Thorne, A. G. and Macumber, P. G. (1972) Discoveries of Late Pleistocene Man at Kow Swamp, Australia. *Nature 238*, 316–319.

Larnach, S. L. (1974) Frontal recession and artificial deformation. *Archaeol. phys. Anthrop. Oceania 9*, 214–216.

Brothwell, D. R. (1975) Possible evidence of a cultural practice affecting head growth in some late Pleistocene East Asian and Australian population. *J. archaeol. Sci. 2*, 75–77.

Thorne, A. G. (1976) Morphological contrasts in Pleistocene Australians. In *The Origin of the Australians*, 95–112. Eds. R. L. Kirk and A. G. Thorne.

Thorne, A. G. and Wilson, S. R. (1976) Pleistocene and Recent Australians: A multivariate comparison. *J. hum. Evol. 6*, 393–402.

Larnach, S. L. (1978) Australian Aboriginal craniology. 2 vols. *Oceania Monogr, 21.*

Brown, P. (1981) Artificial cranial deformation; a component in the variation in Pleistocene Australian Aboriginal crania. *Archeol. Oceania 16*, 156–167.

Thorne, A. G. and Wolpoff, M. H. (1981) Regional continuity in Australasian Pleistocene hominid evolution. *Am. J. phys. Anthrop. 55*, 337–349.

Kennedy, G. E. (1984) Are the Kow Swamp hominids 'archaic'? *Am. J. phys. Anthrop. 65*, 163–168.

PART III
Essays on Fossil Man

The Australopithecine Problem

The discovery of the Taung skull (*q.v.*) just over 60 years ago provoked a widespread controversy because of the hominid features of the skull and the dentition. Those opposed to Dart's assessment regarded the hominid features as due to parallel evolution and of little significance. The specimen was also obviously juvenile. Such a small cranial capacity and superficially ape-like features in an infant seemed sure indication of a small adult brain size and grossly anthropoid features on the grounds of paedomorphosis. Subsequent finds proved Dart right and his opponents wrong. Perhaps the hominid form of the first permanent molar tooth should, in retrospect, have cautioned Dart's critics.

Between 1936 and 1949 Broom, who had supported Dart's opinion, discovered three new sites in the Transvaal—Sterkfontein, Kromdraai and Swartkrans (*q.v.*) from which, with the help of Robinson, he recovered a great deal of material including skulls, hundreds of teeth and a number of postcranial bones including a pelvis with bipedal features. Further north at Makapansgat (*q.v.*), Dart also obtained many new specimens from similar deposits.

Following the study of these remains it became clear that the material could be divided into two broad groups. They comprise the remains of a small generalized light-framed form represented from Taung, Sterkfontein and Makapansgat, and the remains of larger, more dentally specialized, robust creatures from Kromdraai and Swartkrans. The smaller form seemed to be derived from deposits that are earlier than those containing the larger form. The species represented by the smaller form was named *Australopithecus africanus*. There was, and is, less agreement about the classification and naming of the larger form. Broom believed that the Kromdraai remains represented a new australopithecine genus and species and named it *Paranthropus robustus*; later finds from Swartkrans were accepted as of the same genus but of a new species, *P. crassidens*.

Robinson (1954 *et seq.*) and Napier (1970) have adhered to the generic separation of the larger and smaller forms and Robinson (1972) suggested that all the more gracile australopithecine material should be placed within the genus *Homo*. This viewpoint is supported by Olson (1981). Other authorities regard the Transvaal material as representative of one genus *Australopithecus*, containing two species *A. africanus* and *A. robustus* (Tobias, 1980; White *et al.*, 1981). The 'single species hypothesis' of australopithecine taxonomy (Wolpoff, 1968, 1970, 1971; Wolpoff and Lovejoy, 1975) regarded all australopithecine material as belonging to one species, *A. africanus*, the large and the small specimens being male and female respectively. The viewpoint now commands little support.

The East African hominid remains from Olduvai (*q.v.*) and Koobi Fora (*q.v.*) have extended the range of the robust australopithecine in the form of specimens such as Olduvai Hominid 5, Koobi Fora KNM–ER 406, 729, 739, and 818. This group of East African robust australopithecines is widely regarded as a variant of the South African robust forms either at specific (*A. boisei*) or subspecific (*A. rob. boisei*) levels. The position of the gracile australopithecines in East Africa is much less clear, if indeed they are present at all as the species *A. africanus* in this region. The early hominids from Olduvai seem to belong to *A. boisei* or to *Homo habilis* as do those from Koobi Fora; on the other hand the early hominid remains from Laetoli (*q.v.*) have been attributed to *A. africanus* (Tobias, 1980). The presence of *A. africanus* at Koobi Fora is also a matter of doubt (Wood, 1985).

The recovery of the remarkable assemblage of hominid fossils from Hadar (*q.v.*) and the subsequent attribution of them all to a new species of australopithecine *Australopithecus afarensis* (Johanson *et al.*, 1978; Johanson and White, 1979) has proved to be a matter of intense debate (Tobias, 1980; White *et al.*, 1981; Olson, 1981, 1985; Logan *et al.*, 1983; Schmid, 1983; Ferguson, 1983, 1984; Zihlman, 1985; Johanson, 1985; Kimbel, 1985). Johanson and his colleagues maintain that all of the Hadar hominids as well as those from Laetoli belong to one species *A. afarensis*—the stem form for all australopithecines and indeed all later hominids. This stem form is seen to lead on the one hand to *A. africanus* and *A. robustus/boisei* and on the other to *Homo habilis*, *Homo erectus* and *Homo sapiens*. Tobias, however accommodates all of the Laetoli and Hadar material in an enlarged range of *A. africanus* which he sees as the true stem form that leads, after a divergence, to *A. robustus/boisei* and to the later hominids along separate lines.

Olson (1981, 1985) takes a third view, on basicranial and other evidence, that does not identify a stem form; he postulates a split at generic level with the Hadar material being of two species the more robust of which leads to *Paranthropus robustus/boisei* and the more gracile of which leads to *Homo africanus*, *H. habilis*, *H. erectus* and *H. sapiens*.

A fourth view, that of Coppens (1983), envisages a pre-australopithecine stage at Hadar and Laetoli that gave rise to three lines, one leading to the genus *Homo*, another to *A. africanus* and *A. robustus boisei* and a third that became extinct.

At the time of writing there is no clear resolution between these conflicting interpretations of australopithecine taxonomy, but there are some points that are in common between all of the phylogenetic schemes that are before us for evaluation. All agree that at about five m.y. B.P., or a little less, a single line of hominids that can be termed australopithecines were present in Africa; also that this line divided into two, or possibly three, branches and that of these branches one became extinct at about one m.y. B.P. This latter is of the robust forms. There is also unanimous agreement that one of the two or three lines eventually gave rise to the genus *Homo*. The differences between the schemes, whilst of intense interest to palaeoanthropologists, are, perhaps not as profound as they may appear.

The australopithecines represent, therefore, a pre-human phase of hominid evolution in which considerable advance was made in the development of the postcranial skeleton for upright bipedalism, in the modification of the dentition for an omnivorous diet whilst expansion of the brain proceeded but slowly. The principal event that took place during this phase of hominid evolution seems to have been a split in the evolving line that led to the development of a robust form which did not succeed and became extinct. Clearly this left the field open to the line that did succeed and led to the origin of our own genus, the genus *Homo*.

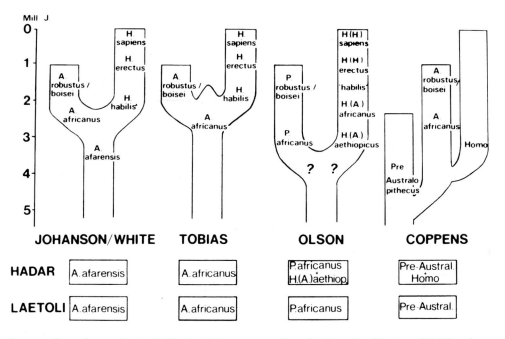

Fig. 132. Four schemes of australopithecine phylogeny currently under discussion. (Courtesy of G. Bräuer.)

There is one dissentient voice to this general conclusion. Oxnard (1975a, 1975b *et seq.*), on the grounds of metrical and statistical studies alone, claims that *Australopithecus* is 'uniquely different' and thus not in any way ancestral to the genus *Homo*. This view has been vigorously contested by drawing attention to the findings of comparative anatomy that are not vitiated by morphometrics alone (Howell *et al.*, 1978).

Additional References

Wolpoff, M. H. (1968) 'Telanthropus' and the single species hypothesis. *Am. Anthrop.* 70, 477–493.

Napier, J. R. (1970) *The Roots of Mankind.* Washington: Smithsonian Institution Press.

Wolpoff, M. H. (1970) The evidence for multiple hominid taxa at Swartkrans. *Am. Anthrop.* 72, 576–607.

Wolpoff, M. H. (1971) Competitive exclusion among Lower Pleistocene hominids: the single species hypothesis. *Man* 6, 601–614.

Oxnard, C. E. (1975a) The place of the australopithecines in human evolution: grounds for doubt? *Nature* 258, 389–395.

Oxnard, C. E. (1975b) *Uniqueness and Diversity in Human Evolution.* Chicago: Chicago University Press.

Wolpoff, M. H. and Lovejoy, C. O. (1975) A rediagnosis of the genus *Australopithecus. J. hum. Evol.* 4, 275–276.

Howell, F. C., Washburn, S. L. and Ciochon, R. L. (1978) Relationship of *Australopithecus* and *Homo. J. hum. Evol.* 7, 127–131.

Johanson, D. C. and White, T. D. (1979) A systematic assessment of early African hominids. *Science* 202, 321–330.

Tobias, P. V. (1980) '*Australopithecus afarensis*' and *A. africanus:* Critique and an alternative hypothesis. *Palaeont. afr. 23*, 1–17.

Olson, T. R. (1981) Basicranial morphology of the extant hominoids and Pliocene hominids: The new material from the Hadar Formation, Ethiopia, and its significance in early human evolution and taxonomy. In *Aspects of Human Evolution*, 99–128. Ed. C. B. Stringer. London: Taylor and Francis.

White, T. D., Johanson, D. C. and Kimbel, W. H. (1981) *Australopithecus africanus:* its phyletic position reconsidered. *S. Afr. J. sci. 77*, 445–470.

Coppens, Y. (1983) Les plus anciens fossiles d'Hominides. *Pontif. Acad. Scient. Scripta Varia 50*, 1–9.

Ferguson, W. W. (1983) An alternative interpretation of *Australopithecus afarensis* fossil material. *Primates 24*, 397–409.

Schmid, P. (1983) Einer Rekonstruktion des skelettes von A. L. 288–1 (Hadar) und deren Konsequenzen. *Folia Primatol. 40*, 283–306.

Kimbel, W. H., White, T. D. and Johnson, D. C. (1985) Craniodental morphology of the hominids from Hadar and Laetoli: Evidence of '*Paranthropus*' and *Homo* in the Mid-Pliocene of Eastern Africa. In *Ancestors*, 120–137. Ed. E. Delson. New York: Alan R. Liss.

Olson, T. R. (1985) Cranial morphology and systematics of the Hadar Formation hominids and '*Australopithecus*' *africanus. Ibid*, 102–119.

Johanson, D. C. (1985) The most primitive *Australopithecus*. In *Hominid Evolution: Past, Present and Future*, 203–212. Ed. P. V. Tobias. New York: Alan R. Liss.

Wood, B. (1985) A review of the definition, distribution and relationships of *Australopithecus africanus. Ibid*, 227–232.

Zihlman, A. L. (1985) *Australopithecus afarensis*: Two sexes or two species? *Ibid*, 213–220.

The Homo erectus *Problem*

Following the initial discoveries of specimens now attributed to *Homo erectus* in Java (Trinil *q.v.*: Sangiran *q.v.*), China (Zhoukoudian *q.v.*) and North Africa (Ternifine *q.v.*) a picture slowly emerged of a group of Asian and African hominines of the Lower to Middle Pleistocene period whose morphology and temporal ranges seemed to be fairly clearly defined. Their morphological characteristics, albeit almost exclusively cranial and dental, were outlined in the writings of Dubois and von Koenigswald and the classic monographs of Black (1931), Weidenreich (1936, 1937, 1941 and 1943) and Arambourg (1963); monographs that are still the foundation studies of this group of fossil men. Since that time the picture has changed radically with new finds attributed to *Homo erectus* from East Africa (Olduvai *q.v.*; Koobi Fora *q.v.*; West Turkana *q.v.*), North Africa (Salé *q.v.*) and Europe (Bilzingsleben *q.v.*). More controversially other remains, both long known and relatively recent finds, from Mauer (*q.v.*), Vértesszöllös (*q.v.*), Arago (*q.v.*) and Petralona (*q.v.*) have been entered into the discussion. A detailed review of much of the material has been given by Howells (1980). No longer is *Homo erectus* a clearly defined taxon temporally, morphologically or even geographically.

Debate centres around almost all of the following topics. Does *Homo erectus* exist as a true taxon or should it be sunk into *Homo sapiens*? Is it a palaeospecies that exists, in classical form, as a segment of the line that emerged from *Homo habilis* and gave rise to *Homo sapiens*? Is *Homo erectus* an extinct form that had no part to play in the evolution of *Homo sapiens*? Is *Homo erectus* a good example of a 'stasis event' in hominine evolution with little or no evolutionary change in its form during its existence? Is there a clear cut example of *Homo erectus* in the European fossil record of man? Finally, are the Asian forms so far removed from the evolution of *Homo sapiens* in Africa to call into question the existence of *Homo erectus sensu stricto* in Africa at all? In addition there are the usual problems that relate to the accuracy of the dating of the sites involved both in relation to each other and to the time scale of the Pleistocene period. All these are profound questions that are answered in differing ways by various authors.

In this situation the question of the definition of *Homo erectus* as a taxon must arise. What are the morphological characteristics of *Homo erectus* that can provide some basis upon which to make a differential diagnosis? The early descriptions of what is now widely known as *Homo erectus* were based on the material known from Java (*Pithecanthropus*), China (*Sinanthropus*) and North Africa (*Atlanthropus*). These descriptions and others of later material from East Africa include the following features that epitomize a *Homo erectus* skeleton: a low and long cranial vault with flattened frontal and parietal bones, an angulated occiput, a strongly marked and continuous supraorbital torus, a small mastoid process with a marked supramastoid crest and a torus angularis on the parietal bone. The vault also shows a frontal and parietal sagittal keel with parasagittal flattenings, a 'tent-shaped' coronal section, a low maximum skull breadth between the supramastoid crests as well as a low triangular squamous portion of the temporal bone.

The vault bones are thick, there is pronounced postorbital constriction and the inion and the opisthocranion coincide. The cranial capacity is between 700–1225 cc.

The face is less well known but it is prognathic with a large interorbital breadth and broad nasal bones. The mandible has no chin, a narrow but rounded dental arcade, thickening of the mandibular body, a large bicondylar breadth and in many cases multiple mental foramina. The teeth are of variable size but are in general robust with shovel-shaped incisors and basal tubercles. Molars and premolars have a cingulum and the molars have a dryopithecine cusp pattern that has a tendency to transformation to the 'plus' pattern by metaconid reduction. The third molar is often reduced in size whilst the permanent molars, premolars and milk molars show some degree of tauro-dontism.

The postcranial bones were poorly represented at first but later finds have improved the sample. The femora are unusual in the great thickness of the cortical bone, they are platymeric, have a low narrow point and a prominent convexity of the medial border of the shaft. The pelvic morphology is also distinctive in having a large aceta-bulum, a stout acetabulocristal buttress and medially rotated ischial tuberosities. The recognition of this femoropelvic complex of features (Weidenreich, 1941; Day, 1971) has disposed of the view held earlier that *Homo erectus* was essentially sapient in its postcranial features.

This general description includes many features referred to by others who have attempted a definition of the species *Homo erectus* (Weidenreich, 1943; Le Gros Clark, 1964; Howell, 1978; Howells, 1980; Day and Stringer, 1982; Rightmire, 1984; Strin-ger, 1984; Wood, 1984) but no attempt has been made here to distinguish between characters of common inheritance and new or derived features unique to *Homo erectus* (autapomorphic features). Those who have sought such unique features have not been too successful (Wood, 1984; Andrews, 1984; Hublin, 1986; Bilsborough and Wood, 1986). The derived features that are usable for a diagnosis of the taxon are very few and their apparent concentration in the Asian specimens has led to doubts about the existence of *Homo erectus* from African sites (Andrews, 1984); these doubts are not entirely shared by Bilsborough and Wood (1986). Hublin goes even further and sug-gests that from a purely cladistic point of view *Homo erectus* does not exist as a taxon, but as a grade it can be defined by features primitive to *Homo sapiens* particularly if evolutionary stasis has occurred. This agrees (perhaps for different reasons) with the view taken earlier by Jelinek (1978, 1981) and Thoma (1973) who argue that *Homo erectus* should be sunk as a taxon into *Homo sapiens*.

A more widely held view sees *Homo erectus* as a palaeospecies or chronospecies that will show evidence of evolution through time from a more primitive ancestor, such as *Homo habilis*, to a more advanced successor such as *Homo sapiens* (Le Gros Clark, 1964; Campbell, 1972; Wolpoff, 1980, 1984; Howells, 1981; Day, 1984).

The question of evolutionary rates, of the punctualist versus the gradualist models, in the hominine fossil record has been raised in relation to *Homo erectus* by those who support the punctuational model (Gould and Eldredge, 1977; Stanley, 1979, 1981; Eldredge and Tattersall, 1982). *Homo erectus* is seen by these authors as a 'true' taxon that did not vary greatly in form during its existence. Some evidence has also been presented for this view from the postcranial skeleton (Kennedy, 1983 (but see Trinkaus,

1984); Day, 1982). Wolpoff (1980, 1984) contends that significant evolution within the taxon can be determined by the examination of cranial, dental and mandibular features. The full description and analysis of the new find from West Turkana will do much to underpin, or otherwise, the contention that *Homo erectus* was in existence from as early as 1·6 m.y. B.P. at that site and lasted until perhaps as recently as 0·3 m.y. B.P. at other sites in both Africa and Asia—a span of more than 1·0 m.y.

The existence of a 'true' example of *Homo erectus* in Europe is another question of debate; denied by Howell (1981, 1982) and not accepted by Stringer (1981) it has been accepted by Wolpoff (1975, 1977) and Vlček (1978, 1983a, 1983b) for fossils such as those from Mauer, Vértesszöllös, Petralona and Bilzingsleben. Rightmire (1980, 1984), however, also holds the view that *Homo erectus* is a 'real' species morphologically distinct from modern humans and that there is no need to define this extinct species of man arbitrarily by reference to chronology or gaps in the fossil record.

The erectus/sapiens transition has also been examined in relation to the Omo I and Omo II skulls from Ethiopia (Day and Stringer, 1982) who conclude that these two, supposedly contemporaneous, skulls can be aligned with modern *Homo sapiens* and *Homo erectus* respectively, or Omo II included in an 'archaic' *Homo sapiens* group that displays a suite of mosaic or intermediate characters.

It is clear, therefore, that the taxon *Homo erectus* is under intense debate in terms of its geographic range, its temporal range, its origin and its evolutionary fate. It is also the subject of discussion in relation to the evolutionary models of punctuation and gradualism as well as the taxonomic approaches of the cladists and the gradists. As in most debates that are pursued with great vigour and determination it is possible, indeed probable, that the truth will lie in part with all the contenders. Only time and research will provide the answers.

Additional References

Campbell, B.G. (1972) Conceptual progress in physical anthropology: fossil man. *Ann. Rev. anthrop. 1*, 27–54.

Thoma A. (1973) New evidence for the polycentric evolution of *Homo sapiens. J. hum. Evol. 2*, 529–536.

Jaeger, J.-J. (1975) The mammalian faunas and hominid fossils of the Middle Pleistocene of the Mahgreb. In *After the Australopithecines*, 399–418. Eds. K.W. Butzer and G.Ll. Isaac. The Hague: Mouton.

Gould, S.J. and Eldridge, N. (1977) Punctuated equilibria: the tempo and mode of evolution considered. *Paleobiol. 3*, 115–151.

Howell, F.C. (1978) Hominidae. In *Evolution of African Mammals*, 154–248. Eds. V.J. Maglio and H.B.S. Cooke. Cambridge, Mass: Harvard University Press.

Jelinek, J. (1978) *Homo erectus* or *Homo sapiens*? In *Recent advances in Primatology*, 419–429. Eds. D.J. Chivers and K.A. Joysey. London: Academic Press.

Stanley, S.M. (1979) *Macroevolution: Pattern and Process*. San Francisco: W.H. Freeman.

Rightmire, G.P. (1980) Middle Pleistocene hominids from Olduvai Gorge, Northern Tanzania. *Am. J. phys. Anthrop. 53*, 225–241.

Wolpoff, M.H. (1980) *Paleoanthropology*. New York: Knopf.

Jelinek, J. (1981) ed. *Homo erectus and his time*. Vol. II. Anthrop Inst. Brno.

Stanley, S.M. (1981) *The new evolutionary timetable*. New York: Basic Books.

Stringer, C.B. (1981) The dating of European Middle Pleistocene hominids and the existence of *Homo erectus* in Europe. *Anthropologie XIX*, 3–14.

Day, M.H. and Stringer, C.B. (1982) A reconsideration of the Omo Kibish remains and the *erectus-sapiens* transition. *Prem. Congr. Internat. Paléont. hum. Nice* Prètirage, 814–846.

Eldredge, N. and Tattersall, I. (1982) *The Myths of Human Evolution*. New York: Columbia University Press.

Kennedy, G. (1983) A morphometric and taxonomic assessment of a hominine femur from the Lower member, Koobi Fora, Lake Turkana. *Am. J. phys. Anthrop.* 61, 429–436.

Trinkaus, E. (1984) Western Asia. In *The Origins of Modern Humans*, 251–292. Eds. F.H. Smith and F. Spencer. New York: Alan R. Liss.

Wolpoff, M.H. (1984) Evolution in *Homo erectus*: the question of stasis. *Paleobiol.* 10, 389–406.

Wood, B.A. (1984) The origin of *Homo erectus*. *Cour. Forsch. Inst. Senckenberg* 69, 99–111.

Bilsborough, A. and Wood, B.A. (1986) The nature, origin and fate of *Homo erectus*. In *Major Topics in Primate and Human Evolution*, 295–316. Eds. B. Wood, L. Martin and P. Andrews. Cambridge, Cambridge University Press.

Hublin, J.-J. (1986) Some comments on the diagnostic features of *Homo erectus*. Spec. Vol. in honour of Jan Jelinek, *Anthropos* (Brno) 23, 175–187.

The Neandertal Problem

From the first recognition of Neandertal man in 1856 his precise evolutionary position has been a source of debate, and the discussion still continues. One of the long-standing puzzles has been their supposed sudden disappearance from the fossil record: their origins and their relationship to a group that has come to be known as anatomically modern man (a.m. *Homo sapiens sapiens*) have been equally difficult problems.

So called 'classic' Neandertalers were first known from European sites and were associated with the Mousterian culture. Their sudden or 'catastrophic' disappearance has been variously attributed to epidemics, conflicts with more advanced peoples, changes in the climate, or to their absorption into the gene pool of incoming migratory peoples. If the Neandertalers did disappear suddenly, and the idea has been seriously questioned (Brace, 1964), there seems no imperative reason to look for a single cause; a combination of circumstances seems possible, even reasonable.

The number of Neandertal fossils from Europe and the Near East has grown remarkably and now includes several hundred specimens. Sites such as Krapina (*q.v.*), Amud (*q.v.*) and Shanidar (*q.v.*) have added enormously to the sample known from the classic sites such as Neandertal (*q.v.*), La Chapelle-aux-Saints (*q.v.*), and La Ferrassie (*q.v.*). The new site of St Césaire (*q.v.*) has revealed a Neandertal burial with a Châtelperronian industry that seems to be of the most recent Neandertaler yet known, at about 30,000–35,000 years B.P.

Clearly the question of the use and definition of terms is of crucial importance when a group such as Neandertal man is being discussed. Hrdlicka (1930) took a cultural view stating that Neandertal man and his period was 'the man and period of the Neandertal culture'. Brace (1964) added a morphological dimension to this later by stating that Neandertalers were 'the men of the Mousterian culture prior to the reduction in size and form of the Middle Pleistocene face'. The dangers of associating hominid categories with cultural traditions, however, have now been exposed by finds such as St Césaire and Jebel Qafzeh (*q.v.*).

Morphological definitions given in the past by Boule and Vallois (1957), Thoma (1965), Le Gros Clark (1966), and Vandermeersch (1972) would limit the term Neandertal to Western European examples of 'classic' morphology. Brose and Wolpoff (1971), however, gave a temporal and morphological definition that included 'all hominid specimens from the end of the Riss to the appearance of a.m. *Homo sapiens.*' This view has been criticized by Howells (1974) and Stringer (1974). Howells used the term 'Neandertal' to include only European 'classic' Neandertal sites plus Tabūn, Shanidar and Amud. He excluded Skhūl (*q.v.*), Jebel Qafzeh (*q.v.*), Jebel Ighoud (*q.v.*) and Petralona (*q.v.*) as well as sub-Saharan finds such as Kabwe (*q.v.*) and those from the Far East such as Ngandong (*q.v.*). In general this view was shared by Stringer (1974) and has become widely accepted.

Trinkaus (1983) defined the Neandertals in general terms as 'a group of Archaic *Homo sapiens* from Europe and western Asia who lived from the end of the last interglacial to the middle of the last glacial and shared a set of morphological characteristics that have traditionally been called "classic Neandertal"'. Lists of these morphological characteristics have been given by Vandermeersch (1972), Heim (1978), Le Gros Clark and Campbell (1978) and Stringer, Hublin and Vandermeersch (1984). These can be epitomized as follows:

1. An inflated skull form with its maximum transverse diameter mid-parietal, a low frontal bone, a suprainiac fossa as well as an occipitomastoid crest. The face is large with voluminous orbits and nasal cavities; the skull is also extensively pneumatized. The mid-face is prognathic showing a retromolar space and the supraorbital torus is divided centrally. There is no chin and the teeth are frequently taurodont. Postcranially the distal limb segments are short with large extremities, the scapula has a dorsal axillary groove and the superior pubic ramus is flat and elongate. In general the skeleton provides evidence of a short, thick-set, muscular individual with large hands and feet and a body form not unlike that of cold-adapted modern man.

2. Some of the features mentioned above share a common inheritance with earlier forms such as *Homo erectus*; others are new characters that are shared between contemporary hominids which, on this basis, can be defined as Neandertal. In the interpretation of Neandertal body form in relation to the environment, however, all of the information is of importance and its combination of features is of taxonomic significance.

3. The history of the Neandertals and their evolutionary position has been given recently (Spencer, 1984). The story is revealing in showing how discoveries and events have influenced the views of scholars over the years. In general terms the phylogeny of Neandertal man can be summarized in three ways at present, the *Neandertal Phase of Man Hypothesis*, the *Preneandertal Hypothesis* and the *Presapiens Hypothesis*. The first two of these are widely held whilst the third is less well supported and is losing ground.

The Neandertal Phase of Man Hypothesis

This view is unilinear and gradualist. It sees the Neandertalers as arising from a Middle Pleistocene predecessor by successive evolution and passing through a Neandertal phase to become modern man. This suggestion was first made by Schwalbe (1904) who saw the Neandertalers as a separate species intermediate between ape and man. Later supporters of this hypothesis (although not quite in the same terms) included Hrdlička (1930) and Weidenreich (1943, 1949). After a period when other views prevailed, a new impetus was given to this theory. Brace (1964 et seq. to Brace *et al.*, 1984) suggested that dental and masticatory evolutionary changes were brought about by tool use which led in turn to cranial morphological changes from Neandertal to modern sapient forms. Others who accept this general hypothesis include Brose and Wolpoff (1971), Wolpoff, (1980), Frayer (1978, 1984) and Smith and Ranyard (1980). In central and eastern Europe Smith also sees local continuity and change between Neandertal and later modern sapiens (Smith, 1982, 1984); he discounts the other two current hypotheses and regards the Neandertalers as reasonable candidates for the ancestors of modern Europeans.

The Preneandertal Hypothesis

This view suggests that the Neandertals arose from a 'Preneandertal' stock that became progressively specialized for resisting cold, underwent severe natural selection and restricted gene flow that led to 'classic' Neandertal isolates exemplified by La Chapelle, La Ferrassie, Neandertal and many others. This specialized Neandertal offshoot represents a group sharing new traits of subspecific taxonomic value. Supporters of this approach include Sergi (1953), Howell (1957), Breitinger (1957), Le Gros Clark (1966), Howells (1975), Hublin (1978), Santa Luca (1978), Stringer (1974, 1978), Trinkaus and Howells (1979), Stringer and Trinkaus (1981). The most recent supporters of the bilinear approach often see that the 'parent' line may have developed outside Europe, and at present Africa is the best candidate for the origin of the Preneandertal line on the basis of early examples of *Homo sapiens* known from Omo (*q.v.*), Laetoli (*q.v.*) and Border Cave (*q.v.*) (Bräuer, 1984a & b, Stringer, Hublin and Vandermeersch, 1984).

The Presapiens Hypothesis

This view holds that a European modern sapient lineage, as exemplified by Swanscombe (*q.v.*) and Steinheim (*q.v.*), existed quite separately from the Neandertals and ultimately gave rise to modern Europeans. The Neandertals then became extinct at the end of the Early Würm Glaciation. The hypothesis originated with Boule (1911/13, 1923) and was taken on by his successor Vallois (1954) as well as others including Weiner (1958), Thoma (1965), Leakey (1972), Vlček (1978) and Saban (1982). Gradually it has become apparent, however, that the Swanscombe and Steinheim skulls also possess Neandertal traits and are no longer widely acceptable as 'anatomically modern' and separate as a lineage (Stringer, 1974; Hublin, 1982; Bräuer, 1984a; Smith, 1984).

These three views of the origins of a.m. *Homo sapiens sapiens* are clearly a simplification—perhaps an oversimplification (Spencer, 1984)—of the various theoretical approaches that have been put forward by the authors cited, but they provide a framework within which to consider the phylogeny of this phase of human evolution.

Additional References

Schwalbe, G. (1904) *Die Vorgeschichte des Menschen*. Braunschweig: Friedrich Vieweg und Sohn.

Boule, M. (1923) '*Les Hommes Fossiles: Elements de Paléontologie Humaine*', 2nd ed. Paris: Masson et Cie.

Weidenrich, F. (1943) The 'Neanderthal Man' and the ancestors of '*Homo sapiens*'. *Am. Anthrop.* 42, 375–383.

Weidenrich, F. (1949) Interpretations of the fossil material. In *Ideas on Human Evolution*. Ed. W. W. Howells 1962. Cambridge, Mass.: Harvard University Press.

Sergi, S. (1953) Morphological position of the 'Prophaneranthropi' (Swanscombe and Fontéchevade). *R. C. Acad. Lincei* 14, 601–608.

Breitinger, E. (1957) On the phyletic evolution of *Homo sapiens*. In *Ideas on Human Evolution*. Ed. W. W. Howells 1962. Cambridge, Mass.: Harvard University Press.

Howell, F.C. (1957) The evolutionary significance of variations and varieties of 'Neanderthal' man. *Quart. Rev. Biol.* 32, 330–347.

Brace, C.L. (1964) The fate of the 'Classic' Neanderthals: a consideration of hominid catastrophism. *Curr. Anthrop.* 5, 3–43.

Thoma, A. (1965) La définition des Néandertaliens et la position des hommes fossiles de Palestine. *Anthropologie 69*, 5–6; 519–534.

Leakey, L. S. B. (1972) *Homo sapiens* in the Middle Pleistocene and the evidence of *Homo sapiens'* evolution. In *The Origin of Homo sapiens*, 25–29. Ed. F. Bordes. Paris: UNESCO.

Vandermeersch, B. (1972) Recentes découvertes de squelettes humains à Qafzeh (Israël): essai d'interpretation. In *The Origin of Homo sapiens*. Ed. F. Bordes. UNESCO (INQUA): Proc. Paris Symp.

Frayer, D. W. (1978) Evolution of the dentition in upper paleolithic and mesolithic Europe. *Univ. of Kansas Publ. Anthrop. 10*, 1–201.

Heim, J.-L. (1978) Le problème de l'Homme de Néandertal. Contribution du massif facial à la morphogenèse du crâne néandertalien. In *Les Origines humaines et les Epoques de l'Intelligence* Fondation Singer-Polignac, 183–215. Paris: Masson.

Hublin, J.-J. (1978) Quelques caractères apomorphes du crâne néandertalien et leur interprétation phylogénétique. *C.r. Acad. Sci. Paris 287*, 923–926.

Trinkaus, E. and Howells, W. W. (1979) The Neanderthals. *Scient. Am. 241*, 118–133.

Smith, F. H. and Ranyard, G. C. (1980) Evolution of the supraorbital region in Upper Pleistocene fossil hominids from South-Central Europe. *Am. J. phys. Anthrop. 53*, 589–609.

Hublin, J.-J. (1982) Les Anténéandertaliens: Présapiens ou Prénéandertaliens. *Geobios* mem. spec. 6, 345–357.

Saban, R. (1982) Les empreintes endocrâniennes des veines méningées moyennes et les étapes de l'évolution humaine. *Ann. paléont. 68*, 171–120.

Bräuer, G. (1984a) The 'Afro-European *sapiens*-hypothesis', and hominid evolution in East Asia during the late Middle and Upper Pleistocene. *Cour. Forsch. Senckenberg 69*, 145–165.

Bräuer, G. (1984b) A craniological approach to the origin of anatomically modern *Homo sapiens* in Africa and implications for the appearance of modern Europeans. In *The Origins of Modern Humans*, 327–410.

Brace, C. L., Shao, X. and Zhang, Z. (1984) Prehistoric and modern tooth size in China. In *The Origins of Modern Humans*, 485–516. Eds. F. H. Smith and F. Spencer. New York: Alan R. Liss.

Frayer, D. W. (1984) Biological and cultural change in the European Late Pleistocene and Early Holocene. In *The Origins of Modern Humans*, 211–250. Eds. F. H. Smith and F. Spencer. New York: Alan R. Liss.

Vandermeersch, B. (1985) The Origin of the Neandertals. In *Ancestors*, 306–309. Ed. E. Delson. New York: Alan R. Liss.

Glossary

Acetabulocristal Buttress   A thickening of the hip bone between the hip socket (acetabulum) and the iliac crest seen in bipedal hominids.

Acheulean   A stone tool culture characterized by distinctive pointed or almond-shaped hand-axes. Type site, St Acheul, Amiens (Somme), Northern France.

Alveolar Prognathism   Forward projection of the portions of the jaws that bear teeth.

Aminoacid Racemization Method   A dating method that depends upon the detection of residual aminoacids in fossil bone.

Angle of the Cranial Base   The angle between the basi-occiput and the body of the sphenoid.

Apomorph   (*n.*), -ous, -ic (*adj.*) A new morphological feature that has appeared in an evolving lineage that may signify a point of divergence.

Appendicular Skeleton   The bones of the limbs and the limb girdles.

Artefacts (Artifacts)   Man-made objects.

Artesian Water   Ground water contained under pressure.

Artiodactyla   The zoological name given to an order of ungulates. The 'even-toed' ungulates, e.g. deer, antelopes, gazelle, buffalo, pigs, oxen, sheep and goats.

Asterion   A point on the skull at which the lambdoid, parietomastoid and occipital sutures meet.

Atlanthropus   The generic name given to a group of North African Middle Pleistocene hominids. After the Atlas range of mountains, North Africa.

Aurignacian   A culture of stone, bone and antler which includes flint side and end scrapers, spear tips and blades. The bone implements include awls and spear points. The culture is associated with the Cro-Magnon people. Type site; Aurignac, Haute Garonne, France.

Australopithecinae   The zoological sub-family which contains the fossil 'ape-men', 'man-apes' and 'near men'.

Australopithecine   (*n.*) A member of the zoological sub-family Australopithecinae. (*adj.*) Pertaining to the zoological sub-family Australopithecinae.

Australopithecus   The generic name given to a group of South and East African Lower Pleistocene hominids. 'Southern ape.'

Autapomorph   (*n.*), -ous, -ic (*adj.*) A new morphological feature confined to one group in an evolving lineage.

Axial Skeleton   The skull, vertebral column and thorax.

b   Breadth.

Basalt   Fine-grained extrusive igneous rock of dark colour, low in silica.

Bentonitic Clay   A clay formed from decomposed volcanic ash.

Bicuspid   (*n.*) A premolar tooth. (*adj.*) Two-cusped.

Bipedal Gait   Two-legged walking.

B.P.   Before present.

Brachycephalic   Having a Cranial Index above 80. 'Broad-headed.'

Breccia   Sedimentary rock composed of angular fragments of derived material embedded in a finer cement.

Bregma   The point at which the coronal and sagittal sutures of the skull meet.

Burin   An Upper Palaeolithic chisel-like stone tool suitable for engraving bone, wood, horn or soft stone.

Caenozoic (Cenozoic)   See geological time scale.

Calcite   The stable crystalline form of calcium carbonate at normal temperatures, hence the commonest mineral form of limestone.

Calcrete   Desert soil cemented with calcium carbonate.

Calotte   The bones of the cranial vault.

Calvaria   A skull which has lost the bones of the face including the mandible.

Cambrian   See geological time scale.

Carabelli's Cusp   An accessory cusp on the lingual surface of the crown of an upper molar tooth.

Carabelli's Pit and Grooves   Features found on the lingual surface of the crown of an upper molar tooth.

Carapace   An external shell.

Carbonatite   An originally molten rock of the crust or upper mantle consisting of calcium carbonate, magnesium carbonate and, rarely, strontium carbonate as well as rare earth minerals.

Catarrhine Monkeys   A sub-group of the order Primates which includes monkeys from Africa and Asia. 'Old-world monkeys.'

Chalcedony   A crystalline variety of silica.

Châtelperronian   An early phase of the Perigordian (*q.v.*).

Chert   A siliceous rock found in limestone of which flint is an example.

Chignon   An occipital 'bun-like' protuberance of the skull characteristic of the Neandertalers of the Fourth Glaciation.

Cingulum   A collar-like ridge of enamel around the base of the crown of a tooth.

Clactonian   A primitive flake culture found in Europe which includes concave scrapers, cores and some flakes with retouched edges. Type site, Clacton-on-Sea, Essex.

Cladistics   A system of taxonomy that seeks to determine evolutionary relationships by the identification of points of divergence in evolutionary lineages.

Cladogram   A diagram that seeks to codify the conclusions of a cladistic analysis,

Conglomerate   Sedimentary rock composed of rounded pebbles of older rocks embedded in a younger cement, e.g. puddingstone.

Cranial Index $\dfrac{\text{Max. Cranial Breadth}}{\text{Max. Cranial Length}} \times 100$

Cranium   That part of the skull forming the brain-case.

Crassidens   The specific name given to a group of South African hominids known from Swartkrans. 'Big-toothed'.

Cyphanthropus   The generic name formerly given to Rhodesian man. 'Stooping-man.'

Dental Caries   A pathological process, with destruction of tooth enamel and dentine, leading to infection and loss of the tooth.

Devonian   See geological time scale.

Diabase   An American term for dolorite. A medium-grained dark igneous rock, low in silica.

Diastema   A gap between the teeth.

Diopside   A colourless or pale green mineral of calcium magnesium silicate.

Dolichocephalic   Having a Cranial Index of less than 75. 'Long-headed.'

Dolomite   1. Mineral calcium magnesium carbonate.
2. Limestone containing more than 50% mineral dolomite.

Dripstone   Crystalline calcium carbonate deposited from water in layers or strata.

Dryopithecine   (*n.*) A member of the genus *Dryopithecus*.
(*adj.*) Pertaining to the genus *Dryopithecus*.

Dryopithecus   The generic name given to a group of Middle Miocene apes. 'Oak-ape.'

Enamel Wrinkling   Secondary folding of the enamel of the occlusal surface of a tooth; consistently found in the molar teeth of the modern orang-utan (*Pongo*), also known in australopithecine and pithecanthropine teeth.

Endocast   A cast of a cavity, displaying internal surface features in relief.

Faunal Break   A sudden change in the character of the fossil fauna encountered during excavation of successive layers of a deposit; possibly due to partial erosion and subsequent redeposition of later material containing a different fauna, or to faunal migration.

Fauresmith   A Palaeolithic stone tool culture found in South Africa consisting of hand-axes and cleavers. Type site, Fauresmith, Orange Free State, Republic of South Africa.

Felspar (Feldspar)   A group of crystalline minerals consisting of silicates of aluminium with sodium, potassium, barium or calcium. Decomposition of felspars produces clays.

Felstone   An obsolete term for compact felspar occurring in amorphous rock masses.

Femoro-Condylar Angle   The angle between the shaft of the femur and a line drawn tangentially to the articular surfaces of the femoral condyles.

Ferricrete   Soil cemented with iron oxide.

Fission Track Method   A radiometric dating method dependent upon the presence of a radio-active constituent in natural glasses.

Fluviatile Deposits   Deposits produced by river action.

Frankfurt Plane   An agreed plane in which skulls may be oriented for comparative purposes. Arranged horizontally, it passes through the lower orbital margin and forms a tangent to the upper margin of the external auditory meatus.

Habilis   The specific name given to a group of East African Lower Pleistocene hominids. 'Able, handy, vigorous, mentally skilful.'

Holocene   See geological time scale.

Hominid   (*n.*) A member of the zoological family Hominidae. (*adj.*) Pertaining to the Zoological family Hominidae.

Hominidae   The zoological family which includes fossil and modern man as well as the fossil 'ape-men', 'man-apes' and 'near-men'.

Homininae   The zoological sub-family which contains fossil and modern man.

Hominine   (*n.*) A member of the zoological sub-family Homininae. (*adj.*) Pertaining to the zoological sub-family Homininae.

Hominoid   (*n.*) A member of the zoological super-family Hominoidea. (*adj.*) Pertaining to the zoological super-family Hominoidea.

Hominoidea   The zoological super-family which contains fossil apes, 'ape-men', 'man-apes', 'near-men' and men, as well as modern great apes and modern man.

Homo   The generic name given to the group of hominids which contains fossil and modern man.

Hypervitaminosis   A condition resulting from a dietary excess of the vitamin concerned.

Hypsodont   Having teeth with tall crowns, e.g. the horse.

Ilmenite   Mineral iron titanium oxide.

Inion   A position on the skull marked by the external occipital protuberance.

Interglacial   A warm period between two major glaciations.

Interpluvial   A dry phase between two rainy periods.

Interstadial   A warm interval within a major glaciation.

Javanthropus   The sub-generic name formerly given to a group of hominids from Ngandong, Java. 'Java-man.'

Karstic Caves   Caves formed in limestone by the action of water.

l   Length.

Lacustrine   Lacustrine deposits are laid down in relatively still water lakes.

Lambda   A point on the skull at which the sagittal and lambdoid sutures meet.

Levalloisian   A Palaeolithic flake tool culture produced by striking serviceable flakes from a prepared core; recognized in Europe, Asia and Africa. Type site, Levallois-Perret, Paris.

Lias (Liassic)   A rock formation consisting of layers of limestone, marl and clay attributed to the Lower Jurassic period. ? Corruption of 'layers'.

Lissoir   A polishing or rubbing tool.

Loam   An iron-rich mixture of clay and silt.

Loess   A fine-grained deposit of wind-blown material.

Magnetostratigraphy   The arrangement of geological strata based upon their residual magnetism compared with the world geomagnetic polarity column.

Mamelon   A small hillock or tuberosity; small elevations found along the free margin of a newly erupted incisor tooth.

Meganthropus   The generic name given to a group of early hominids from Java and East Africa. 'Big-man.'

Travertine   Almost pure calcium carbonate rock deposited around lime-rich springs and lakes.

Tropical Savannah   Tropical grassland containing scattered trees, such as the Baobab in Africa.

Tufa   A calcareous deposit, usually spongy in texture formed near lime-rich springs and rivers.

Tuff   A consolidated deposit of volcanic ash often laid down in water.

Villafranchian   1. A faunal assemblage containing new types of mammals such as *Elephas* (*Archidiskodon*), *Equus*, *Bos* (*Leptobos*) and *Camelus*, which appeared suddenly during the Lower Pleistocene. Type site, Villafrancha d'Asti, Italy.

2. Pertaining to the Lower Pleistocene.

Wormian Bones   Sutural bones formed from isolated centres of ossification between major components of the skull vault. Commonly found between the occipital and parietal bones.

Zinjanthropus   The generic name given to an East African Lower Pleistocene hominid. 'East African man.'

Index